CELEBRATING DIVERSITY

CELEBRATING DIVERSITY
A Multicultural Reader

Lee Brandon

Mount San Antonio College

D. C. Heath and Company
Lexington, Massachusetts   Toronto

Address editorial correspondence to:

D. C. Heath and Company
125 Spring Street
Lexington, MA 02173

Acquisitions Editor:	Paul A. Smith
Developmental Editor:	Linda M. Bieze
Production Editor:	Bryan Woodhouse
Designer:	Kenneth Hollman
Photo Researcher:	Billie Porter
Production Coordinator:	Charles Dutton
Permissions Editor:	Margaret Roll

Cover: *Recess* by Woodie Long. Private Collection.

Published simultaneously in Canada.

Printed in the United States of America.

International Standard Book Number: 0-669-35081-8

Library of Congress Catalog Number: 94-77432

10 9 8 7 6 5 4 3 2 1

To my many multicultural students,
who have taught me to celebrate diversity

TO THE INSTRUCTOR

The multicultural readings that comprise *Celebrating Diversity* vary in perspective, subject, form of discourse, genre, and length. Yet they all reflect—and celebrate—cultural diversity in its broadest sense. A major criterion in selecting these readings was that they have universal application for college composition students—that they suggest a common ground for all cultures, rather than making diversity a barrier between cultures. (See the To the Student section for more on my intentions in selecting these readings.) Views on race, culture, sexual preference, handicaps, prison life, class, poverty, gender, and age are included.

Each thematic chapter also focuses on a single form of discourse. For example, the readings in Chapter 2, "Pivotal Moments in American Experience," are all narratives, and the writing instruction focuses on narration. However, instructors can simply concentrate on the themes of the readings without calling attention to forms or rhetorical modes. Flexibility in subject matter, form, and writing assignments is a hallmark of *Celebrating Diversity*.

The genres represented by these selections include essays, short stories, paragraphs, and poems. Most essays are short to moderate in length, and most single- and multiparagraph Brief Views are between two hundred and five hundred words. Along with eighty-two excellent readings from published sources are forty-three wonderfully fresh student pieces written by individuals with rich multicultural backgrounds.

In addition to providing a wide range of culturally diverse views, these readings have been selected for three pedagogical reasons: to promote in-class discussion, to stimulate students' ideas for reading-related writing, and to provide models of good writing. The readings are supported by vocabulary study suggestions, where appropriate, and by guide questions for both discussion and writing. At the end of each chapter are suggestions for collaborative learning and writing assignments that encourage students to make connections among chapter readings. An appendix includes a brief guide to documented writing and the research paper.

Following an introductory chapter on writing, the first nine thematic chapters of readings offer different views on aspects of our multicultural society: "Pivotal Moments in American Experience" (Chapter 2), "Home: Sweet and Sour" (Chapter 3), "Love, Sex, and Marriage" (Chapter 4), "Celebration: Song, Food, Ceremony" (Chapter 5), "Youth in Crisis" (Chapter 6), "Families: For Better or Worse" (Chapter 7), "Culture: Blends and Clashes" (Chapter 8), "Types and Stereotypes" (Chapter 9), and "Discrimination: Playing the Exclusion Game" (Chapter 10). Finally, Chapter 11, "America: What Is It? What *Should* It Be?" serves as a capstone, giving students an opportunity to develop and express their own opinions on these questions.

The *Instructor's Guide* provides suggestions for collaborative learning, suggested answers to the text's Critical Reading and Discussion questions, and reproducible quizzes for selected readings.

Acknowledgments

Reviewers: I am grateful to the following instructors who reviewed *Celebrating Diversity:* Don Blankenship, West Valley College; Beverly Chin, University of Montana; Margaret DeHart, Trinity Valley Community College; Sarah L. Dye, Elgin Community College; David E. Hartman, St. Petersburg Junior College; Priscilla Homola, Alpena Community College; Jane Maher, Nassau Community College; Patricia Ross, Moorpark College; Barbara Speidell, Southwestern College; Joanne M. Sullivan, Middlesex Community College; Andrea J. Westcott, Kingwood College; and Joyce Zaritsky, LaGuardia Community College. Thanks also to the faculty members at Mt. San Antonio College who reviewed this text and suggested readings to me: Lydia Alvarez, Suzanne Arakawa, Pamela Arterburn, Virginia Burley, Keith Cole, Debra Farve, Jean Garrett, Julian Medina, and Mark Fernandez. I am also grateful to the students at Mt. San Antonio College and the California Institution for Women, who reacted helpfully to early drafts of the manuscript and contributed paragraphs and essays.

D. C. Heath and Company: Thanks also to the staff at D. C. Heath and Company: Paul A. Smith, Senior Acquisitions Editor; Linda Bieze, Developmental Editor; Margaret Roll, Senior Permissions Editor; Bryan Woodhouse, Senior Production Editor; Kenneth Hollman, Senior Designer; and Paul Durantini, Sales Representative.

Family: Finally, I am grateful to my family for their encouragement and humor: my son Kelly, daughter-in-law Jeanne, and grandson Shane; my daughter Erin and son-in-law Michael; and especially my wife Sharon.

Lee Brandon

TO THE STUDENT

The title *Celebrating Diversity* conveys the intent and tone of this book. Cultural diversity ("assortment, medley, variety") is growing in importance and touches your life daily; it characterizes America today and is as basic as saying that the only constant is change. We can use this diversity either to increase our awareness, to energize us, and to unite us; or to divide us into separate groups, each viewing others as peculiar, threatening, or even un-American. The idea underlying this book is that, in looking at other cultures, we can begin to appreciate and even celebrate differences, while learning that, under the veneer of culture, we are all much more alike than different.

The diverse views in this book appear here in many forms, as well. Along with eighty-two excellent essays, short stories, and poems from published sources are forty-three wonderfully fresh student pieces written by individuals representing different races, cultures, sexual preferences, states of handicap, genders, social classes, and ages. Following Chapter 1, "The Written Response," which offers strategies for writing effective paragraphs and essays, the readings are arranged thematically as follows:

Chapter 2: "Pivotal Moments in American Experience"
Chapter 3: "Home: Sweet and Sour"
Chapter 4: "Love, Sex, and Marriage"
Chapter 5: "Celebration: Song, Food, Ceremony"
Chapter 6: "Youth in Crisis"
Chapter 7: "Families: For Better or Worse"
Chapter 8: "Culture: Blends and Clashes"
Chapter 9: "Types and Stereotypes"
Chapter 10: "Discrimination: Playing the Exclusion Game"
Chapter 11: "America: What Is It? What *Should* It Be?"

Considering these groups of readings in a classroom setting will give you an opportunity to think, discuss, and write. Each chapter of readings also demonstrates familiar writing forms such as narration, description, exposition, and argumentation. The last chapter encourages you to synthesize what you have read throughout the book and to develop your own view of cultural diversity: What do you think America is now, and what do you think it should become? Possibly no two views in your class will be exactly the same, but that's what diversity is about.

I have chosen these particular selections with the belief that we all are curious to learn about other cultural views and that, if we bring light without heat to those views, we will be more ready to understand, tolerate, learn about, and borrow from others. A colleague in South Dakota told me that his Native American students refer to an atmosphere in which one can talk about one's culture without fear of ridicule or antagonism as a "safe house." This book promotes that concept. Let the celebration begin!

Lee Brandon

CONTENTS

    "The sacred sweat ceremony has always been at the center of my life. Here at prison it has taken on a special meaning."

Brief Views

    "The children stood near by, drawing figures in the dust with bare toes, and the children sent exploring senses out to see whether men and women would break."
    "She quickened her pace to escape, but another handful of gravel hit her and the laughter continued."

*Student Writing

Chapter 5 Celebration: Song, Food, Ceremony 147

Chapter 6 Youth in Crisis 175

"A traditional Chinese wife has to abandon her original family, please her in-laws, and obey her husband."

Extended Views

Chapter 8 Culture: Blends and Clashes 253

Brief Views

Extended Views

Chapter 9 *Types and Stereotypes* 293

Brief Views

Chapter 10 Discrimination: Playing the Exclusion Game 338

Brief Views

Extended Views

Chapter 11 America: What Is It? What Should It Be? 376

Brief Views

Extended Views

ALTERNATE TABLE OF CONTENTS

African-American Culture

Asian-American Culture

Hispanic-American Culture

Native American Culture

Other Ethnic Cultures

CELEBRATING DIVERSITY

1

The Written Response

As treated in this book, reading, thinking, and writing are inseparable. How can you learn to read better? By learning to think more clearly.
How can you learn to think more clearly? By working out logical patterns
in your writing. How can you learn to write better? By reading more and
by thinking more clearly. In other words, each reinforces the other, and
each depends on the other.

The reading selections in this book invite you to think and to write.
Therefore, this opening chapter deals with writing—forms, strategies, and
the relationship of writing to reading and thinking. Many of your college
writing assignments, both while you use this book and in other classes,
will be short statements such as the *developmental paragraph* and longer
statements such as the *essay*.

THE DEVELOPMENTAL PARAGRAPH

Defining the word *paragraph* is no easy task, because there are different
kinds of paragraphs: introductory, developmental, transitional, and concluding. Each is a short unit of material based on a single idea. The developmental paragraph, which concerns us here, is a multisentence unit that
expands on an idea. You can use it in two ways: (1) as a complete answer to
a short writing assignment and (2) as a middle or body paragraph in an

essay. The following paragraph both defines and illustrates the developmental paragraph.

<table>
<tr><td>topic sentence
support

support

support</td><td>The developmental paragraph contains three parts: the subject, the topic sentence, and the support. The *subject* is what one will write about. It is likely to be broad and must be focused or qualified for specific treatment. The *topic sentence* contains both the subject and the treatment, meaning what one will do with the subject. It carries the central idea to which everything else in the paragraph is subordinated. For example, the first sentence of this paragraph is a topic sentence. Even when not stated, the topic sentence as an underlying concept unifies the paragraph. The *support* is the evidence and/or reasoning by which a topic sentence is developed. It comes in several basic patterns and serves any of the four typical purposes of communication:</td></tr>
</table>

> narration (What happened?)
> description (What is it like?)
> exposition (What does it mean?)
> argumentation (What should we believe?)

<table>
<tr><td>restated topic sentence (with the complete definition)</td><td>These communication purposes, or forms of discourse, can also be combined in thought and writing. The developmental paragraph, therefore, is a group of sentences, each with the function of stating or supporting a single, controlling idea that is contained in the topic sentence.</td></tr>
</table>

Usually the developmental paragraph will be indented only one time: however, you will note in your reading that some writers, especially journalists, indent more than once in developing a single idea. That arrangement, called a *paragraph unit,* is fairly common in magazine and newspaper articles but less so in college writing. Two effective forms of conventional paragraph structure are shown in Figure 1.1.

Figure 1.1 Effective Paragraph Structures

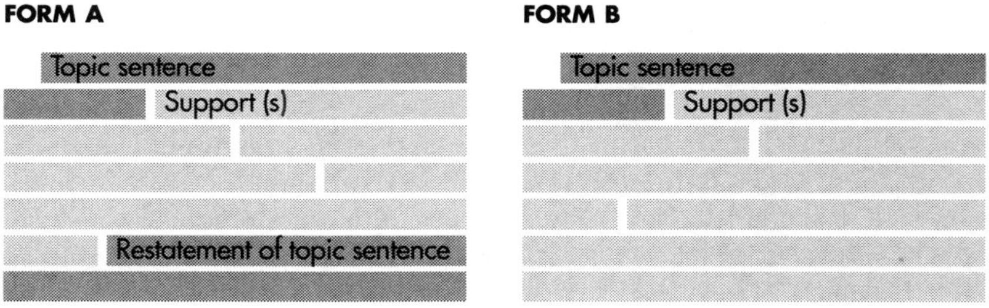

Example of Form A

topic sentence

I can see myself today as a person historically defined by law and custom as being forever alien. Being neither "free white," nor "African," our people in California were deemed "aliens, ineligible for citizenship," no matter how long they intended to stay here. Aliens ineligible for citizenship were prohibited from

support

owning, buying, or leasing land. They did not and could not belong here. The voice in me remembers that I am always a *Japanese*-American in the eyes of many. A third-generation German-American is an American. A third-generation Japanese-American is a Japanese-American. Being Japanese means being a danger to the country during the war and knowing how to

restatement

use chopsticks. I wear this history on my face.

Kesaya E. Noda,
"Growing Up Asian in America"

Example of Form B

topic sentence

But now I can say that I am a Japanese-American. It means I have a place here in this country, too. I have a place here on the

support (example)

East Coast, where our neighbor is so much a part of our family that my mother never passes her house at night without glancing at the lights to see if she is home and safe; where my

support (example)

parents have hauled hundreds of pounds of rocks from fields and arduously planted Christmas trees and blueberries, lilacs,

support (example)

asparagus, and crab apples, where my father still dreams of angling a stream to a new bed so that he can dig a pond in the

support (example)

field and fill it with water and fish. "The neighbors already came for their Christmas tree?" he asks in December. "Did they like it? Did they like it?"

Kesaya E. Noda,
"Growing Up Asian in America"

THE ESSAY

The essay is as difficult to define as the paragraph, but the paragraph definition gives us a framework.

The developmental paragraph is a group of sentences, each with the function of stating or supporting a controlling idea called the topic sentence.

The main parts of the developmental paragraph are the topic sentence (subject and treatment), support (evidence and reasoning), and, often, the restated topic sentence at the end. Now let's use that framework for the essay:

> The essay is a group of paragraphs, each with the function of stating or supporting a controlling idea called the thesis.

The main parts of the essay are:

Introduction: carries the thesis, which states the controlling idea—much like the topic sentence for a paragraph but on a larger scale.

Development: evidence and reasoning—the support.

Transition: points out divisions of the essay (seldom used in the short essay).

Conclusion: an appropriate ending—often a restatement of or reflection on the thesis.

Thus, considered structurally, the paragraph is often an essay in miniature. That does not mean that all paragraphs can grow up to be essays or that all essays can shrink to become paragraphs. For college writing, however, a good understanding of the parallel between well-organized paragraphs and well-organized essays is useful. As you learn the properties of effective paragraphs—those with strong topic sentences and strong support—you also learn how to organize an essay, if you just magnify the procedure.

Recall the developmental paragraphs on cultural identity. Following is another paragraph that is similarly organized, with a topic sentence, the development, and the restatement of the topic sentence, in this example on the fans of Elvis. The annotations show how it could also have been developed into a whole essay if the author, Jim Miller, had wanted to amplify his supporting ideas.

topic sentence (subject and treatment)	A messiah, a jester, a reckless jerk—or a soulful singer from the Deep South—Elvis at different times to different people was all these things. <u>His fans mirror every facet of their idol.</u> "I liked
support 1	him because of his looks," says Sue Scarborough, forty-nine, of Lexington, Kentucky, as she waits with her husband to tour
support 2	Graceland. "He didn't put on airs," says Jeff Graff, twenty, of Cleveland, Ohio. "He went out of his way to help people." "I

support 3

support and
reflection on topic
sentence

met him in 1960 when I was twelve years old," says Billie Le
Jeune of Memphis, who visits Graceland once or twice a
month: "He asked me what my favorite subject was." On the
pink fieldstone wall outside Graceland, which for years has
functioned as an unauthorized bulletin board, the graffiti runs
like this: ELVIS IS LOVE; I DID DRUGS WITH ELVIS; and most cryptic
of all—ELVIS DIDN'T DESERVE TO BE WHITE.

Jim Miller,
"Forever Elvis"

By taking a bit of license to fabricate, one can easily expand this into a
short essay. The fabricated parts are in parentheses.

Good King Elvis

introductory
paragraph

thesis

A messiah, a jester, a reckless jerk—or a soulful singer
from the Deep South—Elvis at different times to different people was all these things. His fans mirror every facet of their
idol.

topic sentence

paragraph of
development 1 from
support 1

For some fans the attraction is appearance. "I liked him
because of his looks," says Sue Scarborough, forty-nine, of Lexington, Kentucky, as she waits with her husband to tour Graceland. (She grins good-naturedly at her husband and gives him
an affectionate nudge in the ribs when he says, "My wife really
likes Elvis, but I'm not jealous because he is dead—I think."
Her response tells all: "My husband's a good man at drivin' a
truck and fishin' for bass, but no one'll ever paint his picture
on velvet.")

topic sentence

paragraph of
development 2 from
support 2

(For others, Elvis was a king with a common touch and
humanitarian instincts.) "He didn't put on airs," says Jeff Graff,
twenty, of Cleveland, Ohio. "He went out of his way to help
people." (His friend nods his head in agreement. "Elvis must've
given away a hundred Cadillacs in his day." Others in line
break-in to tell stories about the generosity of this good man
who once walked among them.)

topic sentence

paragraph of
development 3 from
support 3

(The speakers at Graceland who get the most attention are
those who actually met Elvis and have information about his
basic goodness.) "I met him in 1960 when I was twelve years
old," says Billie Le Jeune of Memphis, who visits Graceland
once or twice a month: "He asked me what my favorite subject
was." (A few others have stories equally compelling. The crowd
listens in awe.)

topic sentence
reflecting

(Along with these talkers at Graceland are the writers,
who sum up the range of Elvis's qualities.) On the pink field-

concluding
paragraph reflecting
on introductory
paragraph and
thesis stone wall outside Graceland, which for years has functioned as an unauthorized bulletin board, the graffiti runs like this: ELVIS IS LOVE; I DID DRUGS WITH ELVIS; and most cryptic of all—ELVIS DIDN'T DESERVE TO BE WHITE.

Ponder that fanciful expansion with our definition in mind: "The essay is a group of paragraphs, each with the function of stating or supporting a controlling idea called the thesis." Note that the introduction carries the thesis, complete with subject and treatment; the developmental paragraphs collectively support the thesis, and each, in turn, has a topic sentence and support; the conclusion recalls the introduction and, in fact, illustrates the thesis.

Like the paragraph, the essay may also assume different patterns. It may be principally one form of discourse: narration, description, exposition, or argumentation. Or it may be a combination, varying from paragraph to paragraph and even within paragraphs. But no matter what its pattern is, it will be unified around a central idea, the thesis. The *thesis* is the assertion or controlling purpose to which all other parts of the essay will be subordinate and supportive. As with the paragraph, the main point, here the thesis, will almost certainly be stated, usually in the first paragraph, and again, more frequently than not, at the end of the essay. The essay on Elvis illustrates this pattern.

The only difference in concept between the topic sentence and the thesis is one of scope: the topic sentence unifies and controls the content of the paragraph, and the thesis does the same for the essay. Because the essay is longer and more complex than the typical paragraph, the thesis may suggest a broader scope and may more explicitly indicate the parts.

SPECIAL PARAGRAPHS WITHIN THE ESSAY

In addition to developmental paragraphs, paragraphs of introduction and conclusion are important parts of the short essay.

Introductions

An introductory paragraph or introductory paragraph unit (a number of paragraphs at the beginning of the essay whose purpose is to introduce the subject) has various functions, including gaining reader interest, indicating or pointing toward the thesis, and moving the reader smoothly into the body paragraphs, the developmental paragraphs. The introductory methods are varied. They include:

- a direct statement of the thesis,
- background,
- definition of term(s),
- quotation(s),
- a shocking statement,
- question(s), and
- a combination of two or more of this list.

You should not decide that some of the methods are good and some are bad. Indeed, all are valid, and the most common one is the last, the combination. Use the approach that best fits each essay. Resist the temptation to find a pat introduction to use for each essay you write.

In each of the following examples, the thesis is quite explicit, and it comes naturally from the whole context of one or more of the recommended methods of introduction. Notice that in some of the theses, the subject and the treatment are not easily separated in space.

Direct Statement of Thesis

Anyone on the road in any city near midnight on Friday and Saturday is among dangerous people. They're not the product of the witching hour; they're the product of the "happy hour." They're called drunk drivers. These threats to our lives and limbs need to be controlled by federal laws with strong provisions.

thesis { subject / treatment

Background

In one five-year period in California (1987–1992), 215,000 people were injured and 43,000 were killed by drunk drivers. Each year, the same kinds of figures come in from all our states. The state laws vary. The federal government does virtually nothing. Drunk driving has reached the point of being a national problem of huge proportions. This slaughter of innocent citizens should be stopped by following the lead of many other nations and passing federal legislation with strong provisions.

thesis { subject / treatment

Definition (as an operation)

Here's a recipe. Take two thousand pounds of plastic, rubber, and steel, pour in ten gallons of gas, and start the engine. Then take one human being of two hundred pounds of flesh, blood, and bones, pour in two glasses of beer in one hour, and put him or her behind the wheel. Mix the two together, and the result may be a drunken driver ready to cause death and destruction. This problem of drunk driving can and should be controlled by federal legislation with strong provisions.

thesis { subject / treatment

Quotation

The National Highway Traffic Safety Administration has stated that 50 percent of all fatal accidents involve intoxicated drivers and that "75 percent of those drivers have a Blood Alcohol Content of .10 or greater." That kind of information is widely known, yet the carnage on the highways continues. This problem of drunk driving should be addressed by a federal law with strict provisions.

thesis { subject / treatment

Shocking Statement and Questions

Almost 60,000 Americans were killed in the Vietnam War. What other war kills more than that number each year? Give up? It's the war with drunk drivers. The war in Vietnam ended about two decades ago, but our DUI war goes on, and the drunks are winning. This deadly conflict should be controlled by a federal law with strong provisions.

thesis { subject / treatment

Questions and a Definition

What is a drunk driver? In California it's a person with a Blood Alcohol Content of .8 or more who is operating a motor vehicle. What do those drivers do? Some of them kill. Every year more than 60,000 people nationwide die. Those are easy questions. The difficult one is, What can be done? One answer is clear: drunk drivers should be controlled by federal laws with strong provisions.

thesis { subject / treatment

Although the preceding methods are effective, some others are ineffective because they are too vague to carry the thesis or because they carry the thesis in a mechanical way. The mechanical approach may have merit in directness and explicitness, but it usually disengages the reader's imagination and interest.

AVOID: The purpose of this essay is to write about the need for strong national laws against drunk driving.

AVOID: I will now write a paper about the need for strong national laws against drunk driving.

The length of an introduction can vary, but the typical one for a student essay is about three to five sentences. If your introduction is shorter than three, be certain that it conveys all that you want to say. If it is longer than five, be certain that it only introduces and does not attempt to expand upon ideas, a function reserved for the developmental paragraphs; a long and complicated introduction may make your essay top-heavy.

Conclusions

In your *concluding paragraph,* give the reader the feeling that you have said all that you want to say about the subject. Like introductory paragraphs, conclusions can be quite varied. Some effective ways of concluding a paper are:

- Conclude with a final paragraph or sentence that is a logical part of the body of the paper; that is, it functions as part of the support. In this case, the paper requires no formal conclusion. This form is more common in the published essay than in the student essay.

One day he hit me. He said he was sorry and even cried, but I could not forgive him. We got a divorce. It took me a while before I could look back and see what the causes really were, but by then it was too late to make any changes.

Maria Campos,
from an essay on divorce

- Conclude with a restatement of the thesis in slightly different words, perhaps pointing out the significance and/or making applications. This type may state or imply a call to action.

Don't blame it on the referee. Don't even blame it on the fight managers. Put the blame where it belongs—on the prevailing mores that regard prize fighting as a perfectly proper enterprise and vehicle of entertainment. No one doubts that many people enjoy prize fighting and will miss it if it should be thrown out. And that is precisely the point.

Norman Cousins,
"Who Killed Benny Paret?"

- Conclude with a review of the main points of the discussion—a kind of summary. This will be appropriate only if the complexity of the essay necessitates a summary.

But even this small slight has carved out a warm place to hide in my memories. For, at my mother's signal, I had moved away from those Saturday hair sessions, as if from a safe harbor, carrying with me: "Child, go look at yourself in the mirror." It was always said as if whatever I saw surpassed good and bordered on the truly wonderful. And I, searching for my own reflection, walked away oblivious to the love and life-sustaining messages which had seeped into my pores as I sat on the floor of my mother's kitchen.

Willi Coleman,
"Closets and Keepsakes"

- Conclude with an anecdote related to the thesis.

I was called to dinner: steam silvered my mother's glasses as she said grace; my brother and sister with their heads bowed made ugly faces at their glasses of powdered milk. I gagged too, but eagerly ate big rips of buttered tortilla that held scooped up beans. Finished, I went outside with my jacket across my arm. It was a cold sky. The faces of clouds were piled up, hurting. I climbed the fence, jumping down with a grunt. I started up the alley and soon slipped into my jacket, that green ugly brother who breathed over my shoulder that day and ever since.

Gary Soto,
"The Jacket"

- Conclude with a quotation related to the thesis.

"We are just not raising kids who can deal with the stresses of living in this wild and crazy society," Spiegel says, "We are producing Teenage Mutant I-don't-know-what . . . We want inner-city kids to make the right choices, but we forget to show them there is a rainbow of choices out there."

Laurie Becklund and Marc Lacey,
from an essay on teenage sex

There are also many ineffective ways of concluding a paper; do not conclude with

- a summary when a summary is unnecessary;
- a complaint about the assignment or an apology about the quality of the work;
- an afterthought—that is, adding something that you forgot to discuss in the body of the paper;
- a tagged conclusion—for example, using *In conclusion, To conclude,* or *I would liked to conclude this discussion;*
- a conclusion that raises additional problems that should have been settled during the discussion.

The conclusion is an integral part of the essay and is often a reflection of the introduction. If you have trouble with the conclusion, reread your introduction, and work for a roundness or completeness in the whole paper.

CRITICAL READING, CRITICAL THINKING, CRITICAL WRITING

Because reading is such an important ingredient in this reading-related writing process, it is useful to consider how reading, thinking, and writing go together, how they are similar, and how ability in one strengthens ability in the others. The comments and marks on the following essay will help you understand the connection between writing and reading. The underlining and annotations show the basic types of organization already presented in this chapter. Following the essay is a topic outline. All three techniques—underlining to indicate main and supporting ideas, annotating to indicate importance and relevance to the task at hand, and outlining to show the relationship of ideas and the underlying structure— aid reading, thinking, and writing.

causes of mental illness—main idea (thesis)

1. inherited depression in family

schizophrenia in family

Far more is known about the symptoms of mental illness and how to treat them than about the causes. But it is known that these problems often don't have a single cause.

Some types of mental illness, or at least a predisposition toward them, can be inherited. For example, depression is more likely to occur in a person with a family history of depression. Similarly, a child with a schizophrenic parent may be more likely to develop schizophrenia than a child with non-schizophrenic parents.

2. triggering factors

personal problems

such as

3. chemical
changes

physical problems
such as

4. feelings: self,
others

guilt

hostile

detached

But though there may be inherited differences in susceptibility to mental illness, some triggering factors, perhaps environmental stress or a particular set of circumstances, must be present for mental illness to manifest itself. For example, one study showed that each of 40 depressed patients had suffered several personal problems in the year preceding breakdown. These included a threat to sexual identity, moving to another community, physical illness, and death of a loved one.

Chemical changes in the body also have to do with how the mind functions. Exactly what these changes are and how they work isn't fully understood. Some mental disorders (known as organic psychoses) are caused by physical problems. Among the possible causes of organic psychoses are congenital defects, prenatal injury, hardening of the arteries in the brain, brain tumors and infections, and severe alcoholism. Glandular disturbances and certain nutritional deficiencies can also produce psychotic symptoms.

Emotional disturbances are also related to how the individuals feel about themselves and the world around them. For example, those who are constantly criticized can develop an exaggerated feeling of guilt. They come to expect everyone will find fault with them and even punish them. Or, if as youngsters they were repeatedly neglected and reprimanded, they may have grown up expecting trouble and rejection. They may have developed a protective reaction of verbally attacking another before the other criticized them. Or perhaps they remain detached and aloof from other people so as not to give others a chance to reject them. For some people these painful feelings are successfully buried till they run into a crisis situation—for example, the loss of a job or the breakup of a marriage—when the feelings surface again.

Judith Ramsey,
"Causes of Mental Illness"

OUTLINING WHAT YOU HAVE READ

After reading, underlining, and annotating the piece, the next step could be to outline. If the piece is well organized, you should be able to reduce it to a simple outline so that you can, at a glance, see the relationship of ideas (sequence, relative importance, and interdependence).

Ramsay's piece can be outlined very easily:

Causes of Mental Illness

  I. Inherited, at least predisposition for
    A. From family with depression
    B. From a parent with schizophrenia
 II. Trigger factor
    A. Environmental stress
    B. Circumstances
      1. Sexual-identity crisis
      2. Physical illness
      3. Death of a loved one.
III. Chemical changes
    A. Congenital defects
    B. Brain tumors
    C. Glandular disturbances
IV. Emotional disturbances
    A. Abuse
    B. Neglect

TYPES OF READING-RELATED WRITING

Much of the writing you did before entering college may have been of a personal nature. The content of personal writing comes from direct and indirect experience (reading and listening), and often involves opinion. Mastering this kind of writing is important because you do have something to say. Most college writing tasks, however, will require you to evaluate and to reflect on what you read, rather than write only about personal experience. You will be expected to read, think, and write. The writing part in these circumstances is commonly called reading related. It includes

- the *summary* (main ideas stated in your own words);
- the *reaction* (usually meaning how what you have read relates specifically to you, your experiences, and attitudes, but also often meaning a critique of the worth and logic of a piece); and
- the *spin-off* (a smaller form of the reaction, in that it takes one aspect of the reading and develops a parallel experience, or simply one that has an interesting connection to the piece of writing).

These kinds of writing have certain points in common; they all

- originate as a response to something you have read;
- refer, to some degree, to content from that piece; and,
- demonstrate an understanding of the piece of writing.

Writing in specific forms such as comparison and contrast, causes and effects, and argument will be featured in individual chapters.

Summary

Your instructor may ask you to summarize a reading selection. If so, preparing an outline will serve as an excellent prelude to your task, because it helps you identify the main ideas and their most basic support. In the summary, concentrate on those main ideas, putting them into your own words while usually reducing the piece by more than two-thirds. You can also use a summary as part of a larger work such as an essay or a research paper. When your summary is derived from an original source, you are obliged to credit that source in your paper. This credit can usually be done informally on a simple class assignment by indicating the title and author, and it can be done formally using parenthetical citations, which are usually just the author's surname and the page number following the summarized passage.

The following guidelines will help you write effective summaries. The summary

1. is usually about one-third the length of the original, though it will vary depending on the content of the original;
2. begins with the main idea (as in developmental paragraphs) and proceeds to cover the major supporting points in the same sequence as the source, always in complete sentences;
3. changes the wording without changing the idea;
4. does not evaluate the content or give an opinion in any way (even if you see an error in logic or fact);
5. does not add ideas (even if you have an abundance of related information);
6. does not refer directly to the writing (do not write, for example, "the author says");
7. does not include any personal comments by the author of the summary (therefore, do not use *I*); and
8. seldom uses quotations (but if so, always with quotation marks).

In the following summary paragraph, the numbered parts indicate guidelines that were not followed:

One cause of mental illness can be heredity, traceable back to families with depression and especially to schizophrenic parents. (I know that to be true
7
because of some family problems I have.) (Then the writer says that another cause is circumstantial in that mental illness may be brought on by various
6   7
kinds of stress.) (I wish the author had given more statistics on this point.) (A third is how chemical changes in the body also have to do with how the mind
7
functions.) These chemical changes can be linked to physical problems, (glan-
3
dular disturbances and certain nutritional deficiencies.) Finally low self-esteem can cause emotional problems, (although it seems to me this is one point that's
7
difficult to prove.) Persons who have been neglected or abused will often withdraw or become hostile.

The following paragraph is an example of an effective summary:

Mental illness has at least four causes. It can be hereditary—that is, traceable to families with depression and especially schizophrenic parents. It can be circumstantial, in that it can be brought on by various kinds of stress. It can be chemical—that is, linked to physical problems, glandular problems, and dietary problems. Finally, it can be caused by low self-esteem or other emotional problems. People who have been neglected or abused often withdraw or become hostile.

Reaction

The reaction is another kind of reading-related writing. Some reactions require evaluation with a critical-thinking emphasis. Some focus on a simple discussion of the content presented in the reading and include summary material. Others concentrate on your experiences as related to the content of the passage.

The following paragraph is an example of a student reaction, and evaluation of, "Causes of Mental Illness."

The article "Causes of Mental Illness" makes sense from my perspective because it does not try to simplify a complex problem. The introductory paragraph points out that "the symptoms of mental illness . . . often don't have a single cause." That admission is perhaps the best insight in the article. The four causes—heredity, stress, chemical, and abuse—often occur in combination. The people I have known with mental illness cannot be diagnosed easily, for they all have complicated backgrounds. For example, a physical problem can cause both stress and low self-esteem. And a person with family mental problems must be concerned about more than heredity problems. That person must also deal with stress and probably with neglect or other forms of abuse. If single causes were the issue, treatment would be much simpler.

Spin-off

The spin-off, a shorter form of the reaction statement, takes one aspect of the reading and develops a parallel experience or one that has an interesting connection to the piece of writing. The following example shows how one student personalized a spin-off response to the reading "Causes of Mental Illness."

One statement in "Causes of Mental Illness" gave me a better understanding of my friend. He is normal in relationships that are well established. With me he is at ease, and we laugh and joke a lot. But when he is around strangers, something seems to snap. He will find points of disagreement and focus on them aggressively until I am embarrassed. Sometimes he will bring up topics about religion or politics in an opinionated way that shuts off all discussion. At first I couldn't understand this Jekyll-and-Hyde behavior, but then I learned that he was self-conscious and afraid of being criticized, so he just launched a first attack. Fortunately in the last year he has become much more successful in his work; hence, he has higher self-esteem. The result is a noticeable improvement in his behavior with strangers.

THE WRITING PROCESS

Regardless of the nature of your writing project, you are likely to go through certain stages in the process of completing it. First, explore your basic idea, whether you are investigating an assigned topic or generating an original one. Then decide what point to make about your topic, with all its specifics and limitations. Next, develop an overall plan with main ideas and support, all arranged in a sequence. Finally, write more than one draft, revising as you go. We will first discuss these strategies—exploring, stating your point, planning, drafting and revising, and editing—and then show examples of each of them, taken from student work.

Exploring

Freewriting, brainstorming, and clustering will help you to generate topics and explore their potential.

Freewriting

Freewriting is an exercise that its originator, Peter Elbow, has called "babbling in print." Using this strategy, you write without stopping, letting your ideas tumble forth. You do not concern yourself with the fundamentals of writing, such as punctuation and spelling. This strategy is especially useful in generating or further exploring topics. Where you start depends on your assignment: working with original topics, working from a restricted list of topics, or working with reading-related topics. If you are at a loss for words on your subject, write in a comment such as "I don't know what is coming next" or "blah, blah, blah," and continue when relevant words come. In doing this exercise, you will shake loose ideas of all kinds to look at on paper. You will get an impression of how much you know and of what your interests are. If practically nothing worthwhile emerges, perhaps it is time to freewrite another topic.

Brainstorming

Another strategy is *brainstorming*. Begin by applying Who? What? Where? When? Why? and How? questions to your subject. Then let your mind run free as you jot down answers in single words or lists. Some of the questions will be more important than others, depending on the purpose of your writing. For example, if you are writing about the causes of some situation, the Why? question could be more important than the others; if you are concerned with how to do something, the How? question would predominate. Sometimes, in order to focus on a particular form of writing, another question will be added to the brainstorming "basic six." If you are writing in response to something you have read (as you will be doing frequently in assignments from this book), confine your thinking to ideas appropriately related to that content. Whatever your focus for questions, the result is likely to be a long list of useful ideas.

Clustering

Still another technique of exploration is *clustering* (also called *mapping*). Begin by "double-bubbling" your topic (writing it down and drawing a double circle around it). Then, in response to the question, What comes to mind? single-bubble other ideas on spokes radiating out from the hub, which contains the topic. Any bubble can lead to another bubble or bubbles in the same fashion. (See the student example at the end of this discussion on the writing process.)

Stating Your Point

The sentence that states your point will be your most important sentence. In the paragraph that sentence is called the *topic sentence;* in the essay, it is called the *thesis.* The two are identical in form. In some instances, the topic sentence or thesis will be a response to an assignment, whereas in others it will be the product of working with exploratory strategies such as freewriting, brainstorming, and clustering. Of course, you must keep in mind what you want to say and to whom—to what audience.

The extent to which you present and explain your topic and the language you use will depend on your purpose, so phrase your topic sentence or thesis with the expected development in mind. The topic sentence or thesis will indicate the subject (what you are concerned with generally) and the treatment of that subject (what aspect of it you intend to discuss).

A narrow factual statement will not bear development.

WRONG: <u>Multicultural studies</u> <u>were introduced in 1965.</u>
            Subject   Treatment

A broad or vague statement cannot be easily developed.

WRONG: <u>Multicultural studies</u> <u>are interesting.</u>
            Subject   Treatment

An effective topic sentence or thesis leads naturally to development. It indicates a topic and shows how it will be treated.

The treatment may be factual:

RIGHT: <u>Multicultural studies</u> <u>have been presented in two distinct ways.</u>
           Subject   Treatment

The treatment may be an opinion:

RIGHT: <u>Multicultural studies</u> <u>have reduced racial tension at Citrus College.</u>
           Subject   Treatment

In some topic sentences and theses, especially in published writing, the subject and treatment may seem to merge, or they may be reversed in order, but you should always be able to separate these parts in your thinking.

Planning

An outline or a focused cluster is likely to follow the formulation of your topic sentence or thesis. You may wish to use an outline as a pattern for showing the relationship of ideas in your paragraph or essay. You can also use it to demonstrate the framework of a reading passage or to show the organization of a piece of writing. In writing about a reading selection, both uses may merge.

The two main forms are the *sentence outline* (each entry is a complete sentence) and the *topic outline* (each entry is a key word or phrase). The topic outline is more common for both paragraph and essay writing.

The placement of words (with indentation), punctuation, and number and letter sequences are important to clear communication. The outline is not basically a creative effort. We do not read it expecting to be surprised by form and content, as we do a poem. We go to the outline for information, and we expect to find ideas easily. Unconventional marks (circles, squares, half parentheses) and items out of order are distracting and therefore undesirable in an outline. The standard form is as easily mastered as a nonstandard form, and it is well worth your time to learn it. Outlining is not difficult; here is the pattern:

Main idea (will usually be the topic sentence for the paragraph or the thesis for the essay)

   I. Major support
     A. Minor support
       1. Details (specific information of various kinds)
       2. Details
     B. Minor support
       1. Details
       2. Details
  II. Major support
     A. Minor support
     B. Minor support
       1. Details
       2. Details
       3. Details

The pattern is flexible and can have any number of levels and parts.

Drafting and Revising

Here are some ideas to consider as you revise. You need not complete these parts in any order or even work on them one at a time.

Coherence

Coherence is progression of ideas, with each idea leading logically and smoothly to the next. It is achieved by numbering parts or otherwise indicating time (*first, second, third; then, next, soon,* and so on), giving directions (spatial, as in "To the right is a map, and to the left of that map is a bulletin board"), using transitional words (*however, otherwise, therefore, similarly, hence, on the other hand, then, consequently, accordingly, thus*), using demonstrative pronouns (*this, that, those*), and moving in a logical or emphatic order (through functional stages, from the least important to the most important or from the most important to the least important).

Language

Language here means the appropriate usage, tone, and diction. *Usage* refers to the level of language appropriate for your topic, your writing task, and your audience; it can be formal or informal, and should be standard (educated) language rather than nonstandard. *Tone* refers to your attitude toward your subject and your audience. Like speech, writing can project diverse tones: playful, serious, objective, sarcastic, cautionary, loving. *Diction* pertains to word choice appropriate for your writing as it addresses a particular audience; word choice will convey your ideas clearly and concisely, usually avoiding slang and cliches.

Unity

Everything in your passage should be related and subordinate to your topic sentence or thesis. Repetition of a key word or phrase can make the unity even more apparent.

Emphasis

Emphasize important ideas by using *position* (the most emphatic parts of a work are the beginning and the end), *repetition* (repeat key words and phrases), and *isolation* (a short, direct sentence among longer ones will usually command attention).

Support

Support is the material that backs up, justifies, or validates your topic sentence or thesis. Work carefully with the material from the outline or outline substitute to ensure that your ideas are well supported. If the paragraph or essay is skimpy and your ideas thin, you probably are generalizing and not explaining how you arrived at your conclusions. Use details and examples; indicate parts and discuss relationships; explain why your generalizations are true, logical, and accurate. Your reader can't accept your ideas unless he or she knows by what reasoning or use of evidence you developed them.

Sentence Structure

Be sure that your sentences are complete (not fragments) and that you have not incorrectly combined word groups that could be sentences (comma splices and run-togethers). Consider using different types of sentences and different sentence beginnings.

Editing

This final stage of the writing process involves a careful examination of your work. Look for basic problems such as capitalization, omissions, punctuation, and spelling. Before preparing the final draft to hand in, read your paper aloud to discover oversights and awkwardness of expression.

A DEMONSTRATION OF THE WRITING PROCESS

Leah, an inmate in a California prison, was enrolled there in a small, low-cost college program. Her assignment was to write a personal essay of 500–800 words. Her instructor suggested that she concentrate on a recent development or event at the prison that had changed her life, for better or worse.

Numerous topics interested Leah. There was the problem of overcrowding: she lived in an institution built for 900 inmates, and the population was now 2,200. She also considered education. After spending some time in routine prison work and aimless activities, she had discovered school and found it highly satisfying. And then there was an accomplishment by her Native American (they refer to themselves as American Indians and Native Americans interchangeably) friends at the prison. After years of arguing their case, they finally convinced the institution to build a sweat lodge for their religious purposes, and it was now in operation. That was a subject she knew well, and it was one for which she held the most enthusiasm.

Exploring

Freewriting

First Leah started freewriting, which enabled her to probe her memory and to measure her inclinations. She would write without stopping, letting her ideas tumble forth in order to liberate and associate the many thoughts she had had on the subject of "sweat lodge."

> For several years I have wanted to worship in the way that I did when I was on the reservation. These people here at prison were discriminating against me, I thought. I knew that the other people here could go to the chaplain and to the chapel and they could do so without people complaining or going to any bother. I didn't know why they did not allow me to follow my own religious preference. Then I talked to the other Indian sisters here at the prison and they told me that they had been working for many years to get a sweat lodge. I started working with them. It took years of work, but it is worth it for now we have a sweat lodge where we can go for our ceremonies. It makes me feel good. I look forward to it. I have used it once a week for most of the last year. When I am nervous and when things are tense on the prison grounds, I think about the sweat lodge and just thinking about it gives me some peace. Then when I go there and sweat for a period of time I seem to feel that I am leaving the prison grounds and I am at peace with the universe. It is a ceremony that is important to me and also to the prison. We even have women who are not Indians who are interested and we teach them about Indian ways and we all learn from what we do. What else is there to say. I could go on and on. That is what I have to say. I love the sweat lodge which we call the sweats. I think it is the most important thing in my life now. I used to be bitter toward the prison for denying me my rights, but now I am even at peace with them—most of the time. I remember when we were trying to get approval and . . .

Brainstorming

After setting up a useful framework of questions, she let herself free-associate with tentative answers.

Who?   American Indian inmates and others
What?   sweat lodge—how it was started—the politics—the
         ceremonies

Where?	California Institution for Women—off the yard
When?	1989, before, after, long time in planning and building
Why?	spiritual, physical, self-esteem, educational

Clustering

Next Leah was ready for some more precise structuring of her thoughts, which would take the form of clustering. She began with a double circle enclosing her topic. Then, in response to the question What comes to mind? she bubbled in ideas on spokes radiating out from the hub. She knew that she was covering more than she could include in her essay, but she wanted to see her topic presented broadly so she could focus her work and proceed. Leah's first bubble cluster is shown in Figure 1.2.

Figure 1.2 Leah's First Bubble Cluster

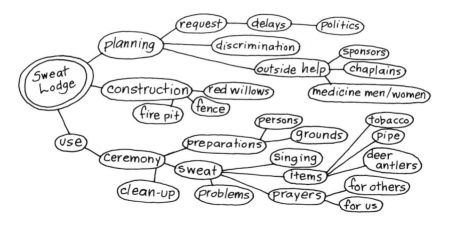

Stating the Point

Now Leah was ready to focus, concentrating on one aspect of her larger topic that could be reasonably developed in an essay of 500–800 words. She also wanted to establish a direction for the essay that would target her audience, who knew little about her topic. It would be necessary to explain her topic in detail so that uninformed readers could easily understand. Moreover, she would avoid any Native American word that her audience might not know. Although the sweat lodge was developed in an atmosphere of controversy in which she and others often had to be persuasive, she anticipated that her readers of this essay would be open-minded and interested. She would simply inform them about her experience with the sweat lodge, giving a personal perspective. She would also have to avoid using prison slang because this essay was for an assignment in a college writing class.

The third attempt at writing the thesis produced a subject and its treatment that pleased her.

> I want to explain how we use the sweats and why.

> Using the prison sweat lodge involves specific practices which contribute to my well-being.

subject
treatment

> I want to discuss the <u>prison sweat lodge</u>, <u>what we do in the preparation period, what we do when we're inside for the ceremony, and what we do afterwards.</u>

Planning

Leah's next task was to organize her material. For this strategy, she went back to her clustering, which she had divided into Planning, Construction, and Use. She had already decided in formulating her topic to work with the "use" aspect and to explain it from her perspective. Therefore, she focused on only one part of the cluster. Her refined bubble cluster is shown in Figure 1.3.

Figure 1.3 Leah's Refined Bubble Cluster

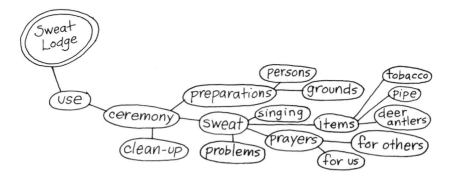

She might have started to write a first draft at this point, but instead she decided she wanted to recall and organize more detail, so she began an outline. She used her own memory and private reference sources for information. Had she been working on a reading-related topic, she would have gone back to the reading. Had she been working on a topic subject to research, she would have consulted library sources.

The outline shows a relationship of ideas, suggesting divisions of the essay according to her thesis and now indicating support. The divisions are Preparation, Ceremony, and Completion. Those items are her Roman-numeral headings.

thesis { subject / treatment }   I want to discuss the <u>prison sweat lodge,</u> <u>what we do in the</u> <u>preparation period, what we do when we're inside for the cere-</u> <u>mony, and what we do afterwards.</u>

     I. Preparation period
       A. Fasting
         1. Duration
         2. Only water
       B. Heat rocks
         1. Thirty to fifty
         2. Build fire
       C. Set up lodge
         1. Permission from sponsor
         2. Cover framework
    II. The ceremony
       A. Movement
         1. Going and coming
         2. Passing sacred objects
       B. Establishing attitude
       C. Sweating
       D. Praying and singing
       E. Purification rites
         1. Tobacco ties
         2. Sage
         3. Sweet grass
   III. Completing the ceremony and site restoration
       A. Personal
         1. Water down
         2. Eat and drink
         3. Change
       B. Site
         1. Remove and store blankets
         2. Move rocks

Drafting and Revising

At this point Leah was ready to write and revise her essay. After completing the first draft, she began revising. She marked problems, but she was mainly concerned with these points:

coherence   one idea leading smoothly to the next
language   usage, tone, and diction
unity   using the thesis to unify the essay parts and the
                        topic sentences to unify the developmental
                        paragraphs
emphasis   principally, repetition of words and phrases and
                        placement of key parts at the beginning or
                        ending of units
support   presenting evidence and reasoning in relation to
                        the thesis and topic sentences
sentence structure   especially, using a variety of beginnings and
                        types, along with avoiding fragments, comma
                        splices, and run-togethers

Editing

After revising her essay (to conserve space here, only one draft appears before the final), Leah began her editing. She knew that after completing the other drafts and doing the revision, a writer can be tempted into laziness. That condition may cause the writer to neglect such fundamentals as capitalization, omissions, punctuation, and spelling, thereby spoiling an otherwise strong project. She had already marked some of the items during the drafting and revising. She read the paper aloud twice to be sure that it flowed well and that she had no awkward phrases. Then she examined it with care. Here is the draft she edited.

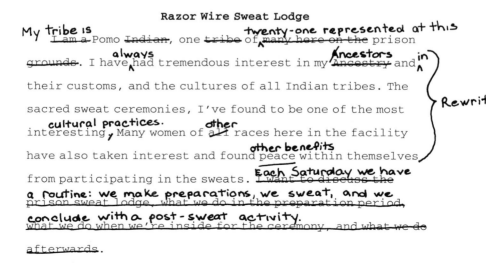

Razor Wire Sweat Lodge

My tribe is ~~I am a~~ Pomo ~~Indian~~, one ~~tribe~~ of ~~many here on the~~ prison twenty-one represented at this ~~grounds~~. I have always had tremendous interest in my ~~Ancestry~~ Ancestors and in their customs, and the cultures of all Indian tribes. The sacred sweat ceremonies, I've found to be one of the most interesting, cultural practices. Many women of ~~all~~ other races here in the facility have also taken interest and found ~~peace within themselves~~ other benefits from participating in the sweats. Each Saturday we have ~~I want to discuss the~~ a routine: we make preparations, we sweat, and we ~~prison sweat lodge, what we do in the preparation period,~~ conclude with a post-sweat activity. ~~what we do when we're inside for the ceremony, and what we do~~ ~~afterwards.~~

Rewrite

The first step to sweating [in our prison facility] ∧ is the preparation period.   } Rewrite for stronger Topic sentence

Before anyone can sweat there are many requirements ~~in~~ [concerning] what we

wear, ~~how we are instructed (depending on how many times we've~~

~~gone)~~, and how we act. [For] ~~T~~wenty-four hours before the sweat ⓪ we

fast. ~~We can only drink~~ [We do not eat anything and drink only] water or juices, but if someone has } coherence

health problems ⓪ we will excuse ~~them~~. [her] ∧ The lava rocks have to [heat] ∧ in

the fire approximately three hours before we start sweating.

The fire has to be built just right in a little house shape.

~~Putting~~ [We put] all the rocks in the middle with the wood standing   ⎞ organize

like a teepee around them; then the paper [is] ∧ stuffed between and   } Be more

around the wood. Once there's a good fire going ⓪ ~~then~~ we ~~start~~   ⎠ concise

tend to the sweat lodge itself. Since we have no tarp to put on

the sweat lodge, the state has provided us with plenty of

blankets. The blankets have to cover the sweat lodge fully. We

put at least three layers of blankets on the sweat lodge. We

make sure we leave about eight inches of blanket around the

bottom of the sweat lodge. [By] ~~Around~~ this time some women have

started making their tobacco ties. These ties are used for

coherence [sending] ~~putting~~ your prayer on. We [must] ~~'ve got to~~ make sure the sponser is

somewhere by the sweat lodge at all times. [As for] ~~Also about~~ the rocks,

we use thirty to fifty of them ⓪ It depends on their size and how

many women are sweating that day. Then the women are told to ⟩ Rewrite

change into only muu muu; [is] the state provides them also. [Finally] Then

[are] we ~~'re~~ ready to go inside. The preparation period is very

important [but] ~~and~~ everyone looks forward to it [s] being over.

[From this point on through the ceremony, everything must]
~~Once everyone is inside the sweat lodge, there are certain~~
[be done according to rules.]
~~things you must do. The way we enter is~~ first we enter counter ∧

clockwise, and [once] ∧ inside we ~~maintain everything we do~~ [conduct all parts of the ceremony] counter ∧

clockwise. There are four rounds in the sweat ∧ [each of] which lasts about

twenty to thirty minutes ~~each~~. We stress that no one should break our
[coherence] circle inside the sweat lodge, but it ~~is possible~~ sometimes happens. Some women
can't handle the heat inside, steam and the so we never make them stay. The   [Rephra]
praying and singing is in the Sioux language since our outside
sponsor is Sioux. Not everyone has to sing or pray. It's up to the
individual. ~~Them.~~ As someone finishes a prayer ~~they say for all their~~ she mentions her relatives
~~relations~~, then the next person prays. ~~Before anyone even~~ we   [Agr]
~~enter the sweat, they have to make sure they have peace and~~
~~good feelings with all other members~~. The tobacco ties hang
over our heads in the sweat or around our necks. Also we take in
sage with us and smudge ourselves with it for purification. After each round,   [Be more concise]
[Verb tense] new hot rocks are brought in. As these rocks are placed in the
fire, sweet grass is put on them. ~~All~~ What we do inside the sweat lodge
is not only for ourselves, but ~~for~~ through our prayers for others. We
maintain ourselves with humility during the whole sweat.

    When the sweat is over we enter the final phase. We come out
and throw our tobacco ties in to the fire pit. and the smoke takes our prayers to the sky Then ~~first thing~~ we ~~do~~
~~is~~ hose ourselves down with plenty of cold water. ~~The~~ and open
refreshments ~~are opened and someone goes after food.~~ we've bought. Once
we've eaten and changed our cloths we start ~~taking down~~ dismantling the
sweat. The blankets have to be taken off the same way they were
put on and folded ~~up good~~ carefully. The left-over wood has to be put
away and ~~on both~~ the blankets and the wood ~~we put their covers~~ must be covered.
Any garbage that's been left around is thrown in to the dumpster.
Then we lock the gate and bid ~~our~~ f farewells ~~until the next~~
~~weekend~~. After its all over ~~you really~~ we feel ~~a sense of~~ physically   [move to end of next ¶]
refreshed ~~ness~~ and clean ~~liness~~ and peaceful ~~ness~~.
Using ~~The~~ sweat lodge is a custom of most ~~ly all~~ Indian tribes.   [Rewrit]
Certain Indian tribes go about it differently ~~than~~ from others but

once they're all inside everyone feels of one whole being. ~~All three of the steps I've gone through are helpful for a successful sweat ceremony.~~ ~~Many of us members~~ Each week we look forward to ~~these~~ this ceremon~~ies every week~~y. ~~They~~ It help~~s~~ us cope better with the prison system.

Final Draft

Razor Wire Sweat Lodge

Leah

My Indian tribe is Pomo, one of twenty-one 1 represented at this prison. I have always had tremendous interest in my ancestors and their customs, and in the cultures of all Indian tribes. The sacred sweat ceremony has always been at the center of my life. Here at prison it has taken on a special meaning. In fact, many women of other races here have also found peace within themselves as a result of participating with me and other

thesis   American Indians in the sweats. Each Saturday we have a routine: we make preparations, we sweat, and we conclude with a post-sweat activity.

topic sentence   Before we sweat, we must prepare ourselves and the facility. For twenty-four 2 hours before the sweat, we fast. We do not eat anything and drink only water or juices, but if someone has a health problem, we will excuse her. As for clothing we wear simple, loose dresses such as the prison-issued muu-muus. We bring tobacco ties, sage leaves, sweet grass, and sometimes a pipe. Preparing the facility is more complicated than preparing ourselves. About thirty-five lava rocks must be heated in a fire approximately three hours before we start sweating. The wood for the fire has to be placed in a tepee shape around the pile of rocks and ignited. Once the fire is hot, we tend to the sweat lodge itself. Since we have no tarp to put on the sweat lodge frame, the state provides us with blankets. We use these to cover the lodge fully, draping it with about three layers and leaving an opening to the east. Finally we are ready to go inside. The preparation period is very important, but everyone looks forward to its being over.

topic sentence   From this point on through the ceremony,   3
everything must be done according to rules.
First we enter counterclockwise, and once inside we conduct all parts of the ceremony counterclockwise. There are four rounds in the sweat, each of which lasts about twenty to thirty minutes. We stress that no one should break our circle inside the sweat lodge, but it sometimes happens. Some women can't handle the steam and the heat, so we

never make them stay. Those who do stay are free to participate in the singing and praying or not. The four rounds are similar. For each, six hot rocks are brought in, and six dippers of water are poured onto the rocks. The number six indicates the four directions and the sky and the ground. As someone finishes a prayer (usually in Sioux because our sponsor is a Sioux), she mentions her relatives, for this ceremony is also for others. Then another person follows. As sweet grass burns outside on the fire, we sit in the hot steam with tobacco ties hanging over our heads or around our necks and rub sage leaves on our bodies for purification. We maintain ourselves with humility during the whole sweat.

topic sentence   When the sweat is over, we enter the final   4
phase. We come out and throw our tobacco ties into the fire pit, and the smoke takes our prayers to the sky. Then we hose ourselves down with plenty of cold water and open the refreshments we brought. Once we've eaten and changed our clothes, we start dismantling the sweat. The blankets have to be taken off the same way they were put up and then folded carefully. The left-over wood has to be put away, and the blankets and wood must be covered. Any garbage that's been left

around is thrown into the dumpster. Then we
lock the gate to our facility and bid our
farewells.

Using a sweat lodge is a custom of most   5
Indian tribes. Certain Indian tribes go
about it differently from others, but in here
when we are together in the lodge, we feel
like one whole being. Each week we look
forward to this ceremony. It helps us cope
better with the prison system. After it's
over, we feel physically refreshed, clean,
and peaceful.

Any of paragraphs 2 through 4 is a good example of a developmental paragraph. Consider paragraph 2 in relation to the outline to see how Leah used the steps in the preparation process to support her topic sentence.

topic sentence	<u>Before we sweat, we must prepare ourselves</u>
step 1: preparing ourselves	<u>and the facility.</u> For twenty-four hours
	before the sweat, we fast. We do not eat
	anything and drink only water or juices, but
	if someone has a health problem, we will
	excuse her. As for clothing we wear simple,
	loose dresses such as the prison-issued muu-
	muus. We bring tobacco ties, sage leaves,
step 2: preparing the facility	sweet grass, and sometimes a pipe. Preparing
	the facility is more complicated than
	preparing ourselves. About thirty-five lava
	rocks must be heated in a fire approximately
	three hours before we start sweating. The

wood for the fire has to be placed in a tepee shape around the pile of rocks and ignited. Once the fire is hot, we tend to the sweat lodge itself. Since we have no tarp to put on the sweat lodge frame, the state provides us with blankets. We use these to cover the lodge fully, draping it with about three layers and leaving an opening to the east. Finally we are ready to go inside. The preparation period is very important, but everyone looks forward to its being over.

2

Pivotal Moments in American Experience

We all have pivotal moments, times when something happens that helps define us. These are experiences that represent growth, or, conversely, even some reduction in what we are or think we are. In short, they nudge us forward or push us back, and we remember them vividly, although we may not recognize their significance immediately. Perhaps only the perspective of time will give us standards for judging such events, but inevitably they represent self-discovery. Of course, pivotal moments always occur within the framework of our society, and, therefore, they reveal many aspects of culture. Elders often dwell upon these moments and pass them down as oral history to their children and grandchildren. This chapter includes accounts of several such moments. Many are about childhood, usually the most impressionable time of life, but defining moments can and do occur at any time. Although these accounts are interesting because they reveal something about particular cultures, they are even more interesting because we know that they have parallels in other cultures and, therefore, are part of the commonality of human experience.

WRITING STRATEGIES AND TECHNIQUES: NARRATION

In our everyday lives, we tell stories and invite other people to do so by asking questions such as "What happened at work today?" and "What did you do last weekend?" We are disappointed when the answer is "Nothing much." We may be equally disappointed when a person doesn't give us enough details—or maybe gives us too many and spoils the effect. After all, we are interested in people's stories and in the people who tell them. We like the narrative.

What is the narrative? *The narrative is an account of an incident or a series of incidents that make up a complete and significant action.* Each narrative has five properties:

- *setup,* which may be quite brief or even implied, but always gives the necessary setting or situation for the action ("It was a Saturday afternoon in the park");
- *conflict,* which is at the heart of each story ("when this mugger came up and grabbed my purse.");
- *struggle,* which adds action to the conflict, though it need not be physical engagement ("He yanked and I yanked back, and then I kicked him in the groin.");
- *outcome,* which is merely the result of the struggle ("He ran away, and I smirked."); and
- *meaning,* which is a significance and may be deeply philosophical or simple, stated or implied ("Don't mess with me!").

These components are present in some way in all of the many forms of the narrative.

Purposes and Forms

Narratives primarily inform or persuade, although they may also entertain. They make up many of the examples we use in explaining ideas, and they engage a reader's feelings and intellect as we persuade readers to accept our views. Narratives can be used in brief paragraph statements and throughout the essay, in the introduction, the developmental paragraphs, and the conclusion.

Narratives come in different lengths and forms. Parts of short stories, novels, essays, ballads, and plays are narrative. Anecdotes and jokes are often purely narrative.

Narrative Technique

Order

Narratives almost always move in chronological order. The progressive action, of course, carries that idea, but transitional words that suggest time change—such as *then, later, soon, finally, last,* and *now*—are also useful. Furthermore, you can specify time change directly by using such phrases as "the next day," "after ten minutes had passed," and "when the smoke had cleared," for example.

Because description is so frequently an ally of narration, you may combine references to space as a technique for giving order to your writing. Space references include the specific noting of movement from place to place by using words such as *here, there,* and *beyond.*

Verb Tense

Because most narratives relate experience in time order, the verb tense is more likely to be past (She *walked* into the room) than present (She *walks* into the room), though you can use either. An unnecessary change in tense may distract or confuse readers.

Two generalizations may be useful as you work with verb tense.

- Most narratives (often summaries) taken from literature are written in *present tense.*

  Tom Sawyer *pretends* that painting the fence *is* a special pleasure. His friends *watch* him eagerly. He *talks* and *displays* his joy. They do his work and *pay* him.

- Most historical events and personal experiences are written in *past tense.*

  We *walked* down the path to the well-house, attracted by the fragrance of the honeysuckle with which it *was covered.* Someone *was* drawing water and my teacher *placed* my hand under the spout. As the cool stream *gushed* over one hand she *spelled* into the other the word *water,* first slowly, then rapidly.

  Helen Keller,
  The Story of My Life

Although Helen Keller chose the conventional past tense for verbs in the last passage, in a different context she might have chosen the present tense for a sense of immediacy.

The two main points about tense are:

- The generalizations about verb-tense selection (using past for the historical and personal and using present for fiction) are useful.
- The change of verb tense in a passage should be made only when the change is needed for clarity or emphasis.

Point of View

Point of view shows the writer's relationship to the material, the subject, and it usually does not change within a passage.

If you are conveying personal experience, the point of view will be *first person*, which can be either involved (a participant) or detached (an observer). The involved perspective uses *I* more prominently than the detached does.

If you are presenting something from a distance, geographical or historical (for example, telling a story about George Washington), the point of view will be *third person*, and the participants will be referred to as "he," "she," and "they."

In the following paragraph the author is present but uninvolved other than as another member of the audience (and even then she is mainly watching the audience). The annotation indicates narrative parts and tense change. Transitional words (those indicating the order of time) are italicized.

	A slick-haired Russian M.C. announced B. B. King ("A great Negritanski musician"), and *then* King was onstage with his well-known guitar—Lucille—and a ten-man ensemble. *As*
conflict introduced	King and the ensemble swung into "Why I Sing the Blues," <u>one could sense the puzzlement of the Russian audience.</u> "Negro" music to them meant jazz or spirituals, but this was something
tense change with a reason: King as a person, aside from the narrative, is discussed in the present tense	else. Also, <u>there was the question of response.</u> B. B. King is a great, warm presence when he performs, and he asks his audiences to pour themselves out to him in return. <u>King teases his audiences,</u> urging them to clap along, to whistle, to hoot their appreciation, like the congregations in the Southern churches in which he grew up. But to Russians, such behavior suggests a
conflict dealt with	lack of culture and an almost frightening disorder. Though obviously impressed, the audience *at first* kept a respectful silence *during* the numbers, as it might at the symphony. (Only the foreigners shouted and stomped out the beat; we found the
conflict dealt with	Russians around us staring at us open-mouthed.) *Then* <u>King played an irresistible riff, stopped, and leaned toward the audi-</u>

<table>
<tr><td>conflict dealt with</td><td>ence with his hand cupped to his ear. The audience caught on and began to clap. <u>King changed the beat, and waited for the audience to catch up.</u> *Then* he changed it again. *Soon* the whole place was clapping along to "Get Off My Back, Woman," and there were even a few timid shouts and whistles. <u>King, who has carried the blues to Europe, Africa, and the Far East, had bro-</u></td></tr>
<tr><td>outcome</td><td><u>ken the ice one more time.</u></td></tr>
</table>

Andrea Lee,
"The Blues Abroad"

Description

A good descriptive writer presents material so that the perceptive reader can read and reexperience the writer's ideas. One device important to that writer is imagery. Images can be perceived through the senses (sight, sound, taste, smell, and touch). A good descriptive writer also gives specific details and presents concrete particulars (actual things) in a convincing way. We read, we visualize, we identify, and *zap!*—connection with a narrative account.

In the following paragraphs the images are italicized to emphasize how the author has made us see, hear, smell, touch, and see. Also note the other specific details.

> Before she had quite arisen, she *called* our names and *issued* orders, and *pushed* her large feet into homemade slippers and *across* the *bare lye-washed wooden floor* to *light* the coal-oil lamp.
>
> The *lamplight* in the Store gave a *soft* make-believe feeling to our world which made me want to *whisper* and walk about on tiptoe. The *odors* of onions and oranges and kerosene had been *mixing* all night and wouldn't be disturbed until the wooded slat was removed from the door and the early morning air forced its way in with the bodies of people who had walked miles to reach the pickup place.

Maya Angelou,
"Cotton-Picking Time"

Note the use of specific information in the next paragraph.

On one recent Saturday afternoon a Latino fifth-grader, wearing the same type of hightop tennis shoes I wore as a 10-year-old on that same street corner, strode up to Señor Farrillas' snow-cone pushcart. The kid pulled out a pocketful of dimes and bought two *raspadas*. One for himself, and one for his school chum—a Vietnamese kid. He was wearing hightops, too. They both ordered strawberry, as I recall.

Luis Torres,
"Los Chinos Discover el Barrio"

Torres presents the material so you can visualize it. Try to picture this, instead: "The other day I saw a youngster buy a refreshment for himself and his friend." Of course, that is what happened, but very little narrative/descriptive communication takes place in this abbreviated version. In Torres's account, you know when and where the action took place. You know what the kids were wearing, and you know that the author (point of view as technique) identifies with the kids. They buy strawberry *raspadas* from Señor Farrillas. The Latino kid pays for the *raspadas* with "a pocketful of dimes." Did you ever, as a kid, put your hand in the pocket of some tight jeans and try to pull out those dimes with a balled fist? We identify, and the imagery registers. We may not have visited that street corner in reality, but vicariously we take a trip with Torres.

The following student-written paragraph and essay illustrate effective uses of narrative.

EGGS TITANIC*

Diana Dill

setup
Every family has stories that its members tell and pass along from generation to generation. My favorite concerns my great-grandfather and great-grandmother, showing how they managed to have a good marriage, though their cultures were different. They both immigrated to America from Europe, he from Ireland and she from Germany. They came through Ellis Island and met a year later, though she knew little English. After two years of courtship and hard work, they were married. He

conflict
wanted her to cook foods that he liked, and she did her best. On one occasion the result was humorous. She had just served him fried eggs when he told her that he would like to have some boiled eggs the next time. She

struggle
had never boiled eggs before, and she thought the whole idea was a bit strange, but she decided to try. First she boiled a pot of water; then she broke some eggs into the

outcome

meaning

water, stirring briskly and cooking the concoction until the eggs were stringy and well-done. When my great-grandfather came home from work, she served him a big bowl of "boiled eggs" and some bread. He thanked her very kindly and ate the eggs bravely with a big spoon. The next day he contacted my great-grandmother's cousin, who spoke good English, and explained what he meant by boiled eggs. He also said he didn't want to hurt his wife's feelings. The following day he came home to a plate of eggs that had been boiled in the shell.

A BEE IN MY BONNET*

Elizabeth Brock

setup

My grandmother, who came from the hill country of   1
Oklahoma, had a wonderful vocabulary of folk expressions and country words. She also had a collection of stories that I got to know by heart. In short, she was my favorite person—the owner of all wisdom and goodness—and whatever she said was, as she would phrase it, "the gospel truth." Of course, as a child before I started to school, I wanted to talk like her. Then in the first grade, I discovered that Grandma's language could get me laughed at.

At the beginning of that school year, we were read-   2
ing little books about many countries, places that I had never heard of. One book was about Greece. It was full of all kinds of difficult words such as "Socrates" and "olympics," and it had pictures of buildings that were on top of hills and looked different from any I'd seen. All of us in the Blue group had copies of the book on Greece, but our teacher had a special book. It was large with colorful paintings and drawings.

conflict

One day she brought it to our table and began to   3
read. Then she got to the word *pillar*. "Does anyone know what the word *pillar* means?" she asked. I was shy and didn't want to answer, but when no one else knew, my hand rose slowly as if I thought someone might slap it at any time. When she called me by name, I said, "A pillar is something you put your head on when you're

going to sleep." For a brief moment there was silence, and I felt proud. I even thought of my grandmother saying, "Take your pillar and go in there and get your nap."

struggle

Then the teacher began laughing. "No, Elizabeth," 4 she said. "You're talking about a pillow. A pillow is what you put under your head." With that explanation, the students began to laugh, and I tried to laugh too, but my face was both frozen and red. The teacher held up her book and pointed to some large round supports on a Greek temple. "These are pillars," she said.

outcome

That one incident would set me back for the whole 5 year in volunteering to answer questions. I could never seem to forget it. But I didn't tell anyone in my family about it. After school, I just went home and stomped around a little, and Grandma said, "You got a bee in your bonnet today, honey?" and I said I did. I still liked the way she talked, but right then I started sorting out the Grandma language from my school language.

meaning

Though Grandma has died, I look back and remem- 6 ber her words with great fondness. They didn't help me in school, but they are my family words—my country grandma words that bring back poignant memories—and those words are some of the best I've ever heard.

WRITER'S CHECKLIST

- Consider personal experience for good subject material.
- Develop your ideas so there is actually a plot structure in segments from conflict to outcome.
- Remember that most narratives are presented in chronological order; space order can also provide coherence.
- Use dialogue when appropriate.
- Use specific descriptions. Make your readers experience—see, smell, taste, hear, touch—vicariously.
- Give details concerning action.
- Be consistent with point of view and verb tense.
- Keep in mind that most narratives written as college assignments will have an expository purpose (they explain a specified idea).
- Consider working with a short time frame for short writing assignments. The scope would usually be no more than one incident of

brief duration for one paragraph. For example, writing about an entire graduation ceremony might be too complicated, but concentrating on the moment when you walked forward to receive the diploma or the moment when the relatives and friends come down on the field could work very well.

DARK DAY IN THE DUST BOWL

John Steinbeck

In the 1930s, a dust storm descended upon the Southwest. The sun disappeared, the chickens went to roost in the middle of the day, a desert invaded the fields, and sand drifted in like snow, in places covering whole houses. Initially, some people, especially those in rural areas, thinking the end of the world was upon them, fled to churches or withdrew into themselves. But then they found the strength to survive, some digging out and digging in, some moving out and away. In Grapes of Wrath, *from which this excerpt is taken, John Steinbeck depicts the people in an early stage of confronting this "natural" disaster.*

The people came out of their houses and smelled the hot stinging air and covered their noses from it. And the children came out of their houses, but they did not run or shout as they would have done after a rain. Men stood by their fences and looked at the ruined corn, drying fast now, only a little green showing through the film of dust. The men were silent and they did not move often. And the women came out of the houses to stand beside their men—to feel whether this time the men would break. The women studied the men's faces secretly, for the corn could go, as long as something else remained. The children stood near by, drawing figures in the dust with bare toes, and the children sent exploring senses out to see whether men and women would break. The children peeked at the faces of the men and women, and then drew careful lines in the dust with their toes. Horses came to the watering troughs and nuzzled the water to clear the surface dust. After a while the faces of the watching men lost their bemused perplexity and became hard and angry and resistant. Then the women knew that they were safe and that there was no break. Then they asked, What'll we do? And the men replied, I don't know. But it was all right. The women knew it was all right, and the watching children knew it was all right. Women and children knew deep in themselves that no misfortune was too great to bear if their men were whole. The women went into the houses to their work, and the children began to play, but cautiously at first. As the day went forward the sun became less red. It flared down on the dust-blanketed land. The men sat in the doorways of their houses; their hands were busy with sticks and little rocks. The men sat still—thinking—figuring.

Vocabulary

bemused
perplexity

Critical Thinking and Discussion

1. Notice how each group looks at something. What do the men look at? What do the women look at? What do the children look at?
2. What is more important, finding a solution or maintaining self-control?
3. Explain how this could be a pivotal moment for any person there, but especially the children.
4. Briefly, what are the situation, the conflict, the struggle, the outcome, and the meaning?
5. How does descriptive detail heighten the tension? In other words, what is emphasized?
6. What words or phrases suggest the passage of time and give chronological order to this piece?

Reading-Related Writing

1. Write about a time when your family was beset by trouble and your parents maintained their composure and dignity even before the problem was dealt with.
2. Rewrite this paragraph from the point of view of one of the children Steinbeck mentions.

WALKING IN OTHERS' SHOES

Katherine Barrett

This pivotal experience is different from the others in this chapter in that it was actually staged. Pat Moore was a young woman who wanted to know what it was like to be old. At twenty-six, she engaged the help of a professional makeup artist and transformed herself into an eighty-five-year-old woman. She went through this transformation more than two hundred times in fourteen different states. Reported by

Katherine Barrett, what follows is only a small incident from Moore's experiences.

It was a slushy, gray day and Pat had laboriously descended four flights of stairs from her apartment to go shopping. Once outside, she struggled to hold her threadbare coat closed with one hand and manipulate her cane with the other. Splotches of snow made the street difficult for anyone to navigate, but for someone hunched over, as she was, it was almost impossible. The curb was another obstacle. The slush looked ankle-deep—and what was she to do? Jump over it? Slowly, she worked her way around to a drier spot, but the crowds were impatient to move. A woman with packages jostled her as she rushed past, causing Pat to nearly lose her balance. If I really were old, I would have fallen, she thought. Maybe broken something. On another day, a woman had practically knocked her over by letting go of a heavy door as Pat tried to enter a coffee shop. Then there were the revolving doors. How could you push them without strength? And how could you get up and down stairs, on and off a bus, without risking a terrible fall?

Vocabulary

laboriously
manipulate
jostled

Critical Reading and Discussion

1. What does Moore have to contend with as an older woman?
2. What seems to be the attitude of others?
3. What does she learn?
4. How do descriptive details heighten the tension?
5. What words or phrases suggest the passage of time and give chronological order to this selection?

Reading-Related Writing

1. Write about a person with a different handicap dealing with a specific problem.
2. Write about the transformed Pat Moore in a different situation, such as getting on a bus or subway, shopping, or walking a crime-ridden street.
3. Create a situation in which Pat Moore actually meets an eighty-five-year-old woman who needs help. In your account, point out what she might learn from such an encounter.

Collaborative Learning

As an exercise in role-playing, duplicate Pat Moore's experience by simulating a handicap. You might choose individuals from the following suggestions, in order to gain some impression of how difficult life can be for others:

Blindness: Wear a blindfold and be led.

Deafness: Wear ear plugs during some activity.

Dyslexia: Create an area in which all signs and instructions are spelled incorrectly.

Second-language problems: Engage a student who speaks a second language to conduct your group meeting in his or her language.

Physical limitation: Try to walk through a crowd or up the stairs on crutches, or try to use a wheelchair.

Either as a group or individually, write about your experiences.

LANGUAGE SET ME FREE

Helen Keller

Helen Keller (1880–1968) was a remarkable person. With the help of her teacher and companion, Anne Sullivan, she conquered the handicaps of blindness and deafness and became one of the most famous and admired persons of her time. Here she writes about perhaps the most important constructive event in her life.

One day, while I was playing with my new doll, Miss Sullivan put my big rag 1
doll into my lap also, spelled "d-o-l-l" and tried to make me understand that "d-o-l-l" applied to both. Earlier in the day we had had a tussle over the words "m-u-g" and "w-a-t-e-r." Miss Sullivan had tried to impress it upon me that "m-u-g" is *mug* and that "w-a-t-e-r" is *water*, but I persisted in confounding the two. In despair she had dropped the subject for the time, only to renew it at the first opportunity. I became impatient at her repeated attempts and, seizing the new doll, I dashed it upon the floor. I was keenly delighted when I felt the fragments of the broken doll at my feet. Neither sorrow nor regret followed my passionate outburst. I had not loved the doll. In the still, dark world in which I lived there was no strong sentiment of tenderness. I felt my teacher sweep the fragments to one side of the hearth,

and I had a sense of satisfaction that the cause of my discomfort was removed. She brought me my hat, and I knew I was going out into the warm sunshine. This thought, if a wordless sensation may be called a thought, made me hop and skip with pleasure.

We walked down the path to the well-house, attracted by the fragrance of 2 the honeysuckle with which it was covered. Someone was drawing water and my teacher placed my hand under the spout. As the cool stream gushed over one hand she spelled into the other the word *water*, first slowly, then rapidly. I stood still, my whole attention fixed upon the motions of her fingers. Suddenly I felt a misty consciousness as of something forgotten—a thrill of returning thought; and somehow the mystery of language was revealed to me. I knew then that "w-a-t-e-r" meant the wonderful cool something that was flowing over my hand. That living word awakened my soul, gave it light, hope, joy, set it free! There were barriers still, it is true, but barriers that could in time be swept away.

Critical Thinking and Discussion

1. What is Keller's condition before the event described?
2. Why is she at first uncooperative?
3. Why is this such a significant time for her?
4. How important is description (especially using the sense of touch) in creating the narrative account?

Reading-Related Writing

This passage relates an epiphany—a moment that reveals an important truth (through setup, incident, and meaning). This one experience transformed Helen Keller's life. Using this passage as a model, write about an epiphany of your own, such as the first time you knew or understood something about a concept such as love, caring, or family. Or write about the moment you first realized you could read or learn another language.

CHILDREN OF THE HARVEST

Lois Phillips Hudson

Children naturally crave stability—the same friends, neighborhood, schools, and activities. Change is the unknown—an unfamiliar territory, perhaps one with no friends, new enemies, and a new set of mysterious rules. But for some, such as these children depicted in

Reapers of the Dust, *change is the only constant, and trying to deal with hostility and prejudice becomes a main occupation.*

When we got to school, the teacher kept me standing at her desk while she 1 called the role and started the class on a reading assignment. When she looked up at me, I got the irrational impression that I had already managed to do something wrong. She asked where I had come from and I said "North Dakota," thinking it would be simpler than trying to tell all the places I had been in the last three months. She gave me the last seat in a row behind a boy in dirty clothes. As she passed by him she made the faintest sound of exhalation, as though she was ridding her nostrils of a disagreeable smell.

At recess a boy in a bright shirt and new cream-colored corduroy pants 2 yelled "North Dakota, North Dakota!" in a funny way as he ran past me to the ball field. The boy who sat ahead of me came up and said confidentially, "We been out all around here for two years. We come from Oklahoma. We're Okies. That's what *you* are too, even if you didn't come from Oklahoma." I knew I could never be anything that sounded so crummy as "Okie," and I said so. "Oh, yeah!" he rejoined stiffly. I walked away before he could argue any more and went to find my sister, but the primary grades had recess at a different time, so I went and stood by the door until the period was over. That afternoon I stayed in my seat reading a history book, but the teacher, who seemed to want to go outdoors herself, said, "It's better for the room if everybody goes outside for recess." So I went out and stood around the fringes of two or three games and wondered what was funny about North Dakota. Somehow I had the feeling that it would hurt my mother if I asked her.

Critical Reading and Discussion

1. Hudson writes about this childhood experience after she is mature. Why does she remember the details so well?
2. Are you surprised that the "Okie" youngster is not more sympathetic? Explain.
3. What did the teacher do to make the new student feel unwelcome?
4. Who made the deepest hurtful impression—the boy who yelled "North Dakota," the boy who called her an "Okie," or the teacher? Discuss each.

Reading-Related Writing

1. Write about this incident from the teacher's point of view.
2. Write about this incident from the "Okie" youngster's point of view.
3. Write about an incident in which you or someone you know was discriminated against in a school situation (perhaps because of family social standing, appearance, race, gender, sexual preference, handicap, or age).

MY SCHOOL NIGHTMARE*

Anna Kuang

Your first day of school anywhere may be a traumatic experience. Your first day of school in a new country may be even more—a nightmare. For a young child a small, seemingly insignificant incident may seem horrendous and permanently damaging. But at such a time an act of kindness may offset the embarrassment and pain and be just as memorable.

My first day of school in America was also the worst nightmare of my life. I still remember that day. I woke up early in the morning, and my uncle took me to school. During the first period, I sat in the classroom and listened, although I couldn't understand what the teacher was talking about. Fifty minutes passed. I saw everybody walk out of the classroom, and I didn't know what they were doing, but I walked out with them. I still didn't realize that the school system in America was different from that in China. In China, the students don't change classrooms every period, but the teachers do. In America, students, rather than teachers, change classrooms. So, I went back to the same classroom again, and I stayed in that room until noon. Lunch hour was coming. In China, everybody goes home for lunch, so I thought people did the same thing here. I left for home, and a school security man stopped me outside of school. He talked to me, and I didn't know what he was talking about. From the time I had arrived at school to the time I tried to leave, strange people had bustled around me and spoken a language that I had never heard. I was frustrated and scared, and I wanted to cry. Some of my schoolmates looked at me as if I were an alien. My face turned red, and my heart was crying, but I hid my tears. Then a Chinese girl came up and talked to me in Chinese. She told me that we had to stay in school until the last period. At that time, I did not know that she would become my best friend, but I did know that she had awakened me from my worst nightmare.

Critical Reading and Discussion

1. Briefly, what are the situation, the conflict, the struggle, the outcome, and the meaning?
2. What words or phrases suggest the passage of time and give chronological order to this piece?
3. In what way is this a memorable and significant moment?

Reading-Related Writing

1. Write about a similar experience you or someone you know has had.
2. Write about your worst "nightmare" experience and how an unexpected friend helped you.
3. Write about this incident from the unexpected friend's point of view.
4. Write about a time when you were an unexpected friend.

THE PIE

Gary Soto

Author and teacher Gary Soto here discusses the time when he gave in to temptation, swapping immediate gratification for ensuing guilt. After committing his act, he returned to his home where he "knew" that others knew. It is the classic story of crime and self-punishment, filtered through childhood perceptions, which, of course, magnify and distort. This is taken from his collection of essays A Summer Life *(1990).*

I knew enough about hell to stop me from stealing. I was holy in almost every 1
bone. Some days I recognized the shadows of angels flopping on the backyard grass, and other days I heard faraway messages in the plumbing that howled underneath the house when I crawled there looking for something to do.

But boredom made me sin. Once, at the German Market, I stood before a 2
rack of pies, my sweet tooth gleaming and the juice of guilt wetting my underarms. I gazed at the nine kinds of pie, pecan and apple being my favorites, although cherry looked good, and my dear, fat-faced chocolate was always a good bet. I nearly wept trying to decide which to steal and, forgetting the flowery dust priests give off, the shadow of angels and the proximity of God howling in the plumbing underneath the house, sneaked a pie behind my coffee-lid frisbee and walked to the door, grinning to the bald grocer whose forehead shone with a window of light.

"No one saw," I muttered to myself, the pie like a discus in my hand, and 3
hurried across the street, where I sat on someone's lawn. The sun wavered between the branches of a yellowish sycamore. A squirrel nailed itself high on the trunk, where it forked into two large bark-scabbed limbs. Just as I was going to work my cleanest finger into the pie, a neighbor came out to the porch for his mail. He looked at me, and I got up and headed for home. I raced on skinny legs to my block, but slowed to a quick walk when I couldn't

wait any longer. I held the pie to my nose and breathed in its sweetness. I licked some of the crust and closed my eyes as I took a small bite.

In my front yard, I leaned against a car fender and panicked about 4 stealing the apple pie. I knew an apple got Eve in deep trouble with snakes because Sister Marie had shown us a film about Adam and Eve being cast into the desert, and what scared me more than falling from grace was being thirsty for the rest of my life. But even that didn't stop me from clawing a chunk from the pie tin and pushing it into the cavern of my mouth. The slop was sweet and gold-colored in the afternoon sun. I laid more pieces on my tongue, wet finger-dripping pieces, until I was finished and felt like crying because it was about the best thing I had ever tasted. I realized right there and then, in my sixth year, in my tiny body of two hundred bones and three or four sins, that the best things in life came stolen. I wiped my sticky fingers on the grass and rolled my tongue over the corners of my mouth. A burp perfumed the air.

I felt bad not sharing with Cross-Eyed Johnny, a neighbor kid. He stood 5 over my shoulder and asked, "Can I have some?" Crust fell from my mouth, and my teeth were bathed with the jam-like filling. Tears blurred my eyes as I remembered the grocer's forehead. I remembered the other pies on the rack, the warm air of the fan above the door and the car that honked as I crossed the street without looking.

"Get away," I had answered Cross-Eyed Johnny. He watched my fingers 6 greedily push big chunks of pie down my throat. He swallowed and said in a whisper, "Your hands are dirty," then returned home to climb his roof and sit watching me eat the pie by myself. After a while, he jumped off and hobbled away because the fall had hurt him.

I sat on the curb. The pie tin glared at me and rolled away when the wind 7 picked up. My face was sticky with guilt. A car honked, and the driver knew. Mrs. Hancock stood on her lawn, hands on hip, and she knew. My mom, peeling a mountain of potatoes at the Redi-Spud factory, knew. I got to my feet, stomach taut, mouth tired of chewing, and flung my frisbee across the street, its shadow like the shadow of an angel fleeing bad deeds. I retrieved it, jogging slowly. I flung it again until I was bored and thirsty.

I returned home to drink water and help my sister glue bottle caps onto 8 cardboard, a project for summer school. But the bottle caps bored me, and the water soon filled me up more than the pie. With the kitchen stifling with heat and lunatic flies, I decided to crawl underneath our house and lie in the cool shadows listening to the howling sound of plumbing. Was it God? Was it Father, speaking from death, or Uncle with his last shiny dime? I listened, ear pressed to a cold pipe, and heard a howl like the sea. I lay until I was cold and then crawled back to the light, rising from one knee, then another, to dust off my pants and squint in the harsh light. I looked and saw the glare of a pie tin on a hot day. I knew sin was what you take and didn't give back.

Critical Thinking and Discussion

1. What is Soto's motive—the real motive—in taking the pie?
2. What occurs between temptation and conscience?
3. What forms does guilt take?
4. How realistic is this story of youthful crime and self-punishment?
5. If you were Soto's parent (or the shop owner) and you knew what he had done and what he had felt, what would you do?

Reading-Related Writing

1. Write about one of your own childhood experiences in which you did something wrong or perceived that you did.
2. Write about this incident from the pie's point of view.
3. Analyze this piece of work in terms of the idea of guilt.

CLOSETS AND KEEPSAKES

Willi Coleman

Certain moments of growing up are indelible, and recalling them can be a comfort, especially when we have problems. Those were the times when someone listened and made us feel special. Willi Coleman had such moments with her mother. Coming across mementos from her childhood brings back with poignant clarity just what her mother did for her. This is about closets, and keepsakes, and pivotal moments.

Closets are the city dweller's storeroom, attic, and basement. Although I've 1 been known to keep boxes under my bed or stuffed behind the sofa, it is the shelves and back recesses of a closet which seem to hold a rare assortment of items. There are some very special memories contained in cardboard boxes and brown paper bags of varying sizes. Such things I make no pretense of wanting to throw away or share with others during sophisticated wine and cheese romps down memory lane. Some things are too precious for either category. Occasionally it is up to scraps of paper and old photographs to link you with yourself through the passing of time and shifts in lifestyles. And so, we move battered boxes and newspaper-protected, oddly shaped bundles into cramped studio or tenth-floor "garden" apartments. Inside these packages are parts of ourselves that we sometimes refuse to share with curious lovers and newfound friends. Decor and lifestyles change, but the stuff in the back of the closet remains a constant beacon calling us back.

Sitting on the floor with the contents of two boxes spread out before me, 2
I feel the weight of a wrinkled brown paper bag. It is heavy and crumpled to
fit the shape of its contents. The straightening comb inside has slightly bent
teeth, contoured by years of being dropped from less than skillful hands and
blackened by just as much use. A few remaining glints of bright metal transport me instantly to a time when I was very small, very southern . . . and
quite happy. There was a time . . . there really was a time when hot combs
were for holidays and permanents did not exist. Political correctness be
damned, we loved the ritual as well as the end results. Both were powerful
lines of love held in the hands of women and shaping the lives of girls. The
route taken was as old as fire and remains equally as irreplaceable.

I remember being eight years old and sitting on the floor, my head even 3
with my mother's knees. She above me, seated on a chair, shifted her weight
from side to side organizing wide tooth comb, brush, pins, straightening
comb and serious hair grease. Her hands pulled, darted, twisted and patted as
if she were directing the Sunday morning choir for "Light of the World"
Baptist Church. Two smart taps on the left side of my head was the signal for
me to turn my head to the right and vice versa. When I allowed my head to
wander out of her reach or without her direction my reward was three sharp
raps on the top of my head. It never hurt, and the ritual never gave way to
verbal directions. It was always three slaps on the head with a wide tooth
comb . . . never two or four.

Mama was a creature of habit and our sessions together could halt time, 4
still waters, and predict the future. Any soul-wrenching childhood catastro-
phe could be borne until it was again my turn on the floor between my
mother's knees. On some occasions the first flap of the comb brought not my
usual obedient response but a sniffle. On the second flap I escalated to a
whimper and the third was almost anticipated by a full-scale yell. Always an
overly dramatic child, I played the sniffle, whimper, yell routine for a full
three minutes to my one-woman audience. In due time I would quiet down
just enough to hear the head tapper inquire in words that never changed . . .
"Lil old negro . . . what in the world is wrong with you?" The sentence had a
rhythm all its own. Negro came out "knee-grow" and world was drawn out as
if to give the sound a chance to circle the entire universe. Mama had her way
of pampering each of her children. She did not like "nobody's rotten kids" and
had no intentions of raising any in her house. Behavior which would not have
been tolerated otherwise received lesser penalties on hair day. The invitation
of her words immediately prompted me to unburden myself. It never crossed
my mind to hold back the hurt, fear, or anger. Long before I was four I knew
that with me on the floor and Mama waving her comb I could get more
mileage out of a mere whimper than a loud wail at any other time.

Except for special occasions Mama came home from work early on Satur- 5
days. She spent six days a week mopping, waxing, and dusting other women's

houses and keeping out of reach of other women's husbands. Saturday nights were reserved for "taking care of them girls' hair" and the telling of stories. Some of which included a recitation of what she had endured and how she had triumphed over "folks that were lower than dirt" and "no-good snakes in the grass." She combed, patted, twisted, and talked, saying things which would have embarrassed or shamed her at other times. There were days when I was sure that she had ceased to be the mother we all knew. The smell of warm oils, clean hair, and a Black working woman's anger had transformed her into some-body else. She talked with ease and listened with undivided attention. Some-times the magic lasted for hours. By the time my sister had taken her place on the floor I had covered the two blocks to the store. With whatever change could be squeezed out of Mama's "four dollars a day plus carfare," I would carefully choose day-old pastry and get back home before my sister's last plait was in place. There never was a time when I did not wonder just what tales and secrets I had missed. The eleven months which separated my sister and me were, I suspected, most evident in what was said during my absence.

But even this small slight has carved out a warm place to hide in my 6 memories. For, at my mother's signal, I had moved away from those Saturday hair sessions, as if from a safe harbor, carrying with me: "Child, go look at yourself in the mirror." It was always said as if whatever I saw surpassed good and bordered on the truly wonderful. And I, searching for my own reflection, walked away oblivious to the love and life-sustaining messages which had seeped into my pores as I sat on the floor of my mother's kitchen.

Vocabulary

sophisticated (1)	contoured (2)	sustaining (6)
decor (1)	escalated (4)	

Critical Thinking and Discussion

1. At what point in Coleman's life did the sessions with her mother become important to her?
2. Were the sessions deliberately planned by her mother?
3. Were the sessions mutually satisfying? Explain.
4. Precisely why were the sessions pivotal experiences for Coleman?

Reading-Related Writing

1. Create one such comfort session. Include specific information that would be believable for both mother and daughter, or father and son, to relate.
2. Write about occasions (work, play, walks, eating out) when you had comfort conversations with grown-ups such as parents or grandparents.

FIFTH CHINESE DAUGHTER

Jade Snow Wong

As Jade Snow Wong discovered the larger world outside her Chinese neighborhood, she began to evaluate the cultural pattern of values, customs, and language into which she was born. As a dutiful Chinese daughter she did as her parents directed, but as a young person seeking her own identity, she yearned for independence well beyond the traditions of the nineteenth-century Chinese family. In this incident, taken from her celebrated book Fifth Chinese Daughter *(1976), she finally confronts her parents and precipitates a classic struggle between generations and cultures.*

One afternoon on a Saturday, which was normally occupied with my house- 1 work job, I was unexpectedly released by my employer, who was departing for a country weekend. It was a rare joy to have free time and I wanted to enjoy myself for a change. There had been a Chinese-American boy who shared some classes with me. Sometimes we had found each other walking to the same 8:00 A.M. class. He was not a special boyfriend, but I had enjoyed talking to him and had confided in him some of my problems. Impulsively, I telephoned him. I knew I must be breaking rules, and I felt shy and scared. At the same time, I was excited at this newly found forwardness, with nothing more purposeful than to suggest another walk together.

He understood my awkwardness and shared my anticipation. He asked 2 me to "dress up" for my first movie date. My clothes were limited but I changed to look more graceful in silk stockings and found a bright ribbon for my long black hair. Daddy watched, catching my mood, observing the dashing preparations. He asked me where I was going without his permission and with whom.

I refused to answer him. I thought of my rights! I thought he surely 3 would not try to understand. Thereupon Daddy thundered his displeasure and forbade my departure.

I found a new courage as I heard my voice announce calmly that I was no 4 longer a child, and if I could work my way through college, I would choose my own friends. It was my right as a person.

My mother heard the commotion and joined my father to face me; both 5 appeared shocked and incredulous. Daddy at once demanded the source of this unfilial, non-Chinese theory. And when I quoted my college professor, reminding him that he had always felt teachers should be revered, my father denounced that professor as a foreigner who was disregarding the superiority of our Chinese culture, with its sound family strength. My father did not spare me; I was condemned as an ingrate for echoing dishonorable opinions which should only be temporary whims, yet nonetheless inexcusable.

The scene was not yet over. I completed my proclamation to my father, who had never allowed me to learn how to dance, by adding that I was attending a movie, unchaperoned, with a boy I met at college. 6

My startled father was sure that my reputation would be subject to whispered innuendos. I must be bent on disgracing the family name; I was ruining my future, for surely I would yield to temptation. My mother underscored him by saying that I hadn't any notion of the problems endured by parents of a young girl. 7

I would not give in. I reminded them that they and I were not in China, that I wasn't going out with just anybody but someone I trusted! Daddy gave a roar that no man could be trusted, but I devastated them in declaring that I wished the freedom to find my own answers. 8

Both parents were thoroughly angered, scolded me for being shameless, and predicted that I would some day tell them I was wrong. But I dimly perceived that they were conceding defeat and were perplexed at this breakdown of their training. I was too old to beat and too bold to intimidate. 9

Vocabulary

incredulous (5)   innuendos (7)
unfilial (5)   intimidate (9)

Critical Reading and Discussion

1. What occasion encouraged Wong to take action?
2. What conflict does she have other than the one with her parents?
3. What different kinds of arguments did her father offer?
4. With what arguments did she counter?
5. What is the main conflict?
6. Is the order based on time, space, or both?
7. Why is the incident pivotal?

Reading-Related Writing

1. Write a narrative about a generational or cultural conflict you have had with your parents.
2. Using your imagination, write about what may have happened when the central character of "Fifth Chinese Daughter" comes home following the date at the movies.
3. Discuss in what way the family might be strengthened by this confrontation.

4. What values from the two perspectives—the traditional Chinese and contemporary American—might be combined in the formation of a strong and independent individual? In other words, how might a person coming from an ethnic minority background have rich and varied potential for self-development?
5. Discuss the possibility that if Wong is not careful in establishing her independence, she may give up much that cannot be regained.

Collaborative Learning

1. Dramatize this entire narrative. You might want to begin with the narrator (the young Wong), who will act as a stage director by describing the scene and giving a bit of background; then present the conversation between her and her parents; and finally allow her to comment a bit on the meaning of this event. Include stage descriptions, movements, and dialogue in the written script.
2. Role-play a scene in which a thoughtful Chinese person (perhaps a Buddhist monk) or a sociology professor sits down with the Chinese daughter and her family and tries to help the family achieve a better understanding of the daughter's behavior. Then write an evaluation or a report of the session.

THE DISCUS THROWER

Richard Selzer

We often think of pivotal experiences as stages in growing up, when we move from childhood to adulthood, when we gain strength and substance as adults, when we learn about ourselves from others. But what about the experience of death? Perhaps we think less about it because it is too painful. And, of course, our own death is something we cannot write about personally. Dr. Richard Selzer writes poignantly about the world of medicine and the ways in which people deal with suffering and death. Selzer entitles this essay "The Discus Thrower." The title is also used for a famous ancient Greek sculpture in which an idealized muscular athlete is poised just before beginning his forward movement to throw the discus. Is there a connection between the two? If so, is it one of mockery or solemn admiration?

I spy on my patients. Ought not a doctor to observe his patients by any 1
means and from any stance, that he might the more fully assemble evidence?
So I stand in the doorways of hospital rooms and gaze. Oh, it is not all that

furtive an act. Those in bed need only look up to discover me. But they never do.

From the doorway of Room 542 the man in the bed seems deeply tanned. 2 Blue eyes and close-cropped white hair give him the appearance of vigor and good health. But I know that his skin is not brown from the sun. It is rusted, rather, in the last stage of containing the vile repose within. And the blue eyes are frosted, looking inward like the windows of a snowbound cottage. This man is blind. This man is also legless—the right leg missing from midthigh down, the left from just below the knee. It gives him the look of a bonsai, roots and branches pruned into the dwarfed facsimile of a great tree.

Propped on pillows, he cups his right thigh in both hands. Now and then 3 he shakes his head as though acknowledging the intensity of his suffering. In all of this he makes no sound. Is he mute as well as blind?

The room in which he dwells is empty of all possessions—no get-well 4 cards, small, private caches of food, day-old flowers, slippers, all the usual kick-shaws of the sickroom. There is only the bed, a chair, a nightstand, and a tray on wheels that can be swung across his lap for meals.

"What time is it?" he asks. 5

"Three o'clock." 6

"Morning or afternoon?" 7

"Afternoon." 8

He is silent. There is nothing else he wants to know. 9

"How are you?" I say. 10

"Who is it?" he asks. 11

"It's the doctor. How do you feel?" 12

He does not answer right away. 13

"Feel?" he says. 14

"I hope you feel better," I say. 15

I press the button at the side of the bed. 16

"Down you go," I say. 17

"Yes, down," he says. 18

He falls back upon the bed awkwardly. His stumps, unweighted by legs 19 and feet, rise in the air, presenting themselves. I unwrap the bandages from the stumps, and begin to cut away the black scabs and dead, glazed fat with scissors and forceps. A shard of white bone comes loose. I pick it away. I wash the wounds with disinfectant and redress the stumps. All this while, he does not speak. What is he thinking behind those lids that do not blink? Is he remembering a time when he was whole? Does he dream of feet? Of when his body was not a rotting log?

He lies solid and inert. In spite of everything, he remains impressive, as 20 though he were a sailor standing athwart a slanting deck.

"Anything more I can do for you?" I ask. 21

For a long moment he is silent. 22

"Yes," he says at last and without the least irony. "You can bring me a pair 23
of shoes."

In the corridor, the head nurse is waiting for me. 24

"We have to do something about him," she says. "Every morning he 25
orders scrambled eggs for breakfast, and, instead of eating them, he picks up
the plate and throws it against the wall."

"Throws his plate?" 26

"Nasty. That's what he is. No wonder his family doesn't come to visit. 27
They probably can't stand him any more than we can."

She is waiting for me to do something. 28

"Well?" 29

"We'll see," I say. 30

The next morning I am waiting in the corridor when the kitchen delivers 31
his breakfast. I watch the aide place the tray on the stand and swing it across
his lap. She presses the button to raise the head of the bed. Then she leaves.

In time the man reaches to find the rim of the tray, then on to find the 32
dome of the covered dish. He lifts off the cover and places it on the stand. He
fingers across the plate until he probes the eggs. He lifts the plate in both
hands, sets it on the palm of his right hand, centers it, balances it. He hefts it
up and down slightly, getting the feel of it. Abruptly, he draws back his right
arm as far as he can.

There is the crack of the plate breaking against the wall at the foot of his 33
bed and the small wet sound of the scrambled eggs dropping to the floor.

And then he laughs. It is a sound you have never heard. It is something 34
new under the sun. It could cure cancer.

Out in the corridor, the eyes of the head nurse narrow. 35

"Laughed, did he?" 36

She writes something down on her clipboard. 37

A second aide arrives, brings a second breakfast tray, puts it on the 38
nightstand, out of his reach. She looks over at me shaking her head and
making her mouth go. I see that we are to be accomplices.

"I've got to feed you," she says to the man. 39

"Oh, no you don't," the man says. 40

"Oh, yes I do," the aide says, "after the way you just did. Nurse says so." 41

"Get me my shoes," the man says. 42

"Here's oatmeal," the aide says. "Open." And she touches the spoon to his 43
lower lip.

"I ordered scrambled eggs," says the man. 44

"That's right," the aide says. 45

I step forward. 46

"Is there anything I can do?" I say. 47

"Who are you?" the man asks. 48

In the evening I go once more to that ward to make my rounds. The head 49
nurse reports to me that Room 542 is deceased. She has discovered this quite

by accident, she says. No, there had been no sound. Nothing. It's a blessing, she says.

I go into his room, a spy looking for secrets. He is still there in his bed. 50 His face is relaxed, grave, dignified. After a while, I turn to leave. My gaze sweeps the wall at the foot of the bed, and I see the place where it has been repeatedly washed, where the wall looks very clean and very white.

Vocabulary

furtive (1)   shard (19)   hefts (32)
facsimile (2)   athwart (20)

Critical Thinking and Discussion

1. Why does the nurse complain to the doctor?
2. Why does the doctor empathize with the patient?
3. Why doesn't the patient have any visitors?
4. Why is the author so fascinated with the patient?
5. What are the implications of the title—comic or heroic?
6. How does the patient define himself?

Reading-Related Writing

1. Write about a moment when someone you know has faced a difficult situation in a memorable way.
2. Discuss whether, by reading this essay, you learn more about the patient, the doctor, or human beings generally. Or did you learn about all equally?
3. Write about how one quality of the patient (courage, self-pity, cowardice, immaturity, self-centeredness) is illustrated.
4. Write about the courage of an individual you know or have known who suffered greatly but struggled to express himself or herself.

HAVE I TOLD YOU LATELY THAT I LOVE YOU?*

Jerry Chandler

We all have experiences when we are growing up that show us what life is really like. Most of us have a collection of them that stand out from other happenings, and sometimes take on even more significance as we

I was very young when I first learned what true love really is. In fact, I didn't just learn; I was taught a lesson. 1

My teacher was the least likely "teacher" in town. She was someone the town barely tolerated. I think other residents secretly wished she lived somewhere else. The town was small, less than five hundred people, and everyone knew everyone. Anna Hoskins, whom we youngsters called Anna Banana, had mental problems. We all knew that she did because she talked to herself as she walked to the store and back, and did all kinds of peculiar things such as having a pet pig that lived in her house. Some people joked that the pig smelled better than she did, and it was true that she had a strong odor. Despite her problems, she had a husband. He worked as a custodian in a large town several hundred miles away and only occasionally came home to spend a few days with her. Years ago they had had two children, who had both died in an automobile accident. 2

It was during summer vacation on the day of my lesson, and my friends and I were swimming naked in a little pool in the creek by the bridge on the road leading from Anna Hoskin's house to town, where she went almost every day to check her mailbox. She always came by at the same time, and when she did, if we were swimming, we mooned her. It always happened the same way. She would come walking by and we would yell and she would look our way and we would turn bare bottoms up. Then she would laugh and say something that we could never understand, and we would laugh and that would be it. 3

On that day we mooned her, she laughed, and so on. Then we talked as foolish young boys will talk, sitting there in the sun and passing around all the Anna Banana stories we had heard from our siblings and others. When we were through swimming and the sun had dried us, we put on our clothes and headed for our homes. The other boys went back toward town, and I walked in the other direction, which would take me past Anna's house. 4

I hadn't walked far when I came across a letter lying there beside the gravel road. I picked it up and saw that it was from Anna's husband and had been opened. I hadn't carried it more than a few steps before I decided to read it. I had never talked to Anna's husband, but it was assumed that he was as bad off as she was or he wouldn't keep coming back. Whatever he wrote would give me and my buddies something to laugh about, and I hurriedly opened the letter and began reading. 5

It was written in pencil in the very awkward style of a third grader with poor coordination. It started off with "My Dear Wife," which was followed with "How are you? I am fine." Then came the words, "Have I told you lately that I love you? Well, darlin I'm tellin you now." That was followed by more 6 of the same kind of thing. He had copied out all the words of an old country love song—for Anna Banana. For a second I pictured him sitting there copying out the song and thinking about her, and what he must have been thinking wasn't anything close to what we thought about her. He really loved her. He loved dirty old Anna Banana, the pig woman, and what did that make me, standing there where I had stopped on the road, reading somebody's private letter?

When I walked by her house, I put the letter in a crack in her gate. I had   7
wanted to take it to her door, but I was too embarrassed. She would never know that by dropping the letter she had taught me more about love than I would learn anywhere else.

Critical Thinking and Discussion

1. When did this incident happen?
2. Chandler doesn't say just what he learned. Is it something that he couldn't put into words? Or is it something that need not be put into words because doing so would spoil the effect of the essay?

Reading-Related Writing

1. Write about an occasion on which you learned an important lesson about grief, sacrifice, dedication, love, kindness, anger, sorrow, price, shame, fear, or pain. You may describe an incident that happened to you or to another person.
2. Write about several occasions that collectively formed your views on one of the concepts listed in suggestion 1.

Collaborative Learning

1. In groups, discuss the different expressions of love found in "Eggs Titanic," "A Bee in My Bonnet," "Closets and Keepsakes," "Fifth Chinese Daughter," and "Have I Told You Lately That I Love You?" Then, either as a group or individually, write about love as defined mainly by examples from these works.
2. In groups, discuss the idea of courage as found in "Dark Day in the Dust Bowl," "Walking in Others' Shoes," "The Discus Thrower," "Fifth Chinese Daughter," and "Closets and Keepsakes." Then, either as a group or individually, write about courage as defined mainly by examples from these works. Begin with a basic definition, such as "courage represents the proven ability to stand up to threatening situations." Take into consideration that, to some extent, a person's courage should be judged by his or

her capacity for struggle; in other words, not everyone has the strength to be heroic in the "Rambo" sense, but a person who struggles with all his or her might can be admirable.

Connections

1. Write about a pivotal experience in your life and relate it to one or more selections in this chapter.
2. Pick two pieces for a comparative study of sources of strength during pivotal moments. Consider ideas such as culture, family, community, and self.
3. Pick two pieces for a comparative study or pick several and discuss the way each handles the concept of how individuals see themselves and how others see them. Suggestions for study: "The Pie," "Children of the Harvest," "Fifth Chinese Daughter," "The Discus Thrower," "Walking in Others' Shoes," and "Have I Told You Lately That I Love You?"

3

Home: Sweet and Sour

*H*omes, neighborhoods, and hometowns do not exist in isolation like backdrops for a drama. They are the products of people, reflecting all aspects of a culture, and they can be understood in human terms only in relation to their inhabitants. Of course, writers shape our ideas about an area by the details they select and, therefore, often reveal as much about themselves as they do about the physical properties they describe.

This chapter presents a variety of selections. Some give a balanced description of both people and places, and others focus mainly on one or the other. Regardless of the treatment, consider these questions as you read each selection:

- What is the dominant impression given by the writer?
- Is the quality of life of the people described here magnified or diminished by their environment?
- What qualities do the most satisfactory homes have in common?
- What do you learn about the residents of a community or members of a family by studying the buildings or furnishings and their condition?
- What universal concerns do you find among these different cultural settings?

WRITING STRATEGIES AND TECHNIQUES: DESCRIPTION

Description means the use of words to represent the appearance or nature of something. Often called a word picture, description is an attempt to reveal a subject to the mind's eye. When writing description, you should not become merely an indifferent camera; instead, you should select details that will convey a good depiction. Just what details you as a descriptive writer select will depend on several factors, especially the type of description and the dominant impression in the passage.

Types of Description

On the basis of treatment of subject material, description is customarily divided into two types: objective and subjective.

Effective objective description presents the subject clearly and directly as it exists outside the realm of feelings. If you are explaining the function of the heart, the characteristics of a computer chip, or the renovation of a manufacturing facility, your description would probably feature specific, impersonal details. Most technical and scientific writing is objective in that sense. It is likely to be practical and utilitarian, making little use of speculation and poetic technique.

Effective subjective description is also concerned with clarity and it may be direct, but it conveys a feeling about the subject and sets a mood while making a point. Because most expression involves personal views, even when it explains by analysis, subjective description (often called "emotional description") has a broader range of uses than objective description.

Descriptive passages can have a combination of objective and subjective description; only the larger context of the passage will reveal the main intent. The following description of a baseball begins with objective treatment and then moves to subjective.

> It weighs just over five ounces and measures between 2.86 and 2.94 inches in diameter. It is made of a composition-cork nucleus encased in two thin layers of rubber, one black and one red, surrounded by 121 yards of tightly wrapped blue-gray wool yarn, 45 yards of white wool yarn, 53 more yards of blue-gray wool yarn, 150 yards of fine cotton yarn, a coat of rubber cement, and a cowhide (formerly horsehide) exterior, which is held together with 216 slightly raised red cotton stitches. Printed certifications, endorsements, and outdoor advertising spherically attest to its authenticity. Like most institutions, it is considered inferior in its present form to its ancient archetypes,

and in this case the complaint is probably justified; on occasion in recent years it has actually been known to come apart under the demands of its brief but rigorous active career. Baseballs are assembled and handstitched in Taiwan (before this year the work was done in Haiti, and before 1973 in Chicopee, Massachusetts), and contemporary pitchers claim that there is a tangible variation in the size and feel of the balls that now come into play in a single game; a true peewee is treasured by hurlers, and its departure from the premises, by fair means or foul, is secretly mourned. But never mind: any baseball is beautiful. No other small package comes as close to the ideal in design and utility. It is a perfect object for a man's hand. Pick it up and it instantly suggests its purpose; it is meant to be thrown a considerable distance—thrown hard and with precision. Its feel and heft are the beginning of the sport's critical dimensions; if it were a fraction of an inch larger or smaller, a few centigrams heavier or lighter, the game of baseball would be utterly different. Hold a baseball in your hand. As it happens, this one is not brand-new. Here, just to one side of the curved surgical welt of stitches, there is a pale-green grass smudge, darkening on one edge almost to black—the mark of an old infield play, a tough grounder now lost in memory. Feel the ball, turn it over in your hand; hold it across the seam or the other way, with the seam just to the side of your middle finger. Speculation stirs. You want to get outdoors and throw this spare and sensual object to somebody or, at the very least, watch somebody else throw it. The game has begun.

marginal note: objective treatment moving to subjective treatment

Roger Angell,
"On the Ball"

Techniques of Descriptive Writing

As a writer of description, you will need to focus your work so as to emphasize a single point, establish a perspective from which to describe your subject, and position the details for coherence. The terms for these considerations are *dominant impression, point of view,* and *order.*

Dominant Impression

Linked closely to purpose, the dominant impression derives from a pattern of details, often involving repetition of one idea with different particulars. Word choice is of paramount importance, and that choice depends on the situation of your writing, which in turn involves your purpose for writing and your audience—two inseparable factors.

If you are eating hamburgers in a restaurant, and you say to your companion, "This food is good," your companion may understand all he or she needs to understand on the subject. After all, your companion can see you sitting there chewing the food, smacking your lips, and wiping the sauce off your chin. But if you write that sentence on a piece of paper and mail it to someone, your reader may be puzzled. Although you may know the reader fairly well, your reader may not know the meaning of "good" (good to eat, good to purchase for others, good to sell), and "this food" (What kind? Where is it? How is it special? How is it prepared? What qualities does it have?).

In order to convey your main concern effectively to readers, you will have to give some sensory impressions, and you may use figures of speech. These sensory impressions, collectively called *imagery,* refer to that which can be experienced by the senses—what we can see, smell, taste, hear, and touch. The figures of speech involve comparisons of unlike things that, nevertheless, have something in common. We will discuss these techniques in more detail following the example.

image (sight) topic sentence	A single knoll rises out of the plain in Oklahoma, north and west of the Wichita Range. <u>For my people, the Kiowas, it is an old landmark, and they gave it the name Rainy Mountain.</u> The
image (touch)	hardest weather in the world is there. Winter brings blizzards, hot tornadic winds arise in the spring, and in summer the
image (sound)	prairie is an anvil's edge. The grass turns brittle and brown, and it cracks beneath your feet. There are green belts along the rivers and creeks, linear groves of hickory and pecan, willow and witch hazel. At a distance in July or August the steaming
image (sight)	foliage seems almost to writhe in fire. Great green-and-yellow grasshoppers are everywhere in the tall grass, popping up like
image (touch)	corn to sting the flesh, and tortoises crawl about on the red earth, going nowhere in the plenty of time. Loneliness is an aspect of the land. All things in the plain are isolate; there is no confusion of objects in the eye, but *one* hill or *one* tree or *one*
note references to time and space	man. To look upon that landscape in the early morning, with the sun at your back, is to lose the sense of proportion. Your imagination comes to life, and this, you think, is where Creation was begun.

N. Scott Momaday,
"The Way to Rainy Mountain"

Through imagery, Momaday has involved the reader in what he has seen, felt, and heard. Only the imagery of smelling and tasting are not included. He also uses figures of speech, including these examples:

Simile: *a comparison using* like   "popping up like corn"
   or as
Metaphor: *a comparison using word*   "the prairie is an anvil's edge"
   replacement
Personification: *an expression*   "Loneliness is an aspect of the
   giving human characteristics to   land."
   something not human

Subjective description is likely to make more use of imagery, figurative language, and words rich in associations than does objective description. But just as a fine line cannot always be drawn between the objective and the subjective, a fine line cannot always be drawn between word choice in one and in the other. However, we can say with certainty that whatever the type of description, careful word choice will always be important. Consider these points about precise diction:

General and Specific Words/Abstract and Concrete Words

To move from the general to the specific is to move from the whole class or body to the individual(s); for example:

General	Specific	More Specific
insects	*grasshoppers*	*great green-and-yellow grasshoppers*
vegetation	*trees*	*hickory, pecan, willow, witch hazel*
landmark	*single knoll*	*Rainy Mountain*

Words are classified as abstract or concrete depending on what they refer to. *Abstract words* refer to qualities or ideas: *good, ordinary, ultimate, truth, beauty, maturity, love. Concrete words* refer to a substance or things; they have reality: *onions, grease, buns, tables, food.* The specific concrete words, sometimes called *concrete particulars,* often support generalizations effectively and convince the reader of the accuracy of the account.

Never try to give all the details when writing description; instead, be selective, picking only those that you need to project a dominant impression, always taking into account the knowledge and attitudes of your readers. Remember, description is not photographic. If you wish to describe a person, select the traits that will project your intended dominant impression. If you wish to describe a landscape, do not give all the details that you might find in a picture; on the contrary, pick the details that support your intended dominant impression. That extremely important dominant impression is directly linked to your purpose and is created by the judicious choice and arrangement of images, figurative language, and revealing details.

Point of View

Point of view shows the writer's relationship to the subject, thereby establishing the perspective from which the subject is described. It rarely changes within a passage. Two terms usually associated with narrative writing, *first person* and *third person*, also pertain to descriptive writing.

If you want to convey personal experience, your point of view will be *first person*, which can be either involved (a participant) or uninvolved (an observer). The involved perspective uses *I* more prominently than the uninvolved.

If you want to present something from a detached position, especially from geographical or historical distance (see "On the Ball"), your point of view will be *third person*, and you will refer to your subjects by name or by third-person pronouns such as *he, she, him, her, it, they,* and *them,* without imposing yourself as an *I*.

Order

The point of view you select may indicate or even dictate the order in which you present descriptive details. If you are describing your immediate surroundings while taking a walk (first person, involved), the descriptive account would naturally follow spatially as well as chronologically—in other words, by space and time.

- For space, give directions to the reader, indicating *next to, below, under, above, behind, in front of, beyond, in the foreground, in the background, to the left,* or *to the right.*
- For time, use words such as *first, second, then, soon, finally, while, after, next, later, now,* and *before.*

Some descriptive pieces may follow the progression of an idea for emphasis and not move primarily through space or time. Whatever appropriate techniques you use will guide your reader and thereby aid coherence.

The three factors—dominant impression, point of view, and order—work together in a well-written description.

N. Scott Momaday's paragraph can also be evaluated for all three factors:

- *Dominant impression:* loneliness (images, figurative language, other diction). The reader experiences the incident vicariously because of the diction. The general and abstract have been made clear by use of the specific and the concrete. Of course, not all abstract words need to be tied to the concrete, nor do all general words need to be transformed into the specific. As you describe, use your judgment to decide which words fit your purposes—those needed to enable your audience to understand your ideas and to be persuaded or informed.

- *Point of view:* first person, involved
- *Order:* space and time

The following student-written paragraph and essay illustrate effective uses of description.

THE ESSENCE OF MORNING IN FIJI[1]*

Pravina Singh

first person point of view

image (smell)

image (sound)

image (sight)

image (touch)

image (touch)

image (taste)

image (taste)

In the mornings, I remember the warm sun bathing me in the cool, soft breeze while I lay in bed staring out the window. I would always awake to the sounds of village men mowing their lawns. The smell of the fresh grass would make me anxious to run barefoot through the wet fields. I would watch the birds maze through the mango tree plucking and picking at the ripe mangos. "Shoo! Shoo!" I would scare the birds away because I wanted to eat the ripe mangos first, but it would be too late. The birds were always up early in the morning before any human being. Besides, that's their home. Like the birds, Ama[2] would be up cooking for the rest of us who sleep in. I remember looking out at Ama's long black braided hair from my room. She stood outside cooking in the warm comforting sun. I could see her, but she couldn't see me because of the bamboo blinds. I've seen her feed the sacred cows with her small hands, the same hands she also fed us with. Ama would make hot ginger tea with biscuits. We would quickly grab the warm biscuits, spread butter on them, and dip them in the tea. That's the way we always ate our biscuits. While we enjoyed our biscuits and tea, Ama would be peeling the soft, yellow-green bananas for us. Sometimes she'd fry the bananas and corn for snacks. Oh, what a taste! I never

[1]Fiji Islands, in the southwest Pacific
[2]mother

remember thanking Ama for all the things she did for us. Occasionally, I would send her a great big smile, and she would smile back.

REDISCOVERED HONG KONG CHILDHOOD*

Helen Li

thesis

During the last Christmas vacation, after being away 1 for ten years, I went back to Hong Kong for a visit. When I passed by the old area where I used to live when I was small, everything I saw brought back memories of my childhood.

image (smell)

From birth until the age of ten, I lived in a building 2 next to a bakery in the city of Hung Hom. Every morning I was wakened by the aroma of fresh-baked bread, cookies, and cakes from the nearby bakery. Then I would go to the pier nearby, the place where many of the kids around that neighborhood met everyday. I was usually the first one to arrive. There I would watch the calm sea across which ships and ferries go. I would also watch waves going up and down along the shore like the satin dress of a little girl dancing in the wind.

image (sight)

figure of speech (simile)

After all the kids had gathered at the pier, we would 3 visit the bakery. The owner of the bakery, who was bald and always looked very serious (but was actually very kind), would give us a bag of cookies that we could share. We would then go back to the pier, sit on the bleachers and share the cookies by playing the stone-scissors-paper game. The one who won the most would get the biggest share.

image (sight)

There we would also watch people fishing. They 4 would put worms on their hooks and then put their fishing lines and hooks in the water. After a few minutes they would pull their poles up with dozens of lively fish struggling and flinging themselves about. Usually the fishermen would put the fish in baskets and take them home. Or they might even sell the fish if they had a big harvest.

image (sight)

<table>
<tr><td>image (sight)</td><td>After the fishermen had left, we usually went to our favorite playground, which was the little yard next to the grocery store. We loved to play there, not only because it was the perfect place for games—sandy with the mild sun shining but not too bright—but also because it was our candyland. The owner of the grocery store, who loved children very much, would usually come out and feed us our favorite candies. Sometimes during special Chinese occasions when people shopped for such things as joss sticks and joss paper to worship their Chinese god, we would even help him in dealing with the customers. It was always extremely crowded with housewives and superstitious old women who yelled out what they needed. I was usually the cashier who counted the money carefully to make sure that I received the right amount.</td></tr>
</table>

After the fishermen had left, we usually went to our ⁵ favorite playground, which was the little yard next to the grocery store. We loved to play there, not only because it was the perfect place for games—sandy with the mild sun shining but not too bright—but also because it was our candyland. The owner of the grocery store, who loved children very much, would usually come out and feed us our favorite candies. Sometimes during special Chinese occasions when people shopped for such things as joss sticks and joss paper to worship their Chinese god, we would even help him in dealing with the customers. It was always extremely crowded with housewives and superstitious old women who yelled out what they needed. I was usually the cashier who counted the money carefully to make sure that I received the right amount.

restated thesis My childhood was filled with happy times and ani- 6 mated scenes that I will never forget.

WRITER'S CHECKLIST

- Use a dominant impression to unify your description.
- Select your point of view (first, involved or third, observer) with care, and be consistent.
- To promote coherence, impose a plan for order by space, time, or emphasis.
- In objective description, use direct, practical language, and (usually) appeal mainly to the sense of sight.
- In emotional description, appeal to the reader's feelings, especially through the use of figurative language and images of sight, sound, smell, taste, and touch.
- Use specific and concrete words if appropriate.

CUBANS DISCOVER NEW YORK

Oscar Hijuelos

Winner of the Pulitzer Prize in 1990 for The Mambo Kings Play Songs of Love, *Oscar Hijuelos was born in New York of Cuban*

*parents. This paragraph depicts young immigrants from Havana
exploring the exciting world of New York.*

And in those days Pablo would drive them around in his Oldsmobile to see
the sights, or the brothers would ride the subway all over the four boroughs,
faces pressed against the windows, as if counting the pillars and flashing
lights for fun. Cesar favored amusement parks, circuses, movie houses,
burlesques, and baseball games, while Nestor, a more quiet, docile, and
tormented man, enjoyed nature and liked going to the places that Pablo's
children loved the most. He liked to take the children to the Museum of
Natural History, where he would revel in walking among the remains of so
many reptiles, mammals, birds, fish, insects which had once vibrated, shim-
mered, crawled, flown, swum through the world and which were now preserved in row after row of glass cases. On one of those days, he, Cesar, Pablo,
and the kids posed proudly for a photograph before the looming skeleton of
Tyrannosaurus Rex. Afterwards they walked over to Central Park, the brothers strolling together as they used to down in Havana. Back then it was
tranquil and clean. Old ladies sunned themselves everywhere and young
men snuggled in the grass with their girls. Picnicking on the green, they ate
thick steak heroes and drank Coca-Colas, enjoying the sunshine as they
watched boats float across the lake. Best was the Bronx Zoo in springtime,
with its lions prowling in their dens, the buffalo with their great horns and
downy fur foaming like whitewater beneath their chins, long-necked giraffes
whose heads curiously peeked high into the skirts of trees. Beautiful days,
beyond all pain, all suffering.

Critical Thinking and Discussion

1. Does the last line ("Beautiful days, beyond all pain, all suffering") serve as
   the dominant impression? Explain.
2. Is the main pattern of organization according to time or place?
3. How is contrast used?
4. What specific information (such as the make of automobile and the
   specific park in New York) makes it easy to imagine what the men,
   especially Nestor, experienced?

Reading-Related Writing

Write about your or somebody else's experiences immediately after moving to a new community, a new area, or a new country. Be specific in
naming places, times, and things. Consider emphasizing cultural shock
and adjustments.

THE KITCHEN

Alfred Kazin

The center of Alfred Kazin's young life was his home, a tenement building in a community inhabited mainly by Jewish immigrants from Eastern Europe. The center of his home was the kitchen. There his mother cooked, sent his father off to work and greeted him at the end of the day, worked at her sewing machine, and talked to neighbors and clients of her dressmaking business. Young Alfred observed all this while doing his homework, eating his meals, and, during the cold months, sleeping there. It is the setting he remembers best, and one in which the deepest lessons about life were taught indirectly. This description is taken from Kazin's essay "Brownsville Schooldays."

The kitchen held our lives together. My mother worked in it all day long, we ate in it almost all meals except the Passover *seder*, I did my homework and first writing at the kitchen table, and in winter I often had a bed made up for me on three kitchen chairs near the stove. On the wall just over the table hung a long horizontal mirror that sloped to a ship's prow at each end and was lined in cherry wood. It took up the whole wall, and drew every object in the kitchen to itself. The walls were a fiercely stippled whitewash, so often rewhitened by my father in slack seasons that the paint looked as if it had been squeezed and cracked into the walls. A large electric bulb hung down the center of the kitchen at the end of a chain that had been hooked into the ceiling; the old gas ring and key still jutted out of the wall like antlers. In the corner next to the toilet was the sink at which we washed, and the square tub in which my mother did our clothes. Above it, tacked to the shelf on which were pleasantly ranged square, blue bordered white sugar and spice jars, hung calendars from the Public National Bank on Pitkin Avenue and the Minsker Progressive Branch of the Workman's Circle; receipts for the payment of insurance premiums, and household bills on a spindle; two little boxes engraved with Hebrew letters. One of these was for the poor, the other to buy back the Land of Israel. Each spring a bearded little man would suddenly appear in our kitchen, salute us with a hurried Hebrew blessing, empty the boxes (sometimes with a sidelong look of disdain if they were not full), hurriedly bless us again for remembering our less fortunate Jewish brothers and sisters, and so take his departure until the next spring, after vainly trying to persuade my mother to take still another box. We did occasionally remember to drop coins in the boxes, but this was usually only on the dreaded morning of "midterms" and final examinations, because my mother thought it would bring me luck. She was extremely superstitious, but embarrassed about it, and always laughed at herself whenever, on the morning of an examination, she counseled me to leave the house on my right foot. "I know it's silly," her smile seemed to say, "but what harm can it do? It may calm God down."

Critical Thinking and Discussion

1. Why do you think Kazin remembers the kitchen so well?
2. What do you learn about the people by reading his description of the room?
3. Is the organization based mainly on time or space?

Reading-Related Writing

Write about the area in your home that left you with the deepest impressions (perhaps the kitchen, your bedroom, the den, the living room, the garage, the yard). Use Kazin's paragraph as a model; include some human behavior such as the mother's acting out her superstitions.

FENG SHUI*

Jean Chew

When a Chinese client asks a real estate agent about a particular house, the questions may derive from ancient culture and be deeply embedded in superstition. For some of us the number 13 is a cause of anxiety; for the Chinese the number is likely to be 4.

When my real estate client, Mrs. Wong, asked me, "Do you know about *Feng Shui?*" I smiled and said, "Of course." Without that knowledge I could not function in my profession. Feng Shui is the name for Chinese superstitions, especially those regarding the interrelationship of a person's birth chart and the home where he or she lives. Thus, describing an ideal house to a client may be more a matter of describing what it should not have rather than what it should have. These are a few of the negative characteristics other than those associated with personal charts. At the entrance facing the front door there should be no tree, for it may bring death or divorce. The front door itself should not face the stairwell because all good fortune may roll right out of the house. The back door should also not face the front door; such an arrangement may allow the money that comes in the front door to go out the back. The house itself should sit on a lot that is square or rectangular; sharp angles will bring bad luck. The land itself should be higher along the fence behind the house to hold in prosperity. Moreover, the house must face the right direction according to the individual's time of birth. This placement can affect a person's destiny. The number of the house may be more easily understood; in Chinese, the number 4 has the same character as *death*. These and many, many more rules of Feng Shui, along with commonsense requirements such as a bright and cheerful feeling and a functional floor plan, are points Mrs. Wong will consider. Because trying to follow all the rules of Feng Shui may keep people from finding an excellent house, I often advise clients not to take them too seriously lest they make life miserable.

Critical Thinking and Discussion

1. What value system underlies most of these rules of Feng Shui?
2. What superstitions do you have? Do they relate to a particular culture? Are some related to buildings? Do they imply a value system?

Reading-Related Writing

1. If you are Chinese or if you know someone who is, write about other rules of Feng Shui.
2. If you have some superstitions, especially those pertaining to a household, discuss them. Regardless of how irrational they are, how do you feel about violating them?
3. Using these rules (and others, if you know them) of Feng Shui, describe an ideal house for a specific person.
4. Discuss the value system implied in this selection.

LOS CHINOS DISCOVER EL BARRIO

Luis Torres

Cautious optimism characterizes the following essay by Luis Torres, who chronicles the cultural changes of this East Los Angeles neighborhood. Note how the concluding scene reflects back on the introductory scene. If, after you have finished reading the piece, you are not certain whether it is optimistic or pessimistic, reread the first and last paragraphs again.

There's a colorful mural on the asphalt playground of Hillside Elementary 1 School, in the neighborhood called Lincoln Heights. Painted on the beige handball wall, the mural is of life-sized youngsters holding hands. Depicted are Asian and Latino kids with bright faces and ear-to-ear smiles.

The mural is a mirror of the makeup of the neighborhood today: Latinos   2
living side-by-side with Asians. But it's not all smiles and happy faces in the
Northeast Los Angeles community, located just a couple of miles up Broadway from City Hall. On the surface there's harmony between Latinos and
Asians. But there are indications of simmering ethnic-based tensions.

That became clear to me recently when I took a walk through the old   3
neighborhood—the one where I grew up. As I walked along North Broadway,
I thought of a joke that comic Paul Rodriguez often tells on the stage. He
paints the picture of a young Chicano walking down a street on L.A.'s East-
side. He comes upon two Asians having an animated conversation in what
sounds like babble. "Hey, you guys, knock off that foreign talk. This is
America—speak Spanish!"

When I was growing up in Lincoln Heights 30 years ago most of us   4
spoke Spanish—and English. There was a sometimes uneasy coexistence in
the neighborhood between brown and white. Back then we Latinos were
moving in and essentially displacing the working-class Italians (to us, they
were just *los gringos*) who had moved there and thrived after World War II.

Because I was an extremely fair-skinned Latino kid I would often over-   5
hear remarks by gringos in Lincoln Heights that were not intended for Latino
ears, disparaging comments about "smelly wetbacks," and worse. The transition was, for the most part, a gradual process. And as I recall—except for the
slurs that sometimes stung me directly—a process marked only occasionally
by outright hostility.

A trend that began about 10 years ago in Lincoln Heights seems to have   6
hit a critical point now. It's similar to the ethnic tug-of-war of yesteryear, but
different colors, different words are involved. Today Chinese and Vietnamese
are displacing the Latinos who, by choice or circumstance, had Lincoln
Heights virtually to themselves for two solid generations.

Evidence of the transition is clear.   7

The bank where I opened my first meager savings account in the late   8
1950s has changed hands. It's now the East-West Federal Bank, an Asian-
owned enterprise.

The public library on Workman Street, where I checked out *Charlotte's*   9
Web with my first library card, abounds with signs of the new times: It's called
"La Biblioteca del Pueblo de Lincoln Heights," and on the door there's a notice
advising that the building is closed because of the Oct. 1 earthquake; it's
written in Chinese.

The white, wood-frame house on Griffin Avenue that I once lived in is   10
now owned by a Chinese family.

What used to be a Latino-run mortuary at the corner of Sichel Street and   11
North Broadway is now the Chung Wah Funeral Home.

A block down the street from the funeral home is a *panadería,* a bakery.   12
As I would listen to radio reports of the U.S. war in faraway Indochina while

walking from class at Lincoln High School, I often used to drop in the *panaderia* for a snack.

The word *panaderia,* now faded and chipped, is still painted on the shop 13 window that fronts North Broadway. But another sign, a gleaming plastic one, hangs above the window. The sign proclaims that it is a Vietnamese-Chinese bakery. The proprietor, Sam Lee, bought the business less than a year ago. With a wave of his arm, he indicates that *La Opinion,* the Spanish-language daily newspaper, is still for sale on the counter. Two signs hang side-by-side behind the counter announcing in Spanish and in Chinese that cakes are made to order for all occasions.

Out on North Broadway, Fidel Farrillas sells *raspadas* (snow-cones) from 14 his pushcart. He has lived and worked in Lincoln Heights "for 30 years and a pinch more," he says, his voice nearly whistling through two gold-framed teeth. He has seen the neighborhood change. Twice.

Like many older Latinos he remembers the tension felt between *los grin-* 15 *gos y la raza* years ago—even though most people went about their business ostensibly coexisting politely. And others who have been around as long will tell an inquiring reporter scratching away in his notebook, "We're going out of our way to treat the *chinos* nice—better than the *gringos* sometimes treated us back then." But when the notebook is closed, they're likely to whisper, "But you know, the thing is, they smell funny, and they talk behind your back, and they are so arrogant—the way they're buying up everything in our neighbor-hood."

Neighborhood transitions can be tough to reconcile. 16

It isn't easy for the blue-collar Latinos of Lincoln Heights. They haven't 17 possessed much. But they had the barrio, "a little chunk of the world where we belonged," as one described it. There may be some hard times and hard feelings ahead as *los chinos* continue to make inroads into what had been an exclusively Latino enclave. But there are hopeful signs as well.

On one recent Saturday afternoon a Latino fifth-grader, wearing the same 18 type of hightop tennis shoes I wore as a 10-year-old on that same street corner, strode up to Señor Farrillas' snow-cone pushcart. The kid pulled out a pocketful of dimes and bought two *raspadas.* One for himself, and one for his school chum—a Vietnamese kid. He was wearing hightops, too. They both ordered strawberry, as I recall.

Vocabulary

depicted (1)	disparaging (5)	*chinos* (15)
simmering (2)	*los gringos y la raza* (15)	barrio (17)
Chicano (3)	ostensibly (15)	enclave (17)
animated (3)		

Critical Thinking and Discussion

1. If the dominant impression of this essay is change, what are some of the descriptive details Torres uses in support?
2. When the author says, "I took a walk through the old neighborhood," what does he imply he will use mainly for organization—time or space?
3. What sense (sight, sound, taste, smell, touch) is appealed to most frequently?
4. Compare the first paragraph with the last paragraph.
5. Is the essay mainly optimistic or pessimistic? Find evidence for both.

Reading-Related Writing

1. Write a descriptive narrative about changes in your neighborhood. Like Torres, you may choose to make this a brief walking tour.
2. Write a descriptive narrative about an incident that reflects cultural tension in your school or neighborhood. Use the idea of change as a dominant impression. Consider both encouraging and discouraging signs.

BARBA NIKOS

Harry Mark Petrakis

The second- and third-generation immigrant may have lost some of his or her heritage along the way, may have even deliberately done so. In his autobiographical novel Stelmark: A Family Recollection *(1970), Petrakis presents a young man who attacks a representation of his heritage and then, beset by guilt, finds himself deeply immersed in learning about his past in a most unusual cultural museum—a Greek grocery store, where the ghosts of ancient legends appear daily.*

There was one storekeeper I remember above all others in my youth. It was 1
shortly before I became ill, spending a good portion of my time with a motley group of varied ethnic ancestry. We contended with one another to deride the customs of the old country. On our Saturday forays into neighborhoods beyond our own, to prove we were really Americans, we ate hot dogs and drank Cokes. If a boy didn't have ten cents for this repast he went hungry, for he dared not bring a sandwich from home made of the spiced meats our families ate.

One of our untamed games was to seek out the owner of a pushcart or a 2
store, unmistakably an immigrant, and bedevil him with a chorus of insults

and jeers. To prove allegiance to the gang it was necessary to reserve our fiercest malevolence for a storekeeper or peddler belonging to our own ethnic background.

For that reason I led a raid on the small, shabby grocery of old Barba 3 Nikos, a short, sinewy Greek who walked with a slight limp and sported a flaring, handlebar mustache.

We stood outside his store and dared him to come out. When he 4 emerged to do battle, we plucked a few plums and peaches from the baskets on the sidewalk and retreated across the street to eat them while he watched. He waved a fist and hurled epithets at us in ornamental Greek.

Aware that my mettle was being tested, I raised my arm and threw my 5 half-eaten plum at the old man. My aim was accurate and the plum struck him on the cheek. He shuddered and put his hand to the stain. He stared at me across the street, and although I could not see his eyes, I felt them sear my flesh. He turned and walked silently back into the store. The boys slapped my shoulders in admiration, but it was a hollow victory that rested like a stone in the pit of my stomach.

At twilight when we disbanded, I passed the grocery alone on my way 6 home. There was a small light burning in the store and the shadow of the old man's body outlined against the glass. Goaded by remorse, I walked to the door and entered.

The old man moved from behind the narrow wooden counter and stared 7 at me. I wanted to turn and flee, but by then it was too late. As he motioned for me to come closer, I braced myself for a curse or a blow.

"You were the one," he said, finally, in a harsh voice. 8

I nodded mutely. 9

"Why did you come back?" 10

I stood there unable to answer. 11

"What's your name?" 12

"Haralambos," I said, speaking to him in Greek. 13

He looked at me in shock. "You are Greek!" he cried. "A Greek boy 14 attacking a Greek grocer!" He stood appalled at the immensity of my crime. "All right," he said coldly. "You are here because you wish to make amends." His great mustache bristled in concentration. "Four plums, two peaches," he said. "That makes a total of 78 cents. Call it 75. Do you have 75 cents, boy?"

I shook my head. 15

"Then you will work it off," he said. "Fifteen cents an hour into 75 cents 16 makes"—he paused—"five hours of work. Can you come here Saturday morning?"

"Yes," I said. 17

"Yes, Barba Nikos," he said sternly. "Show respect." 18

"Yes, Barba Nikos," I said. 19

"Saturday morning at eight o'clock," he said. "Now go home and say   20
thanks in your prayers that I did not loosen your impudent head with a solid
smack on the ear." I needed no further urging and fled.

Saturday morning, still apprehensive, I returned to the store. I began by   21
sweeping, raising clouds of dust in dark and hidden corners. I washed the
windows, whipping the squeegee swiftly up and down the glass in a fever of
fear that some member of the gang would see me. When I finished I hurried
back inside.

For the balance of the morning I stacked cans, washed the counter, and   22
dusted bottles of yellow wine. A few customers entered, and Barba Nikos
served them. A little after twelve o'clock he locked the door so he could eat
lunch. He cut himself a few slices of sausage, tore a large chunk from a loaf of
crisp-crusted bread, and filled a small cup with a dozen black shiny olives
floating in brine. He offered me the cup. I could not help myself and gri-
maced.

"You are a stupid boy," the old man said. "You are not really Greek, are   23
you?"

"Yes, I am."   24

"You might be," he admitted grudgingly. "But you do not act Greek.   25
Wrinkling your nose at these fine olives. Look around this store for a minute.
What do you see?"

"Fruits and vegetables," I said. "Cheese and olives and things like that."   26

He stared at me with a massive scorn. "That's what I mean," he said. "You   27
are a bonehead. You don't understand that a whole nation and a people are in
this store."

I looked uneasily toward the storeroom in the rear, almost expecting   28
someone to emerge.

"What about olives?" he cut the air with a sweep of his arm. "There are   29
olives of many shapes and colors. Pointed black ones from Kalamata, oval
ones from Amphissa, pickled green olives and sharp tangy yellow ones. Achilles carried black olives to Troy and after a day of savage battle leading his
Myrmidons, he'd rest and eat cheese and ripe black olives such as these right
here. You have heard of Achilles, boy, haven't you?"

"Yes," I said.   30

"Yes, Barba Nikos."   31

"Yes, Barba Nikos," I said.   32

He motioned at the row of jars filled with varied spices. "There is origa-   33
non there and basilikon and daphne and sesame and miantanos, all the marvelous flavorings that we have used in our food for thousands of years. The
men of Marathon carried small packets of these spices into battle, and the
scents reminded them of their homes, their families, and their children."

He rose and tugged his napkin free from around his throat. "Cheese, you   34
said. Cheese! Come closer, boy, and I educate your abysmal ignorance." He

motioned toward a wooden container on the counter. "That glistening white delight is feta, made from goat's milk, packed in the wooden buckets to retain the flavor. Alexander the Great demanded it on his table with his casks of wine when he planned his campaigns."

He walked limping from the counter to the window where the piles of tomatoes, celery, and green peppers clustered. "I suppose all you see here are some random vegetables?" He did not wait for me to answer. "You are dumb again. These are some of the ingredients that go to make up a Greek salad. Do you know what a Greek salad really is? A meal in itself, an experience, an emotional involvement. It is created deftly and with grace. First, you place large lettuce leaves in a big, deep bowl." He spread his fingers and moved them slowly, carefully, as if he were arranging the leaves. "The remainder of the lettuce is shredded and piled in a small mound," he said. "Then comes celery, cucumbers, tomatoes sliced lengthwise, green peppers, origanon, green olives, feta, avocado, and anchovies. At the end you dress it with lemon, vinegar, and pure olive oil, glinting golden in the light." 35

He finished with a heartfelt sigh and for a moment closed his eyes. Then he opened one eye to mark me with a baleful intensity. "The story goes that Zeus himself created the recipe and assembled and mixed the ingredients on Mount Olympus one night when he had invited some of the other gods to dinner." 36

He turned his back on me and walked slowly again across the store, dragging one foot slightly behind him. I looked uneasily at the clock, which showed that it was a few minutes past one. He turned quickly and startled me. "And everything else in here," he said loudly. "White beans, lentils, garlic, crisp bread, kokoretsi, meat balls, mussels and clams." He paused and drew a deep, long breath. "And the wine," he went on, "wine from Samos, Santorini, and Crete, retsina and mavrodaphne, a taste almost as old as water . . . and then the fragrant melons, the pastries, yellow diples and golden loukoumades, the honey custard galatobouriko. Everything a part of our history, as much a part as the exquisite sculpture in marble, the bearded warriors, Pan and the oracles at Delphi, and the nymphs dancing in the shadowed groves under Homer's glittering moon." He paused, out of breath again, and coughed harshly. "Do you understand now, boy?" 37

He watched my face for some response and then grunted. We stood silent for a moment until he cocked his head and stared at the clock. "It is time for you to leave," he motioned brusquely toward the door. "We are square now. Keep it that way." 38

I decided the old man was crazy and reached behind the counter for my jacket and cap and started for the door. He called me back. From a box he drew out several soft, yellow figs that he placed in a piece of paper. "A bonus because you worked well," he said. "Take them. When you taste them, maybe you will understand what I have been talking about." 39

I took the figs and he unlocked the door and I hurried from the store. I 40
looked back once and saw him standing in the doorway, watching me, the
swirling tendrils of food curling like mist about his head.

I ate the figs late that night. I forgot about them until I was in bed, and 41
then I rose and took the package from my jacket. I nibbled at one, then ate
them all. They broke apart between my teeth with a tangy nectar, a thick
sweetness running like honey across my tongue and into the pockets of my
cheeks. In the morning when I woke, I could still taste and inhale their
fragrance.

I never again entered Barba Nikos's store. My spell of illness, which began 42
some months later, lasted two years. When I returned to the streets I had
forgotten the old man and the grocery. Shortly afterwards my family moved
from the neighborhood.

Some twelve years later, after the war, I drove through the old neighbor- 43
hood and passed the grocery. I stopped the car and for a moment stood before
the store. The windows were stained with dust and grime, the interior bare
and desolate, a store in a decrepit group of stores marked for razing so new
structures could be built.

I have been in many Greek groceries since then and have often bought 44
the feta and Kalamata olives. I have eaten countless Greek salads and have
indeed found them a meal for the gods. On the holidays in our house, my
wife and sons and I sit down to a dinner of steaming, buttered pilaf like my
mother used to make and lemon-egg avgolemono and roast lamb richly sea-
soned with cloves of garlic. I drink the red and yellow wines, and for dessert I
have come to relish the delicate pastries coated with honey and powdered
sugar. Old Barba Nikos would have been pleased.

But I have never been able to recapture the halcyon flavor of those figs he 45
gave me on that day so long ago, although I have bought figs many times. I
have found them pleasant to my tongue, but there is something missing. And
to this day I am not sure whether it was the figs or the vision and passion of
the old grocer that coated the fruit so sweetly I can still recall their savor and
fragrance after almost thirty years.

Vocabulary

mettle (5)	apprehensive (21)	desolate (43)
impudent (20)	abysmal (34)	halcyon (45)

Critical Thinking and Discussion

1. Why are the young men trying to act as if they were "really Americans"?
   What does the narrator mean by "American"?

2. Why do he and his fellow gang members attack one of their own ethnic group?
3. Why does he go back?
4. What does he learn?
5. Why does eating Greek food make him remember this experience? Why have the figs never tasted the same as they did that day he worked in the grocery store?
6. How many specific items of food are mentioned in paragraphs 29–37?

Reading-Related Writing

1. Discuss a childhood experience visiting a grocery store or restaurant that offered items that were ethnically, culturally, or regionally "yours." Be very specific in listing and describing items, and discuss their significance.
2. If you have parents or grandparents from "the old country" or even from a different part of the country or from a different class, have you ever felt some embarrassment when they were among people of a different background? What did you do? Describe an incident and how you felt about it later.
3. Discuss why the youngsters were motivated to attack someone of their own ethnic group.

TUESDAY MORNING

William Least Heat-Moon

William Trogdon, of English-Irish-Osage ancestry, writes under the pen name William Least Heat-Moon. Traveling around the country in the old van he calls Ghost Dancing, he sought out locales on secondary highways marked in blue on road maps, and a collection of his subsequent descriptions of these adventures became the best-selling book Blue Highways. *Here he travels across two Indian reservations as history, geography, anthropology, and whimsy merge.*

Tuesday morning: the country east of Heber was a desert of sagebrush and globe-shaped junipers and shallow washes with signs warning of flash floods. I turned north at Snowflake, founded by Erastus Snow and Bill Flake, and headed toward the twenty-five thousand square miles of Navajo reservation (nearly equal to West Virginia) which occupies most of the northeastern corner of Arizona. The scrub growth disappeared entirely and only the distant outlines of red rock mesas interrupted the emptiness. But for the highway, the land was featureless.

Holbrook used to be a tough town where boys from the Hash Knife cattle 2 outfit cut loose. Now, astride I-44 (once route 66), Holbrook was a tourist stop for women with Instamatics and men with metal detectors; no longer was the big business cattle, but rather rocks and gems.

North of the interstate, I entered the reserve. Although the area has been 3 part of the Navajo homeland for five hundred years, settlers of a century before, led by Kit Carson, drove the Navajo out of Arizona in retribution for their raids against whites and other Indians alike. A few years later, survivors of the infamous "Long Walk" returned to take up their land again. Now the Navajo possess the largest reservation in the United States and the one hundred fifty thousand descendants of the seven thousand survivors comprise far and away the largest tribe. Their reservation is the only one in the country to get bigger—five times bigger—after it was first set aside; their holdings increased largely because white men had believed Navajo land worthless. But in fact, the reservation contains coal, oil, gas, uranium, helium, and timber; these resources may explain why Navajos did not win total control over their land until 1972.

Liquor bottles, beercans, an occasional stripped car littered the unfenced 4 roadside. Far off the highway, against the mesa bottoms, stood small concrete-block or frame houses, each with a television antenna, pickup, privy, and ceremonial hogan of stone, adobe, and cedar. Always the hogan doors faced east.

In a classic scene, a boy on a pinto pony herded a flock of sheep and 5 goats—descendants of the Spanish breed—across the highway. A few miles later, a man wearing a straw Stetson and pegleg Levi's guided up a draw a pair of horses tied together at the neck in the Indian manner. With the white man giving up on the economics of cowpunching, it looked as if the old categories of cowboys and Indians had merged; whoever the last true cowboy in America turns out to be, he's likely to be an Indian.

At the center of the reservation lay Hopi territory, a large rectangle with 6 boundaries the tribes cannot agree on because part of the increase of Navajo land has come at the expense of the Hopis. A forbidding sign in Latinate English:

> YOU ARE ENTERING THE EXCLUSIVE
> HOPI RESERVATION AREA. YOUR
> ENTRANCE CONSTITUTES CONSENT
> TO THE JURISDICTION OF THE HOPI
> TRIBE AND ITS COURTS.

Although the Hopi have lived here far longer than any other surviving 7 people and consider their mile-high spread of rock and sand, wind and sun, the center of the universe, they are now, by Anglo decree, surrounded by their old enemies, the Navajo, a people they see as latecomers. In 1880, Hopis held two and one half million acres; today it has decreased to about a half million.

Holding on to their land has been a long struggle for the Hopi. Yet for a 8 tribe whose name means "well behaved," for Indians without war dances, for a group whose first defense against the conquistadors was sprinkled lines of sacred cornmeal, for a people who protested priestly corruption (consorting with Hopi women and whipping men) by quietly pitching a few padres over the cliffs, Hopis have done well. But recently they have fought Navajo expansion in federal courts, and a strange case it is: those who settled first seeking judgment from those who came later through laws of those who arrived last.

Because the Navajo prefer widely dispersed clusters of clans to village 9 life, I'd seen nothing resembling a hamlet for seventy-five miles. But Hopi Polacca almost look like a Western town in spite of Indian ways here and there: next to a floral-print bedsheet on a clothesline hung a coyote skin, and beside box houses were adobe bread ovens shaped like skep beehives. The Navajos held to his hogan, the Hopi his oven. Those things persisted.

Like bony fingers, three mesas reached down from larger Black Mesa into 10 the middle of Hopi land; not long ago, the only way onto these mesas was by handholds in the steep rock heights. From the tops, the Hopi look out upon a thousand square miles. At the heart of the reservation, topographically and culturally, was Second Mesa. Traditionally, Hopis, as do the eagles they hold sacred, prefer to live on precipices; so it was not far from the edge of Second Mesa that they built the Hopi Cultural Center. In the gallery were drawings of mythic figures by Hopi children who fused centuries and cultures with grotesque Mudhead Kachinas wearing large terra-cotta masks and jack-o-lantern smiles, dancing atop spaceships with Darth Vader and Artoo Deetoo.

At the Center, I ate *nokquivi*, a good hominy stew with baked chile pep- 11 pers, but I had no luck in striking up a conversation. I drove on toward the western edge of the mesa. Not far from the tribal garage (TRIBAL VEHICLES ONLY) stood small sandstone houses, their slabs precisely cut and fitted as if by ancient Aztecs, a people related to the Hopi. The solid houses blended with the tawny land so well they appeared part of the living rock. All were empty. The residents had moved to prefabs and double-wides.

I couldn't see how anyone could survive a year in this severe land, yet 12 Hopis, like other desert life, are patient and clever and not at all desperate; they have lasted here for ten centuries by using tiny terraced plots that catch spring rain and produce a desert-hardy species of blue corn, as well as squash, onions, beans, peppers, melons, apricots, peaches. The bristlecone pine of American Indians, Hopis live where almost nothing else will, thriving long in adverse conditions: poor soil, drought, temperature extremes, high winds. Those give life to the bristlecone and the Hopi.

Clinging to the southern lip of Third Mesa was ancient Oraibi, most 13 probably the oldest continuously occupied village in the United States. Somehow the stone and adobe have been able to hang on to the precipitous edge since the twelfth century. More than eight hundred Hopis lived at Oraibi in 1901—now only a few. All across the reservation I'd seen no more than a dozen people, and on the dusty streets of the old town I saw just one bent woman struggling against the wind. But somewhere there must have been more.

To this strangest of American villages the Franciscan father, Tomás 14 Garces, came in 1776 from Tucson with gifts and "true religion." Hopis permitted him to stay at Oraibi, looking then as now if you excluded an occasional television antenna, but they refused his gifts and god, and, on the fourth day of July, sent him off disheartened. To this time, no other North American tribe has held closer to its own religion and culture. Although the isolated Hopi had no knowledge of the importance of religious freedom to the new nation surrounding them, several generations successfully ignored "the code of religious offenses"—laws designed by the Bureau of Indian Affairs to destroy the old rituals and way of life—until greater bureaucratic tolerance came when Herbert Hoover appointed two Quakers to direct the BIA.

A tribal squadcar checked my speed at Hotevilla, where the highway 15 started a long descent off the mesa. The wind was getting up, and tumbleweed bounded across the road, and sand hummed against the Ghost. West, east, north, south—to each a different weather: sandstorm, sun, rain, and bluish snow on the San Francisco Peaks, that home of the Kachinas who are the spiritual forces of Hopi life.

Tuba City, founded by Mormon missionaries as an agency and named 16 after a Hopi chieftain although now mostly a Navajo town, caught the sandstorm full face. As I filled the gas tank, I tried to stay behind the van, but gritty gusts whipped around the corners and stung me and forced my eyes shut. School was just out, and children, shirts pulled over their heads, ran for the trading post, where old Navajo men who had been sitting outside took cover as the sand changed the air to matter. I ducked in too. The place was like an A&P, TG&Y, and craft center.

In viridescent velveteen blouses and violescent nineteenth-century skirts, 17 Navajo women of ample body, each laden with silver and turquoise bracelets, necklaces, and rings—not the trading post variety but heavy bands gleaming under the patina of long wear—reeled off yards of fabric. The children, like schoolkids anywhere, milled around the candy; they spoke only English. But the old men, now standing at the plate glass windows and looking into the brown wind, popped and puffed out the ancient words. I've read that Navajo, a language related to that of the Indians of Alaska and northwest Canada, has no curse words unless you consider "coyote" cursing. By comparison with other native tongues, it's remarkably free of English and Spanish; a Navajo mechanic, for example, has more than two hundred purely Navajo terms to describe automobile parts. And it might be Navajo that will greet the first extraterrestrial ears to hear from planet Earth: on board each *Voyager* spacecraft traveling toward the edge of the solar system and beyond is a gold-plated, long-playing record: following an aria from Mozart's *Magic Flute* and Chuck Berry's "Johnny B. Goode," is a Navajo night chant, music the conquistadors heard.

Intimidated by my ignorance of Navajo and by fear of the contempt that 18 full-bloods often show lesser bloods, I again failed to stir a conversation. After the storm blew on east, I followed the old men back outside, where they squatted to watch the day take up the weather of an hour earlier. To one with a great round head like an earthen pot, I said, "Is the storm finished now?" He looked at me, then slowly turned his head, while the others examined before them things in the air invisible to me.

I took a highway down the mesa into a valley of the Painted Desert, 19 where wind had textured big drifts of orange sand into rills, U.S. 89 ran north along the Echo Cliffs. Goats grazed in stubble by the roadsides, and to the west a horseman moved his sheep. Hogans here stood alone; they were not ceremonial lodges but homes. For miles at the highway edges sat little cardboard and scrapwood ramadas, each with a windblasted sign advertising jewelry and cedar beads. In another era, white men came in wagons to trade beads to Indians; now they came in stationwagons and bought beads. History may repeat, but sometimes things get turned around in the process.

Critical Thinking and Discussion

1. Why must Willian Least Heat-Moon, himself a Native American, write about these reservations as an outsider?
2. What does he say about the roles of cowboys and Indians in paragraph 5?
3. What specific items from nontraditional Native American culture are mentioned in paragraphs 4 and 5?
4. How do the cultures merge in paragraph 10?
5. In what way are the Hopis the "bristlecone pines" of American Indians (paragraph 12)?
6. What types of images (sight, sound, touch, taste, smell) are used in paragraphs 16 and 17?
7. What role reversal is mentioned in the last paragraph?

Reading-Related Writing

1. Write about your neighborhood. Through description and observation, show how homes, landscaping, and other features reveal values and a

way of life in general. Include people in your study, and consider using the framework of an incident.

2. From the point of view of one of the Navajos or Hopis (an older person or one of the youths in the trading post), give a brief profile of Least Heat-Moon and his behavior. Because you probably do not know what he looks like, use your imagination.

SOFT MORNINGS AND HARSH AFTERNOONS

Maya Angelou

In this narrative passage from her celebrated book I Know Why the Caged Bird Sings, *Maya Angelou introduces you to people and situations from her childhood. She also introduces you to a full range of her emotions, from reverential love to bitter anger. Early mornings and late evenings frame the passage, but they represent more than just the time of day.*

Each year I watched the field across from the Store turn caterpillar green, then gradually frosty white. I knew exactly how long it would be before the big wagons would pull into the front yard and load on the cotton pickers at daybreak to carry them to the remains of slavery's plantations.

During the picking season my grandmother would get out of bed at four o'clock (she never used an alarm clock) and creak down to her knees and chant in a sleep-filled voice, "Our Father, thank you for letting me see this New Day. Thank you that you didn't allow the bed I lay on last night to be my cooling board, nor my blanket my winding sheet. Guide my feet this day along the straight and narrow, and help me to put a bridle on my tongue. Bless this house, and everybody in it. Thank you, in the name of your Son, Jesus Christ, Amen."

Before she had quite arisen, she called our names and issued orders, and pushed her large feet into homemade slippers and across the bare lye-washed wooden floor to light the coal-oil lamp.

The lamplight in the Store gave a soft make-believe feeling to our world which made me want to whisper and walk about on tiptoe. The odors of onions and oranges and kerosene had been mixing all night and wouldn't be disturbed until the wooded slat was removed from the door and the early morning air forced its way in with the bodies of people who had walked miles to reach the pickup place.

"Sister, I'll have two cans of sardines."

"I'm gonna work so fast today I'm gonna make you look like you stand- 6
ing still."

"Lemme have a hunk uh cheese and some sody crackers." 7

"Just gimme a coupla them fat peanut paddies." That would be from a 8
picker who was taking his lunch. The greasy brown paper sack was stuck
behind the bib of his overalls. He'd use the candy as a snack before the noon
sun called the workers to rest.

In those tender mornings the Store was full of laughing, joking, boasting 9
and bragging. One man was going to pick two hundred pounds of cotton,
and another three hundred. Even the children were promising to bring home
fo' bits and six bits.

The champion picker of the day before was the hero of the dawn. If he 10
prophesied that the cotton in today's field was going to be sparce and stick to
the bolls like glue, every listener would grunt a hearty agreement.

The sound of the empty cotton sacks dragging over the floor and the 11
murmurs of waking people were sliced by the cash register as we rang up the
five-cent sales.

If the morning sounds and smells were touched with the supernatural, 12
the late afternoon had all the features of the normal Arkansas life. In the
dying sunlight the people dragged, rather than their empty cotton sacks.

Brought back to the Store, the pickers would step out of the backs of 13
trucks and fold down, dirt-disappointed, to the ground. No matter how much
they had picked, it wasn't enough. Their wages wouldn't even get them out of
debt to my grandmother, not to mention the staggering bill that waited on
them at the white commissary downtown.

The sounds of the new morning had been replaced with grumbles about 14
cheating houses, weighted scales, snakes, skimpy cotton and dusty rows. In
later years I was to confront the stereotyped picture of gay song-singing
cotton pickers with such inordinate rage that I was told even by fellow Blacks
that my paranoia was embarrassing. But I had seen the fingers cut by the
mean little cotton bolls, and I had witnessed the backs and shoulders and
arms and legs resisting any further demands.

Some of the workers would leave their sacks at the Store to be picked up 15
the following morning, but a few had to take them home for repairs. I winced
to picture them sewing the coarse material under a coal-oil lamp with fingers
stiffening from the day's work. In too few hours they would have to walk back
to Sister Henderson's Store, get vittles and load, again, onto the trucks. Then
they would face another day of trying to earn enough for the whole year with
the heavy knowledge that they were going to end the season as they started it.
Without the money or credit necessary to sustain a family for three months.
In cotton-picking time the late afternoons revealed the harshness of Black
Southern life, which in the early morning had been softened by nature's
blessing of grogginess, forgetfulness and the soft lamplight.

Critical Thinking and Discussion

1. What does Angelou's grandmother represent to her?
2. What opposing feelings does Angelou express?
3. What times of the day are featured? What characterizes each?
4. What is emphasized—the security of the store or the oppression of the farm? Or are they treated equally?

Reading-Related Writing

(Although these assignments are mainly descriptive, they are likely to work best when they are used within a story framework.)

1. The author reveres her grandmother. Using this essay as a model, write a descriptive piece in which you show your admiration for someone.
2. Write a descriptive piece in which you present another group of workers who are exploited in the fields, factories, or streets.
3. Describe the store from the perspective of one of the field workers.

RULES OF THE GAME

Amy Tan

This passage is taken from The Joy Luck Club, *a book comprising sixteen tales that reflect a young girl's life in San Francisco. Here, in brief narrative and rich descriptive treatment, she reveals a young girl's ties to her community and her mother.*

I was six when my mother taught me the art of invisible strength. It was a   1
strategy for winning arguments, respect from others, and eventually, though neither of us knew it at the time, chess games.

"Bite back your tongue," scolded my mother when I cried loudly, yanking   2
her hand toward the store that sold bags of salted plums. At home, she said, "Wise guy, he not go against wind. In Chinese we say, Come from South, blow with wind—poom!—North will follow. Strongest wind cannot be seen."

The next week I bit back my tongue as we entered the store with the   3
forbidden candies. When my mother finished her shopping, she quietly plucked a small bag of plums from the rack and put it on the counter with the rest of the items.

My mother imparted her daily truths so she could help my older brothers   4
and me rise above our circumstances. We lived in San Francisco's Chinatown.

Like most of the other Chinese children who played in the back alleys of restaurants and curio shops, I didn't think we were poor. My bowl was always full, three five-course meals every day, beginning with a soup full of mysterious things I didn't want to know the names of.

We lived on Waverly Place, in a warm, clean, two-bedroom flat that sat 5 above a small Chinese bakery specializing in steamed pastries and dim sum. In the early morning, when the alley was still quiet, I could smell fragrant red beans as they were cooked down to a pasty sweetness. By daybreak, our flat was heavy with the odor of fried sesame balls and sweet curried chicken crescents. From my bed, I would listen as my father got ready for work, then locked the door behind him, one-two-three clicks.

At the end of our two-block alley was a small sandlot playground with 6 swings and slides well-shined down the middle with use. The play area was bordered by wood-slat benches where old-country people sat cracking roasted watermelon seeds with their golden teeth and scattering the husks to an impatient gathering of gurgling pigeons. The best playground, however, was the dark alley itself. It was crammed with daily mysteries and adventures. My brothers and I would peer into the medicinal herb shop, watching old Li dole out onto a stiff sheet of white paper the right amount of insect shells, saffron-colored seeds, and pungent leaves for his ailing customers. It was said that he once cured a woman dying of an ancestral curse that had eluded the best of American doctors. Next to the pharmacy was a printer who specialized in gold-embossed wedding invitations and festive red banners.

Farther down the street was Ping Yuen Fish Market. The front window 7 displayed a tank crowded with doomed fish and turtles struggling to gain footing on the slimy green-tiled sides. A hand-written sign informed tourists, "Within this store, is all for food not for pet." Inside, the butchers with their bloodstained white smocks deftly gutted the fish while customers cried out their orders and shouted, "Give me your freshest," to which the butchers always protested, "All are freshest," On less crowded market days, we would inspect the crates of live frogs and crabs which we were warned not to poke, boxes of dried cuttlefish, and row upon row of iced prawns, squid, and slippery fish. The sanddabs made me shiver each time; their eyes lay on one flattened side and reminded me of my mother's story of a careless girl who ran into a crowded street and was crushed by a cab. "Was smash flat," reported my mother.

At the corner of the alley was Hong Sing's, a four-table café with a 8 recessed stairwell in front that led to a door marked "Tradesmen." My brothers and I believed the bad people emerged from this door at night. Tourists never went to Hong Sing's since the menu was printed only in Chinese. A Caucasian man with a big camera once posed me and my playmates in front of the restaurant. He had us move to the side of the picture window so the photo would capture the roasted duck with its head dangling from a juice-covered rope. After he took the picture, I told him he should go into Hong Sing's and eat dinner. When he smiled and asked me what they served, I shouted, "Guts and duck's feet and octopus gizzards!" Then I ran off with my friends, shrieking with laughter as we scampered across the alley and hid in the entryway grotto of the China Gem Company, my heart pounding with hope that he would chase us.

My mother named me after the street that we lived on: Waverly Place Jong, 9 my official name for important American documents. But my family called me Meimei, "Little Sister." I was the youngest, the only daughter. Each morning before school, my mother would twist and yank on my thick black hair until she had formed two tightly wound pigtails. One day, as she struggled to weave a hard-toothed comb through my disobedient hair, I had a sly thought.

I asked her, "Ma, what is Chinese torture?" My mother shook her head. A 10 bobby pin was wedged between her lips. She wetted her palm and smoothed the hair above my ear, then pushed the pin in so that it nicked sharply against my scalp.

"Who say this word?" she asked without a trace of knowing how wicked I 11 was being. I shrugged my shoulders and said, "Some boy in my class said Chinese people do Chinese torture."

"Chinese people do many things," she said simply. "Chinese people do 12 business, do medicine, do painting. Not lazy like American people. We do torture. Best torture."

Vocabulary

imparted (4)	eluded (6)	deftly (7)
curio (4)	embossed (6)	cuttlefish (7)
saffron (6)	festive (6)	grotto (8)
pungent (6)		

Critical Thinking and Discussion

1. What is the dominant impression of this story?
2. What is the effect of beginning and ending the description with comments from the narrator's mother?
3. How many of the senses (sight, smell, taste, hearing, and touch) are represented here?
4. What is the narrator's "best playground"? Why?

Reading-Related Writing

Describe your neighborhood as it was when you were growing up. Populate it with one or more of the people (not necessarily family members) who influenced you. Limit your description in time or place, and unify your description around a dominant impression.

BARRIO AFTER DARK*

Yvette Lohayza

Reading a newspaper account of violence in the inner city is not quite the same as reading an account by an insider. Student Yvette Lohayza knows what it is like. She's not just covering a story; she once lived there.

L.A.'s barrio, in the east-central part of a chaotic city, is a fortress of frantically 1 terrified residents. During a hot summer's day, while the sun is still shining bright, the children of the barrio are dispersed within the driveways, streets, and alleys, merrily playing such sports as kickball and handball. This is a safe time for the children's activities, as well as the adults' social hour among neighborly friends. But once the sun begins to set and the cool winds begin to blow, signs of danger commence, and the happy barrio is about to become a bestial barrio.

Suddenly the laughter of the children playing in the streets and the 2 chattering of the older Latina women start to diminish as peculiar bird-like whistles fill the air, and hoards of Latino youths begin to emerge from various alleys, walkways, and sometimes their own homes, like cucarachas crawling out of crevices in a scurry for some food. A boy no older than thirteen throws his arms up to motion some letters that are recognized by his gang members. Anarchy fills the air as the children scurry home to the crying demand of their mothers. The older women begin to hobble to their homes and immediately begin locking their front doors. What once appeared to be a normally decent neighborhood has now been converted into a fortress of criminal activity.

With nightfall the day has just begun for these nocturnal creatures of the 3 Los Angeles barrio. Like a ritual, these youths gather at a particular cul-de-sac which is located in the very center of the barrio for what appears to be a "gathering" (gang gathering). You could not miss this place they call the "circle" because of its historically beautiful paintings on the walls, which, under a scattering of graffiti, depict various scenarios of Aztec Indians and Latino people engaging in interracial encounters of handshaking and peaceful gestures. The painters of these murals are also residents here, and they know all about the hardships that these young boys are vulnerable to. So they paint peaceful encounters on these walls as an attempt to somehow psychologically influence this younger generation that has gone so wrong. Standing amid the broken beer bottles, one may not notice at first glance the old blood stains and the pockmarks of bullets inflicted by gunshots from rival gang members.

The marks on and around these walls, the wailing walls of my people, 4 could tell a thousand horrid stories of violence that took place here. Once all the members of this barrio gang have gathered here, the smell of cheap cologne fills the air as these young boys begin to play their rap music. The girls have now joined the boys, and their giggling punctuates the stories of the young boys who describe in mixed Spanish and English what happened last night and what will happen tonight or tomorrow night. One boy begins to brag to a girl whom he is interested in how he stabbed a rival gang member and points to a particular dark stain. It's almost as if he were some great fisherman displaying a remnant of the biggest catch of the day.

Meanwhile, the other people stay inside. The barrio is a place where 5 hardship rules, and for the young gangsters, sharing a common bond of being somebody in this place that is nowhere is what they live and die for. The barrio is a place of eternal tragedies.

Critical Thinking and Discussion

1. What is Lohayza's thesis?
2. Is the organization of this essay based more on time or space?
3. What is the effect of comparison and contrast in this descriptive piece?
4. What one word would you use to describe the tone of this essay?
5. What is the dominant impression of this description?

Reading-Related Writing

1. Describe your neighborhood before and after dark.
2. Describe your neighborhood—the good, bad, beautiful, ugly.
3. If you live in an area similar to the one described by Lohayza, write about it, concentrating on the daylight activities or, following her lead, focusing on activities after dark.

MY NAVAJO HOME IN LOS ANGELES*

Thomas Whiterock

The traditional Navajo home is a hogan, and it would be located somewhere on the huge Navajo reservation. But what kind of home does the Navajo who lives off the reservation have? Student Thomas

Whiterock's home is in Los Angeles County, and inside are cultural reminders that he is a Navajo.

On a warm summer day, my friend Tung and I walked into my mother's 1 house. It was a relief to be out of the heat and to feel the coolness of home. I immediately began to walk across the living room to get to the stack of homework waiting for me. Out of the corner of my eye, I noticed that Tung was not behind me, but was still standing in the doorway, staring at the opposing wall. "What is that?" he asked, pointing to the wall. "That," I said, "is Navajo. Just look around, and you'll see Navajo items everywhere."

Across from where Tung stood hung a large painting of pottery and corn 2 on a table top. The pottery, white and brown, is decorated with bold, black lines and birds. The corn is made up of vivid squares of white, yellow, maroon, brown, and black wrapped in pale husks. One one side of the painting is a bushel of "Indian" corn, the same as depicted in the painting. I explained that the corn is as important to our diet as rice is to his. When the white man put us on reservations to change our religion and language, he also tried to change our food. We were given corn in equal rations with wheat, which was foreign to us. We had to fight for our corn. On the other side of the painting hangs a bushel of long, red chili peppers. The chili was introduced to us by the Spanish, but today is still consumed with each meal in most Navajo families.

Next, Tung pointed to the ladder leaning against the wall, a crude ladder 3 made of bare wood. The rungs were held tightly in the notches with straps of leather. "Why do you have a ladder in the house?" he asked. "This, too, is Navajo," I explained. Though there were different kinds of houses, or hogans, the most common was the square, one-room house made of logs and adobe. These homes had lofts for the children to sleep in, and leading up to these lofts were ladders. Even though we had no loft, the ladder was here. The ladder was a relic of older times and a reminder of our heritage.

I then unfolded a rug that hung over the third rung. "This rug is pur- 4 posely red," I said, "because red represents wisdom, which is very important in our culture." He then asked what the other rugs were for, referring to the rug on the table, the one on the couch and another on the wall. The colors have various meanings, depending on their use, I explained. The largest rug is turquoise, which represents spiritual goodness. The designs are of the "holy" people who will protect us. The black and red rug means knowledge, and the lines and diamond shapes are symbolic for corn stalks, which produce the main parts of our diet.

Together we looked closely at the smaller painting on the side of the 5 entry way to the dining room. One painting is of a Navajo woman weaving, a second is a child at play, and a third is a man herding sheep. Tung picked up the pottery from the shelf to get a closer look, but something else caught his eye. After putting the pottery down carefully, he slowly walked to the corner of the room and picked up the stick that lay there. The sound it made amazed him. He tilted the stick back and forth. This always holds the most fascination for guests, and it's something my family is used to explaining. I told him, "That is the cause of ignorant statements and stereotypes and makes us the butt of many jokes. But is also means much to my people." He moved it back and forth, listening. "Yes, there really is a rain dance," I continued. "Not like you see in cartoons or in old movies made by white men, though. This is a ceremony performed by the Zuni, the Hopi, and the Navajo. It was vital to their harvest." Tung was holding the rainstick used in the ceremony. The simulated sound of rainfall as the seeds rolling through the small tunnels of the hollow stick made Tung smile. "Put the stick down," I joked, "before it starts to rain."

Caught up in the excitement of explaining my culture that I walk by 6
every day without noticing, I finally dragged Tung to the kitchen. I pointed to the sunflowers that are sprinkled around the room. I told him the story of the sunflowers' disappearance from our region for a few years, which was understood to be a bad sign. When the flower returned, it was proof that the spirits were happy with us. I pointed to the ceramic mushrooms on the table and on the counter and explained that they are used for visionquests or wisdomquests. I was on a roll! Before he could ask, I stepped quickly to the window and stood underneath a large, silk butterfly on the curtain. "This," I said, "represents two things in our art: dead warriors rising to the great hunting ground, and here," I paused to point to the butterfly, "the butterfly is taking our prayers to heaven."

I later walked Tung to the door after long hours of studying. He took 7
another look around the room and smiled. "I like it here," he said. "It feels like a true home in every way." I opened the door. The sky had become overcast. It looked as if it just might rain after all.

Critical Thinking and Discussion

1. What is the dominant impression of this essay?
2. What is the main sensory image used here—sight or sound?
3. Is time or space used as the main frame for organization?

Reading-Related Writing

1. Write about your own home, discussing art, pictures, furniture, and other items that show the diversity of your household.
2. If you know an interracial family, describe their home to show how more than one culture is represented.

3. If your family has strong cultural ties, reflected in interior decoration or landscaping (yard design or items in a garden), follow Thomas Whiterock's lead and describe your house or yard to a visitor.

Collaborative Learning

This project is designed for several small groups. Each group will be responsible for reading and evaluating one or more of this chapter's descriptive selections about a home, building, neighborhood, or area. Consider whether the place

- is nurturing or harmful
- is restrictive or not
- has multicultural implications or not
- implies or states universal values
- is significant to the writer

Of course, these selections are short and written by individuals with focused views. It would be unfair to judge any group or location on the basis of one set of impressions. Perhaps the tendency to do that could also be discussed in your group as you employ critical-thinking skills.

Connections

1. Write about your own region, town, or neighborhood. Refer to some of the places described in this chapter for comparisons and contrasts.
2. Write about scenes in a book, a movie, or a television program, explaining the cultural implications and the relationship between individuals and their environment.

4

Love, Sex, and Marriage

*T*he idea of love is pervasive. *Love* is one of the most frequently used words in the English language—and in the language of any other cultural group considered here. Love is probably the most common subject of songs, sermons, and spats. When lovers aren't loving, they may very well be contemplating love—love as theory, love as behavior, love as an illusion.

This chapter brings together diverse expressions of love, sex, and marriage. Some relationships include all three, and some don't. Moreover, the sequence may vary: love, marriage, sex; love, sex, marriage; sex, love, marriage; or marriage, sex, love. But love is always present in these selections. The examples of love come from different cultures, different perspectives. You will read about glandular love, love according to psychological perspective, lesbian love, confirming love, love C.O.D. for mail-order brides, and the consummate love of two passionate people.

WRITING STRATEGIES AND TECHNIQUES: EXEMPLIFICATION

Exemplification is simply using examples to develop ideas. We all know of the effectiveness of examples. In the 1992 presidential campaign, the candidates made much use of this technique. On one occasion, Ross Perot announced he had received thousands of letters from supporters. Then he offered an example. He made the example specific and concrete by reading the letter and stating the supporter's name. He made his example even more specific and concrete by showing a photograph of the supporter, a young girl he called "the future of America." If she had been there, he might have held her up as a live, specific, concrete example, squirming and protesting in embarrassment, before the audience of reporters and photographers. His technique worked, at least in one way: we remember the event.

You will, of course, note that the previous paragraph used an example to explain the effectiveness of examples. In fact, glance back at the paragraph and try to imagine how it could be developed well without an example.

All perceptive readers appreciate and even expect well-chosen examples. One recurring complaint English instructors hear from instructors in other departments is that student writers use generalizations without support. These unsupported generalizations are likely to be uninteresting, unclear, and unconvincing.

Consider these two statements on the same subject.

> College coaches know the importance of finding talented athletes for intercollegiate sports programs, and they know all the techniques for attracting such athletes to their schools. Ironically, one technique is the appeal to the athletes' desire for an education. To that end, the coaches will highlight the tutorial help and other learning assistance that are available in their schools. Some of these athletes have learning disabilities, some of them were not serious students in high school, and some attended inferior schools. Unfortunately, some of these athletes are promised more than will be delivered. The school will make millions on its athletic program, but the athletes will be neglected as students.

Dull, isn't it? Now read another version.

> As any coach knows, the outcome of a season is often determined before the opening tip-off of the first game. It begins with the high school players recruited by the school. A single talented player can be worth hundreds of thousands of dollars to a college —and, indirectly, to a coach. The NCAA prohibits recruiters from offering money to prospective players. But many student athletes say recruiters offered them cash, cars and jewelry. For some young players, and especially for their families, the promise of educational help can swing their decision. It is not only the larger schools that have problems.
>
> Take the case of Reggie Ford. As a 6-ft. 4-in. senior at Marion High School in rural South Carolina three years ago, Reggie was an All-State center. More than a dozen universities salivated over his 22-points-a-game average. They

paid little mind to his scant 2.0 grade-point average. It was Bob Battisti, coach of Northwestern Oklahoma State University, who persuaded Reggie to attend his school. What won him over, said Reggie, was Battisti's promise that a tutor would be available to help him through the difficult academic times ahead. "I knew I wasn't no A student," explains Reggie. For the Ford family, it was a shining moment. They are poor. Reggie's mother is disabled from a car accident, his father from a stroke. Reggie was the first member of his family to go to college.

Initially, the coaches were attentive. Reggie remembers they joked with him and invited him into their homes. But each time Reggie asked about a tutor, he was put off. Then he injured his knee, and everything changed, he said. The coaches ignored him, and the invitations dried up. His grades dropped; the scholarship was withdrawn. "After I hurt my knee, it seemed like they were trying to tell me there wasn't much I could do for them, so I got up and left," says Reggie. Now 21, he lives with his family in South Carolina, and is collecting unemployment.

Ted Gup, "Foul"

One example here in the second version makes the topic idea come alive. The second and following paragraphs in this unit support the idea by providing an example, a specific, named subject. With this kind of development, we are more likely to be interested, informed, and convinced, and we are more likely to remember.

Sources of Examples

For the personal essay, the best source of examples is your own knowledge. If you know your subject well, from either reading or experience, you will be able to recall many examples through your writing strategies of freewriting, brainstorming, and clustering. Good examples are likely to come from something you know well. If you have worked in a fast-food restaurant, you probably have dozens of stories about activities there. Some of these stories might be appropriate for illustrating a topic on human behavior. Although a reader has not shared an experience with a writer, he or she will almost certainly be able to judge and appreciate its authenticity. Professional writers working outside their specialties often interview (and sometimes pay) ordinary individuals in order to obtain concrete particulars to color and enliven their work. Television-crime-show writers, for instance, regularly collect information from police officers.

A more academic topic, such as one on a novel, might be researched by scrutinizing the book itself for incidents, statements, or descriptions. A history topic might be researched in a textbook or in library sources.

Connecting Examples with Purpose

Examples, by their very definition, are functional. They are representative of something, or they illustrate something. Their purpose may be to explain, convince, or amuse. The connection between this purpose and the example must be clear. If your example is striking, yet later your reader can remember the example but not the point being illustrated, then you have failed in your basic task. Writing good exemplification begins with a good topic sentence or thesis.

BROAD: People seeking plastic surgery have various motives.

                        Subject   *Treatment*
FOCUSED: Some people seeking plastic surgery are driven by irrational
          emotional needs that can never be met.

In the following paragraph on essentially that focused idea, the author uses an example effectively by stating the purpose (topic sentence), connecting it with the example, and restating the purpose while relating it, in turn, directly to the example.

topic sentence — Leigh Lachman, a plastic surgeon in Manhattan, notes that "some patients are never satisfied." One of his clients, a 45-year-old woman, came to him for a facelift, then a nose job, and then a breast reduction. She now insists that her breasts are too small and she wants them augmented. Then she plans

extended example — to get an eye-lift. She started bringing in friends to see Lachman. "Her attitude seems to be that she's bringing me business, so I should continue to operate on her," Lachman says. "These

restatement of topic sentence — kinds of patients can be very difficult to help, because it becomes obvious that they want more than a surgical correction can provide."

Holly Hall,
"Scalpel Slaves"

Examples: Kinds, Choices, Patterns

Specific

"Take the case of Reggie Ford" begins the paragraph on exploitation of student athletes. "One of his clients, a 45-year-old woman, came to him for a facelift" highlights the paragraph on plastic surgery. Both examples are specific and concrete. The first names a person and discusses him for several paragraphs; the second refers directly to a woman and in a short paragraph discusses her in relation to the topic sentence. Each example illustrates an idea and fulfills a purpose. The examples are effective because readers can see the subjects both as individuals and as representatives of groups. Each is interesting and appropriate. Specific examples can be powerful tools in writing to explain and persuade.

The following three examples came from "The Business of Selling Mail-Order Brides" by Venny Villapanda.

<table>
<tr><td>a specific correspondent</td><td>When he receives a letter and the appropriate fees from a prospective groom, Broussard sends off a catalogue. One of his correspondents describes the process: "I selected fourteen ladies to send introductory letters to. To my amazement, I received fourteen replies and am still corresponding with twelve of them." One of the reasons why letters so often succeed is the detailed coaching both parties receive. For instance Broussard and Pomeroy publish a 130-page pamphlet entitled</td></tr>
<tr><td>two specific pamphlets</td><td>"How to Write to Oriental Ladies." There is also one for women called "The Way to an American Male's Heart."</td></tr>
</table>

Typical

The typical differs from the specific in that it shows what is generally true.

<table>
<tr><td>typical mail-order brides</td><td>In the present matches brides-to-be are generally Asian and husbands-to-be are Caucasians, mostly American, Australian, and Canadian. A majority of the women are poor and because of economic desperation become mail-order brides. Racial, as well as economic, factors define the marriage however. The new wife is relegated to a more inferior position than her picture bride counterpart. Plus the inequity of the partnership is further complicated by the mail-order bride's immigrant status. Consequently she is a foreigner not only to the culture, language, and society, but to her husband's race and nationality as well.</td></tr>
</table>

Hypothetical

Another kind of example is the hypothetical. At times we will offer an example that is presented in an "imagine that" or "what if" posture. In other words, we make up something and offer it to the reader, who understands that it is contrived, made up, for the purpose of discussion. An author could write,

an imagined
woman

Erroneous ideas continue to thrive. An Asian woman dreams she will meet and marry someone rich and powerful, someone to rescue her and free her from poverty-stricken bondage. She hopes to live the rest of her life in a land of plenty. An American man dreams he will meet and marry someone passive, obedient, nonthreatening, and virginal, someone to devote her entire life to him, serving him and making no demands. Only a strong women's movement, one tied to the exploited underdeveloped country's struggle for liberation and independence, can challenge these ideas and channel the aspirations and ambitions of both men and women in a more positive and realistic direction.

an imagined man

Choosing the Kinds

Whether you use the specific, the typical, or the hypothetical example will depend on your purpose, your audience, and the context. No firm rules can apply here; you must consider the complete situation, reflect on the properties of each example, and exercise judgment. However, keep in mind that a specific example dealing with a concrete particular that the reader can conceptualize is a powerful aid in developing ideas.

Number and Arrangement

Exemplification can be used with single or multiple examples. The section on exploitation of student athletes uses only one example and extends it through several paragraphs. The paragraph on plastic surgery also uses only one example but extends it just within the paragraph. The paragraph on erroneous ideas about mail-order spouses uses two hypothetical examples. Certainly there are no formulas regarding the number of examples you should employ. However, short essays of five paragraphs are often developed with three examples presented in the middle three paragraphs, and one example is sometimes extended and presented in logical three-paragraph units in the same kind of essay. These organizational patterns can also be applied to simple paragraphs, although you should always think about the types of examples you need rather than select a design before you work with your ideas.

Order

Once you have selected examples, proceed to work on the order in which you will relate the extended example or in which you will present the multiple examples.

The three basic ways of establishing order—time, space, and emphasis—also apply here. The extended example may be a narrative account: therefore, **time** order (using words such as *next, then, soon, later, last, finally*) will be appropriate. When movement is a component of the example, **space** references (*up, down, left, right*) are used. The third method, **emphasis**, simply means that one point leads to the next in logical thought. Emphasis may move from the general to the specific, from the specific to the general, or from the least important to the most important. In this regard, a writer who has two extraordinary examples and two others that are good but not spectacular might lead with a lively one to attract attention, use the two serviceable ones for conventional support, and finish with the remaining lively one for emphasis. Experiment; consider what principles apply, if any. Experiment with your outline or your cluster; rework the organization in your drafts as you go back and forth in your recursive writing.

The following student-written paragraph and essay illustrate effective uses of exemplification.

THE FIGHTING FOUNDING MOTHERS*

Maxine Johnson

topic sentence

People argue a lot about the prospects of women in the military fighting in combat, but in the War of Independence, several women distinguished themselves in combat situations. In 1775, Paul Revere got the main credit for riding to warn the Patriots that the British were coming on a military move on Concord and Lexington, Massachusetts. The fact is that although he did warn some Patriots, he was stopped by the British. Who did get

specific example

through? Several people, including Sybil Ludington, a teenage woman who fearlessly rode her horse like the wind. Another famous woman was known as Molly

specific example

Pitcher. Her real name was Mary Hayes. She, like many women, went with her husband to the battlefield, where she brought the men pitchers of water (hence her nickname) and helped load the cannon her husband fired. When her husband was shot at the Battle of Monmouth in 1778, she took over the cannon and fought bravely. At the end of the battle, won by the Patriots, she carried a wounded man for two miles. More than two hundred years ago, these women proved that their gender can be soldiers in every sense.

YOUNG LOVE, PAST AND PRESENT*

Yvette Lohayza

thesis

It was a warm summer night, and my three teenage girls, 1 who range from sixteen to nineteen, anxiously scurried around their bedroom for something to wear to a concert that they had been awaiting for several weeks. As I stood in the hallway—just outside their bedroom door—wearing my flannel nightgown and fluffy pink slippers, my hair in rollers, and holding a hot cup of cocoa in my hands, I suddenly began to envision myself in their place and to feel the excitement that they were feeling. I began to slip back into my era—the fifties— and relive my teenage years.

Oh, how much fun we had preparing ourselves 2 before leaving the house for a similar concert! The dress fashion at that time was a waist-tight—almost like a cincher—skirt that flared out below the knees. As we listened to Frankie Valli or heartthrob Dion on the radio, we would dance the twist with each other around the bedroom to the beat while getting ready for the night. We would put on our ankle-high white (always white) bobby socks and penny loafers, and we would leave the house at approximately five o'clock with three dollars each in our pockets for the evening. We would reassure our parents, both reclined in their favorite front-room chairs watching a rerun of "Ozzie and Harriet," that we would return home at a decent hour—no later than eleven o'clock. We would jump in my sister's '56 Chevy and cruise down to the nearest burger stand where waitresses on roller skates served orders. We would choose our traditional root beer floats that we always drank when going out.

This is where we would meet our dates for the con- 3 cert, since we were not allowed to date until the age of eighteen (I was shy by one year.). After chatting about the evening that we had all planned ahead of us, we

thesis

example

examples

examples

example

example

would slurp down our root beer floats and begin driving from our neighborhood of San Gabriel to El Monte where there was a dance hall called El Monte Legion. This is where live performances of singers were held weekly on Saturday night and all the teenyboppers would flock.

Little Richard and the Skyliners would be appearing 4 tonight. Although the entrance fee was one dollar and fifty cents, we felt it was worth the price and anxiously anticipated the show. We would all dance the twist to Little Richard's "Good Golly, Miss Molly," and we would continue to dance the whole night through. When it came time to return home our knees would still be quivering from all the dancing.

Arriving in front of our parents' house, I turned and 5 shyly thanked my date for the dances. We both had seemed to lock eyes in our thank you's, and I felt my heart racing against my chest while my palms suddenly became light and clammy. This would be my first goodnight kiss ever. As our lips came closer and closer, we suddenly . . .

I was abruptly brought back to reality by the tug- 6 ging of my youngest daughter's hand at my flannel nightgown. "Mommy, I need to use the bathroom," my fouryear-old said. After I helped her and returned to my teenager's room, where I resumed my previous catatonic position, I suddenly realized the changes that have occurred between my teenage life and the teenage life that my girls were living.

They were listening to a Rod Stewart song on the 7 radio, which sounded as if we were in a live concert, with the resonance and amplification of the sounds very rich and loud. "Do ya think I'm sexy?" was playing while the girls danced around their room in a rather unladylike fashion. They were excited because it was a Rod Stewart concert that they were getting ready for this evening. They had paid $35 for a ticket to see this man with a raspy voice and shoulder-length hair. This idea was almost inconceivable to me.

As they shook their long permed hair out, I realized 8 how differently they were dressed. "What happened to the embroidered skirts?" I questioned. "Oh, mother, get real," one replied. Then they rushed out the door with faded jeans, open shirts, and cowboy boots as their

example

example

example

example

attire. This was something that only the Marlboro Man on those large billboards would wear back in my time. God forbid that a woman should ever be clothed in such drab material! In these times it is all right for the girls to pick up their dates for the concert—they reassured me of this.

Off they went for their dates, none of whom were older than seventeen. For a moment I felt a culture shock, but these are the times, and times change. After having some chocolate-chip cookies and milk with my four-year-old, I was walking her to her room to tuck her in for the night when suddenly a ghastly feeling came over me as I looked at her open-eyed: What will be popular in *her* time? 9

I immediately banished that scary thought from my mind and went to bed exhausted. 10

WRITER'S CHECKLIST

- Pick the kind of example that will best support your ideas; don't overlook the power of the specific example (name, place, etc.).
- Don't overlook personal experience as a source of good examples.
- Select an example or examples that are representative and interesting.
- Consider how much members of your audience know about your example or examples and how they are likely to react to them.
- Establish and maintain a clear relationship between the supporting example or examples and the main idea.
- In the extension of an example or in the use of several examples, consider order of presentation, such as time, space, emphasis, and logic.

PASSION AT FIRST SIGHT

John Updike

To what extent is first love, young love, glandular? Was Georg Lichtenberg right more than a hundred years ago when he said, "What they call 'heart' is located far lower than the fourth waistcoat button"? In this paragraph taken from the famous short story "A & P" by John

Updike, the central character, named Sammy, who clerks in a super-
market, is "checking out" some very welcome customers.

[T]he girls had circled around the bread and were coming back, without a pushcart, back my way along the counters, in the aisle between the checkouts and the Special bins. They didn't even have shoes on. There was this chunky one, with the two-piece—it was bright green and the seams on the bra were still sharp and her belly was still pretty pale so I guessed she just got it (the suit)—there was this one, with one of those chubby berry-faces, the lips all bunched together under her nose, this one, and a tall one, with black hair that hadn't quite frizzed right, and one of these sunburns right across under the eyes, and a chin that was too long—you know, the kind of girl other girls think is very "striking" and "attractive" but never quite makes it, as they very well know, which is why they like her so much—and then the third one, that wasn't quite so tall. She was the queen. She kind of led them, the other two peeking around and making their shoulders round. She didn't look around, not this queen, she just walked straight on slowly, on these long white prima-donna legs. She came down a little hard on her heels, as if she didn't walk in her bare feet that much, putting down her heels and then letting the weight move along to her toes as if she was testing the floor with every step, putting a little deliberate extra action into it. You never know for sure how girls' minds work (do you really think it's a mind in there or just a little buzz like a bee in a glass jar?) but you got the idea she had talked the other two into coming in here with her, and now she was showing them how to do it, walk slow and hold yourself straight.

Critical Thinking and Discussion

1. What is Sammy's apparent interest in these girls?
2. To what extent does he stereotype females?
3. Do you learn more from this paragraph about the girls or about the boy who is describing the girls?

Reading-Related Writing

1. Assume the perspective of one of the girls and describe Sammy by imply-ing or directly stating that he is an example of a certain kind of person. If you have not read the entire story, use your imagination.
2. Use the content of this piece as an example to develop a topic idea about a certain kind of attraction or infatuation.
3. Write about a similar experience of your own. Use that experience as an example of a generalization you offer regarding love, sex, or relationships.

LOVE OR AFFECTION

Ernest van den Haag

Love and affection are the key words in "Marriage: the Invention That Isn't Working," an essay by Ernest van den Haag. He suggests that one of the problems with marriage is that people enter it with emphasis on the wrong idea.

Perhaps this [marriage] sounds grim. But it needn't be if one marries for affection more than for love. For affection, marital love may grow with knowledge and intimacy and shared experience. Thus marriage itself, when accepted as something other than a love affair, may foster affection. Affection differs from love as fulfillment differs from desire. Further, love longs for what desire and imagination make uniquely and perfectly lovable. Possession erodes it. Affection, however—which is love of a different, of a perhaps more moral and less aesthetic kind—cares deeply also for what is unlovable without transforming it into beauty. It cares for the unvarnished person, not the splendid image. Time can strengthen it. . . . Whereas love stresses the unique form perfection takes in the lover's mind, affection stresses the uniqueness of the actual person.

Vocabulary

erodes
unique

Critical Thinking and Discussion

1. Why can marrying for affection rather than love be a solution to the problem of divorce?
2. How is affection defined?
3. How is love defined?
4. What examples does van den Haag use?

Reading-Related Writing

1. Apply van den Haag's ideas about love and affection to specific examples from your direct experience or observation.
2. Apply these ideas to other selections in this chapter.

YEARNING FOR LOVE*

Chantra Shastri

Having lived in America for five years, Chantra Shastri asks for free-
dom—freedom to make a choice in marriage, a choice based on love.

I need not go beyond myself to find examples of love, at least the yearning for love. My home is now America, but I have not left India far behind. There, in ways still cherished by my traditional family, freedom is based on gender, and I am a female. My parents expect women to cook, clean, and nurture. My parents expect me to marry the man of their choice, although my brother will have the freedom to choose his own mate. If I disobey, I will no longer be recognized by my parents. It is easy to give in to such a custom; it is difficult to disobey. My parents have always believed as they do. I cannot change them, nor do I want to, but I wish they would accept my difference in this different country. I think my mother understands. Last week, I saw her crying while she ironed our clothes. When I asked her why she was crying, she wiped the warm tears off her thin, soft cheeks and pretended not to hear me as she sang. Her singing made me sad because I knew why she had cried, and she knew I knew. I seized the opportunity to say, "I don't want an arranged marriage," but she sang on even louder, singing a song of a distant home. In times such as these, like my father, she too covers her ears with the thick dried mud of tradition. She doesn't want to hear me. It is easier that way.

Critical Thinking and Discussion

1. Why did Shastri's mother cry?
2. What chance does Shastri have to make her own choice?
3. What would you advise her to do?
4. How does the specific example of her mother crying imply more than it actually says?

Reading-Related Writing

1. Assume the role of the mother who cried and write about her thoughts.
2. Imagine what will happen to Shastri and write about her situation ten years after this paragraph was written.
3. Using an example or examples, write about similar marriage customs of a culture other than Indian.

HOW DO I LOVE THEE?

Robert J. Trotter

How one loves depends on many things, including who is loving and who is being loved, but each love has certain components. Robert Trotter, using the system developed by R. J. Sternberg, details the different types of love by giving explanations and by providing examples.

Intimacy, passion and commitment are the warm, hot and cold vertices of Sternberg's love triangle. Alone and in combination they give rise to eight possible kinds of love relationships. The first is nonlove—the absence of all three components. This describes the large majority of our personal relationships, which are simply casual interactions. 1

The second kind of love is liking. "If you just have intimacy," Sternberg explains, "that's liking. You can talk to the person, tell about your life. And if that's all there is to it, that's what we mean by liking." It is more than nonlove. It refers to the feelings experienced in true friendships. Liking includes such things as closeness and warmth but not the intense feelings of passion or commitment. 2

If you just have passion, it's called infatuated love—the "love at first sight" that can arise almost instantaneously and dissipate just as quickly. It involves a high degree of physiological arousal but no intimacy or commitment. It's the 10th-grader who falls madly in love with the beautiful girl in his biology class but never gets up the courage to talk to her or get to know her, Sternberg says, describing his past. 3

Empty love is commitment without intimacy or passion, the kind of love sometimes seen in a 30-year-old marriage that has become stagnant. The couple used to be intimate, but they don't talk to each other any more. They used to be passionate, but that's died out. All that remains is the commitment to stay with the other person. In societies in which marriages are arranged, Sternberg points out, empty love may precede the other kinds of love. 4

Romantic love, the Romeo and Juliet type of love, is a combination of intimacy and passion. More than infatuation, it's liking with the added excitement of physical attraction and arousal but without commitment. A summer affair can be very romantic, Sternberg explains, but you know it will end when she goes back to Hawaii and you go back to Florida, or wherever. 5

Passion plus commitment is what Sternberg calls fatuous love. It's Hollywood love: Boy meets girl, a week later they're engaged, a month later they're married. They are committed on the basis of their passion, but because intimacy takes time to develop, they don't have the emotional core necessary to 6 sustain the commitment. This kind of love, Sternberg warns, usually doesn't work out.

Companionate love is intimacy with commitment but no passion. It's a   7
long-term friendship, the kind of committed love and intimacy frequently
seen in marriages in which the physical attraction has died down.

When all three elements of Sternberg's love triangle come together in a   8
relationship, you get what he calls consummate love, or complete love. It's the
kind of love toward which many people strive, especially in romantic relationships. Achieving consummate love, says Sternberg, is like trying to lose
weight, difficult but not impossible. The really hard thing is keeping the
weight off after you have lost it, or keeping the consummate love alive after
you have achieved it. Consummate love is possible only in very special relationships.

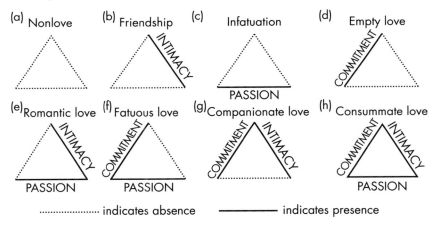

.... indicates absence   ———— indicates presence

Vocabulary

dissipate (3)
fatuous (6)
consummate (8)

Critical Thinking and Discussion

1. What are the eight different types of love described by Trotter?
2. What examples does Trotter use? Which ones are general and which are
   specific? What additional examples can you think of, taken from what
   you have read and what you have seen in movies and on television?
3. What examples can you think of for the types of love for which Trotter
   does not provide his own examples?

4. Does this description of the types of love hold up well when applied in a broad multicultural sense, or is it more applicable to Western cultures?

Reading-Related Writing

1. Select one of the types of love and discuss it in more detail, providing an extended example or numerous examples.
2. Discuss this system as it relates to other cultures. Would each of the three components be important? Be specific.
3. Select another piece of writing from this chapter or from another chapter and discuss the love described in it as an example of one of these categories.

GET IT IF YOU CAN

Roy Rivenburg

In 1993, Lakewood High School in Southern California was the scene of a teenage sex scandal that attracted national media attention. A group of boys, the Spur Posse, was being investigated for its sexual activity, which involved keeping score of sexual conquests. One result was a number of interviews and studies. While many teens say the Lakewood High case is an aberration, they also say the public's reaction shows that people don't realize how common sex is in their daily lives. "Sex, to us, is like taking vitamins," says Sharon Osornio, 16, "because if you don't have sex, you're not gonna grow up right." This article from the Los Angeles Times *describes some male viewpoints. The selection following this one, "Girls Also Use Sex," is an interview with some teenage girls.*

The truth about what happened at Lakewood High School may never be known. But the claim that some members of the "Spur Posse" slept with dozens of girls—and used points to tally their sexual encounters—has provoked amazement, outrage and fear. It's not that "scoring" sex is something new, but it seems to have taken on new dimensions. Getting to "first base," "second base" or "going all the way" has apparently given way to the faster pace of basketball—or even Nintendo. The leading Don Juan of the Spur Posse claims almost 70 points—meaning sex with 70 different girls.

Is Lakewood just an isolated case, or are adults oblivious to the realities of teen-age sex? Experts (read: grown-ups) and teenagers from other schools say both answers are correct. The Spurs, although atypical, aren't alone. "Seventy points —I think they exaggerated on that," says Anthony Sanford, 18, a student at the Metropolitan Skills Center, a Los Angeles high school. "That's not average." But Sanford's estimate of what *is* average might still surprise the average parent. In his case, he says, it's "about 30." Sex, Sanford says, has become "one of the main things in how we're growing up. It's just an everyday thing."

To be sure, many teens don't have dozens of sexual partners—and many   3 don't engage in sex at all—but for a sizable number of others, sex has become commonplace. According to a study released last year by the national Centers for Disease Control, 54% of U.S. students in grades nine through 12 have had sex—and seven out of 10 high school seniors. The stereotpye about men and sexual conquests has always been around. And there is precedent for a "point" system—at least if one believes the reported sexual exploits of public figures such as Earvin "Magic" Johnson and Wilt Chamberlain. But the Lakewood episode has left many wondering about the level of sexual involvement among teenagers and their attitude toward it. A 1988 survey of sexually active males, age 15 to 19, found that 27% has had six or more partners.

Los Angeles psychiatrist Mark Goulston says part of the problem is an   4 "escalation of everything that plays to the senses": Roller coasters of the 1990s dwarf the roller coasters of the 1950s, scary movies are far more gory than their predecessors and "what was kinky in the 1950s or '60s is now on prime-time television." The 1990s, he adds, are "more of a time of urgency than the 1950s or '60s. [Teens] are more concerned with grabbing onto something than holding on because you can't hold on to anything. Parents can't hold on to their marriages or their jobs . . . so [youngsters] grab for the quick score instead of holding on for the longer-lasting ride." Or, as Sanford's classmate Tony Ramirez puts it: "While you're young, have fun." For Ramirez, 18, that means sleeping with a girl a maximum of two times before moving on. After that, he and some other boys agree, it gets "boring" or the girl starts to get jealous or nag.

And they seem to have no regrets about using a girl for sex. "We're just   5 not sentimental," says Christian Urbina, 17. "That's why we're men. . . . We like girls, we don't love them. . . . You see a girl and you just think, yeah, she's really pretty and the first thing that comes to mind is you want to have sex." Once that happens, Urbina says, many boys dump the girl. Says Goulston, "A lot of boys don't know how they really feel about a girl until they have sex with her. There's so much sexual tension that they can't [analyze the situation or] think about anything else." After the liaison, "they often don't respect the girl because of [the old maxim]: Why belong to a club that would have me as a member."

Girls, of course, are often wise to the routine—so boys have devised any   6 number of methods to win—and later lose—their prey. "Get them drunk," one teen says. "Sweet-talk them," offers another. "Keep them laughing . . . [and] be a gentleman." Urbina suggests playing on the girls' own sexual desires."You start kissing her and hugging her and little by little you start touching her." Adds Sanford: "They want it just the same as we do. All it takes is a little conversation." After the deed, some dump the girl immediately. Others spend a few weeks "making up excuses" or ignoring the girl to "let her off easy," Urbina says. Sanford sometimes creates "a false argument" and then uses it to justify breaking off the relationship. "Girls get mad, but they don't take it hard," Urbina says. "They live with it." And they can't really complain to others, Ramirez adds, or they'll be viewed as "sluts."

Goulston says the sexual conquests allow the boys to feel manly—to 7 compare themselves favorably with men in their 20s and older. The teens seem to agree, although they express it in less sophisticated terminology: "It gives you confidence," Sanford says. "It makes you feel good," adds Urbina. And point systems like the one used at Lakewood High aren't even necessary. "You're not racing against nobody," Urbina says. "It's not like a competition to see who can get the most. It's just get it if you can."

Critical Thinking and Discussion

1. Is this a scientific study? How accurate do you think it is?
2. What does Christian Urbina say about love and sex?
3. How do the boys manipulate the girls?
4. How typical are the views of the boys interviewed?

Reading-Related Writing

1. Do your own study of sexual activity in a particular age group and write about the results. Include some specific examples.
2. Write about love and sex, using examples from this article for some of your support.
3. Compare the views in this article with those you have encountered. Consider that these interviews were conducted with youths from an urban school in Southern California.

GIRLS ALSO USE SEX

Michael Quintanilla

To see how teen-age girls view sex, Times staff writer Michael Quintanilla talked 1
*with a group of students from two Los Angeles high schools, the Metropolitan Skills
Center and the Downtown Business Magnet.*

Q: Why have sex? 2

Dee Dee McDaniel, 17: Ideally, a girl enters a relationship for intimacy. 3 "When you have sex in a relationship it does bring you closer. And many times a girl feels if she doesn't have sex with him, 'I'm gonna lose him.' But if you're just messing around, then it's not for love. That's why you see a lot of girls *kicking it* [hanging out] right along with the guys."

As for guys, "a lot of them don't want to have anything to do with you 4 after you have sex with them. They don't want to take you out. The guys use you for sex, but then the girls also use sex and guys for money and their cars. If you ask a guy for money, like to get your nails done, then you probably have to 'give it up' to him. And girls will do that."

Q: Is that common? 5

Chiquita Scott, 17: Yes. "Your girlfriends will say, 'You better give him 6 some because he won't do anything for you if you don't.' "

Rebecca Quezada 17: "If a guy is cute and fine, then you want to have 7 him. And then later on you get pressured into having sex. And then after that, he'll throw it in your face when he wants to get it again. He'll say to you 'I give you this. I give you that. And you don't give me something I want.' "

Chiquita: "Some guys look at a girl's body and say 'I'm gonna get some of 8 that.' They don't look at her personality. But, in fairness, girls do the same thing. They'll look at a guy and think the same thing: 'I'm gonna get some of that.' "

Wendy, 17 [wanted last name withheld]: "To be honest with you we want 9 the same thing we're giving them."

Glenda Montes, 17: "There's girls who feel 'I like this guy, he's real cute and 10 I would like to be with him. He's a player.' The girl wants to be with him and he knows it, so he teases her. He says, 'What's that, baby, you want to go here or there with me?' He'll tease you."

Q: In many cases, you say you go out with guys who are older—at 11 least by three years or more. Why?

Glenda: "Guys our own ages are immature. They have no job, no car, no 12 experience with their words and no experience knowing how to treat a female." Montes says, adding that when she was 11 years old she hung around with older friends, "When I was 13 I felt like I was 17. Now I feel like I'm 20."

Wendy: "When I was 13, I went out with 20-year-olds. We partied." 13

Sharon Osornio, 16: "Older guys know how to push the right buttons. 14 Even they'll sometimes tell you 'It would be so wonderful having a baby together.' Once you become pregnant, they split. I've seen that happen to many friends." By the same token, "Girls will have sex to have a baby with the guy thinking 'I'm gonna be more than just a girlfriend. Now he's gonna stay with me.' But that doesn't happen. He isn't gonna stay with you."

Glenda: A girl will get sweet-talked into having sex with a guy because 15
he'll throw *drags* [pick-up lines] on you. "He'll say 'I won't do you wrong,
baby. I'm gonna treat you right. I'm gonna treat you like no one has before.
You're not gonna regret this.' Sometimes you fall for it."

Sharon: "Sometimes girls drag on guys. Among the most popular lines: 16
'I'll be faithful. I only have eyes for you. You've got everything I want in a
man.'"

Q: What did you think of the Lakewood High sex posse? 17

Rachel Rios, 15: "It's disgusting. For a while I've heard about [posses like 18
that] . . . If a girl has sex, you're considered a slut, but guys can't be sluts."

Q: Do girls talk about sex and assess the performance of their part- 19 ners?

Chiquita: "Girls talk about *it*. We'll be saying, 'Oh, he didn't do this, but 20
he does do this and he's not a good kisser or he's a great kisser.'"

Sharon: Having sex is "like a habit. Sometimes you have sex because you 21
want to keep the guy. If you love him or if you think you love him you'll have
sex. Then sometimes you're with a guy and you're thinking 'I don't want to
have sex with him,' but he's saying, 'If you love me, prove it to me' and he
means having sex. So you do it because you don't want to hear him saying 'So
why don't you want to do it? Is it because you're bored with me? You don't
love me? Are you getting it from someone else?'"

Glenda: "A guy will ask, 'Why are you playing this now?' when a girl 22
doesn't want to have sex. He'll say, 'See how you are.' So you feel bad and you
do it to satisfy *him*. Nowadays a relationship with somebody is like you are
married. A guy wants to have you *on check* [know where you are]. You're not
boyfriend and girlfriend. You're not gonna see holding hands and pecks on
the cheek. You're gonna see grabbing and having sex. Mostly now, guys are
rough with girls. They put one hand around your waist and the other hand is
going everywhere."

Q: How do you stop this, if you don't like it? 23

Vehanush Karapetyan, 17: "It's all up to the girl to say 'No' if she doesn't 24
want to do it."

Q: Are you saying it's always the woman's fault? 25

Chiquita: "My mother always told me sex is something for you and some- 26
one else to enjoy. My mother told me when you have sex try to use protection
and enjoy it at the same time. It's up to you. It's your body. If you can't stop a
guy, then you want it. You have to be straight with him from the start."

Glenda: "Whatever happens to you, it's your fault because you look for it, 27
you ask for it. Sex is something real serious, but people are taking it as a joke.
It's dangerous: gonorrhea, syphilis, AIDS . . . young people are having sex.
Guys are just doing it. [Most] girls are teases, they lead guys on, the girl backs
off when the guy comes on. . . . "

Q: Isn't sex supposed to be something special?

Vehanush: "Sex is no big deal because girls think it's cool to sleep with a   29
guy. Some of the girls who sleep with guys aren't even boyfriend and girlfriend. They just do it to say, 'Oh, I slept with him.' And the guy can say, 'I'm
a macho man.' "

Critical Thinking and Discussion

1. According to these girls, to what extent are girls used by boys?
2. To what extent do girls use sex to get what they want?
3. How do these girls see intimacy, love, and sex?
4. What examples do they use to explain what they mean?

Reading-Related Writing

1. Compare the girls' views of sex with that of the boys; use examples.
2. This interview was with inner-city girls. Do girls from suburbs or small
   towns think or behave differently? Discuss with examples.

THE BUSINESS OF SELLING
MAIL-ORDER BRIDES

Venny Villapando

*Where does one find a wife? At school. At a singles bar. At church. In
the neighborhood. At work. At a dance. At an exercise club. All of those
may be good places, but there is at least one more—through a mail-
order catalog. No, you can't order through Penney's or Spiegel's, but the
procedure is similar. You look at a picture, you fill out the forms, you
pay the price, and you wait for your bride to arrive. Most customers
are white Americans; most brides are impoverished Asian women. Is
anything wrong with this transaction?*

The phenomenon is far from new. Certainly in the Old West and in other   1
frontier situations such as the labor camps at the sugar farms in Hawaii, the
colonization of Australia, or even in the early Irish settlements of New York,
there were always lonely men who would write to their homeland for a bride.
These women would come on the next train or on the next boat to meet their
husbands for the very first time.

For Japanese immigrants traditional marriages were arranged in Japan   2
between relatives of the man and the prospective bride. Information was

exchanged between the two families about the potential union, and photographs were exchanged between the couple. If both parties agreed, then the marriage was legalized in the home country, and the bride came to America.

While these marriages occurred in less than ideal situations, a number of 3 them were successful. For example the Japanese sugar worker who once waited on the Honolulu pier for the arrival of his picture bride, today enjoys the company of a family clan that spans at least two generations. That is indeed an achievement considering the picture bride of yesteryear, just like the contemporary mail-order bride, has always been at a disadvantage. She comes to the marriage from far away, without the nearby support of her family or a familiar culture. The distance that she has traveled is measured not so much in nautical as in emotional miles. She is not quite the happy bride who has been courted and wooed, freely choosing her groom and her destiny.

Today's mail-order brides are products of a very complex set of situations 4 and contradictions. They are confronted by far more complicated conditions than the picture brides of years past. They do not quite fit the simple pattern of a marriage between a lonely man stranded in a foreign land and a woman who accepts him sight unseen.

In the present matches brides-to-be are generally Asian and husbands-to- 5 be are Caucasians, mostly American, Australian, and Canadian. A majority of the women are poor and because of economic desperation become mail-order brides. Racial, as well as economic, factors define the marriage however. The new wife is relegated to a more inferior position than her picture bride counterpart. Plus the inequity of the partnership is further complicated by the mail-order bride's immigrant status. Consequently she is a foreigner not only to the culture, language, and society, but to her husband's race and nationality as well.

Why Men Choose Mail-Order Brides

"These men want women who will feel totally dependent on them," writes Dr. 6 Gladys L. Symons of the University of Calgary. "They want women who are submissive and less intimidating." Aged between thirty and forty, these men grew up most likely before the rise of the feminist movement, adds Symons. She partially attributes the resurgence of the mail-order bride to a backlash against the 1980s high-pressure style of dating.

Dr. Davor Jedlicka, a sociology professor from the University of Texas, 7 notes in his study of 265 subscribers of mail-order bride catalogues that "very many of them had extremely bitter experiences with divorce or breakups or engagements." His research also shows the median income of these men to be higher than average—65 percent of them had incomes of over $20,000. According to Jedlicka, the average age was thirty-seven, average height five feet seven inches, and most were college educated. Only five percent never finished high school.

The Japanese American Citizens League, a national civil rights group, 8
confirms this general profile of the typical male client and adds other findings. According to its recent position paper on mail-order brides, the group
found that men tend to be white, much older than the bride they choose,
politically conservative, frustrated by the women's movement, and socially
alienated. They experience feelings of personal inadequacy and find the traditional Asian value of deference to men reassuring.

In her interview in the Alberta Report, Symons points out that the men 9
are also attracted to the idea of buying a wife, since all immigration, transpor-
tation, and other costs run to only about two thousand dollars. "We're a
consumer society," says Symons. "People become translated into commodities
easily." And commodities they are.

Gold at the End of the Rainbow

Contemporary traders in the Asian bride business publish lists sold for twenty 10
dollars for a catalogue order form to twenty thousand dollars for a deluxe
videotaped presentation. Perhaps the most successful company is Rainbow
Ridge Consultants run by John Broussard and his wife Kelly Pomeroy. They
use a post office box in Honakaa, Hawaii. Explains Broussard:

> Basically, we just sell addresses. . . . We operate as a pen pal club, not a front
> for the slave trade, although some people get the wrong idea. We're not a Sears
> catalogue from which you buy a wife. You have to write and win the heart of
> the woman you desire.

For providing this service, Broussard and Pomeroy reported a net profit in
1983 of twenty-five thousand dollars, which catapulted to sixty-five thousand
in 1984.

Rainbow Ridge Consultants distribute three different publications, of 11
which the top two are *Cherry Blossoms* and *Lotus Blossoms*. These differ from
the Sears catalogue only because an issue is only twenty-eight pages long, not
several hundred, and photos are black and white, not glossy color. A typical
entry reads: "If you like 'em tall, Alice is 5'9", Filipina, social work grad,
average looks, wants to hear from men 25–40. $4." For the stated dollar
amount, interested men can procure an address and a copy of her biographi-
cal data.

Broussard and Pomeroy's sister publication *Lotus Blossoms* has twice the 12
number of names, but Broussard admits that *Lotus* is a "second string" brochure, offering pictures of women who do not have the same looks as those in
Cherry Blossoms.

Six months of subscription to the complete catalogues of Rainbow Ridge   13
will cost the wife-seeker $250. A special service will engage Broussard and
Pomeroy in a wife hunt at the rate of $50 per hour and includes handling all
details, even writing letters and purchasing gifts when necessary. Should the
match succeed, the business pockets another fee of $1,000.

Kurt Kirstein of Blanca, Colorado, runs Philippine-American Life Part-   14
ners, which offers one thousand pictures of Filipino women looking for
American men. Louis Florence of the American Asian Worldwide Service in
Orcutt, California, provides men with a similar catalogue for $25; another
$630 will permit the bride-seeker to correspond with twenty-four women, of
whom any fifteen will be thoroughly investigated by the service. The California business reports an annual gross income of $250,000.

Selling Asian women is a thriving enterprise because the number of   15
American men who seek Asian brides continues to grow. Broussard estimates
the total number of daily inquiries is five hundred. In 1984 the Gannett News
Service reported that seven thousand Filipino women married Australians,
Europeans, and Americans. The *Wall Street Journal* noted that in 1970, only
34 Asians were issued fiancée-petitioned visas; while in 1983, the figure
jumped dramatically to 3,428.

Broussard says that he receives one hundred letters a day from Asian and   16
other women. He publishes about seven hundred pictures every other month
in his catalogues. Still, Broussard reports that the chances of a man finding a
wife through his service is only about one in twenty.

When he receives a letter and the appropriate fees from a prospective   17
groom, Broussard sends off a catalogue. One of his correspondents describes
the process: "I selected fourteen ladies to send introductory letters to. To my
amazement, I received fourteen replies and am still corresponding with
twelve of them." One of the reasons why letters so often succeed is the
detailed coaching both parties receive. For instance Broussard and Pomeroy
publish a 130-page pamphlet entitled "How to Write to Oriental Ladies."
There is also one for women called "The Way to an American Male's Heart."

The Japanese American Citizens League points out the disadvantage to   18
women in these arrangements because of the inequality of information dis-
seminated. Under the traditional arranged marriage system, family investiga-
tion and involvement insured equal access to information and mutual
consent. Now only the women must fill out a personality evaluation which
asks very intimate details about their life-style and history, and is then shared
with the men. Prospective grooms do not have to submit similar information
about themselves. Some companies, in fact, even discourage their male clients
from disclosing certain types of personal facts in their correspondence,
including such potentially negative characteristics as being black or having
physical disabilities.

The Economics of Romance

Coaching or no coaching, the mail-order brides business succeeds partly 19
because it takes advantage of the economic deprivation faced by women in
underdeveloped Asian countries. The Broussard brochure categorically states:

> We hear lots of stories about dishonest, selfish and immature women on both
> sides of the Pacific. Perhaps women raised in poverty will have lower material
> expectations and will be grateful to whoever rescues them and offers a better life.

One Caucasian man who met his wife through the mail says: "They don't 20
have a whole lot of things, so what they do have they appreciate very much.
They appreciate things more than what the average American woman would."
In other words, they are properly grateful for whatever the superior male
partner bestows on them.

"Filipinas come because their standard of living is so low," asserts Pome- 21
roy. In 1984 the per capita income in the Philippines was $640. "Most of the
women make no secret of why they want to marry an American: money." An
Australian reporter who has studied the influx of Filipino mail-order brides to
her country agrees: "Most Filipinas are escaping from grinding poverty."
Indeed, most Asian governments that are saddled with chronic unemployment, spiraling cost of living, malnutrition, and political turmoil are faced
with the problem of emigration and a diminishing labor force. In contrast,
Japan, the economic and technological leader of Asia, has very few women
listed in mail-order catalogues.

The *Chicago Sun-Times* describes Bruce Moore's visit to the family home 22
of his mail-order bride, Rosie, in Cebu, Philippines:

> "All of a sudden, we were driving through the jungle. There was nothing but
> little huts. I really started worrying about what I got myself into." . . . The
> house turned out to be an unpainted concrete building with no doors, plumb-
> ing or electricity. . . . Rosie had worked in a factory, eight hours a day, making
> 75 to 80 cents a day.

Because the Filipinas who avail themselves of mail-order bride service 23
may not have much, Broussard's instructional brochures advise men to use
caution in describing their financial status. The woman may turn out to be "a
con artist after your money or easy entry into the United States." Despite the
poverty, though, many of the women are truly sincere in their responses. The
Broussard customer who is still writing to twelve of the fourteen women who
wrote him notes:

> They all appeared genuine, and not one has asked me for money or anything
> else. In fact, in two instances, I offered to help with postage, and in both cases,

it was declined. One of the ladies said she could not accept postal assistance, as that would lessen the pleasure she felt in the correspondence.

Regardless of the sincerity of the parties involved, one women's rights 24 group in the Philippines has denounced the promotion of relationships through "commerce, industry, negotiation or investment." Their protests, however, do not seem to affect the business.

Racial Images and Romance

Added to economic exploitation, a major cornerstone of the mail-order bride 25 business, is the prevalence of racial stereotypes. They have a widespread effect on the treatment of women and influence why so many men are attracted to mail-order romance. "These men believe the stereotypes that describe Oriental women as docile, compliant, and submissive," says Jedlicka. His 1983 survey showed that 80 percent of the respondents accept this image as true.

One Canadian male, who asked not to be identified, was quoted as 26 saying: "Asian girls are not as liberated as North American or Canadian girls. They're more family-oriented and less interested in working. They're old-fashioned. I like that."

The California-based American Asian Worldwide Service perpetuates the 27 stereotypes when it says in its brochure: "Asian ladies are faithful and devoted to their husbands. When it comes to sex, they are not demonstrative; however, they are inhibited. They love to do things to make their husbands happy."

This company began after owner Louis Florence began his search for a 28 second wife. He says that friends had touted how their Asian wives "love to make their men happy" and finally convinced him to find a wife from Asia.

Another mail-order pitch describes Asian women as "faithful, devoted, 29 unspoiled and loving." Broussard confirms this popular misconception by saying these women are "raised to be servants for men in many Oriental countries." Referring to the Malaysian and Indonesian women who have recently joined his list of registrants, Broussard insists: "Like the Filipinas, they are raised to respect and defer to the male. . . . The young Oriental woman . . . derives her basic satisfaction from serving and pleasing her husband."

Virginity is a highly sought virtue in women. Tom Fletcher, a night 30 worker in Ottawa, Canada, who dislikes North American women because they "want to get out [of the house] and work and that leads to break-ups," is especially appreciative of this sign of purity. "These women's virginity was a gift to their husbands and a sign of faithfulness and trust." One mail-order service unabashedly advertises virginity in a brochure with photos, home addresses, and descriptions of Filipino women, some of whom are as young as seventeen. "Most, if not all, are very feminine, loyal, loving . . . and virgins!" its literature reads.

Many of the Asian countries affected by the revived mail-order bride 31
business have a history of U.S. military involvement. Troops have either
fought battles or been stationed in Korea, the Philippines, and countries in
Southeast Asia. During their stays, the soldiers have often developed strong
perceptions of Asian women as prostitutes, bargirls, and geishas. Then they
erroneously conclude that Asian American women must fit those images,
too. Consequently, the stereotype of women servicing and serving men is
perpetuated.

The Japanese American Citizens League objects to the mail-order bride 32
trade for that very reason. "The marketing techniques used by the catalogue
bride companies reinforce negative sexual and racial stereotypes of Asian
women in the U.S. The negative attitude toward Asian women affects all
Asians in the country." Further, the treatment of women as "commodities"
adds to the "non-human and negative perception of all Asians."

Romance on the Rocks

A marriage made via the mail-order bride system is naturally beset by a whole 33
range of problems. In her testimony before the U.S. Commission on Civil
Rights, Professor Bok-Lim Kim, then with the University of Illinois, noted that
negative reactions and attitudes toward foreign Asian wives "exacerbate marital problems," which result in incidences of spouse abuse, desertion, separation, and divorce. In addition, writes an Australian journalist, most of the
men they marry are social misfits. "Many of them drink too much; some beat
their wives and treat them little better than slaves."

The Japanese American Citizens League asserts: 34

> Individually, there may be many cases of couples meeting and marrying
> through these arrangements with positive results. We believe, however, that for
> the women, there are many more instances in which the impetus for leaving
> their home countries and families, and the resulting marriage relationships,
> have roots and end results which are less than positive.

Many of the Caucasian men who marry what they believe are stereotypi- 35
cal women may be in for some surprises. Psychiatry professor Joe Yamamoto
of the University of California at Los Angeles says: "I've found many Asian
women acculturate rather quickly. These American men may get a surprise in
a few years if their wives pick up liberated ways."

One legally blind and hard-of-hearing American, married to a Korean 36
woman, was eventually bothered by the same problems that plague other
couples: in-laws and lack of money. "She gets frustrated because I don't hear
her," complains the man about his soft-spoken Asian wife. In response, she

says, "The main problem is [his] parents. I can't adapt to American culture. I was going to devote my life for him, but I can't."

Another area which specifically affects foreign-born brides is their immi- 37 grant status. According to the Japanese American Citizens League, "these foreign women are at a disadvantage." This civil rights group targets the women's unfamiliarity with the U.S. immigration laws as one of the most disturbing aspects of the business. "As a result [of the ignorance], they may miss an opportunity to become a naturalized citizen, forfeit rights as a legal spouse, or live under an unwarranted fear of deportation which may be fostered by their spouse as a means of control."

Conclusion

Despite the constant stream of criticism, the mail-order bride system will pre- 38 vail as long as there are consumers and profit, and as long as underdeveloped countries continue failing to meet the economic, political, and social needs of their people. Indications show the business is not about to collapse now.

Erroneous ideas continue to thrive. An Asian woman dreams she will 39 meet and marry someone rich and powerful, someone to rescue her from poverty-stricken bondage. She hopes to live the rest of her life in a land of plenty. An American man dreams he will meet and marry someone passive, obedient, nonthreatening, and virginal, someone to devote her entire life to him, serving him and making no demands. Only a strong women's movement, one tied to the exploited underdeveloped country's struggle for liberation and independence, can challenge these ideas and channel the aspirations and ambitions of both men and women in a more positive and realistic direction.

Vocabulary

intimidating (6)	exploitation (25)	exacerbate (33)
resurgence (6)	perpetuates (27)	impetus (34)
deference (8)	inhibited (27)	prevail (38)
influx (21)	unabashedly (30)	

Critical Thinking and Discussion

1. How are current mail-order brides different from those in the past?
2. How are the mail-order brides at a disadvantage in dealing with their husbands?
3. What is the profile of the typical male customer?
4. What information is usually exchanged by the man and woman?
5. What racial stereotyping is often involved?

6. What are some of the negative findings about the mail-order bride system?
7. As immigrants, how are the brides often at a disadvantage?

Reading-Related Writing

1. If you know of any situations involving mail-order brides or if you know someone who has information on the topic, write a piece with a view supported by examples.
2. Write a piece about the sexual stereotyping involved in the mail-order bride system. Do many men want individuals or types? If they want types, then what types? Explain why there is often dissatisfaction on both sides.
3. Write a piece about matchmaking, incorporating economic considerations. Use examples from history, others, or your own experience illustrating the role of money in choosing marriage partners.
4. Write a piece in which you give your own views on the mail-order bride system. Refer directly to this article.
5. Write a proposal with regulations that might improve the mail-order bride system.

MARRIAGE AS A RESTRICTED CLUB

Lindsy Van Gelder

In this article, which appeared first in Ms. in the 1980s, Linsy Van Gelder asks that the definition of marriage be enlarged to include members of the homosexual community who form lasting bonds of affection. While discussing her own situation and views, she points out that, ironically, lesbians and gays are often criticized for not being what laws prevent them from being—married.

Several years ago, I stopped going to weddings. In fact, I no longer celebrate   1
the wedding anniversaries or engagements of friends, relatives, or anyone else, although I might wish them lifelong joy in their relationships. My explanation is that the next wedding I attend will be my own—to the woman I've loved and lived with for nearly six years.

Although I've been legally married to a man myself (and come close to   2
marrying two others), I've come, in these last six years with Pamela, to see heterosexual marriage as very much a restricted club. (Nor is this likely to change in the near future, if one can judge by the recent clobbering of what was actually a rather tame proposal to recognize "domestic partnerships" in San Francisco.) Regardless of the *reason* people marry—whether to save on

real estate taxes or qualify for married students housing or simply to express love—lesbians and gay men can't obtain the same results should they desire to do so. It seems apparent to me that few friends of Pamela's and mine would even join a club that excluded blacks, Jews, or women, much less assume that they could expect their black, Jewish, or female friends to toast their new status with champagne. But probably no other stand of principle we've ever made in our lives has been so misunderstood, or caused so much bad feeling on both sides.

Several people have reacted with surprise to our views, it never having 3 occurred to them that gay people *can't* legally marry. (Why on earth did they think that none of us had bothered?) The most common reaction, however, is acute embarrassment, followed by a denial of our main point—that the about-to-be-wed person is embarking on a privileged status. (One friend of Pamela's insisted that lesbians are "lucky" not to have to agonize over whether or not to get married.) So wrapped in gauze is the institution of marriage, so ingrained the expectation that brides and grooms can enjoy the world's delighted approval, that it's hard for me not to feel put on the defensive for being so mean-spirited, eccentric, and/or politically rigid as to boycott such a happy event.

Another question we've fielded more than once (usually from our most 4 radical friends, both gay and straight) is why we'd want to get married in the first place. In fact, I have mixed feelings about registering my personal life with the state, but—and this seems to me to be the essence of radical politics—I'd prefer to be the one making the choice. And while feminists in recent years have rightly focused on puncturing the Schlaflyite[1] myth of the legally protected homemaker, it's also true that marriage does confer some very real dollars-and-cents benefits. One example of inequity is our inability to file joint tax returns, although many couples, both gay and straight, go through periods when one partner in the relationship is unemployed or makes considerably less money than the other. At one time in our relationship, Pamela—who is a musician—was between bands and earning next to nothing. I was making a little over $37,000 a year as a newspaper reporter, a salary that put me in the 42 percent tax bracket—about $300 a week taken out of my paycheck. If we had been married, we could have filed a joint tax return and each paid taxes on half my salary, in the 25 or 30 percent bracket. The difference would have been nearly $100 a week in our pockets.

Around the same time, Pamela suffered a months'-long illness which 5 would have been covered by my health insurance if she were my spouse. We were luckier than many; we could afford it. But on top of the worry and expense involved (and despite the fact that intellectually we believe in the ideal of free medical care for everyone), we found it almost impossible to

[1]Phyllis Schlafly, a political activist, opposed the Equal Rights Amendment. [Ed.]

avoid internalizing a sense of personal failure—the knowledge that *because of who we are, we can't take care of each other*. I've heard of other gay people whose lovers were deported because they couldn't marry them and enable them to become citizens; still others who were barred from intensive-care units where their lovers lay stricken because they weren't "immediate family."

I would never begrudge a straight friend who got married to save a lover 6 from deportation or staggering medical bills, but the truth is that I no longer sympathize with most of the less tangible justifications. This includes the oft-heard "for the sake of the children" argument, since (like many gay people, especially women) I *have* children, and I resent the implication that some families are more "legitimate" than others. (It's important to safeguard one's children's rights to their father's property, but a legal contract will do the same thing as marriage.)

But the single most painful and infuriating rationale for marriage, as far 7 as I'm concerned, is the one that goes, "We wanted to stand up and show the world that we've made a *genuine* commitment." When one is gay, such sentiments are labeled "flaunting." My lover and I almost never find ourselves in public settings outside the gay ghetto where we are (a) perceived to be a couple at all (people constantly ask us if we're sisters, although we look nothing like each other), and (b) valued as such. Usually we're forced to choose between being invisible and being despised. "Making a genuine commitment" in this milieu is like walking a highwire without a net—with most of the audience not even watching and a fair segment rooting for you to fall. A disproportionate number of gay couples do.

I think it's difficult for even my closest, most feminist straight women 8 friends to empathize with the intensity of my desire to be recognized as Pamela's partner. (In fact, it may be harder for feminists to understand than for others; I know that when I was straight, I often resented being viewed as one half of a couple. My struggle was for an independent identity, not the cojoined one I now crave.) But we are simply not considered *authentic*, and the reminders are constant. Recently at a party, a man I'd known for years spied me across the room and came over to me, arms outstretched, big happy-to-see-you grin on his face. Pamela had a gig that night and wasn't at the party, my friend's wife was there but in another room, and I hadn't seen her yet. "How's M———?" I asked the man. "Oh, she's fine," he replied, continuing to smile pleasantly. "Are you and Pam still together?"

Our sex life is against the law in many states, of course, and like all 9 lesbians and gay men, we are without many other rights, both large and small. (In Virginia, for instance, it's technically against the law for us to buy liquor.) But as a gay couple, we are also most likely to be labeled and discriminated against in those very settings that, for most heterosexual Americans, constitute the most relaxed and personal parts of life. Virtually every tiny public act of togetherness—from holding hands on the street to renting a hotel room to dancing—requires us constantly to risk humiliation (I think, for example, of the two California women who were recently thrown out of a restaurant that had special romantic tables for couples), sexual harassment (it's astonishing how many men can't resist coming on to a lesbian couple), and even physical assault. A great deal of energy goes into just expecting possible trouble. It's a process which, after six years, has become second nature for me—but occasionally, when I'm in Provincetown or someplace else with a large lesbian population, I experience the *absence* of it as a feeling of virtual weightlessness.

What does all this have to do with my friends' weddings? Obviously, I can't   10 expect my friends to live my life. But I do think that lines are being drawn in this "profamily" Reagan era, and I have no choice about what side I'm placed on. My straight friends do, and at the very least, I expect them to acknowledge that. I certainly expect them to understand why I don't want to be among the rice-throwers and well-wishers at their weddings; beyond that, I would hope that they would commit themselves to fighting for my rights—preferably in personally visible ways, like marching in gay-pride parades. But I also wish they wouldn't get married, period. And if that sounds hard-nosed, I hope I'm only proving my point—that not being able to marry isn't a minor issue.

Not that my life would likely be changed as the result of any individual   11 straight person's symbolic refusal to marry. (Nor, for that matter, do all gay couples want to be wed.) But it's a political reality that heterosexual live-together couples are among our best tactical allies. The movement to repeal the state sodomy laws has profited from the desire of straight people to keep the government out of *their* bedrooms. Similarly, it was a heterosexual New York woman who went to court several years ago to fight her landlord's demand that she either marry her live-in boyfriend or face eviction for violating a lease clause prohibiting "unrelated" tenants—and whose struggle led to the recent passage of a state rent law that had ramifications for thousands of gay couples, including Pamela and me.

The right wing has seized on "homosexual marriage" as its bottom-line   12 scare phrase in much the same way that "Would you want your sister to marry one?" was brandished twenty-five years ago. *They* see marriage as their turf. And so when I see feminists crossing into that territory of respectability and "sinlessness," I feel my buffer zone slipping away. I feel as though my friends are taking off their armbands, leaving me exposed.

Vocabulary

ingrained (3)	internalizing (5)	milieu (7)
eccentric (3)	tangible (6)	empathize (8)
boycott (3)	rationale (7)	authentic (8)
essence (4)		

Critical Thinking and Discussion

1. What reasons does Van Gelder have for wanting to be married to her homosexual partner? Are some reasons more important than others?
2. Is she right in boycotting marriage ceremonies? Why or why not?
3. How well is she coping with her situation?
4. How would you answer her questions about the unfairness of laws regarding homosexual unions?
5. Should such laws be changed? If so, to what extent?

Reading-Related Writing

1. Use your own examples to agree or disagree with Van Gelder's views.
2. Examine the logic of her argument and the quality of her critical thinking. Refer directly to the essay.
3. Assume the role of someone who has invited Van Gelder to a wedding and received a copy of this essay as a response. Then write an answer to Van Gelder in which you either agree or disagree with her.

THE STORY OF AN HOUR

Kate Chopin

Until you've read this story, it wouldn't be right for me to discuss it.
"Why?" you ask.
"Because it has a special twist," I answer.
You persist. "Well, it is by a famous author, and it is a love story, sort of. . . ."

Knowing that Mrs. Mallard was afflicted with a heart trouble, great care was taken to break to her as gently as possible the news of her husband's death.

It was her sister Josephine who told her, in broken sentences, veiled hints that revealed in half concealing. Her husband's friend Richards was there, too, near her. It was he who had been in the newspaper office when intelligence of the railroad disaster was received, with Brently Mallard's name leading the list of "killed." He had only taken the time to assure himself of its truth by a second telegram, and had hastened to forestall any less careful, less tender friend in bearing the sad message.

She did not hear the story as many women have heard the same, with a paralyzed inability to accept its significance. She wept at once, with sudden, wild abandonment, in her sister's arms. When the storm of grief had spent itself she went to her room alone. She would have no one follow her.

There stood, facing the open window, a comfortable, roomy armchair. 4
Into this she sank, pressed down by a physical exhaustion that haunted her
body and seemed to reach into her soul.

She could see in the open square before her house the tops of trees that 5
were all aquiver with the new spring life. The delicious breath of rain was in
the air. In the street below a peddler was crying his wares. The notes of a
distant song which some one was singing reached her faintly, and countless
sparrows were twittering in the eaves.

There were patches of blue sky showing here and there through the 6
clouds that had met and piled above the other in the west facing her window.

She sat with her head thrown back upon the cushion of the chair quite 7
motionless, except when a sob came up into her throat and shook her, as a
child who has cried itself to sleep continues to sob in its dreams.

She was young, with a fair, calm face, whose lines bespoke repression 8
and even a certain strength. But now there was a dull stare in her eyes, whose
gaze was fixed away off yonder on one of those patches of blue sky. It was not
a glance of reflection, but rather indicated a suspension of intelligent thought.

There was something coming to her and she was waiting for it, fearfully. 9
What was it? She did not know; it was too subtle and elusive to name. But she
felt it, creeping out of the sky, reaching toward her through the sounds, the
scents, the color that filled the air.

Now her bosom rose and fell tumultuously. She was beginning to recog- 10
nize this thing that was approaching to possess her, and she was striving to
beat it back with her will—as powerless as her two white slender hands
would have been.

When she abandoned herself a little whispered word escaped her slightly 11
parted lips. She said it over and over under her breath: "Free, free, free!" The
vacant stare and the look of terror that had followed it went from her eyes.
They stayed keen and bright. Her pulses beat fast, and the coursing blood
warmed and relaxed every inch of her body.

She did not stop to ask if it were not a monstrous joy that held her. A 12
clear and exalted perception enabled her to dismiss the suggestion as trivial.

She knew that she would weep again when she saw the kind, tender 13
hands folded in death; the face that had never looked save with love upon
her, fixed and gray and dead. But she saw beyond that bitter moment a long
procession of years to come that would belong to her absolutely. And she
opened and spread her arms out to them in welcome.

There would be no one to live for during those coming years; she would 14
live for herself. There would be no powerful will bending her in that blind
persistence with which men and women believe they have a right to impose a
private will upon a fellow-creature. A kind intention or a cruel intention
made the act seem no less a crime as she looked upon it in that brief moment
of illumination.

And yet she had loved him—sometimes. Often she had not. What did it   15
matter! What could love, the unsolved mystery, count for in face of this
possession of self-assertion which she suddenly recognized as the strongest
impulse of her being!

"Free! Body and soul free!" she kept whispering.   16

Josephine was kneeling before the closed door with her lips to the key-   17
hole, imploring for admission. "Louise, open the door! I beg; open the door—
you will make yourself ill. What are you doing, Louise? For heaven's sake
open the door."

"Go away. I am not making myself ill." No; she was drinking in a very   18
elixir of life through that open window.

Her fancy was running riot along those days ahead of her. Spring days,   19
and summer days, and all sorts of days that would be her own. She breathed
a quick prayer that life might be long. It was only yesterday she had thought
with a shudder that life might be long.

She arose at length and opened the door to her sister's importunities.   20
There was a feverish triumph in her eyes, and she carried herself unwittingly
like a goddess of Victory. She clasped her sister's waist, and together they
descended the stairs. Richards stood waiting for them at the bottom.

Some one was opening the door with a latchkey. It was Brently Mallard   21
who entered, a little travel-stained, composedly carrying his grip-sack and
umbrella. He had been far from the scene of accident, and did not even know
there had been one. He stood amazed at Josephine's piercing cry; at Richards's
quick motion to screen him from the view of his wife.

But Richards was too late.   22

When the doctors came they said she had died of heart disease—of joy   23
that kills.

Critical Thinking and Discussion

1. What is Mrs. Mallard's first reaction in hearing of her husband's death?
2. What is her second reaction?
3. Why hasn't she considered freedom before?
4. Did her husband love her? Did she love him?
5. Did he abuse her?
6. Is this story mainly about women's rights, freedom, or some other subject?
7. Why does she die?

Reading-Related Writing

1. Write a diary account of some of the experiences Mrs. Mallard went
   through in her marriage—experiences that made her long for freedom.

2. Pose as the husband and write a eulogy that he would deliver at his wife's funeral. Include samples of the love they shared. Through his words, have him reveal what type of husband he was. For instance, he may reveal himself as a well-intentioned yet controlling person, but he will not recognize himself as such.
3. Write a piece in which you argue that her reaction is far more likely to be experienced by a woman than by a man; or argue against that view.
4. Discuss the issue of whether, if the roles were reversed, he could die of the same shock that killed her.

THE WOOING OF ARIADNE

Harry Mark Petrakis

Born in St. Louis, Missouri, to parents from the island of Crete, author Harry Mark Petrakis writes especially about ordinary first- and second-generation Greek immigrants who happen to have an enormous capacity for experiencing life with passion. In an earlier story, "Barba Nikos," you discovered that the contemplation of Greek food could be a lesson in cultural history and geography. In this story, Petrakis imparts the same monumental dimensions to love—love between two strong and proud people. Ariadne's spirited resistance fuels Marko's passion, and two undistinguished people become engaged in a clamorous romance, sometimes resembling epic combat. Katherina from Shakespeare's The Taming of the Shrew *and Zorba from Kazantzakis'* Zorba the Greek *come to mind as comparisons, but Ariadne and Marko are their own people.*

I knew from the beginning she must accept my love—put aside foolish female protestations. It is the distinction of the male to be the aggressor and the cloak of the female to lend grace to the pursuit. Aha! I am wise to these wiles. 1

I first saw Ariadne at a dance given by the Spartan brotherhood in the Legion Hall on Laramie Street. The usual assemblage of prune-faced and banana-bodied women smelling of virtuous anemia. They were an outrage to a man such as myself. 2

Then I saw her! A tall stately woman, perhaps in her early thirties. She had firm and slender arms bare to the shoulders and a graceful neck. Her hair was black and thick and piled in a great bun at the back of her head. That grand abundance of hair attracted me at once. This modern aberration women have of chopping their hair close to the scalp and leaving it in fantastic disarray I find revolting. 3

I went at once to my friend Vasili, the baker, and asked him who she was. 4

"Ariadne Langos," he said. "Her father is Janco Langos, the grocer."   5

"Is she engaged or married?"   6

"No," he said slyly. "They say she frightens off the young men. They say   7
she is very spirited."

"Excellent," I said and marveled at my good fortune in finding her   8
unpledged. "Introduce me at once."

"Marko," Vasili said with some apprehension. "Do not commit anything   9
rash."

I pushed the little man forward. "Do not worry, little friend," I said. "I am   10
a man suddenly possessed by a vision. I must meet her at once."

We walked together across the dance floor to where my beloved stood.   11
The closer we came the more impressive was the majestic swell of her breasts
and the fine great sweep of her thighs. She towered over the insignificant
apple-core women around her. Her eyes, dark and thoughtful, seemed to be
restlessly searching the room.

Be patient, my dove! Marko is coming.   12

"Miss Ariadne," Vasili said. "This is Mr. Marko Palamas. He desires to   13
have the honor of your acquaintance."

She looked at me for a long and piercing moment. I imagined her gaug-   14
ing my mighty strength by the width of my shoulders and the circumference
of my arms. I felt the tips of my mustache bristle with pleasure. Finally she
nodded with the barest minimum of courtesy. I was not discouraged.

"Miss Ariadne," I said, "may I have the pleasure of this dance?"   15

She stared at me again with her fiery eyes. I could imagine more timid   16
men shriveling before her fierce gaze. My heart flamed at the passion her rigid
exterior concealed.

"I think not," she said.   17

"Don't you dance?"   18

Vasili gasped beside me. An old prune-face standing nearby clucked her   19
toothless gums.

"Yes, I dance," Ariadne said coolly. "I do not wish to dance with you."   20

"Why?" I asked courteously.   21

"I do not think you heard me," she said. "I do not wish to dance with   22
you."

Oh, the sly and lovely darling. Her subterfuge so apparent. Trying to   23
conceal her pleasure at my interest.

"Why?" I asked again.   24

"I am not sure," she said. "It could be your appearance, which bears   25
considerable resemblance to a gorilla, or your manner, which would suggest
closer alliance to a pig."

"Now that you have met my family," I said engagingly, "let us dance."   26

"Not now," she said, and her voice rose. "Not this dance or the one after.   27
Not tonight or tomorrow night or next month or next year. Is that clear?"

Sweet, sweet Ariadne. Ancient and eternal game of retreat and pursuit. 28
My pulse beat more quickly.

Vasili pulled at my sleeve. He was my friend, but without the courage of a 29
goat. I shook him off and spoke to Ariadne.

"There is a joy like fire that consumes a man's heart when he first sets 30
eyes on his beloved," I said. "This I felt when I first saw you." My voice
trembled under a mighty passion. "I swear before God from this moment that
I love you."

She stared shocked out of her deep dark eyes and, beside her, old prune- 31
face staggered as if she had been kicked. Then my beloved did something
which proved indisputably that her passion was as intense as mine.

She doubled up her fist and struck me in the eye. A stout blow for a 32
woman that brought a haze to my vision, but I shook my head and moved a
step closer.

"I would not care," I said, "if you struck out both my eyes. I would 33
cherish the memory of your beauty forever."

By this time the music had stopped, and the dancers formed a circle of 34
idiot faces about us. I paid them no attention and ignored Vasili, who kept
whining and pulling at my sleeve.

"You are crazy!" she said. "You must be mad! Remove yourself from my 35
presence or I will tear out both your eyes and your tongue besides!"

You see! Another woman would have cried, or been frightened into 36
silence. But my Ariadne, worthy and venerable, hurled her spirit into my
teeth.

"I would like to call on your father tomorrow," I said. From the assem- 37
bled dancers who watched there rose a few vagrant whispers and some rude
laughter. I stared at them carefully and they hushed at once. My temper and
strength of arm were well known.

Ariadne did not speak again, but in a magnificent spirit stamped from the 38
floor. The music began, and men and women began again to dance. I permitted Vasili to pull me to a corner.

"You are insane!" he said. He wrung his withered fingers in anguish. "You 39
assaulted her, like a bandit! Her relatives will cut out your heart!"

"My intentions were honorable," I said. "I saw her and loved her and told 40
her so." At this point I struck my fist against my chest. Poor Vasili jumped.

"But you do not court a woman that way," he said. 41

"*You* don't, my anemic friend," I said. "Nor do the rest of these sheep. But 42
I court a woman that way!"

He looked to heaven and helplessly shook his head. I waved good-by and 43
started for my hat and coat.

"Where are you going?" he asked. 44

"To prepare for tomorrow," I said. "In the morning I will speak to her 45
father."

I left the hall and in the street felt the night wind cold on my flushed 46
cheeks. My blood was inflamed. The memory of her loveliness fed fuel to the
fire. For the first time I understood with a terrible clarity the driven heroes of
the past performing mighty deeds in love. Paris stealing Helen in passion, and
Menelaus pursuing with a great fleet. In that moment if I knew the whole
world would be plunged into conflict I would have followed Ariadne to Hades.

I went to my rooms above my tavern. I could not sleep. All night I tossed 47
in restless frenzy. I touched my eye that she had struck with her spirited
hand.

Ariadne! Ariadne! my soul cried out.   48

In the morning I bathed and dressed carefully. I confirmed the address of 49
Langos, the grocer, and started to his store. It was a bright cold November
morning, but I walked with spring in my step.

When I opened the door of the Langos grocery, a tiny bell rang shrilly. I 50
stepped into the store piled with fruits and vegetables and smelling of cab-
bages and greens.

A stooped little old man with white busy hair and owlish eyes came 51
toward me. He looked as if his veins contained vegetable juice instead of
blood, and if he were, in truth, the father of my beloved I marveled at how he
could have produced such a paragon of women.

"Are you Mr. Langos?"   52

"I am," he said and he came closer. "I am."   53

"I met your daughter last night," I said. "Did she mention I was going to 54
call?"

He shook his head somberly.   55

"My daughter mentioned you," he said. "In thirty years I have never seen 56
her in such a state of agitation. She was possessed."

"The effect on me was the same," I said. "We met for the first time last 57
night, and I fell passionately in love."

"Incredible," the old man said.   58

"You wish to know something about me," I said. "My name is Marko 59
Palamas. I am a Spartan emigrated to this country eleven years ago. I am
forty-one years old. I have been a wrestler and a sailor and fought with the
resistance movement in Greece in the war. For this service I was decorated by
the king. I own a small but profitable tavern on Dart Street. I attend church
regularly. I love your daughter."

As I finished he stepped back and bumped a rack of fruit. An orange 60
rolled off to the floor. I bent and retrieved it to hand it to him, and he cringed
as if he thought I might bounce it off his old head.

"She is a bad-tempered girl," he said. "Stubborn, impatient and spoiled. 61
She has been the cause of considerable concern to me. All the eligible young
men have been driven away by her temper and disposition."

"Poor girl," I said. "Subjected to the courting of calves and goats." 62

The old man blinked his owlish eyes. The front door opened and a 63 battleship of a woman sailed in.

"Three pounds of tomatoes, Mr. Langos," she said. "I am in a hurry. 64 Please to give me good ones. Last week two spoiled before I had a chance to put them into Demetri's salad."

"I am very sorry," Mr. Langos said. He turned to me. "Excuse me, Mr. 65 Poulmas."

"Palamas," I said. "Marko Palamas." 66

He nodded nervously. He went to wait on the battleship, and I spent a 67 moment examining the store. Neat and small. I would not imagine he did more than hold his own. In the rear of the store there were stairs leading to what appeared to an apartment above. My heart beat faster.

When he had bagged the tomatoes and given change, he returned to me 68 and said, "She is also a terrible cook. She cannot fry an egg without burning it." His voice shook with woe. "She cannot make pilaf or lamb with squash." He paused. "You like pilaf and lamb with squash?"

"Certainly." 69

"You see?" he said in triumph. "She is useless in the kitchen. She is thirty 70 years old, and I am resigned she will remain an old maid. In a way I am glad because I know she would drive some poor man to drink."

"Do not deride her to discourage me," I said. "You need have no fear that 71 I will mistreat her or cause her unhappiness. When she is married to me she will cease being a problem to you." I paused. "It is true that I am not pretty by the foppish standards that prevail today. But I am a man. I wrestled Zahundos and pinned him two straight falls in Baltimore. A giant of a man. Afterward he conceded he had met his master. This from Zahundos was a mighty compliment."

"I am sure," the old man said without enthusiasm. "I am sure." 72

He looked toward the front door as if hoping for another customer. 73

"Is your daughter upstairs?" 74

He looked startled and tugged at his apron. "Yes," he said. "I don't know. 75 Maybe she has gone out."

"May I speak to her? Would you kindly tell her I wish to speak with her." 76

"You are making a mistake," the old man said. "A terrible mistake." 77

"No mistake," I said firmly. 78

The old man shuffled toward the stairs. He climbed them slowly. At the 79 top he paused and turned the knob of the door. He rattled it again.

"It is locked," he called down. "It has never been locked before. She has 80 locked the door."

"Knock," I said. "Knock to let her know I am here." 81

"I think she knows," the old man said. "I think she knows." 82

He knocked gently. 83

"Knock harder," I suggested. "Perhaps she does not hear." 84

"I think she hears," the old man said. "I think she hears." 85

"Knock again," I said. "Shall I come up and knock for you?" 86

"No, no," the old man said quickly. He gave the door a sound kick. Then 87 he groaned as if he might have hurt his foot.

"She does not answer," he said in a quavering voice. "I am very sorry she 88 does not answer."

"The coy darling," I said and laughed. "If that is her game." I started for 89 the front door of the store.

I went out and stood on the sidewalk before the store. Above the grocery 90 were the front windows of their apartment. I cupped my hands about my mouth.

"Ariadne!" I shouted. "Ariadne!" 91

The old man came out the door running disjointedly. He looked franti- 92 cally down the street.

"Are you mad?" he asked shrilly. "You will cause a riot. The police will 93 come. You must be mad!"

"Ariadne!" I shouted. "Beloved!" 94

A window slammed open, and the face of Ariadne appeared above me. 95 Her dark hair tumbled about her ears.

"Go away!" she shrieked. "Will you go away!" 96

"Ariadne," I said loudly. "I have come as I promised. I have spoken to 97 your father. I wish to call on you."

"Go away!" she shrieked. "Madman! Imbecile! Go away!" 98

By this time a small group of people had assembled around the store and 99 were watching curiously. The old man stood wringing his hands and uttering what sounded like small groans.

"Ariadne," I said. "I wish to call on you. Stop this nonsense and let 100 me in."

She pushed farther out the window and showed me her teeth. 101

"Be careful, beloved," I said. "You might fall." 102

She drew her head in quickly, and I turned then to the assembled crowd. 103

"A misunderstanding," I said. "Please move on." 104

Suddenly old Mr. Langos shrieked. A moment later something broke on 105 the sidewalk a foot from where I stood. A vase or a plate. I looked up, and Ariadne was preparing to hurl what appeared to be a water pitcher.

"Ariadne!" I shouted. "Stop that!" 106

The water pitcher landed closer than the vase, and fragments of glass 107 struck my shoes. The crowd scattered, and the old man raised his hands and wailed to heaven.

Ariadne slammed down the window. 108

The crowd moved in again a little closer, and somewhere among them I 109 heard laughter. I fixed them with a cold stare and waited for some one of them to say something offensive. I would have tossed him around like sardines, but they slowly dispersed and moved on. In another moment the old man and I were alone.

I followed him into the store. He walked an awkward dance of agitation. 110
He shut the door and peered out through the glass.

"A disgrace," he wailed. "A disgrace. The whole street will know by 111
nightfall. A disgrace."

"A girl of heroic spirit," I said. "Will you speak to her for me? Assure her 112
of the sincerity of my feelings. Tell her I pledge eternal love and devotion."

The old man sat down on an orange crate and weakly made his cross. 113

"I had hoped to see her myself," I said. "But if you promise to speak to 114
her, I will return this evening."

"That soon?" the old man said. 115

"If I stayed now," I said, "it would be sooner." 116

"This evening," the old man said and shook his head in resignation. "This 117
evening."

I went to my tavern for a while and set up the glasses for the evening 118
trade. I made arrangements for Pavlakis to tend bar in my place. Afterward I
sat alone in my apartment and read a little of majestic Pindar to ease the
agitation of my heart.

Once in the mountains of Greece when I fought with the guerrillas in the 119
last year of the great war, I suffered a wound from which it seemed I would
die. For days high fever raged in my body. My friends brought a priest at
night secretly from one of the captive villages to read the last rites. I accepted
the coming of death and was grateful for many things. For the gentleness and
wisdom of my old grandfather, the loyalty of my companions in war, the years
I sailed between the wild ports of the seven seas, and the strength that flowed
to me from the Spartan earth. For one thing only did I weep when it seemed I
would leave life, that I had never set ablaze the world with a burning song of
passion for one woman. Women I had known, pockets of pleasure that I
tumbled for quick joy, but I had been denied mighty love for one woman. For
that I wept.

In Ariadne I swore before God I had found my woman. I knew by the 120
storm-lashed hurricane that swept within my body. A woman whose majesty
was in harmony with the earth, who would be faithful and beloved to me as
Penelope had been to Ulysses.

That evening near seven I returned to the grocery. Deep twilight had 121
fallen across the street, and the lights in the window of the store had been
dimmed. The apples and oranges and pears had been covered with brown
paper for the night.

I tried the door and found it locked. I knocked on the glass, and a 122
moment later the old man came shuffling out of the shadows and let me in.

"Good evening, Mr. Langos." 123

He muttered some greeting in answer. "Ariadne is not here," he said. "She 124
is at the church. Father Marlas wishes to speak with you."

"A fine young priest," I said. "Let us go at once." 125

I waited on the sidewalk while the old man locked the store. We started 126
the short walk to the church.

"A clear and ringing night," I said. "Does it not make you feel the wonder 127
and glory of being alive?"

The old man uttered what sounded like a groan, but a truck passed on 128
the street at that moment and I could not be sure.

At the church we entered by a side door leading to the office of Father 129
Marlas. I knocked on the door, and when he called to us to enter we walked in.

Young Father Marlas was sitting at his desk in his black cassock and with 130
his black goatee trim and imposing beneath his clean-shaven cheeks. Beside
the desk, in a dark blue dress sat Ariadne, looking somber and beautiful. A
bald-headed, big-nosed old man with flint and fire in his eyes sat in a chair
beside her.

"Good evening, Marko," Father Marlas said and smiled. 131

"Good evening, Father," I said. 132

"Mr. Langos and his daughter you have met," he said and he cleared his 133
throat. "This is Uncle Paul Langos."

"Good evening, Uncle Paul," I said. He glared at me and did not answer. I 134
smiled warmly at Ariadne in greeting, but she was watching the priest.

"Sit down," Father Marlas said. 135

I sat down across from Ariadne, and old Mr. Langos took a chair beside 136
Uncle Paul. In this way we were arrayed in battle order as if we were opposing armies.

A long silence prevailed during which Father Marlas cleared his throat 137
several times. I observed Ariadne closely. There were grace and poise even in
the way her slim-fingered hands rested in her lap. She was a dark and lovely
flower, and my pulse beat more quickly at her nearness.

"Marko," Father Marlas said finally. "Marko, I have known you well for 138
the three years since I assumed duties in this parish. You are most regular in
your devotions and very generous at the time of the Christmas and Easter
offerings. Therefore, I find it hard to believe this complaint against you."

"My family are not liars!" Uncle Paul said, and he had a voice like hunks 139
of dry hard cheese being grated.

"Of course not," Father Marlas said quickly. He smiled benevolently at 140
Ariadne. "I only mean to say—"

"Tell him to stay away from my niece," Uncle Paul burst out. 141

"Excuse me, Uncle Paul," I said very politely. "Will you kindly keep out 142
of what is not your business."

Uncle Paul looked shocked. "Not my business?" He looked from Ariadne 143
to Father Marlas and then to his brother. "Not my business?"

"This matter concerns Ariadne and me," I said. "With outside interfer- 144
ence it becomes more difficult."

"Not my business!" Uncle Paul said. He couldn't seem to get that through 145
his head.

"Marko," Father Marlas said, and his composure was slightly shaken. 146
"The family feels you are forcing your attention upon this girl. They are
concerned."

"I understand, Father," I said. "It is natural for them to be concerned. I 147
respect their concern. It is also natural for me to speak of love to a woman
I have chosen for my wife."

"Not my business!" Uncle Paul said again, and shook his head violently. 148

"My daughter does not wish to become your wife," Mr. Langos said in a 149
squeaky voice.

"That is for your daughter to say," I said courteously. 150

Ariadne made a sound in her throat, and we all looked at her. Her eyes 151
were deep and cold, and she spoke slowly and carefully as if weighing each
word on a scale in her father's grocery.

"I would not marry this madman if he were one of the Twelve Apostles," 152
she said.

"See!" Mr. Langos said in triumph. 153

"Not my business!" Uncle Paul snarled. 154

"Marko," Father Marlas said. "Try to understand." 155

"We will call the police!" Uncle Paul raised his voice. "Put this hoodlum 156
under a bond!"

"Please!" Father Marlas said. "Please!" 157

"Today he stood on the street outside the store," Mr. Langos said excit- 158
edly. "He made me a laughingstock."

"If I were a younger man," Uncle Paul growled, "I would settle this 159
without the police. Zi-ip!" He drew a callused finger violently across his
throat.

"Please," Father Marlas said. 160

"A disgrace!" Mr. Langos said. 161

"An outrage!" Uncle Paul said. 162

"He must leave Ariadne alone!" Mr. Langos said. 163

"We will call the police!" Uncle Paul said. 164

"Silence!" Father Marlas said loudly. 165

With everything suddenly quiet he turned to me. His tone softened. 166

"Marko," he said and he seemed to be pleading a little. "Marko, you must 167
understand."

Suddenly a great bitterness assailed me, and anger at myself, and a terri- 168
ble sadness that flowed like night through my body because I could not make
them understand.

"Father," I said quietly. "I am not a fool. I am Marko Palamas and once I 169
pinned the mighty Zahundos in Baltimore. But this battle, more important to
me by far, I have lost. That which has not the grace of God is far better in
silence."

I turned to leave and it would have ended there. 170

"Hoodlum!" Uncle Paul said. "It is time you were silent!" 171

I swear in that moment if he had been a younger man I would have flung 172
him to the dome of the church. Instead I turned and spoke to them all in fire
and fury.

"Listen," I said. "I feel no shame for the violence of my feelings. I am a 173
man bred of the Spartan earth and my emotions are violent. Let those who
squeak of life feel shame. Nor do I feel shame because I saw this flower and
loved her. Or because I spoke at once of my love."

No one moved or made a sound. 174

"We live in a dark age," I said. "An age where men say one thing and 175
mean another. A time of dwarfs afraid of life. The days are gone when mighty
Pindar sang his radiant blossoms of song. When the noble passions of men
set ablaze cities, and the heroic deeds of men rang like thunder to every
corner of the earth."

I spoke my final words to Ariadne. "I saw you and loved you," I said 176
gently. "I told you of my love. This is my way—the only way I know. If this
way has proved offensive to you I apologize to you alone. But understand
clearly that for none of this do I feel shame."

I turned then and started to the door. I felt my heart weeping as if waves 177
were breaking within my body.

"Marko Palamas," Ariadne said. I turned slowly. I looked at her. For the 178
first time the warmth I was sure dwelt in her body radiated within the circles of
her face. For the first time she did not look at me with her eyes like glaciers.

"Marko Palamas," she said and there was a strange moving softness in the 179
way she spoke my name. "You may call on me tomorrow."

Uncle Paul shot out of his chair. "She is mad too!" he shouted. "He has 180
bewitched her!"

"A disgrace!" Mr. Langos said. 181

"Call the police!" Uncle Paul shouted. "I'll show him if it's my business!" 182

"My poor daughter!" Mr. Langos wailed. 183

Uncle Paul shouted, "Ruffian!" 184

"Please!" Father Marlas said. "Please!" 185

I ignored them all. In that winged and zestful moment I had eyes only for 186
my beloved, for Ariadne, blossom of my heart and black-eyed flower of my
soul!

Critical Thinking and Discussion

1. What is the effect of the central character telling the story? How would it be different if the story were told from another point of view?
2. Why does Marko love Ariadne?
3. Why are they a good match?
4. In what ways are they similar?
5. Why hasn't Ariadne experienced romance before?
6. What is the source of the humor in the story? What does humor contribute to the story?
7. Why is it consistent with Marko's character that he read poetry in times of stress?
8. What do the references to Greece and Greek mythology contribute to the story?
9. Why does Marko give in to the demands of Ariadne's family?
10. Why does she change her mind? Is the change believable?
11. Ariadne's mind changes, but does her character change?

Reading-Related Writing

1. Summarize the story or selected parts of the story from Ariadne's first-person point of view.
2. Discuss how they are suited for each other. Use direct references and short quotations.
3. Analyze either Marko or Ariadne in terms of their main traits—spirit, impulsiveness, courage, strength, determination, sincerity, and so forth.
4. Discuss the events from the priest's point of view.
5. Project Ariadne and Marko a year or more into the future and write about the progress of their love.
6. Discuss why Ariadne changed her mind.

Collaborative Project

1. In your classroom, transform this short story into a one-act play; Petrakis has actually done this in another version of the story. Deciding how to interpret each part will help you learn even more about these well-drawn characters. For example, Petrakis has said that Marko is not a bombastic person; instead, he is a person of "exhuberant dignity." Using one of the following approaches, whichever is most feasible for your class, produce this story as a play:

   • Write the script (it need not be complicated), gather some simple props and arrange the "stage," and perform the play.

- Produce this story as a classroom reading: select several students to read the various dialogue parts, and have another to read the narration.
- Individually write reviews of the play or reading.

2. Stage a reception for the wedding of Ariadne and Marko (based on assumption, speculation, and projection). Bring in some Greek food and drinks. Have a few toasts to the bride and groom, including some by characters appearing in the story. Relate some stories of the "wooing of Ariadne." Have both Ariadne and Marko deliver toasts celebrating their love for each other.

AN ARRANGED MARRIAGE AND THE SWITCHED BRIDE

Sandra Pei

Although this marriage, described by student Sandra Pei, was formally approved by the family, the groom actually was in control—at least he thought he was.

Love in our dreams may be something that takes place in a moment, at first 1 sight. We meet the gaze of someone across a crowded room and that's it—for life. For most people, falling in love for life is much less spectacular. It may even follow disappointments. My Uncle George and Aunt Hua had that experience, and they are the leading characters in my favorite love story of all time.

Uncle George lived in Singapore when he fell deeply in love. At least he 2 thought so. As a member of a traditional Chinese family, he worked hard and established himself in business before he would permit himself to think about marriage. When he was thirty, he was finally secure, and ready; so he started looking around and discovered that just next door was a beautiful young single woman. They exchanged glances, and being sure that he was in love, he asked his parents to talk to her parents about a wedding.

In about two months, the arrangements had been made and Uncle 3 George was content. He would have his beautiful bride, and life would be perfect. He worked with his family and made all the plans for a new house. He never talked directly to the girl, but he continued to look at her as she worked about her house, often accompanied by her older, plain sister.

On the day of the wedding, Uncle George was very happy, and when the 4 music played, he entered the temple to accept his bride. As he joined her at the altar, he shyly turned to look at her lovely face. But to his consternation, he saw instead the plain sister. Someone had switched brides, and he was furious in his protest.

The families quickly called a conference to solve the problem, and tea 5 was served amid much talking and even yelling. The other family had switched brides, with the permission of Uncle George's family. They all wanted the older daughter to get married first. They argued and argued and argued with Uncle George. The prospective bride was tearful and embarrassed. Uncle George gave in and married the plain daughter, Hua.

The word *Hua* means flower in Chinese, and that's what she was, a flower 6 that, as Uncle George's wife, blossomed and, to him, became very beautiful. They have had a loving marriage for more than thirty years now. To Uncle George love was not something that he saw; it was something that happened—with a little help.

Critical Thinking and Discussion

1. Did Uncle George feel he was in love with the young neighbor? If so, what was the basis of his love?
2. What did he discover about the meaning of love?
3. Is this something that could happen only in Chinese culture?
4. How many examples does Sandra Pei use in this essay on love? List them.

Reading-Related Writing

1. Write about someone you know who didn't marry a first choice and yet found love and a lasting relationship.
2. Write about this marriage from Aunt Hua's point of view.
3. Write about this marriage from Uncle George's point of view.

Collaborative Learning

1. Set up a "Geraldo"-type show on teenage love and sex. Have a panel made up of role-playing students, teachers, and psychologists. Students who are not on stage would be audience members, who ask questions. You can make this simple (without rehearsal or scripting) or complex (with some rehearsal and a partially prepared script—and even video cameras). Finally, as individuals or groups, write a review of the production.
2. Stage an "Oprah"-type show for Valentine's Day and have the panel represent the views expressed by individuals who either wrote or are featured in the articles, paragraphs, essays, and short stories in this chapter. Then, as a correspondent for a newspaper or magazine, write an account of the show for general readers.

Connections

1. Referring to several readings write about the universal, cross-cultural nature of love. Suggested readings: "The Wooing of Ariadne," "Yearning for Love," "Young Love—Past and Present," and "How Do I love Thee?"

2. Use several readings to show how women often are the victims in love relationships. Suggested readings: "The Story of an Hour," "Yearning for Love," and "The Business of Selling Mail-Order Brides."

3. Use several readings to show that love and sex have a complicated relationship. Suggested readings: "Get It If You Can," "Girls Also Use Sex," and "Love as a Restricted Club," "The Business of Selling Mail-Order Brides," "Passion at First Sight," and "How Do I Love Thee?"

4. Apply the ideas in "How Do I Love Thee?" to other readings, showing how the situation or problem can be explained by examining it in terms of the formulas offered by Trotter. Suggested readings: "Love as a Restricted Club," "The Business of Selling Mail-Order Brides," "Passion at First Sight," "The Story of an Hour," and "An Arranged Marriage and the Switched Bride."

5. Compare the ideas in "Yearning for Love" with those in "An Arranged Marriage and the Switched Bride."

5

Celebration: Song, Food, Ceremony

*I*f you want to know what a culture values, study its celebrations. What holidays does it have? What songs does it sing? What dances does it do? What foods does it consume, especially in the name of celebration?

Except for those of Native Americans, all of these customs were brought to America by immigrants, brought as surely as baggage, picture albums, and language. The practices may become Americanized over the years, but that does not mean they lose their meaning. Even back in the home lands, different regions practiced their own variations, and towns and families have always individualized customs to some extent.

Travel across America and you will encounter various festivals—the German Octoberfest in Milwaukee and other cities, the Kolache Festival begun by the Czechs who settled in Oklahoma a hundred years ago, the Hispanic-American Cinco de Mayo in East L.A., the numerous Native American corn festivals across the Southwest, the elaborate family reunions of African-Americans (especially in the South), and hundreds more.

Many of these ceremonies are simple and appeal to the basic human instinct to enjoy life. When we study the celebrations of another culture, we feel a special warmth, and we immediately relate it to something that we do in our own family. We may learn that a Thanksgiving Day in the fall exists in many cultures, and that spring festivals abound also, and even the small behaviors give us pause and delight.

Last summer I traveled to Russia where I had an opportunity to visit people who lived in villages and on collective farms. They were friendly, but because I knew practically no Russian and they knew little English, we had some difficulty in communicating, usually resorting to gestures, grunts, and body language. Remarkably, this exercise in charades worked pretty well. One incident stands out.

I was on a country road near Smolensk, somewhere between Moscow and Poland, when I came upon a woman and two small girls. The children were prettily dressed, and I gestured for permission to take their picture. The mother agreed, and I posed the children with the village well in the background. The little girls stood there, looking very serious. In order to break through their reserve and shyness, I picked a common flower from the roadside and handed it to one. She looked down, smiled, and began plucking the petals, saying merrily, "*Lubit, ne lubit. Lubit, ne lubit. Lubit, ne lubit.*" I picked another flower and also began plucking the petals, saying, "She loves me, she loves me not. She loves me, she loves me not." The girls giggled, and I laughed. For a moment the *amerikanets* and the *russkiye* were one. The simplest of cultural connections had been established.

WRITING STRATEGIES AND TECHNIQUES: PROCESS ANALYSIS

If you have any doubt about the frequency of the use of process analysis, just think about how many times you have heard people say, "How do you do it?" or "How is [was] it done?" Even when you are not hearing those questions, you are posing them yourself when you need to make something, cook a meal, assemble an item, take some medicine, repair something, or figure out what happened. In your college classes, you may have to discover how osmosis occurs, how a rock changes form, how a mountain was formed, how a battle was won, or how a bill goes through the legislature.

If you need to explain in writing how to do something or how something is (was) done, you will write a paper of *process analysis*. You will break down your topic into stages, explaining each so that your reader can duplicate or understand the process.

Do not underestimate the complexity of this form because of its directness. Try this scenario:

Someone calls you on the phone and says he needs to tie a tie. You try to explain. Even though you have tied ties hundreds of times and have become proficient in the art, you find yourself fumbling with words. If the person were here, you could demonstrate with a tie. You could stand behind him while he looks in a mirror. He could ask questions the moment something goes awry. But he isn't here, and so your hand moves to your neck in pantomime as you try to recall the steps. Your confidence shaken, you ask him to hold the phone. You hurriedly get a tie from the closet. You put your phone on speaker and say, "Drape the tie around your neck with the fat end on your right. Then you . . .

Try another scenario, this time without a phone and without props:

You have to write instructions on how to tie shoes, and put the instructions in the mail—or maybe on your instructor's desk. [Use your imagination to complete this.]

Two Types of Process Analysis: Directive and Informative

The questions How do I do it? and How is (was) it done? will lead you into two different types of process analysis—directive and informative.

Directive process analysis explains how to do something. As the name suggests, it gives directions and tells the reader how to do something. It says, for example, "Read me, and you can bake a pie (tune up your car, read a book, write an essay, take some medicine)." Because it is presented directly to the reader, it usually addresses the reader as "you," or it implies the "you" by saying something like, "First [you] purchase a large, fat wombat, and then [you] . . . " In the same way, this textbook addresses you or implies "you" because it is a long how-to-do-it (directive process analysis) statement.

Informative process analysis explains how something is (was) done by giving data (information). Whereas the directive process analysis tells you what to do in the future, the informative process analysis tells you what has occurred or what *is* occurring. If the process is something that takes place in nature, such as the formation of a mountain, you can read and understand the process by which it occurred, but, of course, you would not be able to make a mountain. If the process in question is how Harry Truman won the presidential election in 1948, you could learn from what happened and perhaps apply your knowledge, but you could not duplicate the experience. Even if the subject is a scientific experiment and you could duplicate the experience, the stress would still be on your *understanding* the process, not on your *doing* the process. Therefore, instead of addressing the reader ("you"), the writer of informative process analysis either discusses his or her own experience (using *I*), or addresses the subject material by using third-person words such as *he, she, they, it,* or *an individual.* For example:

DIRECTIVE: When you encounter a person at a party who starts to tell jokes with racial slurs, you should take certain steps. First, you should not laugh at the jokes, even though you may embarrass that person. Then . . .

INFORMATIVE: Last weekend at a party, a man started telling racial jokes. I decided it was time to take a stand, and I developed some strategies I intend to use from now on. First, I didn't laugh at his jokes. Then . . .

Directive process analysis and informative process analysis are sometimes combined, especially in longer works, such as this book, and in personalized paragraphs and essays, in which the writer tells "how to" but also discusses his or her experiences.

Blending Process Analysis with Other Forms

The directive and informative types of process analysis often overlap with other forms of discourse presented in this book. These are some examples:

DEFINITION: If you need to explain what a taco is, you may decide to simply recite a recipe, which would include the ingredients and their transformation into a dish.

PERSUASION: As a persuasive statement, you could present the steps for getting adequate exercise in relation to good health.

NARRATION: You could explain how your neighborhood has changed.

CAUSE AND EFFECT: You could explain why the United States became involved in the Vietnam conflict, stage by stage.

In fact, a single form of discourse is seldom used alone, although one may be dominant. That is our concern here: the use of directive or informative process analysis as the dominant form to satisfy a how-to or how-it-is-done purpose.

Considering the Audience

Knowledge

Your audience's knowledge about the topic will determine the depth of your explanation. If you are trying to explain how to tune a car to readers who have never worked on a car or learned anything about gasoline engines, your task is much larger than if you were addressing readers who were somewhat knowledgeable. In explaining to the poorly informed, avoid technical words, provide definitions, and go into more detail about the location of parts, the use of tools, and the need for certain precautions.

Attitude

Equally important to knowledge in many cases is the attitude of your audience—that is, how they feel about your topic. Your audience may be open and even eager for the instruction, or uninterested, or even hostile. Anticipate the likely reaction to your subject, and write with the appropriate tone as you attempt to inform or persuade.

Working with the Stages

Preparation

In this first stage of the directive type of process analysis, list the materials or equipment needed for the process and discuss the necessary setup arrangements. For some topics, this stage will also provide technical terms and definitions. The degree to which this stage is detailed will depend on both the subject itself and the expected knowledge and experience of the projected audience.

The informative type of process analysis may begin with background or context rather than with preparation. For example, a statement explaining how mountains form might begin with a description of a flat portion of the earth made up of plates that are arranged like a jigsaw puzzle.

Steps

The actual process will be presented here. Each step must be explained clearly and directly, and phrased to accommodate the audience. The language, especially in directive process analysis, is likely to be simple and concise; however, avoid dropping words such as *and, a, an, the,* and *of,* and thereby lapsing into "recipe language." The steps may be accompanied by explanations about why certain procedures are necessary and how not following directions carefully can lead to trouble.

Order

The order will usually be chronological (time based) in some sense. Certain words are commonly used to promote coherence: *first, second, third, then, soon, now, next, finally, at last, therefore, consequently,* and—especially for informative process analysis—words used to show the passage of time, such as hours, days of the week, and so on.

The following student-written paragraph and essay illustrate effective uses of process analysis.

VIETNAMESE NEW YEAR*

Khanh Nguyen

preparation

steps

The Vietnamese New Year holiday, which is called Tet ("the new year"), occurs on the first day of the first month of the lunar calendar. We prepare for the day for two weeks. First, we clean our houses very carefully because all brooms are hidden away until the fifth day of the new year. People believe that any sweeping on that day will bring money. Second, we display a lot of flowers throughout the house; they symbolize happiness. Third, because food is a very important part of this holiday, we cook a food that is a special symbol of prosperity: Tet cakes. The cakes are made of pork, sweet rice, and mung beans; they are wrapped in banana leaves and boiled for ten hours. Their shape is either square or round. On New Year's Eve, all families stay up for almost an entire night cooking Tet cakes and exploding fireworks to scare away evil spirits. On Vietnamese New Year's day, we greet each other warmly. Adults give children red envelopes containing money. These envelopes express good wishes. Families have an early lunch of Tet cakes, meat, vegetables, and candies. This special meal symbolizes good fortune for the coming year. After lunch we go out to visit relatives and friends and to watch "Dragon

Dances." The whole day is full of excitement and joy, and the holiday season continues for sixteen days.

SABZI POLO MAHI*

Maysim Mondegaran

In Iran, families like to celebrate the beginning of the 1 New Year each spring with a meal called Sabzi Polo Mahi, which means fish with vegetables and rice. The preparation is as important as the cooking.

In order to make this special dish, one must first 2 know how to pick the right fish, rice, and vegetables. A fresh fish is required for the main part of the meal. It should have shiny bright eyes, nonsticky light gray skin, and pale pink meat. Salmon is recommended. In my

preparation

family we usually buy one that weighs about eight kilograms. It is best to pick a male fish because the meat is more tender and tastier than that of the female. The males always have several black round dots that look like moles on top of their heads. Second, the rice must be excellent, and the best is grown in Astara, in Northern Iran. Although my mother is Chinese, she likes to follow the Iranian custom, so every now and then we drive six hours to Astara and buy several big bags of Astarian rice with long grains and a good scent.

steps 1

To get the best results, the rice must be soaked in 3 salty water for twelve hours before it is cooked. When the rice is almost through soaking, the fish is placed in the oven preheated to about 350 degrees and baked.

2

From time to time it should be basted. The baking time will vary, depending on the size of the fish. The fish is done when the flesh is white and flaky but still moist.

3

While the fish is cooking, the rice should be boiled and drained. While the rice is draining, the vegetables should be prepared. The vegetables (in my family, mainly leafy green ones like spinach or parsley) are

4
5
6

chopped fine and stir-fried with garlic. After the vegetables are done, they should be combined with the rice and steamed so that the flavors mix. After they are steamed, melted butter and ground saffron mixed with a few drops of water are poured over them. Saffron has a bright yellow color and a rich flavor. My mother buys it raw and grinds it specially for this meal.

At last the Sabzi Polo Mahi is ready—the succulent 4 baked fish and the mixture of spicy green vegetables and rice, now made vibrant yellow and flavorful by the saffron and butter. This is one of my favorite dishes, and I look forward to the next time when I can have it with my family.

WRITER'S CHECKLIST

* Decide on whether your process-analysis type is mainly directive or informative, and be appropriately consistent in using pronouns and other designations:

Use second person for the directive as you address the reader (*you, your*);

Use first person for the informative; do not address the reader (use *I*); or

Use third person for the informative; do not address the reader (use *he, she, it, they, them, individuals,* the name of your subject).

* In explaining the stages and using technical terms, take into account whether your audience will be mainly well informed, moderately informed, or poorly informed.
* Explain reasons for procedures whenever you believe explanations will help.
* Select an appropriate tone (such as objective, humorous, argumentative, cautionary, playful, ironic, ridiculing), and be consistent.
* Use transitional words indicating time or other progression (such as *first, second, then, soon, now, next, after, before, when, finally, at last, therefore, consequently,* and—especially for the informative process analysis—words used to show passage of time, such as hours, days of the week, and so on).
* Avoid recipe language; in other words, do not drop *the, a, an,* or *of.*
* Indicate major stages by main headings on your outline or main bubbles in your cluster.

FIESTA

Octavio Paz

Well-known Mexican poet, essayist, critic, and social philosopher Octavio Paz has written extensively about his country and its patterns of thought and behavior. Here he writes about the Mexicans' love of fiestas.

In all of these ceremonies—national or local, trade or family—the Mexican opens out. They all give him a chance to reveal himself and to converse with God, country, friends or relations. During these days the silent Mexican whistles, shouts, sings, shoots off fireworks, discharges his pistol into the air. He discharges his soul. And his shout, like the rockets we love so much, ascends to the heavens, explodes into green, red, blue, and white lights, and falls dizzily to earth with a trail of golden sparks. This is the night when friends who have not exchanged more than the prescribed courtesies for months get drunk together, trade confidences, weep over the same troubles, discover that they are brothers, and sometimes, to prove it, kill each other. The night is full of songs and loud cries. The lover wakes up his sweetheart with an orchestra. There are jokes and conversations from balcony to balcony, sidewalk to sidewalk. Nobody talks quietly. Hats fly in the air. Laughter and curses ring like silver pesos. Guitars are brought out. Now and then, it is true, the happiness ends badly, in quarrels, insults, pistol shots, stabbings. But these too are part of the fiesta, for the Mexican does not seek amusement: he seeks to escape from himself, to leap over the wall of solitude that confines him during the rest of the year. All are possessed by violence and frenzy. Their souls explode like the colors and voices and emotions. Do they forget themselves and show their true faces? Nobody knows. The important thing is to go out, open a way, get drunk on noise, people, colors. Mexico is celebrating a fiesta. And this fiesta, shot through with lightning and delirium, is the brilliant reverse to our silence and apathy, our reticence and gloom.

Critical Thinking and Discussion

1. Why do Mexicans behave as they do at fiestas?
2. What does the behavior of Mexicans reveal about their true nature?
3. Through what stages does a fiesta develop?

Reading-Related Writing

1. Select a particular ceremony that illustrates Paz's idea of the fiesta and discuss it as an informative process analysis.

2. Write about another cultural group and its characteristic behavior at a particular festival.
3. If you are familiar with Mexican-American culture, write about one holiday you have witnessed, in relation to Paz's observations.

PERUVIAN NEW YEAR, MIAMI STYLE*

Julio Montez

After leaving Peru because of terrorism, student Julio Montez and his family moved to Miami, Florida, where he joined a small group of his fellow expatriates. The following New Year's Day they gathered in one person's house and celebrated in the Peruvian fashion.

Last year in Miami, Florida, I helped a group of people burn an effigy of an old man. It wasn't an act of terrorism or of protest. It was part of a New Year's Eve ceremony my family brought with us from Peru. This one was not quite the same as the ones we experienced in Peru, but it nevertheless gave us a good feeling. In Peru we would have joined many neighbors, friends, and relatives to make a dummy, *el año viejo*, the old year. We would have dressed him in tattered old rags and carried him to a barrio or a nearby plaza. We would have run around singing, laughing, blowing whistles, shouting, and throwing firecrackers. Next we would have propped him up in a chair and begun reading the "old year's testament." It would be a funny reading, as people would donate items for the dummy, items like an old shoe for someone who always dresses well or a woman's wig for a bald man, and so on. Meanwhile people would be putting firewood around him. Finally at exactly midnight, someone would set fire to the dummy and everyone would throw their oldest clothes into the flames. The bells from the churches would toll, the fire stations would turn on their sirens, and all the neighbors and visitors would hug and kiss each other and shout out wishes for a happy New Year. That was the background for last year, when we held a scaled-back version with about a dozen people present in the backyard of our hosts. We made an effigy, and we burned it, but we didn't have the firecrackers, bells, and sirens. We did, however, have the feelings. We brought a little bit of Peru with us to our new country.

Critical Thinking and Discussion

1. What transitional words does Montez use to show the progression of thought or the passage of time?
2. What are the stages of the New Year's ceremony in Peru?

Reading-Related Writing

1. If you are an immigrant, write about the first time you held a traditional ceremony after you arrived in your new country.
2. Interview someone who has had a similar experience and write about it.

FESTIVAL OF THE DEAD*

Teresita Castellanos

On November 2, Mexicans celebrate the Festival of the Dead. It is a time of joy when the living go to cemeteries to pay homage to the dead. Children eat candies shaped like skulls, adults clean tombstones, and they all remember and pray. Student Teresita Castellanos, an immigrant from Mexico, knows this day well from her childhood experiences.

The Day of the Dead, which falls on November 2 each year, is a great national holiday in Mexico. Introduced into Mexico by the Spaniards after the Conquest, it is one of the most peculiar and important Mexican religious celebrations. Several days before the occasion, markets and bakeries are filled with special breads baked in human forms, sweets shaped into skulls, and toy coffins, skeletons, and masks made of papier-mâché. Flower shops overflow with marigolds, the flower that in Aztec times was sacred to the dead. On that day Mexicans carry gifts of food and flowers to the graves of those who have died. But they do not feel sad, for they believe that the dead return to earth in spirit on this special day. People clean tombstones, set out offerings of treats, salt, and sugar, and welcome the dead as honored guests. Then people celebrate by eating the food and by wearing masks that look like grinning skulls. The children pretend to frighten each other with jack-in-the-boxes that look like skeletons jumping out of their coffins. This celebration helps people not to be afraid of the dead and of death itself.

Critical Thinking and Discussion

1. Why is the Festival of the Dead not an occasion of sadness?
2. What are the basic steps in the celebration?

Reading-Related Writing

1. Write about your experience with the Festival of the Dead or another holiday that also has a long history.

2. If the Festival of the Dead is not part of your culture, write about your initial reaction to it and your reaction to it after you learned of its history and meaning.

3. Because of the close proximity of Halloween and the Festival of the Dead, the two may be celebrated by the same people at almost the same time. Some Hispanics may feel that the wildness of Halloween tends to corrupt the seriousness of their holiday. Interview a few Hispanics (incorporating your own view if you are Hispanic), and write a report on the issue. Include comments on any blending that occurs.

KWANZAA: HOLIDAY OF "PRINCIPLES TO LIVE BY"

Eugene Morris

Kwanzaa is an invented holiday, one that expresses the joy, pride, dedication, and values of many African-American people. It pays respect to African origins and celebrates the uniqueness of African-American culture.

Alice Lovelace said her five children don't complain each holiday season 1 when they get handmade African toys and books written by African-American authors instead of computerized laser games and combat-fighter planes. They also understand why their home is decorated with candles, fruit, and place mats instead of a Christmas tree and stockings. Like millions of other black Americans, the Lovelace family celebrates *Kwanzaa* (also spelled *Kwanza*), a holiday when African-Americans give thanks for their heritage. Beginning [December 26], Kwanzaa is celebrated the seven days after Christmas.

Derived from an East African Swahili phrase, *matunda ya kwanza* or "first 2 fruits," Kwanzaa is neither an African holiday nor a black Christmas. It is an African-American cultural celebration that draws on African harvest festival traditions, like giving thanks for the first crops of the year. It also stresses principles for better living and offers guides to achieve inner peace.

"We started celebrating Kwanzaa as an alternative to the commercializa- 3 tion of Christmas and because Kwanzaa is grounded in moral and cultural values," said Ms. Lovelace, executive director of an art gallery. "Kwanzaa teaches principles to live by," she said, "and we thought that was more valuable than celebrating Christmas, which has become so commercial."

Kwanzaa was founded in 1966 by Dr. Maulana Karenga, a black studies 4 professor at California State University campuses in Los Angeles and Long Beach. Karenga initiated the holiday because he felt blacks needed a holiday that had historical relevance for blacks and Africans. Longtime Kwanzaa observers said small celebrations also began about the same time in Atlanta in the homes of some blacks. Other programs and celebrations were held at community centers, black college campuses, and other sites. . . . National Kwanzaa officials said more than 13 million African-Americans celebrate Kwanzaa. In Atlanta, Kwanzaa . . . celebrations . . . include displays and demonstrations throughout the city. . . .

Kwanzaa was founded under seven principles, referred to as the *Nguzo* 5 *Saba.* They are unity, self-determination, collective work and responsibility, cooperative economics, purpose, creativity, and faith. During Kwanzaa, traditional holiday decorations are replaced by red, black, and green African colors of liberation. Kwanzaa symbols are placed upon a *mkeka* or place mat, which represents the African foundation of the holiday. A *kinara* (seven-piece candleholder) and the *mishumaa saba* (seven candles) are also displayed. One candle is lighted each day. Other displays include *vibunzi* (corn), which symbolizes children, *mazao* (fruits, nuts, and vegetables), which represent the holiday's origins, African harvest, the rewards of collective efforts, and the *zawadi* (gifts) primarily given to the children. However the gifts should be creative, cultural, and educational and not merely for entertainment. Each night some families sip a libation (or *tambiko*) from a unity cup (or *kikombe*) to honor black ancestors. Songs and dances are also performed.

Although Ikenna Ubaka and her daughter celebrate Kwanzaa and Christ- 6 mas, Ms. Ubaka stresses the religious impact of Christmas and downplays its commercialization. "We try to send the message during Kwanzaa that it is more important to give of yourselves than to spend money on presents," she said. "Kwanzaa deals with our heritage and our culture."

Dr. Omowale Amuleru-Marshall, a member of the Atlanta Chapter of the 7 Association of Black Psychologists and the faculty of the Morehouse School of Medicine, said his family celebrates Kwanzaa because of a disillusionment with Christmas. "My rejection of Christmas is not a rejection of Christ," he said, "just the way the holiday creates a psychological denial of one's own self and one's own culture."

Critical Thinking and Discussion

1. What does the word *Kwanzaa* mean?
2. What is the basis of Kwanzaa?
3. What are the basic steps of the ceremony?
4. What message does Ms. Ubaka stress?

Reading-Related Writing

1. If you have participated in a Kwanzaa ceremony, write an account.
2. If you have not participated in this ceremony, interview someone who has and write about it.

3. Kwanzaa is a relatively new holiday, having begun in 1966. Invent a new holiday of your own that celebrates your culture, and discuss its meaning, basis, and ceremonial steps.

THE LOUDEST VOICE

Grace Paley

Sometimes an immigrant group may find itself in the middle of a cultural experience that is fundamentally alien to their thinking. In this short story, Grace Paley writes of first-generation Jewish people participating in a play celebrating the birth of Jesus Christ. Ever eager to avoid offending the citizens of their host country, most of the parents and children cooperate, with ironic results.

There is a certain place where dumb-waiters boom, doors slam, dishes crash; 1 every window is a mother's mouth bidding the street shut up, go skate somewhere else, come home. My voice is the loudest.

There, my own mother is still as full of breathing as me and the grocer 2 stands up to speak to her. "Mrs. Abramowitz," he says, "people should not be afraid of their children."

"Ah, Mr. Bialik," my mother replies, "if you say to her or her father 'Ssh,' 3 they say, 'In the grave it will be quiet.' "

"From Coney Island to the cemetery," says my papa. "It's the same sub- 4 way; it's the same fare."

I am right next to the pickle barrel. My pinky is making tiny whirlpools 5 in the brine. I stop a moment to announce: "Campbell's Tomato Soup. Campbell's Vegetable Beef Soup. Campbell's S-c-otch Broth . . . "

"Be quiet," the grocer says, "the labels are coming off." 6

"Please, Shirley, be a little quiet," my mother begs me. 7

In that place the whole street groans: Be quiet! Be quiet! but steals from 8 the happy chorus of my inside self not a tittle or a jot.

There, too, but just around the corner, is a red brick building that has been 9 old for many years. Every morning the children stand before it in double lines which must be straight. They are not insulted. They are waiting anyway.

I am usually among them. I am, in fact, the first, since I begin with "A." 10

One cold morning the monitor tapped me on the shoulder. "Go to Room 11 409, Shirley Abramowitz," he said. I did as I was told. I went in a hurry up a down staircase to Room 409, which contained sixth-graders. I had to wait at the desk without wiggling until Mr. Hilton, their teacher, had time to speak.

After five minutes he said, "Shirley?" 12

"What?" I whispered.   13

He said, "My! My! Shirley Abramowitz! They told me you had a particu- 14
larly loud, clear voice and read with lots of expression. Could that be true?"

"Oh yes," I whispered.   15

"In that case, don't be silly; I might very well be your teacher someday. 16
Speak up, speak up."

"Yes," I shouted.   17

"More like it," he said. "Now, Shirley, can you put a ribbon in your hair or 18
a bobby pin? It's too messy."

"Yes!" I bawled.   19

"Now, now, calm down." He turned to the class. "Children, not a sound. 20
Open at page 39. Read till 52. When you finish, start again." He looked me
over once more. "Now, Shirley, you know, I suppose, that Christmas is coming. We are preparing a beautiful play. Most of the parts have been given out.
But I still need a child with a strong voice, lots of stamina. Do you know what
stamina is? You do? Smart kid. You know, I heard you read 'The Lord is my
shepherd' in Assembly yesterday. I was very impressed. Wonderful delivery.
Mrs. Jordan, your teacher, speaks highly of you. Now listen to me, Shirley
Abramowitz, if you want to take the part and be in the play, repeat after me, 'I
swear to work harder than I ever did before.'"

I looked to heaven and said at once, "Oh, I swear." I kissed my pinky and 21
looked at God.

"That is an actor's life, my dear," he explained. "Like a soldier's, never 22
tardy or disobedient to his general, the director. Everything," he said, "absolutely everything will depend on you."

That afternoon, all over the building, children scraped and scrubbed the 23
turkeys and the sheaves of corn off the schoolroom windows. Goodbye
Thanksgiving. The next morning a monitor brought red paper and green
paper from the office. We made new shapes and hung them on the walls and
glued them to the doors.

The teachers became happier and happier. Their heads were ringing like 24
the bells of childhood. My best friend Evie was prone to evil, but she did not
get a single demerit for whispering. We learned "Holy Night" without an
error. "How wonderful!" said Miss Glacé, the student teacher. "To think that
some of you don't even speak the language!" We learned "Deck the Halls" and
"Hark! The Herald Angels". . . . They weren't ashamed and we weren't
embarrassed.

Oh, but when my mother heard about it all, she said to my father: 25
"Misha, you don't know what's going on there. Cramer is the head of the
Tickets Committee."

"Who?" asked my father. "Cramer? Oh yes, an active woman." 26

"Active? Active has to have a reason. Listen," she said sadly, "I'm sur- 27
prised to see my neighbors making tra-la-la for Christmas."

My father couldn't think of what to say to that. Then he decided: "You're 28 in America! Clara, you wanted to come here. In Palestine the Arabs would be eating you alive. Europe you had pogroms. Argentina is full of Indians. Here you got Christmas. . . . Some joke, ha?"

"Very funny, Misha. What is becoming of you? If we came to a new 29 country a long time ago to run away from tyrants, and instead we fall into a creeping pogrom, that our children learn a lot of lies, so what's the joke? Ach, Misha, your idealism is going away."

"So is your sense of humor." 30

"That I never had, but idealism you had a lot of." 31

"I'm the same Misha Abramovitch, I didn't change an iota. Ask anyone." 32

"Only ask me," says my mama, may she rest in peace. "I got the answer." 33

Meanwhile the neighbors had to think of what to say too. 34

Marty's father said: "You know, he has a very important part, my boy." 35

"Mine also," said Mr. Sauerfeld. 36

"Not my boy!" said Mrs. Klieg. "I said to him no. The answer is no. When 37 I say no! I mean no!"

The rabbi's wife said. "It's disgusting!" But no one listened to her. Under 38 the narrow sky of God's great wisdom she wore a strawberry-blond wig.

Every day was noisy and full of experience. I was Right-hand Man. Mr. 39 Hilton said: "How could I get along without you, Shirley?"

He said: "Your mother and father ought to get down on their knees every 40 night and thank God for giving them a child like you."

He also said: "You're absolutely a pleasure to work with, my dear, dear 41 child."

Sometimes he said: "For God's sakes, what did I do with the script? 42 Shirley! Shirley! Find it."

Then I answered quietly: "Here it is, Mr. Hilton." 43

Once in a while, when he was very tired, he would cry out: "Shirley, I'm 44 just tired of screaming at those kids. Will you tell Ira Pushkov not to come in till Lester points to that star the second time?"

Then I roared: "Ira Pushkov, what's the matter with you? Dope! Mr. 45 Hilton told you five times already, don't come in till Lester points to that star the second time."

"Ach, Clara," my father asked, "what does she do there till six o'clock she 46 can't even put the plates on the table?"

"Christmas," said my mother coldly. 47

"Ho! Ho!" my father said. "Christmas. What's the harm? After all, history 48 teaches everyone. We learn from reading this is a holiday from pagan times also, candles, lights, even Chanukah. So we learn it's not altogether Christian. So if they think it's a private holiday, they're only ignorant, not patriotic. What belongs to history, belongs to all men. You want to go back to the Middle Ages? Is it better to shave your head with a secondhand razor? Does it hurt

Shirley to learn to speak up? It does not. So maybe someday she won't live between the kitchen and the shop. She's not a fool."

I thank you, Papa, for your kindness. It is true about me to this day. I am foolish but I am not a fool. 49

That night my father kissed me and said with great interest in my career, "Shirley, tomorrow's your big day. Congrats." 50

"Save it," my mother said. Then she shut all the windows in order to prevent tonsillitis. 51

In the morning it snowed. On the street corner a tree had been decorated for us by a kind city administration. In order to miss its chilly shadow our neighbors walked three blocks east to buy a loaf of bread. The butcher pulled down black window shades to keep the colored lights from shining on his chickens. Oh, not me. On the way to school, with both my hands I tossed it a kiss of tolerance. Poor thing, it was a stranger in Egypt. 52

I walked straight into the auditorium past the staring children. "Go ahead, Shirley!" said the monitors. Four boys, big for their age, had already started work as propmen and stagehands. 53

Mr. Hilton was very nervous. He was not even happy. Whatever he started to say ended in a sideward look of sadness. He sat slumped in the middle of the first row and asked me to help Miss Glacé. I did this, although she thought my voice too resonant and said, "Show-off!" 54

Parents began to arrive long before we were ready. They wanted to make a good impression. From among the yards of drapes I peeked out at the audience. I saw my embarrassed mother. 55

Ira, Lester, and Meyer were pasted to their beards by Miss Glacé. She almost forgot to thread the star on its wire, but I reminded her. I coughed a few times to clear my throat. Miss Glacé looked around and saw that everyone was in costume and on line waiting to play his part. She whispered, "All right . . ." Then: 56

Jackie Sauerfeld, the prettiest boy in first grade, parted the curtains with his skinny elbow and in a high voice sang out: 57

"Parents dear
We are here
To make a Christmas play in time.
It we give
In narrative
And illustrate with pantomime."

He disappeared. 58

My voice burst immediately from the wings to the great shock of Ira, Lester, and Meyer, who were waiting for it but were surprised all the same. 59

"I remember, I remember, the house where I was born . . ." 60

Miss Glacé yanked the curtain open and there it was, the house—an old 61 hayloft, where Celia Kornbluh lay in the straw with Cindy Lou, her favorite doll. Ira, Lester, and Meyer moved slowly from the wings toward her, sometimes pointing to a moving star and sometimes ahead to Cindy Lou.

It was a long story and it was a sad story. I carefully pronounced all the 62 words about my lonesome childhood, while little Eddie Braunstein wandered upstage and down with his shepherd's stick, looking for sheep. I brought up lonesomeness again, and not being understood at all except by some women everybody hated. Eddie was too small for that and Marty Groff took his place, wearing his father's prayer shawl. I announced twelve friends, and half the boys in the fourth grade gathered round Marty, who stood on an orange crate while my voice harangued. Sorrowful and loud, I declaimed about love and God and Man, but because of the terrible deceit of Abie Stock we came suddenly to a famous moment. Marty, whose remembering tongue I was, waited at the foot of the cross. He stared desperately at the audience. I groaned, "My God, my God, why hast thou forsaken me?" The soldiers who were sheiks grabbed poor Marty to pin him up to die, but he wrenched free, turned again to the audience, and spread his arms aloft to show despair and the end. I murmured at the top of my voice, "The rest is silence, but as everyone in this room, in this city—in this world—now knows, I shall have life eternal."

That night Mrs. Kornbluh visited our kitchen for a glass of tea. 63

"How's the virgin?" asked my father with a look of concern. 64

"For a man with a daughter, you got a fresh mouth, Abramovitch." 65

"Here," said my father kindly, "have some lemon, it'll sweeten your dispo- 66 sition."

They debated a little in Yiddish, then fell in a puddle of Russian and 67 Polish. What I understood next was my father, who said, "Still and all, it was certainly a beautiful affair, you have to admit, introducing us to the beliefs of a different culture."

"Well, yes," said Mrs. Kornbluh. "The only thing . . . you know Charlie 68 Turner—that cute boy in Celia's class—a couple others? They got very small parts or no part at all. In very bad taste, it seemed to me. After all, it's their religion."

"Ach," explained my mother, "what could Mr. Hilton do? They got very 69 small voices; after all, why should they holler? The English language they know from the beginning by heart. They're blond like angels. You think it's so important they should get in the play? Christmas . . . the whole piece of goods . . . they own it."

I listened and listened until I couldn't listen any more. Too sleepy, I 70 climbed out of bed and kneeled. I made a little church of my hands and said, "Here, O Israel . . . " Then I called out in Yiddish, "Please, good night, good night. Ssh." My father said, "Ssh yourself," and slammed the kitchen door.

I was happy. I fell asleep at once. I had prayed for everybody: my talking 71
family, cousins far away, passersby, and all the lonesome Christians. I expected
to be heard. My voice was certainly the loudest.

Vocabulary

a tittle or a jot (8)   pogroms (28)   harangued (62)
stamina (20)   resonant (54)   declaimed (62)

Critical Thinking and Discussion

1. What is the conflict in this story?
2. What is the significance of the setting (where the story takes place)?
3. Who is the main character?
4. Why are Shirley Abramowitz's beliefs unshaken by this experience?
5. This story has a humorous tone. What makes it funny? Might the same
   basic story be told in a different tone for a very different effect?
6. What does having Shirley tell the story contribute to its effect?
7. Why does Shirley speak softly at times?
8. What is her father's view? her mother's view?

Reading-Related Writing

1. Write about a time when you were expected to do something (religious,
   cultural) that made you feel uncomfortable. Using informative process,
   explain how the incident took place.
2. Compare and contrast Shirley's mother and father.
3. Write about events in this story as examples of cultural confrontation.
   Include comments on sensitivity and insensitivity, toleration and intolera-
   tion.

JAPANESE TEA CEREMONY

Vance Horne

*An American tries to understand a ritual that is totally alien to him in
intent and execution. But he knows that in learning about this ceremony he will gain insight into another culture. And he knows that there
he will find a reflective experience that he can use in his own life.*

So Choku Naoko, usually known as Mrs. Gower, is kneeling on a Japanese 1 *tatami* mat in her tea room, trying to tell two Westerners about tea. The Westerners are kneeling, too, and their knees are hurting. "If on the one hand people stop striving to achieve more, civilization will stop," she says. "But on the other hand, you have to accept yourself as you are." She pauses long enough for the Westerners to quit thinking about their knees and contemplate this unshakeable paradox. "This is what you have to learn," she says, smiling at the dry humor of it.

She is dressed in a beautiful kimono and, except for her eyeglasses, there 2 is nothing about her or her tea room to suggest the modern world. This is what she does for a living, showing people how to leave this world briefly through the Japanese tea ceremony. In January she performed parts of the ceremony at The Evergreen State College's Tribute to Japan. I had written a few words telling the public that she would do that. Afterwards she invited me to her Burien home to partake of a full ceremony.

I am writing this in the first person because I was one of the two Wes- 3 terners in the tea room and because I want to confess that the tea ceremony not only impressed me, it baffled me. The centuries-old ceremony is as tidy as algebra but as full of gestures as an opera. It probably is the most Japanese thing there is. Mrs. Gower, a certified teacher, comes from a tea ceremony school in Japan that has 12,000 students, and she estimates that there are 20 to 30 such schools. For years I have heard that if you want to understand Japan, you must understand the tea ceremony.

Mrs. Gower's tea room is perhaps 10 feet by 10 feet and a little over 6 feet 4 high. Inside, you see only wood, bamboo, grass mats, rice paper, a sunken pit for a water pot, a small simple chest that holds tea utensils, and a calligraphy scroll. She built the room inside her son's bedroom when he went to college. After years of living in America with her importer/exporter husband, William, she wanted a room that was totally Japanese. It is too small for Westerners to gather in comfortably, but that is part of what the ceremony is about, learning to co-exist. "One-on-one human relationships aren't hard," she says. "But if you have more people, it can become difficult."

The ceremony is a way of making a group of people harmonious in a 5 little space, she explains. Basically, it is done by feeding them and giving them tea. She enters the tea room on her knees, bowing. Her guests are against one wall, kneeling, and they must know when they, too, must bow. A girls enters, bearing small but beautiful servings of food in black lacquer serving trays. The guests bow over the food, just as the girl bows. Everyone is in equality, because everyone must know and follow the rituals. Although the girl seems to be a servant, the guests must obey the same rules as she does. Picking up a food bowl, the guests observe the food as if it were a painting. They turn and inspect the bowls in precise gestures. Eating is a dance, and not a simple one.

"Tea ceremony has certain unavoidable rules," Mrs. Gower says. "We are living in a do-your-own-thing world. This is totally the reverse."

As they finish with a food bowl, the guests take folded paper from their 6 kimonos and wipe the bowl. Then they appreciate its beauty. The girl pours wine in shallow bowls, and the guests drink, but it's not much wine. "Tea ceremony was begun by men," Mrs. Gower explains. "About 100 years ago we had a big cultural revolution in Japan, and men no longer control everything. Today, 95 to 97 percent of the tea industry is controlled by females. Traditionally, the men drank a lot. Now we don't drink so much; we eat instead." She laughs about this turn of events.

Everything moves slowly in the ceremony, and it takes a long time to get 7 to the tea part of it. The Japanese relish their time in the tea room. "We are leading a very stressful life," Mrs. Gower says, "and people are trying to escape in many ways. As you walk in a Japanese garden, you leave your stresses behind, and once you enter the tea room you're in a very ideal world. In an ideal world we talk only of pleasant subjects, to make people happy. I am actually leading you to a utopian life. I am leading you to the beauty of life." But such beauty evades the hand or brain that would enclose it. It is the beauty of *u gen*—the unknown. But although the beauty is of the unknown, it isn't necessarily unearthly. In trying to explain it Mrs. Gower even speaks of the beauty of an unknown woman's body beneath her clothes.

When Mrs. Gower finally comes to the tea, she carefully opens the chest 8 and takes implements from it. Before she uses them, she inspects them for their beauty, turning them this way and that in a ritual of observation. There is a small ceramic bowl for the tea, a small container holding bright green powdered tea, a simple wood implement that works like a spoon for measuring the tea, a long-handled wooden dipper for getting water from the pot and a curious whisk device for stirring the tea.

Her tea room actually is a school room, and she teaches Japanese-Ameri- 9 cans the use of these utensils and the rituals of the ceremony as a whole. There are maybe 18 certified teachers in the Seattle area, she thinks, but she has one of only two tea rooms. Actually, she has one American student, a man. The fact that there is but one American makes it clear how Japanese the ceremony is. To the learn the ceremony fully usually takes three years.

Using her utensils of ancient design, she makes the tea. It is hard to say 10 in words how careful she is. Perhaps it is what one would imagine heart surgery to be. With appropriate bowing on all parts, she serves the tea, and the participants turn the bowls in their hands, admiring them, and at last they drink the bright green and pleasantly bitter tea, and then they clean their bowls.

Not much has happened in the physical sense. A simple meal that might 11 take 15 minutes has been drawn out to two hours. Although there is much ritual, there is no invoking of gods, no trading of Zen jests. Mrs. Gower talks of it as a matter of her entertaining guests. "Primarily, entertainment is the love of giving," she says. "Entertainment means nothing if you just call up the caterer. You must give your time and, if I may say it, your compassion."

In the end, it is important to see Mrs. Gower as she is. She is not a   12 mysterious and delicate being, conversing only in Buddhistic subtleties. She is an outgoing woman full of humor, and she loves to use American slang. I came away glad to be out of the tea room, because I am not used to such confinement or to such silent ritual or such foreignness. Yet I would like to go back. I am intrigued. A plane ticket to Tokyo and two weeks in a hotel might not take me as close to Japan. In the end, the ceremony reminds me a little of baseball, which is a sport of ritual and of careful geometry, where almost nothing ever happens but it takes a long time. It too is popular in Japan.

Vocabulary

tatami (1)
paradox (1)
subtleties (12)

Critical Thinking and Discussion

1. What is the author's background?
2. What is the teacher's background?
3. What is significant about the size and furnishings of the room?
4. Who is subject to the rules in the room?
5. What is most important—the utensils, the food and drink, or the ceremony?
6. What do Japanese people try to escape through the tea ceremony?
7. What in American culture gets in the way of the writer's appreciation?
8. What preparations are made and what is their significance?
9. What are the steps of the Japanese tea ceremony?

Reading-Related Writing

1. Write about another ceremony (perhaps religious) in which the consumption of food and/or drink may be less important than the ritual.
2. Write about a toast that is associated with a certain culture, one that is made to health, longevity, relationships, or something else. An example is the Greek custom of breaking wine glasses after a toast.
3. Write about other ceremonies that invite contemplation. For example, Native Americans pass a ceremonial pipe.

4. The Japanese seem to escape from the problems of this world by slowing time and withdrawing; according to Octavio Paz in "Fiesta," Hispanics escape from the problems of this world by rushing time and expressing emotions in an extremely uninhibited manner. Write about a ceremony different from the Japanese tea ceremony and include comments on the apparent motives (they may not be obvious to most participants) and their fulfillments. If you would like to do some primary research, check your local newspaper for cultural festivals—Armenian, Ukrainian, Greek, Polish, Bohemian, Chinese, Arab, and so on.

THANKSGIVING

Linda Hogan

Prominent Native American writer and member of the Chickasaw Nation, Linda Hogan writes reverently of a time of thanksgiving for her and her people. But for the Native Americans she writes of, the celebration is not one meal, one ceremony, one day. For them Thanksgiving is a series of dances that are held throughout the growing season. These ceremonies bind her people to the land in a deeply spiritual and cultural fashion. She conveys how Native Americans love the land, the products of the land, and their brothers and sisters, who are all part of nature.

In Pueblo country, throughout the yearly growing season, the corn dances 1 take place. The dancing begins at the time of planting and ends with the time of harvest.

It is a serious dance, a long and hard barefoot dance on burning hot 2 southwestern earth. It is a dance of community, not only between people, but a larger sense of community that includes earth, the new young plants, and the fiery sun. It's a dance of human generosity, as the dancers lend their energy to the kernels sowed in newly turned soil. There is drumming and singing. There is feasting on loaves of bread baked outdoors in clay ovens, on watermelons the color of the mountains, on meats, and varieties of chile sauces. But mostly there is prayer in the dance, and thankfulness.

A few years ago I was asked, as part of a ceremony, to grind light-giving 3 blue corn with a grinding stone and metate. I didn't know then that corn was as dependent on people as people have been, throughout history, on corn. But 90-year-old writer Meridel Le Sueur has written that ancient women gatherers were free travelers who loved the tiny grass of early corn, hand-pollinated it, and "created the great cob of nutrition which cannot free itself from the cob without the hand of human."

During that ceremony, I also drank bitter tea, telling the herb in the cup, ₄
thank you, telling the sun, *thank you,* and thanking the land. Gratitude and a
human connectedness with food is part of many ceremonies of life that are
centered on hunting, picking, planting, and healing.

In my own tribal history, too, corn has meant life. The people eat corn- ₅
bread and ear corn, parched corn, cornmeal mush. My grandmother, like
many other Chickasaw women, made hominy with lye and ashes in a large
black kettle on the wood stove. Still, in a single kernel of that swollen white
corn, people swallow the light of sun and the rich mineral earth, eat of the
rains in the milky sweetness of yellow corn, eat the rich loamy smell of
turned earth, of planter's moons, of seeds planted in the sacred land.

The reciprocity among land, food, and people also exists farther north ₆
where ricers' boats move among the wild rice plants in the swampy, humid
land as the boat is pushed with a pole through lily pads and plants and the
distant call of a loon. In the diffuse, soft light of the sun, the people are
covered with rice dust and dried pollen and insects. They, too, sing their
thankful song to the rice, and the songs, like those of others, come to life
within the food.

Here a woman works with a digging stick. There a child chases crows ₇
away from the crops. Old men break ground and turn the soil. Women plant
by the moon. There are the berry-pickers, and the grateful people who bring
in the twisting, shining fish from the river. The herb gatherers know to pick
plants at certain times of the year and month, and they speak with the plants
as they work, thanking them. And there is the native woman I met in Hawaii;
it fell to her to be the traditional hunter of wild pigs, to take only what was
needed, to feed others, and be thankful. Sometimes in the hurry sickness of
our time, we forget to return the gift of what we've taken from the rich land
that feeds us. Sometimes we do not remember that millions of years of life
have grown from this verdant, muddy, yielding terrain where we live in the
land of our ancestors. We forget the long years of hunger, the starving times
of history we have survived, and the years of living on lard and flour. We
forget the meaning of food, which is both beginning and end of a divine
alchemy, an infinite movement of sun into fruit, of windborne seeds falling to
earth, seeds being carried in the fur of animals and the stomachs of birds, of
rain water, of life rising up again. In our food all things come together in an
elemental dance of magic and mystery; brother water, sister light, mother
land, and the sacred fire all rise up in stalks and stems, opening a blossom
and becoming red fruit of grass eaten by the deer, or the ripening yellow ears
of corn planted and harvested by our short-lived hands.

Now it is autumn, and in the cool, plastered corners of houses are the ₈
seed pots. The pots are smooth, rounded clay that has been painted with lines
thin as a strand of corn silk and they hold the seeds of pumpkin, beans, and
squash in a loving embrace before they go back to land. Even last summer's

sun is held there, dormant and ready to turn over and surge to life in incredible germinations of renewal.

Near here grew the green spring pastures with onions growing at the 9 borders. Now, in autumn, they are the golden stubble of harvested hay, the road is damp and silty with fallen red leaves that are turning back into soil, waiting for spring's rich rains and sun. On the next hill are the five wild turkeys I saw last month as they walked through the tall, dry grasses, and beyond them are the caves of mineral salt that generations of people have used. This is the vulnerable land shared among us. Not far from here the ancient plants are listening and moving again toward the ripening.

Vocabulary

metate (3)   verdant (7)   dormant (8)
reciprocity (6)   alchemy (8)

Critical Thinking and Discussion

1. Hogan writes about more than the process of the dances that take place during the corn growing and harvesting season. She writes about the intricate relationship between human beings and all aspects of nature and even the spiritual world. She sees a reciprocal relationship, an interdependency. What are some of those interdependencies? How do they represent process?
2. What do the dances relate to?
3. How have corn and people been interdependent?
4. In the Southwest, how do different family members participate in corn production? What process is described here?
5. In her next-to-last sentence, she says, "This is the vulnerable land shared among us." Although she is concerned about the life-sustaining forces of larger nature, what understated idea does she bring up here?

Reading-Related Writing

1. If you are familiar with Native American culture, write a process piece about a particular ceremony that is consistent in thought with Hogan's essay.
2. Write a process piece about gratitude and a feeling of interdependence written from any perspective other than Native American.
3. Write about the interdependency Hogan considers.
4. Write about the American Thanksgiving in terms of its original idea and current practice.

5. Discuss the relevance of Hogan's statement "This is the vulnerable land shared among us" to current environmental problems.
6. Discuss how the Native American Thanksgiving as presented by Hogan is different from the American Thanksgiving.

GRANDMA'S TAMALES*

Yvette Lohayza

Student Yvette Lohayza writes about the collaborative activity of her Hispanic family preparing tamales for Christmas.

Every Christmas Eve at Grandma's house is an eventful moment to remember. 1 Christmas Eve is the time for Grandma to make her wonderfully palatable tamales, which take several hours of preparation by all of the female family members.

This is a very warm and joyous time for all of the females of my Spanish 2 family—a time for bonding. The special things to be taken care of for this occasion begin at the break of dawn when the early morning air is cool and the morning dew is still very visible on the nearby plants. Grandma awakes us at five o'clock in the morning with a freshly brewed pot of coffee and some *dulce.*[1]

Soon after our coffee, we drive off to a special market called the *mercado,* 3 where Grandma does all of the shopping for the tamales. First, she visits the butcher, whose name is Pepe. He is awaiting her arrival, just as he does every year. He has put aside his freshest beefsteaks just for Grandma. Grandma carefully chooses the reddest and the most visibly fat-free steaks available. According to Grandma, the meat must be bright red because this is a clear indication of its freshness, and its freshness is what the tamales depend on.

Next, we wander off to a section in the mercado where Grandma meticu- 4 lously searches through large piles of *ojas,* or corn leaves. Corn leaves are what is used to wrap and cook the tamales in. The size of the leaves is very important; they should be of only two sizes—large and medium. Before leaving the mercado, we stop at the canned-food section for what is known as *chili de las palmas,* a red sauce that is spicy and hot and is used to mix the meat after it has been steam-cooked. Finally, we visit a section of the market that prepares and sells *masa,* which is cornmeal. This will be used as the outer layer of the tamales to encase the inner meat portion.

---

[1]sweet bread

As soon as we arrive back home, at nearly eight in the morning, 5 Grandma, like a colonel, delegates duties to everybody present. Now begins the tamale preparation. Two twenty-five-gallon cooking pots are set atop the stove, filled with four inches of water, and warmed. Inside each pot is a wire rack that is mounted about four inches above the bottom of the pot. The tamales are placed on top of these racks for steam-cooking.

Next, the meat is boiled with a few cloves of garlic embedded in it for 6 taste. It will take approximately two hours before the meat is cooked. Meanwhile, the older women sort out the corn leaves, large from medium, as the younger girls wash them and put them in separate stacks to dry. By the time the leaves have dried, the boiled meat is ready for shredding. Grandma watches over our shoulders while we work, laboriously shredding the meat very fine with our bare hands. The aroma of the freshly shredded meat fills the kitchen and the ambience becomes cheerful.

Once the meat has been shredded, the chili sauce, and perhaps some 7 olives, are added and mixed. After the meat is thoroughly mixed, the leaves are set in two piles, large leaves on the left and medium leaves on the right of the six-foot-long table. At this point everybody uses a butter knife to spread masa on the corn leaves. A large leaf is placed on the bottom and masa is spread thinly but generously over it.

Next, a couple of heaps of meat are forked up and spread atop the masa. 8 After this is done, the medium leaf is also topped with a thin but generous layer of masa and placed over the larger leaf, which is filled with the meat. Carefully, we roll the edges of the larger leaf over the edges of the medium leaf to seal the tamale, so that no meat leaks out while it is cooking. This continual spreading and rolling of the tamales will go on for the next two to three hours.

Once all of the tamales have been rolled, they are carefully stacked in the 9 large cooking pots and a wet hand towel is placed on top of the tamales to trap the steam while they are cooking. Four to six hours of steam-cooking will pass before the tamales are ready for consumption, By this time we will all have insatiable appetites and will be ready for this well-deserved meal.

Critical Thinking and Discussion

1. Is this process analysis mainly directive, informative, or a combination?
2. What preparation must be done? Why must it be done with care?
3. What are the steps?

Reading-Related Writing

1. Write about one of your family meals in which you join with others in the preparation and serving.

2. Write about any project—building a house, painting, roofing, landscaping, repairing a car, planning a block party, coaching, directing youth activities, managing a church or temple—that involves cooperation between friends, family members, or neighbors.

Collaborative Learning

1. Make a list of all the cultures in your class and establish committees to organize a multicultural holiday—a Thanksgiving, a New Year, or one that you invent. Select ethnic foods for the meal—salads, soups, appetizers, main courses, desserts, and drinks (before, during, and after the meal). Then make a list of ethnic activities, especially dances, music, and games. Next invent, adapt, or borrow ceremonies or rituals. Finally, combine these elements in a report, using collaborative techniques as directed by your teacher. If time and other circumstances permit, celebrate the holiday, complete with food, song, and activities, and invite other classes or friends.

2. Divide the class into four groups, with each selecting a reading from this chapter showing process, especially a ceremony, that reveals much about a particular culture. Then concentrate on that reading, probing for what it reveals about such ideas as family, mature, religion, and philosophy. A single group may choose more than one reading; for example, several readings reflect Hispanic perspectives. Readings especially appropriate for this activity include "Grandma's Tamales," "Kwanzaa," "Japanese Tea Ceremony," and "Thanksgiving."

Connections

Write about the holiday(s) that have the most cultural significance to you. Comment on how they have been altered by time and by exposure to other cultures. Compare and contrast your holiday with some of those described in this chapter.

6

Youth in Crisis

The topic of this chapter, youth in crisis, embraces much more than cultural groups. But because when trouble hits, certain cultural groups are likely to take the heaviest blows, it is an appropriate topic for this book. The eleven readings in this chapter cover the topics of school dropouts, suicide, immaturity, eating disorders, age discrimination, violence on campus, guns, girls and crime, divorce, child abuse, and drugs. All of these issues relate significantly to the young.

WRITING STRATEGIES AND TECHNIQUES: CAUSES AND EFFECTS

Causes and effects deal with reasons and results; they are sometimes discussed together and sometimes separately. As with other forms of writing to explain, your thought processes are basic to writing about causes and effects. The shortest, and arguably the most provocative, poem in the English language—"I/Why?"—poses a causal question. Children are preoccupied with delightful and often exasperating "why" questions. Daily we encounter matters of causes and effects. The same subject may raise questions for both:

CAUSE: The car won't start. Why?

EFFECT: The car won't start. What now?

At school, from the biology lab to the political science classroom, and at work, from maintaining relationships to changing procedures, causes and effects are pervasive.

Determining Your Purpose

Your purpose in analyzing by causes and effects will probably be to inform or persuade. Usually your work will emphasize either causes or effects. Your initial exploration of ideas will allow you to decide on that purpose and emphasis, as is appropriate for accommodating your interests and background and for meeting the assignment.

Freewriting on an idea that appeals to you will reveal your knowledge and interest, perhaps along with some possibilities for development.

Brainstorming will give you more specific information. In this strategy you should emphasize the *why?* part (for causes) and add a *what happened?* or *what happens?* part (for effects).

Then comes the most important strategy in your exploration of ideas: the *clustering*. For causes and effects, begin with a double bubble for your subject (the situation, circumstance, or trend), and then arrange bubbles to the left for causes and to the right for effects. Consider the partial cluster on "Joining a Gang" shown in Figure 6.1. You will note that

Figure 6.1   A Partial Cluster

"Joining a Gang" is not the effect; it is the subject. As a subject, it can have both causes and effects, which are both sets of emphases. Thus the *subject* is what you are writing about; your *emphasis* will be on causes, effects, or a combination of both; and your *purpose* will be to inform or persuade.

It is at this point in your writing that you will decide whether your topic should mainly inform or mainly persuade. If you intend to inform, your tone should be coolly objective. If you intend to persuade, your tone should be subjective. You should consider the views of your audience as you phrase your ideas. You should also take into account how much your audience understands about your topic and develop your ideas accordingly.

Composing the Topic Sentence or Thesis

Now that you have ideas lined up on either side of the double bubble, you are ready to focus on causes, on effects, or, occasionally, on both.

Your topic sentence or thesis statement might be one of causes: "People join gangs for three main reasons." Later, as you use the idea as a topic sentence in a paragraph or a thesis in an essay, you might rephrase it to make it less mechanical, allowing it to become part of the flow of your discussion. If you want to personalize the work—thereby probably making it more interesting—you could write about someone you know who joined a gang. And you could use the same basic framework, indicating why this person joined a gang.

Your selection of a topic sentence or thesis takes you to the next writing phase: organization. There you need to consider three closely related points.

Considering Kinds of Causes and Effects

Both causes and effects can be primary or secondary, immediate or remote.

Primary or Secondary

Primary means "major," and *secondary* means "minor." A primary cause may be sufficient to bring about the situation (subject). For example, infidelity may be a primary (and possibly sufficient by itself) cause of divorce for some people but not for others, who regard it as secondary. In another example, if country X is attacked by country Y, the attack itself, as a primary cause, may be sufficient to bring on a declaration of war. But a diplomatic blunder regarding visas for workers may be of secondary importance and, though significant, certainly not sufficient to justify starting a war.

Immediate or Remote

Causes and effects often occur at a distance in time from the situation. The immediate effect of sulfur in the atmosphere may be atmospheric pollution, but the long-range, or remote, effect may be acid rain. The immediate cause of the greenhouse effect may be the depletion of the ozone layer, whereas the long-range, or remote, cause is the use of CFCs (commonly called Freon, which is found in such items as Styrofoam cups). The ultimate cause may be the people who use the products containing Freon.

Evaluating the Importance of Sequence

The sequence in which events occur may or may not be significant. When you are dealing with several sequential events, determine whether the sequence of events has causal connections. Specifically, does one cause bring about another?

Consider this sequence of events: Joe's parents get divorced, and Joe joins a gang. We know that one reason for joining a gang is family companionship. Therefore, we may conclude that Joe joined the gang in order to satisfy his need for family companionship, which he lost when his parents were divorced. But if we do so, we may have reached a wrong conclusion, because Joe's joining the gang after the family breakup does not necessarily mean that the two events are related. Maybe Joe joined the gang because of drug dependency, low self-esteem, or a need for protection. In examining the whole situation, we may discover that other members of his family, going through the same family turmoil, did *not* join gangs.

In each case, examine the connections. To assume that one event following another is caused by the other is called a *post hoc* ("after this") fallacy. An economic depression may occur after a president takes office, but that does not automatically mean that the depression was caused by the new administration. It might have occurred anyway, perhaps in an even more severe form. (See Chapter 10 for more information on flawed reasoning.)

Order

The order of the events you discuss in your paper will be based on time, space, emphasis, or a combination of these:

- *Time:* If, as in the case of a paper discussing the causes and effects of upper-atmosphere pollution, one stage leads to another, your paper would be organized best by time.
- *Space:* In some instances, causes and effects are best organized by their relation in space. For instance, the causes of an economic recession could be discussed in terms of local factors, regional factors, national factors, and international factors.
- *Emphasis:* Some causes and effects may be more important than others. For instance, if some causes of divorce are primary (perhaps infidelity and physical abuse) and others are secondary (such as annoying habits and laziness), a paper about divorce could be organized from secondary to primary in order to emphasize the most important causes.

In some instances, two or more factors (such as time and emphasis) may be linked; in that case, select the order that best fits what you are trying to say, or combine orders.

Introducing Ideas and Working with Patterns

The introduction of your topic, whether in a topic sentence and its appropriate context for a paragraph or in an introductory paragraph with a thesis for an essay, will almost certainly perform two functions:

1. *Discuss your subject.* For example, if you are writing about the causes or effects of divorce, begin with a statement about divorce as a subject.
2. *Indicate whether you will concentrate on causes or effects or combine them.* That indication should be made clear early in the paper. Concentrating on one—causes or effects—does not mean you will not mention the other; it only means you will emphasize one of them.

The most likely pattern for your work is one of those shown in Figure 6.2.

Figure 6.2   Patterns for Paragraph and Essay

FOR PARAGRAPH

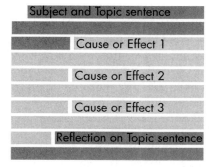

FOR ESSAY

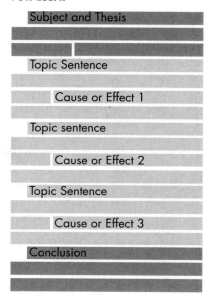

The following student-written paragraph and essay illustrate effective uses of causes and effects.

DEATH BY GANGBANGING*

Aida Gonzales (pseudonym)

topic sentence

causes

He was one of seventeen killed in one gangbanging weekend in a place called "the city of angels." Lying there in the casket, he looked peaceful, as he left behind a world of violence and turmoil. *Sorting out the causes of his becoming a gang member is not easy.* He got off to a bad start because his father was a gang member. Once when a very naive teacher tried to tell the father that his son might be a gang member, he said, "My kid's not a gang member. He's just a wannabe. I'm a gang member." The young man idolized his father, and when his father was killed at a party, the family tradition of gang membership didn't die. A few years later the young man would resent the stepfather who came into his home, and, in turn, the stepfather was unkind. Then fights started between the neighborhood gang and the young man. Finally he laughed and said, "If you can't beat'em, join'em." And he did. He said he found family and protection there. He wasn't bad. Deep down he had good feelings, and he could be funny and warm. He just had too much going against him. I should know. I'm his mother.

GROWING UP WITH DRUGS AND ALCOHOL*

Sergio Ramos

The use of drugs and alcohol from grade school through 1 high school has been a major concern in recent years. Myriads of young kids turn to stealing for the means of satisfying their addictions. The high school drop-out rate is at an all-time high across the nation, and one of the main causes is alcohol and drug abuse. Most of the convicts in prison were locked up because of drug-related crimes. The repeated use of drugs and alcohol at an early age sets a pattern and leads to failure during adulthood; that's what happened to some of my close friends.

thesis

I had a friend named Gerardo who drank beer and 2 smoked marijuana when he was in the fifth grade. He was influenced by his older brother Luis. The only thing that Gerardo talked about at school all day was that he could not wait to get home to smoke marijuana with his brother in their clubhouse. I lived next door, and I would usually go over to watch them get high. They constantly attempted to convince me to try it, but to their dismay, they always failed. Once it was time for Gerardo to do his homework, he would eagerly ask me for help. When Gerardo was sent to the store to buy items for his mother, he would usually steal the items and keep the money to buy beer or marijuana.

effects

When I got to junior high school, I really began to 3 notice the heavy use of drugs and alcohol. I saw students "snort" cocaine behind their open books in class while the teachers wrote notes on the board. I also saw students smoking angel dust on the physical education field during lunchtime. They brought alcoholic beverages on campus and many students smoked a joint before their classes began. Most of these youngsters eventually were caught and expelled from school. Luis was a football player in high school while Gerardo and I were in junior high. Luis "snorted" half a gram of cocaine before every game he played. Gerardo had begun to sniff typewriter correction fluid just for fun.

Once when we were in the eighth grade, we decided that we were going to smoke a marijuana cigarette with two girls from school. After school, at the clubhouse, we could not find the joint we had promised the girls. I felt extremely happy that I was not going to go through with it. Then the two girls began to get upset, and said that we had lied to them. Gerardo immediately handed each of them a sandwich bag with typewriter correction fluid inside. After the three of them began inhaling the substance, they began behaving erratically. Then one of the girls, whom I had an extremely strong crush on, handed me her bag and asked me to try it. I had never felt peer pressure as strong as I did that day. I hesitated at first, but after she moved close and kissed me, I felt obligated to try. It was the worst hallucinating effect I have ever experienced. Gerardo began crawling on the ground because he could not walk, and we all laughed at him.

Luis and Gerardo both dropped out of high school because of their addiction to drugs. They both became crack addicts, and Luis was also an alcoholic. Gerardo ended up in prison for robbery, which he did often in order to support his expensive drug habit. After his release, he went through counseling and treatment, and he was able to stop smoking crack, but he still drinks beer and smokes marijuana. Luis remains a crack addict and an alcoholic. He continues to live at home, and he refuses to get treatment for his disease. Working as a security guard, he spends his entire paycheck on drugs and alcohol. These are only two examples of the tragedies that exist all across this nation.

[margin annotations: effects; effect; cause; effects; effects]

[margin numbers: 4; 5]

WRITER'S CHECKLIST

- State your subject (situation, circumstance, or trend) specifically.
- Clearly indicate your intention of writing about causes, effects, or a combination, and repeat key words, such as *causes, effects, reasons, results, consequences,* and *outcomes.*
- In selecting the causes, effects, or both, for the main thrust of your paper, usually select immediate over remote and primary over secondary causes and effects.
- Organize your work for coherence by using the principles of time, space, or emphasis.
- Be consistent in tone (how you want to treat your topic and your readers—objectively, humorously, persuasively, indignantly, or ironically).
- Avoid pitfalls in logic such as the *post hoc* fallacy (A follows B; therefore, A is caused by B).

WHY KIDS QUIT SCHOOL

David Levine

Every day, somewhere in America, three thousand high school students give up—for good. They push open the doors and walk out. Why do they do it? In this paragraph from his Seventeen *article "I'm Outta Here," David Levine offers six causes.*

Within this larger puzzle are the individual pieces—the reasons why kids quit school. According to the Department of Education, there are six things that put students at higher risk. They include having a dropout sibling, coming from a single-parent family, coming from a household with an income below $15,000, being home alone more than three hours a day, not speaking English well, and having parents who didn't finish high school. What makes any student actually quit is harder to assess. Caroline Abbott, sixteen, who lives in Charlotte, North Carolina, never stopped going to school entirely, she just missed a lot of days. "I'd sit home, go to a friend's house," she says. "A good friend of mine dropped out, and I wanted to, too. I just wanted to be with her."

Critical Thinking and Discussion

1. What is the topic sentence?
2. Is this mainly a paragraph of causes or effects?

3. What are the causes?
4. Why is it hard to assess what makes a particular student quit?

Reading-Related Writing

1. Write about someone you know who quit school. Concentrate on the causes.
2. Write about someone you know who quit school. Concentrate on the effects.
3. Write about someone you know who quit school for reasons that were cultural (attitude, prejudice, obligation, tradition, conditioning, language barriers, or some other reason).

THE CAUSES OF TEEN-AGE SUICIDE

David Shaffer

Although suicide among youths is alarming, David Shaffer says it does not typically occur among all groups. Instead, he explains, suicide victims can be classified according to types of people who are suicide-prone. These types of people experience the same kinds of situations that we all do, but because of their psychological states, they react differently.

As I have focused my professional life on the mental state—the thoughts and feelings—of suicidal teen-agers over the years, I have been struck by the fact that teen-age suicide victims do not represent a cross-section of the population. Rather, they fall into a small number of groups. The largest is a group of unpredictably aggressive, hotheaded males, who lose control with very little provocation. A second group is quite different: teen-agers who are chronically and irrationally anxious, and who may commit suicide just before some feared event. A third group consists of teen-agers who are simply clinically depressed; they see no good in themselves, and feel hopeless about the future.

Critical Thinking and Discussion

1. According to Shaffer, what are the three groups of individuals who are suicide prone?
2. Which group is most likely to get attention prior to a suicide attempt?
3. Assuming that each group needs therapy, what kind of help would you offer to each group?

Reading-Related Writing

1. Select one group of suicide-prone teens and elaborate on the characteristics of its likely members.
2. Discuss any ethnic, cultural, class, or gender circumstances that might make a group or groups suicide prone and perhaps even difficult to help with therapy.

A TIME FOR JUVENILES

Eric Hoffer

A self-educated former dock worker, Eric Hoffer became a well-known social historian and critic. His most famous work, The True Believer, *discussed the personality makeup of the extremist. Here, he writes of the young we read about in history—those who lived at a time when teenagers were not only in turmoil but also in charge.*

The history of less ancient periods, too, reveals the juvenile character of their chief actors. Many observers have remarked on the smallness of the armor which has come down to us from the Middle Ages. Actually, the men who wore this armor were not grown-ups. They were married at thirteen, were warriors and leaders in their late teens, and senile at thirty-five or forty. Without some familiarity with the juvenile mentality and the aberrations of juvenile delinquency it would be difficult to make sense of the romanticism, trickery, and savagery which characterized the Middle Ages. Nor did things change markedly in the sixteenth century. Montaigne tells us that he hardly ever met a man as old as fifty. In the first half of the sixteenth century, Charles V became Holy Roman Emperor at the age of twenty, Francis I became King of France at twenty-one, and Henry VIII King of England at eighteen.

Critical Thinking and Discussion

1. What is the topic sentence of this paragraph?
2. What causes and effects are discussed?
3. In sentence 5, what does the author imply about juveniles?
4. What is the main difference between juveniles then and now?
5. What do you make of the omission of the role of women?

Reading-Related Writing

1. In your estimation, what would be the effects if juveniles were in charge now?
2. What problems of juveniles today can be traced to their lack of opportunity for leadership of even involvement?
3. Discuss the prevailing views held by several cultures on the proper role of juveniles in society. Include some comments on the causes and effects of those views.

I AM ANOREXIC*

Linda Johnson

The youth culture celebrates the young look—the kind that goes with trim, physically fit bodies of certain dimensions. In order to acquire that look, a person can't be overweight. It's a problem, and the person who thinks about it too much may acquire a psychological disorder such as anorexia or bulimia. Student Linda Johnson describes a lifelong condition that, despite her understanding of its causes and effects, is not going away.

My obsession with my weight has always been a factor in my life. My mother and her sisters have been overweight ever since I can remember. Even in elementary school, I associated being a mother with being fat. So I decided not to be a mother. In my teens I began comparing myself with other girls, and if they were thinner than I, I would go on a diet. But after a week or two, I would gain the weight back and feel even worse about myself. As time passed, the situation only got worse, and I started to make myself throw up the food I ate. I suffered from insomnia and became a very moody person. I told myself I wasn't bulimic because I didn't overeat and didn't make myself throw up very often. I started losing my friends because of my moodiness. Even my mother noticed a change in my personality. I didn't want to go anywhere, including school. Although I considered my mother my best friend because we could talk about almost anything, I just couldn't talk to her about this because she was overweight, and I didn't want to offend her. Then one day I realized my obsession was controlling my life, so I told myself I had to stop, and I did. Now, five years later, it's starting all over again. I find myself doing those same things. I weigh myself about five times a day, and if I wake up at night, I go straight to the scale to weigh myself. If I don't see what I want to see, I become depressed. I'm not happy, and everything seems to bother me. I can't focus on anything. I can be reading an article for school, and I'll start thinking of my weight. My husband doesn't understand why I can't get close to him, but I just don't feel good enough about myself. I'm afraid he will want to leave me. My obsession with weight and its effects causes a lot of fights between us. I guess I feel I'm going to lose him later in life if I do get fat, so I may as well lose him now and save myself the agony.

Critical Thinking and Discussion

1. What is the topic sentence of this paragraph?
2. Is this mainly a paragraph of causes or effects, or is it a balanced treatment?
3. In your estimation, is the preoccupation with slenderness an American issue or does it exist in all countries and cultures?
4. Why do you think Johnson was able to solve her problem temporarily but is unable to do so now that it has recurred?
5. What would you suggest that she do or consider?

Reading-Related Writing

1. Write about the causes within society (such as advertising) that promote the idea of slenderness.
2. There have been times in history when the fuller figure was more admired. Do a bit of research and write a piece about the causes of that view.
3. Write about eating and weight from culturally diverse points of view, or from any point of view other than mainstream America.

EMANCIPATED

Emelyn Cruz Lat

Seeking legal independence at seventeen is no easy task, regardless of the circumstances. A child of Filipino immigrant parents, Emelyn Cruz Lat yearned to be part of her American peer group, but her family wanted her to follow strict old-country rules. What occurred was conflict, arguments, and even physical abuse, and she sought help. Here she gives an account of the causes of her seeking emancipation and the effects.

I spent most of my adolescent years surrounded by policemen, social work- 1 ers, and counselors. I have been arrested, detained, and interrogated more times than I can remember. I wasn't a drug or criminal offender. I was a teenage runaway.

My parents were first-generation immigrants who had difficulty accepting 2 the fact that their daughter was becoming "Americanized." They tried to keep me a traditional Filipino woman by dictating exactly what my social life would entail. I, on the other hand, was trying to gain acceptance from my peers and wanted to do things like attend slumber parties and go out on dates.

There were heated, often hateful words exchanged. Sometimes there was 3 physical violence. The conflict, however, was always kept within the household walls and carefully concealed from our middle-class neighbors.

When I looked for help from the law, I was ignored. Ultimately, the law 4 functions as a form of damage control—protection is only offered after abuse has taken place. When I was fifteen, my father chased me out of the house. I ran off, barefoot, wearing only a nightdress. Luckily, I found my way to a friend's house for the night. The very next day, the police escorted me back home.

Shortly thereafter, I called the Alameda County Child Protective Services 5 and told a social worker that my father had beaten me. It took them almost a week to see me. By that time, my bruises had faded and were hardly noticeable. It was a catch-22. My father had no criminal record. I had no evidence. There was no case.

This scenario, with slight variations, repeated itself throughout the course 6 of my high-school years. Each time I looked to the law for help, I was treated more like the offender than the victim. Each time, jumbled thoughts filled my mind: This isn't fair. How can I fight this? Don't I have any rights? After all, I, too, am a person.

I came to see "youth rights" as an oxymoron—youths have almost no 7 rights, separate from their parents. I was treated as a nonperson, an extension of my parents' will. Some individuals, like my high-school counselor and my therapist, bent the rules to help me. With my counselor's efforts, I managed to maintain my 3.9 grade point average and gain entrance to the University of California at Berkeley. My therapist assisted me on his own time, allowing me to visit him free of charge.

On the whole, however, the system did not provide me with any real 8 assistance and gave me very few options. Everyone assumed that the problem was with me and not my parents.

When I was seventeen, I started the legal process of emancipation, which 9 would release me from my parents' custody. This procedure, far from simple, was one of the few options available to me under the law. I still needed my parents' consent, and if they refused, I would have been subject to a drawn-out court battle.

I finally emancipated myself only to find that I was unable to rent my 10 own apartment. Department stores and banks refused to extend credit to me, even though I had a job and was financially qualified. It became painfully apparent that society had no room for someone like me.

Even the yearly ritual of filling out financial-aid forms for college turned 11 into a great bureaucratic hassle. I didn't fit into their present category of an "independent" student (i.e., a student at least twenty-four years old, or self-supporting for five years or more).

In the end, I was able to make all my transactions through a network of 12 informal arrangements. I rented a room in a friend's house and asked relatives or friends for loans when money was short. I had to work three jobs and go to school full-time. I barely got enough sleep, and my social life suffered severely.

Social workers and policemen have been of little help. They urged me to 13 stick it out until I turned eighteen, to take advantage of my parents' financial support and make plans for college. I feel bitter and terribly wronged. They did not understand the pain and despair of my situation. Their system does not work for those it claims to help. At least it didn't work for me.

Recently, I graduated from college, after being on my own for six years. 14 Having lived most of my life under everyone else's conditions, I feel like I didn't just graduate—I survived.

Vocabulary

interrogated (1)
oxymoron (7)

Critical Thinking and Discussion

1. What is the thesis of this article? Is it expressed in a single sentence?
2. Does Lat stress the causes of her seeking emancipation, the difficulty of her achieving emancipation, or the effects of her achieving emancipation?
3. In what ways was she not protected by the law before she was emancipated?
4. How was she treated unfairly after she was emancipated?
5. To what extent was this a cultural issue and to what extent was it not?
6. At what point should young people be allowed to declare their financial independence from their parents?

Reading-Related Writing

1. Write a cause-and-effect piece about a situation you are familiar with concerning youth and parental rights.

2. Write about this situation as if you were Lat's father, now sorry for what he did, or as if you were her mother, who felt almost as powerless as her daughter.
3. Using information from this essay, discuss Lat's situation and characterize her as fully as you can.
4. Evaluate the processes used for evaluating Lat's situation within the family and as a student who needed financial aid.

CHILDREN OF DIVORCE

Anthony Brandt

We all know that divorce has an extreme effect on children. The extent of that effect has been studied by Judith Wallerstein, a coauthor of Second Chances: Men, Women, and Children a Decade After Divorce. *Anthony Brandt discusses Wallerstein's major findings.*

I asked Sharon,[1] who is 45, to describe her most vivid memory of her parents' 1 divorce. A specific image came immediately to her mind. "I remember my father framed in the doorway, leaving." She was five years old at the time. Right after that, her mother's new boyfriend and second-husband-to-be moved in.

Soon after this new arrangement was in place, Sharon had a nightmare 2 that would recur for years. "I dreamt that I was alone in the apartment and 'it' was coming after me," she says. "I never saw 'it,' though when I woke up in the dream, the beds were made but no one was there. The dream was so awful that at dusk I would start to get knots in my stomach, I was so afraid of going to sleep. I was terrified of being abandoned."

Sometimes Sharon would hide in closets to escape her fears. "But my 3 mother ignored the signs of distress," she says. "The fact is, her emotional energy was not focused on helping me and my brother adjust to the divorce. She was more interested in making her new relationship work." Sharon's mother and father each remarried within several years of their divorce, so there were stepparents in both of her homes. "I had the feeling that I didn't belong anywhere—that I never came first."

It has taken Sharon years of therapy to come to terms with all of this. She 4 has been through a divorce of her own, and has had a great deal of trouble getting started in any sort of career. "My parents' divorce drove me crazy half of my life," she says. "My mother and father made me feel responsible for

[1]These names have been changed.

them. The only way I could be OK was to make them feel OK." There is anger in her voice. "If it weren't for therapy, I wouldn't be doing anything at all with my life right now."

Sharon's emotional difficulties may seem extreme, but the situation in 5 which she found herself certainly is not. We all know the figures: If recent trends continue, fully 50 percent of marriages in this country will end in divorce. Compare that to a divorce rate of 30 percent in 1950, and you begin to see how dramatically the American family has been transformed over the past 40 years. In my own extended family, for instance, there was only one divorce in my parents' generation, and it so shocked my family that it was literally unspeakable. No one would talk about it; no one would even mention it. Today, at least four members of my generation have been divorced, including me, my brother, and two cousins, and no one is blinking an eye.

In the midst of this social revolution, we've also been fairly cavalier about 6 the effect that divorce is having on our children. Perhaps it's wishful thinking, or a kind of willed ignorance, but people tend to assume that while children certainly will be disturbed by the breakup of their parents, they'll adjust in time, and whatever emotional scars they've acquired will eventually disappear. Indeed this optimistic attitude was justified by what, until recently, was considered the major scientific study of divorce in this country. Conducted in the late seventies by E. Mavis Hetherington at the University of Virginia, the study found that while divorce did have a destabilizing effect on preschool children—both at home and in school—they generally recovered within a two-year period.

Considering the lifelong devastation that other family traumas, such as 7 child abuse or drug addiction, can cause, two years seemed like a manageable amount of time. Then along came Judith Wallerstein, executive director of the Center for the Family in Transition, in Corte Madera, California. In 1971 she began the longest running study in the country of the effects of divorce on children. She is the Columbus of her field, and the news she is bringing back from the world of divorce is sobering. Among her most shattering findings: Without adequate guidance and love, the psychological damage of divorce on children of all ages can be severe and longlasting. Furthermore, Wallerstein observed what she calls a "sleeper effect" of divorce; that is, even when children may seem to have adjusted quite well, it suddenly becomes clear, ten years later, that they have not. They hit some crisis point, often when romantic relationships become central in their lives, and all the fear and anger come back. Girls, especially, seem to suffer from this kind of delayed reaction.

The point that Wallerstein would like everyone to hear is not that parents 8 should feel guilty about their marital trouble, or even that they should stay together for the sake of the children. In fact, she feels strongly that an unhappy marriage can be just as harmful to a child as a divorce. But what parents often forget, she says, is that divorce is not a one-time event in the lives of their children: It lasts forever. Parents must realize that long after Mom and Dad have emotionally recovered, and perhaps even remarried, their children may still bear the scars of the divorce, and that tending to those scars—for as long as it takes—is something the adults must take responsibility for. Through the work she does at her family counseling center, and which she describes in her book (coauthored with Sandra Blakeslee), *Second Chances: Men, Women, and Children a Decade After Divorce*, Judith Wallerstein has set out to help parents do just that.

The Long-Term Effects

Human psychology is complicated, and the effects of divorce that Wallerstein 9 describes are diverse. But one thread runs through them all, she writes. "These children all say that their lives have been overshadowed by their parents' divorces and that they feel deprived of a range of economic and psychological supports. . . . They feel less protected, less cared for, less comforted." Many of them said that their parents' divorce marked the end of their childhood.

Children of high-conflict divorces suffer the most, but according to Wal- 10 lerstein, no one is totally immune. Teresa Peck, a clinical psychologist at Wallerstein's center, is conducting a research program in some of the local schools to investigate the relationship between divorce and adolescent underachievement. "What I've found is that 78 percent of the underachievers—kids with grade averages in the A–B range in the lower schools, who had fallen into the D–F range in high school—came from families of divorce, compared to only 30 percent of the achieving kids—those who maintained an A–B average consistently over the years," Peck explains. "And when you break the figures down by gender, boys did much worse. None of the male achievers came from families of divorce."

Underachievement is a way for kids to reach out to their parents for help, 11 says Peck. But it's also a way of showing anger: " 'You've messed up my life, so I'm just going to mess it up more to show you.' And these weren't delinquents. These were basically decent kids whose life had taken a turn they couldn't adjust to," she says. Nearly half of the boys in Peck's study continued to fare poorly after leaving school.

Wallerstein also found, in her long-term study, that boys didn't seem to 12 recover very well over time. Ten years after their parents' divorce, many of them were "unhappy and lonely, and had had few, if any, lasting relationships with women," she adds. A significant number of the girls, on the other hand, the same ones who seemed to have adjusted quite well to the divorce, were now suffering from the sleeper effect. Wallerstein explains that this typically occurs when "the man/woman relationship moves into center stage in their lives. All the ghosts rise from the basement at that point." Many of the women

Wallerstein observed destroyed their own relationships with men before they got too close, or simply did not want to get involved at all. Some became sexually promiscuous without forming attachments to anyone in particular.

Veronica, 25, is someone who's experiencing the sleeper effect with a ven- 13
geance. Her parents were divorced when she was six years old, and a year ago she would have said the divorce had no effect on her at all. "There were always conflicts between my parents, but I didn't think I had any scars." Recently, though, her boyfriend raised the issue of marriage, and all of a sudden she "started to panic." She even had an anxiety attack at a friend's wedding.

"I was totally unprepared for how difficult it was for me to trust him," 14
Veronica explains. Eventually she went into therapy, which brought it all back: her parents' divorce, her father's leaving the country for four years, her own insecurity at the time, her mother's emotional withdrawal. "I developed this fear back then that my parents weren't going to be there." Sometimes when her mother would go out for the evening, Veronica would call 911 in a panic, trying to find out if she had been in an accident. Today, Veronica says, she keeps putting off her boyfriend—apparently out of a similar fear of abandonment. "He tells me that he loves me and wants to marry me, but I just can't believe him. I have no trust at all. Marriage feels like an enormous, scary thing to me."

Separating with Sensitivity

Beleaguered parents who already feel bad about the breakup of their marriage 15
won't be eager, of course, to hear all this discouraging news. Indeed, critics often charge that Wallerstein simply makes people feel more guilty. But she insists that that's not her intention. In fact, she agrees with the conclusions of the seminal British study released to the press last June. For the first time ever, more than 17,000 children were observed over a period of several years, both before and after some of their parents had divorced. Researchers found that in the divorced families, the children were already suffering from behavioral and psychological problems long before their parents actually broke up.

These findings might seem to call into question the premise of Waller- 16
stein's study—that divorce itself is to blame for the problems children suffer when families split apart. Wallerstein, though, sees no contradiction whatsoever. "This just confirms what we've known all along, that trouble in the family doesn't begin the day the papers are filed. Divorce is simply the climactic event in the life of the unhappy family." But—and it is an extremely important but—even though she doesn't believe that parents who can't get along should stay together for the sake of the children, Wallerstein thinks that they "have to divorce better than they're doing. That's the whole issue."

In 1980, Wallerstein founded the Center for the Family in Transition 17
to do what no other agency in the country was doing: provide services

specifically designed for divorcing families and their children. For the last 11 years, every couple with children who's filed for a divorce in Marin County, California, has received a letter from Judith Wallerstein inviting them to come in and discuss their problems. "The center provides an educational and a counseling service combined," she explains. "It's based on the simple principle that if you're going to have a society where divorce is so accessible, you have an equal responsibility to provide services to help both the children and the parents."

Couples who seek help at the center are first counseled on how to get 18
through the actual divorce. Wallerstein believes that the manner in which a family separates can help determine the way everyone involved will adjust for years to come, so this is a pivotal part of the therapy. As she explains in *Second Chances*, the hardest, and perhaps the most important, task for parents who are breaking up is to give their children permission to love both of them equally. "Children need to feel that they have a right to their own feelings, and that they are not being asked to ally with one parent against the other." William Voltaire, a father of two in Sausalito, California, who used the center to help him through his divorce, found this to be a crucial first step. "It took plenty of time and reinforcement, but when my kids realized that they could have feelings that were independent of mine—if they were missing their mom, for instance, or wanted to spend an extra night at her house—and I would not feel betrayed, they began to relax."

Wallerstein also stresses how important it is for parents to present the 19
divorce as a rational solution to an unhappy situation—something meant to restore peace and order, not just break the family apart. Then, once the divorce is final, parents are advised on how to be as direct and detailed as possible about all the changes that will result from the split. And, Wallerstein adds, they must take an active role in the process. If a four-year-old is going to visit her father, for instance, Wallerstein suggests that the mother prepare her enthusiastically. If possible, call the father and find out where he plans to take the child, and talk about it with her ahead of time. Give her permission, in other words, to have fun. When the child returns, the mother should observe her to determine what would most help her to settle back in.

Voltaire calls it "mood reading." Many kids like to be greeted at the door, 20
for instance, while others need to be left alone for a while before reconnecting. Some of the children in Wallerstein's study would walk all around the house, touching the furniture just to make sure it was still there.

The point that Wallerstein cannot emphasize enough is that this vigilance 21
toward their children is something divorced parents will need to maintain indefinitely. Whether there's a new school in the offing, a move, new caretaking arrangements, or, perhaps the most traumatic of all, a new parental relationship, it is the parents' job—not the child's—to initiate discussion and try to smooth the way.

But what about parents who don't have access to Judith Wallerstein's 22
center? Wallerstein admits that she is "very, very worried about families in
America, since there just doesn't seem to be any commitment on the part of
society to taking care of the children of divorce." Hers is the only program of
its kind in the country, and even some of her funding for low-income families
has been cut. Wallerstein suggests that, whenever possible, a divorcing couple
seek some kind of counseling or consult books on divorce for ideas about
how to do it themselves. The first and most important step, though, is simply
to acknowledge that their children are hurting, and accept responsibility
for it.

At this point Wallerstein draws her encouragement from the children 23
themselves; most of them show marked improvement with the loving attention they receive at the center. What heartens her the most, though, is that
they haven't given up on the idea of the family: If anything, they just want to
do it better than their parents did. "These children want a family of their
own," Wallerstein says. "And they don't want their children to go through
what they went through, so above all, they don't want a divorce."

If our children are ready to learn from our mistakes, maybe we can, too. 24

Vocabulary

cavalier (6)
destabilizing (6)
traumas (7)

Critical Thinking and Discussion

1. To the children involved, what is more important, the causes of divorce
   or the effects of divorce?
2. What seems to be the common assumption about the effects of divorce
   on children?
3. At what point do children "get over" the pains caused by divorced
   parents?
4. What is the one common thread that runs through the lives of children of
   divorce?
5. To what extent is there a correlation between school achievement and
   being children of divorce?
6. What does Wallerstein mean by saying that people should "divorce
   better"?
7. How does one give a child "permission to have fun"?
8. Is Wallerstein mainly pessimistic or optimistic about society dealing with
   children of divorce?
9. Is this an antidivorce article? Explain.

10. Put the thesis of this article into your own words.
11. Is this article mainly about causes or effects? Explain.

Reading-Related Writing

1. Reduce this article to a succinct piece in which you emphasize the effects of divorce. Relate them to situations with which you are familiar.
2. Can there be multicultural factors involved in divorce or in subsequent remarriage? Discuss the possible effects on the children of divorce and explain how those effects can be softened.

A BOY AND HIS GUN

John D. Hull

Gun violence among teenagers is pervasive. Even Omaha has it. But until recently, many whites there thought it was an African-American problem. Then an incident occurred. John D. Hull, reporting for Time, *begins with a welter of causes and ends with a litany of devastating effects.*

Saying no to guns is still easy for any self-respecting teenager with a little 1
sense, but dealing with guys who do have guns is an excruciating business. Steve, 14, stopped walking home alone from school last year when many of his fellow seventh-graders at Hale Junior High started talking up guns. "Some guys just started to change. It became cool to say you could get a gun," he says. "Nobody messes with you if they even think you may have a gun." Polite, clean-cut and still displaying the awkwardness of adolescence, Steve says he lives in almost constant apprehension. "Oh boy, summer is really the worst," he says. "You always have to deal with troublemakers who will push you around for no reason, but now it's really scary. I know I look like a fool if I get in an argument and walk away, but these days it's too dangerous to fight."

Some days, guns are just a defense against boredom that comes from a 2
lack of guidance and direction. Asked to name a single hobby, Doug, who is remarkably guileless for a gunslinger, is stumped. He concedes the craziness of him and his classmates shooting at one another, but wonders how it could be any different. "Parents just don't understand that everything has changed," he says. "You can't just slug it out in the schoolyard anymore and be done with it. Whoever loses can just get a gun.

Doug looks for affirmation of his own violent impulses in such movies as 3 *South-Central* and *Boyz 'N the Hood*. He misses their point, embracing the life-style they portray rather than heeding any cautionary tale they offer. His favorite book is *Do or Die*, an account of the lives of gang members in Los Angeles. "If there were more books like that, I'd read a lot more," he says, without a hint of sarcasm.

Doug floors his Ford truck through a yellow light, turns sharply and then 4 slows, carefully checking out the other cars as he cruises the largely white working-class neighborhoods of Benson. He points to a light blue, wood-frame house. Dozens of pellet holes from two shotgun blasts scar the wall on either side of the front door. In the driveway, an elderly man tinkers with a blue Chevy Caprice, which is also riddled with holes. Doug drives by slowly, confident he won't be recognized. "We did that three months ago. Monday night about 2 A.M. me and six other guys just fired from the street." He shakes his head. "That old man's son has a problem with stealing cars." Doug puts an Ice-T disc on his car CD player and cranks up the volume. "There's a lot of rappers that make a lot of sense," he says. His friend Scott nods reverently. But neither Doug nor Scott can explain what the songs mean to them. While the lyrics may address inner-city issues, the tone resonates among white teen-agers like them simply because it's the angriest stuff on the market.

"Now, let's say we were going to shoot that house," says Doug, pointing 5 down the street. "Just about now I'd cut the lights and slow down. Then bang, bang, bang, and I'd punch it out of there." The truck lurches forward. Doug turns the stereo louder.

Most Omaha residents used to dismiss teenage gunplay as a problem 6 confined to the north side of Omaha, which is largely black and poor. That comfortable notion was shattered last August by a seven-minute fire fight among mostly white teenagers in Benson. "I've lived in this area all my life, and now boys are shooting at each other for the hell of it," says Bonnie Elseman, a single mother in the neighborhood. "I now realize that I owe the blacks in Omaha an apology for ignoring all the shootings because I thought it was just their problem. I could just weep for these kids."

Norman Johnson carries no gun anymore, but for a different reason. One 7 afternoon last May, as he rode in the backseat of his cousin's Ford Escort on a city street, a car pulled up and the occupants opened fire. "I was just laying in the backseat, you know, resting, when my friend says there's a car right on our tail. Next thing you know, I felt this incredible shock. No noise, just shock." A bullet slammed into the back of Johnson's neck, crushing two vertebrae. "I looked up, and I saw bullet holes in the window," he says, speaking in a raspy voice and pausing frequently to gasp for air. "I looked down at my body, and, well, I didn't feel anything."

Almost completely paralyzed from the neck down, Johnson, who is 6 feet 8
3 inches and 20 years old, spent the first month after the shooting on a
breathing machine. He lost 50 pounds. Between hours of physical therapy
each day, Johnson has had plenty of time to rethink his attitude toward guns.

The youngest of six and a high school dropout, Johnson drifted into 9
gangs for support and identity. Asked why he was shot, he says, "It's a long
story," which means someone was out for revenge. Recalling the streets, he
tries to cling to some of his former toughness. "I guess I was just in the wrong
place at the wrong time," he says. "It could happen to anyone." But that's not
enough. "Sometimes it's so hard," he whispers. "I get high temperatures and
real sweaty, and I get these pains." He breathes on his own through a hole in
his trachea, which a nurse closes with a plug when Johnson wants to talk. "At
first I wanted to die. Now I'm happy to be alive, but I just want to get more
feeling back." His voice is meek, beaten, almost hollow. When talk turns to
football and basketball, he makes gulping, swallowing noises. Among cards
and photos taped to the wall of his hospital bed, an old award certificate is
proudly displayed. It reads, BANQUET OF CHAMPIONS FOR LITTLE PRO BASKETBALL.
BOYS' CLUB OF OMAHA. 1984. "I always loved sports, you know. I mean I was
pretty good." He pauses for air. "I had speed," he murmurs. He is too tired to
continue. The nurse pulls the trachea plug so he can breathe.

Vocabulary

excruciating (1)   affirmation (3)
guileless (2)   resonates (4)

Critical Thinking and Discussion

1. Why do kids carry guns?
2. How knowledgeable are the kids interviewed by Hull?
3. What are the effects of gun violence?
4. Is gun violence, both in those who commit it and the victims, related to a single culture or several cultures?
5. How does the author use examples in order to show both causes and effects?
6. How successful is the last example (of Norman Johnson)? Explain.

Reading-Related Writing

1. Explain the effects of the presence of use of guns in your community or another community you know of.
2. Use examples from your own experience, from the media, or what you have been told to discuss the causes and effects of gun violence.

3. Present your solution to gun violence. Refer to this article for at least part of your support.
4. Write a piece in which you agree or disagree with the thesis of Hull's essay.

GIRL TROUBLE

Linda Stahl

The "weaker sex"? The "peacemakers"? Clinical psychologist Deborah Grisham Blair tells newspaper reporter Linda Stahl, "I see girls acting out violently in all groups that I treat. I see East End kids fighting with their parents, hitting, kicking, and getting into physical confrontations. I see girls using violent language and getting into nasty arguments with authorities at school. I didn't used to see girls like this. I really didn't."

On March 26 at 8:30 A.M., two girls walking to Cochran Elementary School   1
encountered two teen-agers breaking bottles in the street.

"I heard you wanna fight me," one of them yelled.   2

Fifth-grader Melissa Jenkins responded, "No, we've never seen you   3
before." With a swiftness she won't forget, one of the two strangers hit her in the jaw and shoved her to the ground. As the other grabbed her purse, she felt the shoulder strap snap. She ran to school with her friend, a second-grader, and told her teacher what happened. Soon Melissa was back in the 600 block of Shipp Avenue explaining it all to her mother, Jackie Beswick, and a 5th District Louisville police officer.

On the sidewalk, the three found Melissa's gum, perfume, lotions and   4
chap stick. They didn't find the purse or its other contents—$3, a collection of trolls, a key chain with an image of Melissa's favorite wrestler and a hairbrush. Her attackers, she explained, were girls, not boys. "I think they were 14 or 15 because they were bigger," said Melissa, who is 11.

"Now she is walking to school with an adult," said Melissa's mother, "And   5
like the school suggested, she's taking the long way on Hill Street where they have crossing guards that watch out for kids."

On Sunday, April 5, at 1 P.M., a 17-year-old Fern Creek High School   6
student who lives in the Newburg area decided to walk to a nearby Dairy Mart to get change for TARC fare. Her plan was to ride the bus to Bashford Manor Mall. She took a shortcut on Kranet Way between some apartment buildings. Suddenly five girls came around the corner of a building. One of them told the 17-year-old that she had heard she planned to stab her. The

17-year-old denied the accusation. "You know, it was 'he-said, she-said' stuff," the girl said, giving her version of the incident. "They beat me in my mouth and eye. They used their fists," she said.

Her mother, who works nights cleaning office buildings, and her father, 7
who works days fixing cars, also have a 6-year-old daughter. They are thinking about moving. "It's a crying shame when your kids can't go to the store without people jumping on them," the mother said. Her daughter didn't want their names used because she fears more attacks. The mother wasn't surprised that the attackers were females. "In this day and age, there's nothing to be surprised about. Too many of the kids out here are ruling their parents, or they don't know where their parents are. It's no surprise they think my daughter's face is a beanbag they can beat up on."

If you think being a neighborhood bully is the exclusive province of 8
troubled male adolescents, you're wrong, said Stanley Whitaker, who oversees discipline for the Jefferson County schools. If you think fistfighting is mostly boy behavior, think again, said Claudia Snider, a counselor at Hazelwood Junior High School in New Albany. "In the parenting class I teach, one of the things the parents are often surprised at is that we have more girls' than boys' fights in the junior-high age group. This fighting among girls has become more pervasive in the last five years," said Snider, who has been working with junior-high students for 17 years.

Traditionally, girls confined their aggressiveness to name-calling and say- 9
ing mean things to each other, while boys got physical. "Then they began to threaten each other with 'I'm going to kick your butt,' and more and more they began to fight—fistfight, scratch and pull hair. No weapons, thank God, but they jump at each other," Snider said. Professionals who work with juveniles can reel off story after story about girls settling disputes with fights.

But there is disagreement about whether the activity is increasing, getting 10
more notice because it's trickling down to a younger group or just being carried out more openly because of a loosening of traditional rules for girls' behavior. The Southern Indiana torture-slaying of 12-year-old Shanda Renee Sharer last January 11 also has provoked introspection about violence in the lives of girls today. Four girls ages 15 to 17 have been charged with her murder. While feuding and fighting were among problems that preceded the death of Shanda, say classmates at Hazelwood Junior High School, many local experts—including police, counselors and school personnel—see the case as far removed from the everyday violence they encounter.

Jefferson County, Kentucky, juvenile authorities dealt with 56 girls 11
charged with aggravated assaults in 1988. By 1991 the number had more than doubled, to 124. Jefferson County, Kentucky, school officials suspended 66 girls for assault in the 1988–89 school year; the number was 100 last school year.

The national picture shows an increase too. According to the FBI the ₁₂ number of girls under the age of 18 who were charged with violent crimes increased from 8,147 in 1987 to 9,803 in 1989. Some experts say that they think some fighting by girls goes unreported because both the public and police tend to view it differently.

Jewelle Taylor Gibbs, a scholar with the Joint Center for Political and ₁₃ Economic Studies in Washington, D.C., believes there is a surge in girls' violence, mainly in large cities. She sees many reasons for this, including a loosening of inhibitions about expressed feelings, more violence in the streets and the media, disintegrating family life and overt materialism that frustrates poor children. She also said some girls misinterpret sexual equality to mean that they should be as aggressive and violent as boys.

But some people caution against drawing conclusions about violent ₁₄ behavior among girls. Meda Chesney-Lind, director of the women's studies program at the University of Hawaii, said the statistics on delinquent girls are "volatile" because they are so small. She accuses the press of "periodically rediscovering the violence committed by girls," which she thinks has been at about the same level since the 1960s. "You really should focus on the heavy, heavy problems girls have—sexual abuse, physical abuse and other forms of victimization," Chesney-Lind said.

Critical Thinking and Discussion

1. What arguments are used by those who say violence by girls is not increasing?
2. What do FBI statistics show about the increase in violence by girls?
3. According to Jewelle Taylor Gibbs, what are the causes for the alleged increase in violence by girls?
4. According to your experience, are girls more violent now than they were ten years ago?
5. Are girls more violent than boys?

Reading-Related Writing

1. Discuss the causes of the increase in violence among girls and present some steps that should be taken by agencies such as the government and schools.
2. Discuss the causes of the increase in violence among girls and explain what parents can do to help their children avoid such problems.
3. Do you regard manipulation as a cause for the increasing violence among girls? Discuss this statement by social worker Valerie Johnson: "I think in a society plagued with so much abuse, there are women who know how

to manipulate a system that doesn't expect aggression from women. I think they learn very young."

4. How do you regard the idea of girls being emotionally different from boys as a cause of girls' violent acts? Is that stereotyping or just a good observation about female behavior? React to this statement by Valerie Johnson: "Girls are passion-filled and have emotion-filled outbursts. Males, oftentimes because of social modeling, aren't prone to be as vulnerable to being angry for long periods of time as girls. Girls tend to act with a heck of a lot more intensity."

ADD TEACHING TO HIGH-RISK JOBS

Donna Webster-Davis

There was a time when "high-risk jobs" were those associated with police and fire departments, military service, and high-wire trapeze acts. No more. The school, once a sanctuary where occasionally mischievous kids threw spit wads, is now under siege, and an important part of a teacher's job is to act as a police officer. Donna Webster-Davis left the Los Angeles school district last year; she now teaches English at Ayala High School in Chino Hills.

I read Thursday's news of the assault on a Pasadena teacher in the light of two   1
images that haunt me: a frantic colleague being gathered up and taken to the school nurse's office after being attacked by one of her failing students, and the anguish on my own students' faces at the announcement of a killing at the school's football bleachers during class time.

These images remain with me not only because of the horror of those   2
moments, but because they are encountered daily by teachers across the country.

The debate rages on as to why violence has invaded our schools: too   3
much television, provocative lyrics in music, the availability of guns. The experts argue—correctly, I feel—that living in this climate of violence desensitizes young people to the reality of pain and death. I am still waiting, however, for these experts to evaluate how this violence affects teachers and the way we do our jobs.

When I started teaching, at Crenshaw High School in South-Central Los   4
Angeles, I could not imagine a more fulfilling profession. I eagerly planned lessons and looked forward to getting my own classroom. I discovered that if I took the time to attend school functions, such as football and basketball games, my students would be more responsive in class. So I didn't mind

driving to away games and getting home late—it was part of my job. Many of my colleagues felt the same, and our social lives revolved around the school. I was transferred to Washington Preparatory High School, where the situation was the same. I found dedicated teachers happy to make the extra commitment.

That was eight years ago. I am not quite sure what has happened but I do 5 know this: Teachers are frightened. Part of attending extracurricular activities includes supervising students. Naturally, their safety comes first. I have "hit the deck" more than once at football games when the bleachers became targets for drive-bys. Consoling frazzled cheerleaders after crawling around in the sand and mud of the track loses its appeal quickly. Traveling on the school bus after the game with our heads buried in our laps until it is safe to come up for air is no joy ride, either. School dances often are one or two hours of fun squeezed in between the brawls that erupt for no real reason. As teachers, we are obligated to break up these fights, and the angry students often turn on us.

The classroom is no better. Even though high schools in Los Angeles 6 have metal detectors, students still carry weapons—and we know that in some cases, they plan to use them. In the teachers' lounge, we joke and say of students these days, "Hey, you can have an A, just don't shoot me!" I laugh, too. It is a way of releasing the immense stress that chips away at our professionalism. My colleagues complain of having nightmares about someone bursting into their classrooms and just "blowing everyone away." With this in mind, the old "duck and cover" earthquake drills we practiced when we were students weren't as silly as we thought. We hear students say that they will "cap" somebody if they are crossed, and while it may seem that they are kidding, we have to wonder.

All of this has to affect the way we teach. Maintaining classroom order 7 takes on a different meaning when the scales are tipped so against us. We aren't as willing to challenge a potentially violent teen any more, opting to call security and pray that the student is taken away, thus risking our credibility with other students because, to them, we appear sheepish. They don't want us to be afraid. They need us to be fearless. How else can they cope? It is a burden. Also, taking that extra interest in students by attending their concert or cheering them on at the game—interest that is crucial to their overall success— becomes a luxury we are too afraid to enjoy. Ultimately, the students lose.

I do not know the answers. I do know, however, that this trend cannot 8 continue. It is a strain to keep up a front of not being afraid. But why should students feel safe when we do not? How can they excel when we are too traumatized to do our jobs completely?

My colleague who was attacked by her student has moved on to what 9 she believes is a safer job: teaching English at a nearby prison. What does that say?

Critical Thinking and Discussion

1. Is this essay concerned mainly with causes or effects?
2. How do violence and the threat of violence affect teaching?
3. How are teachers affected individually?
4. What has happened to the teacher-student relationships as a result of violence?
5. How do the observations of Webster-Davis relate to your experiences?
6. Webster-Davis has no solutions. Do you? Discuss.
7. The author doesn't discuss multicultural tension in schools, though it is often mentioned in news accounts. To what extent is it a problem in schools you are familiar with and how might that tension be reduced?

Reading-Related Writing

1. Write a piece about the safety and security of a school you have attended. Use some specific examples.
2. Write a proposal in which you present some solutions to school violence.
3. Write about how you or people you know have been affected by violence or the fear of violence in schools.
4. Write about how racial tension often contributes to an unsafe atmosphere in schools.
5. In violent incidents in which racial tension was a factor, explain how it might be reduced.

THE STORY OF AN ABUSED BOY*

Glen Perkins (pseudonym)

No doubt Glen Perkins was regarded by some—his peers, the police, school personnel—as one who was too free. They very naturally were concerned with effects, but here Perkins concentrates on why he became what he is, and those causes go back to the first twelve years of his life and the abuse he experienced. Perkins is now a college student and is performing well in his studies, yet his experiences have left him with persistent problems.

How can parents put their children through pain, instead of protecting and nurturing them? There is no answer. I continue, even today, almost ten years later, to ask this question regarding my childhood. Rather than focusing on why or how my parents did this to me, I would rather focus on how the abuse shaped my personality and how it still affects my life. At times, I use my parents as scapegoats for the problems I inflict upon myself, but there are inescapable connections between my being abused and my becoming the person I am. Wanting to put my life in order, I have thoroughly categorized the characteristics attributed to my abusive past, along with the ways I have begun to deal with them.

I was abused, both physically and mentally, until I reached the age of 2 twelve. At that point, I began running away from home. Then I continued the abuse to myself that my parents had ended, with drugs. Because of generous friends and the connections I made, drugs were always available. I started on speed at age thirteen, then gradually progressed to stronger, more addictive drugs—cocaine, PCP, and so on. When I hit 16, my life was spiraling out of control, and it took the loss of my best friend to make me pull myself out. I began attending Narcotics Anonymous (N.A.). Getting out seemed impossible. I was so terrified of withdrawal that I twice tried to end it all. It took waking up in a hospital with a tube down my throat and machines all around to make me realize that I had to get out to prove to myself and everyone else that I could do it. Another motive was that I had to prove to my parents I could survive without them. Well, I succeeded. I cleaned up and returned to school, and I have continued pretty well up until this very day, four years later.

The abuse and neglect, though, had an impact upon me that I may never 3 surpass. One problem is that I'm afraid of falling in love or even really caring about someone. I find that if I truly begin to care, then this person I care about will begin to treat me just as did those I loved the most—my parents. Therefore, I tend to dissociate myself from those I care for, which hurts, but not nearly as intensely as the hurt which they may be capable of. This way of thinking is related to lack of trust. I'm not capable of trusting those I love with intimacy, with personal, delicate information about myself. I don't believe any woman can honestly love me for being me and not out of sympathy.

The worst trait attributed to my past, which I'm most concerned about 4 changing, is that I can become very violent, but only toward men. When I rage, my first intent is to hit, kill, or destroy something or someone. I must control it before it destroys all that I've accomplished.

The final childhood-earned trait is my low self-opinion. I do not honestly 5 feel that any woman deserves to become involved with someone of my stature. I am a loser, a degenerate, a freak, whatever. I don't wish to inflict my "disease" upon my worst enemy.

As insane as it may appear, there are some traits I attribute to my abusive 6 past that cause me to stand apart from society. I feel they make me a better person, but not a good one. First is that I'm very open and tolerant toward other peoples of the world. I sympathize with those who have struggled to accomplish what they have. Whether they struggle because of race, nationality, or just being in an unconventional environment, I respect them all equally. It is what I expect. The only people who treat me well, though, are those who can identify with my past. The other thing I find positive is that I have learned to be self-reliant, which means doing for myself. I'm proud of my accomplishments because I did it for me. If I had done it for somebody else, then I would not have made it this far.

To put a child through what I've been through is the worst sin any parent   7
can commit. What they must have conceived of as minor or trivial drastically affected me as a child. I was lucky to survive. I have five friends who didn't, but now they are at peace with themselves—dead. At least I will not do to others what has been done to me, because the final consequence of my childhood goes back to family: I don't foresee having children, out of fear of becoming like my father. Although I really love both my parents, I have absolutely no respect for them. Maybe it's better that way.

Critical Thinking and Discussion

1. To what extent has Perkins been successful in dealing with the effects of the abuse he received?
2. To what extent has he been unsuccessful in dealing with those effects?
3. Who does he think understands him best?
4. In what way does he see himself as strong because of the abuse and its consequences?
5. What would you suggest he do for his own mental health?

Reading-Related Writing

1. Write a response to this essay in which you offer Perkins suggestions for coping with the effects he writes about. Use examples from what you have experienced, witnessed, or heard about.

MOTHER AT FIFTEEN*

Ana Reyes

Student Ana Reyes, writing about a friend, explains that having a baby at fifteen may produce effects that will not be recognized for several years or more.

Roxanne was only a fifteen-year-old sophomore in high school when she   1
became pregnant. Her boyfriend was the same age, but his emotional matu-

rity was even lower. While she was dealing with being pregnant, he was going out with his friends and getting into trouble, even having serious fights with other youngsters. The causes of her getting pregnant would be much simpler than the results.

Roxanne and her boyfriend had been dating since the eighth grade, and her boyfriend had always been the type to hang out with the guys. She told me that she often felt insecure and was afraid of losing him. Therefore, she began sleeping with him, thinking that he would love her more and want to spend more time with her. But her plan didn't work. He roamed and she became pregnant. After her pregnancy, she dropped out of regular school and enrolled in home studies. Soon she was living with a daughter named Jessica and working for the school district, making $4.25 an hour. While Roxanne left her daughter every day at home with her mother, the father of the child did nothing but get into trouble with the law and even his family. Roxanne was not emotionally ready for her role as a mother, so Roxanne's mother took on the duty of raising Jessica.

Roxanne is not alone in becoming a young teenage mother. Many young girls are getting pregnant because they don't know any better. They have parents who don't emphasize enough that raising a child is difficult. However, many teenagers are careless and think of nothing but having fun. They believe that by sleeping with their boyfriend and getting pregnant, they will establish a bond, but love and affection require a stronger foundation. Others like the attention they get for being pregnant while so young, or they feel lonely and want someone to love them. They may feel that there is no hope ahead and that having a baby is one way of making a statement. But in most cases, if the teenager gave any thought whatsoever to motive, the baby does not fulfill the need the teenager had when she became pregnant.

A lot of times, when the teenage mother becomes an adult who was never really around for her baby while the baby was growing up, their relationship becomes distant. As for my friend Roxanne, she never concentrated enough on raising her daughter alone. And now that she is twenty years old and her daughter is five, she wants her daughter to listen to her and do what she says. But Jessica has been raised by her grandmother, whom she considers her mother. She calls her grandmother "mom" and Roxanne "Roxanne." When Roxanne tries to make Jessica refer to her as mother, Jessica just laughs as if Roxanne were joking, or she starts to cry when Roxanne becomes angry.

Teenage pregnancy has always been a big issue, especially in the past several years. During the times Roxanne and I have talked about raising a child at such an early age, she has said that she often regrets having a child. She says if she could go back and do it again, she would completely change her life. Far too often, that is what happens. The person regrets having a baby, and it is really sad because the baby is not at fault, and will often have a difficult time growing up.

Critical Thinking and Discussion

1. Is this mainly an essay of causes or effects, or is it balanced?
2. What was the main cause of her pregnancy, according to Roxanne?
3. What were the immediate effects of the teenage pregnancy and what were the long-range effects?
4. Who suffered more in this, the child or the mother?
5. In what way is Jessica fortunate?

Reading-Related Writing

1. The problems of teenage pregnancy and unwed motherhood exist in all cultures in America. Discuss these problems in relation to one culture or in relation to different generations in one culture.

Collaborative Learning
Project 1: *60 Minutes*

First Stage

Divide the class into small groups. One group will represent the producers of *60 Minutes,* and the other groups will represent the staffs of reporters (such as Mike Wallace, Ed Bradley, Leslie Stahl, and Morley Safer). In some fair and reasonable way, choose one reading (or two, if they are on the same topic) for each reporter group and make plans to present it as the subject for a segment on *60 Minutes.* The entire hour of an upcoming program will be devoted to "Youth in Crisis," but there will be space for only three or four topics. (Use a different number if you like, depending on the size of your class and the number of groups, but make the exercise competitive, as it is in the news business.) The objective of each reporter group will be to sell its idea to the producer group.

Cover these points:

- What is the basic content of your piece?
- Why is your piece relevant?
- Why is your piece highly significant?
- What would be the opportunities for interviews (consider those who would be involved, such as teachers, counselors, police, parents, spouses, and so on). You might want to write out or even perform a sample segment.
- What would be the opportunities for some action or atmosphere shots?

Follow-up

Make the presentation. The producer group will ask questions, hold a "closed-door" meeting, and then announce its decisions, perhaps with guidelines and restrictions.

Another Possible Follow-up

Write scripts and film some segments. Involve the producer group as you choose.

Writing Component

Write about the segment or activity you were involved in or, as a group, write about your segment or the whole procedure.

Project 2: Mock radio or television interview

Divide into groups of no more than five persons each and proceed in this fashion:

1. Thoroughly discuss one piece in this chapter. Avoid selecting a piece chosen by another group.
2. Choose one member of your group to pose as one of the individuals written about or referred to in the piece.
3. Interview that person. You may merely ask questions, or you may offer advice. The individuals asking questions may also be posing as someone else, perhaps as another person mentioned in the article or as a person who would naturally be involved in the issue being discussed in the piece. Be creative.
4. You may want to rehearse this interview and make a presentation to the class.
5. Write up an account of this project, either individually or collaboratively, as directed by your instructor.

Connections

1. Write your own evaluation of the problems of growing up in the 1990s. Include suggestions for easing the problems. Refer to readings in this chapter. The topics for the readings are school dropouts, suicide, immaturity, eating disorders, age discrimination, violence on campus, guns, girls and crime, divorce, child abuse, drugs, and teenage motherhood.
2. Prepare a time capsule for the year 2099. Along with various artifacts, include an essay entitled "Growing Up in the 1990s Was Not Easy." In the essay, refer to at least four of the sources in this chapter.

7

Families: For Better or Worse

*D*efinitions of abstractions are never easy. For example, by the time one broadens the definition of a poem to include every expression one wants to call a poem, nothing very definitive remains. The same can be said of *family,* if one is to consider the common use of the word. Traditional American families are under enormous pressure. Ian Robertson points out in *Sociology* that "one in every five American births is to an unmarried mother, usually a teenager. The number of unmarried couples living together has tripled in less than two decades. Americans are staying single longer than ever, and more than one adult in five now lives alone. About half of American marriages are expected to end in divorce." After also factoring in the issues of sexual preference, adults-only units, and various religious, cultural, and philosophical considerations, one comes up with many variations and classes. This collection of readings is concerned with families in that broad sense.

WRITING STRATEGIES AND TECHNIQUES: DIVISION AND CLASSIFICATION

Division and classification are similar in that they analyze, but they are different in that division separates a unit into parts (for example, the parts of a clock), whereas classification creates groups organized according to a common characteristic (such as types of students according to intention: vocational, academic, and specialty).

If you need to explain how something works or exists as a unit, you will write a paper of division, also called a functional analysis. You will break down your subject into its parts and explain how each part functions in relation to the operation or existence of the whole.

Moving from Subject, to Principle, to Division, to Relationship

Almost anything can be analyzed for function—for example, how the parts of the ear work in hearing, how the parts of the eye work in seeing, or how the parts of the heart work in pumping blood throughout the body. Subjects such as these are all approached with the same systematic procedure.

Step 1.   Begin with something that is a unit.
Step 2.   State the principle by which that unit functions.
Step 3.   Divide the unit into parts according to that principle.
Step 4.   Discuss each of those parts in relation to the unit.

This is the way you might apply that procedure to a leaf:

Unit	leaf
Principle of function	food manufacturer
Parts based on the principle	(1) the blade (including the food-making cells, the veins, and the molecules of chlorophyll) and (2) the petiole (the stalk by which the leaf is attached to the stem of the plant)
Discussion	an explanation of how each part contributes to the manufacturing of food

A leaf can represent another concept: you could say a leaf is a beautiful object. In this case, you would follow the same procedure, but the particulars would be different.

Unit	leaf
Principle of function	beautiful object
Parts based on the principle	texture, shape, color
Discussion	an explanation of how the three parts function together to produce that which we call "beautiful object"

Those two approaches are equally valid. But if we mix them by applying more than one principle at a time, we will have an illogical functional analysis. For example, if we say that a leaf has a blade, a petiole, and the eye-catching color of a ripe tangerine, we will have trouble in performing a functional analysis.

The important point here is that subjects can often be considered from different perspectives according to function. A sound division must begin with that function clearly in mind. Institutions such as churches, governments, families, and schools can have different functions. So can art forms such as short stories, poems, plays, novels, and songs. A particular person can be analyzed according to all his or her functions collectively as an entity, or, more likely, according to a particular function—independent individual, worker, family member, or friend.

Order

Your organizational pattern for the functional analysis will vary, depending on the nature of the unit. Following are some considerations:

Time	Something may function in a sequential fashion, one thing naturally leading to another. You would analyze a legislature passing a law using time as an organizational pattern.
Space	If you were analyzing a baseball team in the fielding, or defensive, mode, you might begin with the pitcher and move to the catcher and then through the infield to the outfield.
Emphasis	The word *function* means working or moving toward an end, and the sequence (time) often provides order or coherence, but in some instances the parts will all function simultaneously. In that case, you may want to move from the most important to the least important or, more likely, from the least important to the most important. Although the first

part of any passage receives special attention, the last is the most emphatic.

Combination   Time and space, especially, can be combined for order.

The following student-written paragraph illustrates an effective use of division.

MAGIC JOHNSON*

Cyrus Norton

topic sentence

part 1: shooter

part 2: passes

part 3: rebounding

part 4: leader

Some National Basketball Association (NBA) players are good because they have a special talent in one area such as shooting, passing, or rebounding. Magic Johnson was great because he had talent in all of those areas and more. As a shooter, few have ever equaled him. He could slam, shovel, hook, and fire from three-point range—all with deadly accuracy. As for free throws, he led all NBA players in shooting percentage in 1988–89. While averaging more than twenty points per game, he helped others become stars. As the point guard (the quarterback of basketball), he was always near the top of the league in assists and was famous for his "no-look" passes, which often surprised even his teammates with their precision. A top rebounding guard is unusual in professional basketball, but Magic, at six feet nine inches, could bump shoulders and leap with anyone. These three qualities made him probably the most spectacular triple-double threat of all time. "Triple-double" means reaching two digits in scoring, assists, and rebounding. Magic didn't need more for greatness in the NBA, but he had more. With his everlasting smile and boundless energy, he was also an inspirational team leader. He always believed in himself and his team. When his team was down by a point and three seconds remained on the game clock, the fans looked for Magic to get the ball. Then they watched as "he dribbled once, he faded, he leaped, he twisted, and he hooked one in from twenty feet!" That was magic. That was Magic.

Classification

To explain by classification, you place persons, places, things, or ideas into groups or classes based on similar and dissimilar characteristics.

Observing Classification in Action

Consider this situation. José is taking a class, and his instructor tells him to write a paper of personal experience. He says he can't think of anything worth writing about. His instructor asks José if he works. José says yes, he does; he works in a department store as a salesperson. His instructor suggests that José write about his customers. Deep in thought, José begins. On an extremely bad day, he might write this:

3,042 Customers

I have been working at my job for three weeks now, and I have had three thousand forty-two customers. The first one was a woman. She said she was only looking, and she didn't buy anything. The next person was a young man, and he also said he was a looker, and he didn't buy anything either. Then the third one was shopping for sales, and she went through the merchandise and picked out three sale items and bought them. The fourth one was looking for a specific item; I showed it to her and she bought it. The fourth, a young girl, was also a looker. The fifth one . . .

Of course, if José were to write that way, he would produce a very long and very boring paper, and the instructor would be sorry he or she made the suggestion. On a better day, José might write this:

Sorting Them Out

the classification
class 1

I've had several kinds of customers at my job at Broadway. Specifically, I can divide most of them into three classes: the looking shoppers, the sales shoppers, and the special-item shoppers. The largest class is the *looking shoppers*. One can see them wandering around all over the store as if they were lost or maybe out for exercise. They stop for discoveries here and there, but they don't want to be bothered by salespersons. They're pretty harmless, except sometimes they bump into each other. And quite infrequently they buy something. The

class 2

next class, the *sales shoppers,* are the ones who have read the advertisements. They may even be carrying an advertisement with them, matching pictures and numbers with items. If a salesperson can help them get to the merchandise before someone else does, they're grateful; otherwise, get out of their way. They are single-minded and ruthless. Beware of verbal assaults and vicious bodily contact at the sales tables. The last group is class 3   my favorite. It is the *special-item shoppers*. They know what they want, but they would like good quality and a good price. They are usually friendly, and they are appreciative of good service. On a given day, one person may move from one group to another, and when the person does, his or her behavior changes. After serving more than three thousand customers, I can identify and classify them almost immediately.

The difference between the two efforts is remarkable. The first considered thousands of persons and discussed some of them (before being mercifully cut off) without producing any discernible order or meaning. The second classified the persons according to a single principle, and the reader can follow the logical arrangement and the meaning of the presentation.

If José wanted to polish his skills in writing a paper of classification, he could write about the arrangement of items in the department store. *Department,* as a word, suggests that items are being grouped according to similar and dissimilar characteristics: footwear, underwear, jewelry, perfume, sports equipment, and so on.

Applying a Principle That Fits the Purpose

The purpose of a paper of classification is to inform or to persuade. The principle on which the division of the classes is based must fit that purpose. José wanted to inform the reader (purpose) about the different types of customers according to their motives (principle). Therefore, the purpose and the principle are quite similar. Had he wanted to persuade the reader, let's say, to avoid working in department stores because of the stress related to dealing with customers, he might have used the idea of stress-provoking customers as a principle and classified certain unsavory customers as thieves, manipulators, and bullies. Those three classes would be discussed according to their capacity for producing stress in salespeople.

The key to organization in the second example paragraph is found in José's application of the principle in relation to the subject. Again, the purpose is to inform, and the principle is the intention of the customers—why they come to the store. In the first paragraph, there is no intention. In the second, the three intentions are (1) looking, (2) sale hunting, and (3) special purchasing. Most customers would fit into those classes.

Avoiding Overlap

After a disastrous beginning, José might have stumbled around a bit in applying the principle of classification. He might have come up with four classes: (1) looking, (2) sale hunting, (3) special purchasing, and (4) being informed. Although a certain percentage of customers are informed in various ways, item number 4 is out of place because it is not based on the principle of intention. In his groups there would be a problem of overlapping because members of the other groups could also be informed. Overlapping is the most common problem in developing a classification.

Working with Good Topics, Average Topics, and Bad Topics

The preceding subhead demonstrates an ineffective set of classes. It is colorless, flat, insipid, boring, unimaginative, and monotonous. It requires no thought to write, read, and forget. Topics with two extremes and a middle position are almost always destined for dullness. Consider some more bad ideas: fast runners, slow runners, and average runners; intelligent thinkers, unintelligent thinkers, and average thinkers; good hamburgers, bad hamburgers, and average hamburgers. Who would want to read material based on those ideas: But what about *intelligence* based on the kind of thinking that is employed: academic intelligence (raw IQ), commonsense intelligence (good practical judgment), and street-smart intelligence (cunning)?

When you write classifications, try to look at subjects in new ways. If you are a hairdresser, you might write about your customers as dogs: some pretty and lovable like the cocker spaniel, some growly and assertive like the doberman, and some feisty and temperamental like the poodle. Instead of writing about different kinds of marriages by giving general and abstract terms, you could label the marriages using the names of well-known television entertainers or programs such as "a Huxtable marriage," "a Roseanne marriage," and "a Bundy marriage."

The following student-written paragraph and essay illustrate effective uses of division and classification, respectively.

MEXICAN FOLK COSTUMES*

Teresita Castellanos

Mexico has a great variety of folk and Indian costumes. There are different popular ceremonial outfits among states and zones in Mexico. From Jalisco comes the *charro*, or horseman's suit, with its fitted jacket and trousers, accented with its rows of silver buttons. This was originally the gala dress of

wealthy ranchers. Mariachi bands adopted the *charro* suit as their official
uniform. The *china poblana* dress consists of a red and green embroidered
skirt, a white blouse, and a *rebozo* worn across the front. This was the costume of Puebla servant girls, then called *chinas*. *Guayaberas* are worn by men
on the Gulf Coast, from Veracruz to Yucatán. These are loose-fitting shirts,
with many pockets and tiny pleats, and can be found in different light colors.
These *guayaberas* keep the men cool. The costumes of Huichol men in the
state of Nayarit are trousers and shirts. Both are made of natural white cotton,
with figures of birds and animals and bands of red and black cross-stitched
embroidery in traditional geometric forms. The *hupil* outfit is a rectangular
dress with openings for the head and arms. It is worn in Oaxaca and Yucatán.
The variety of *hupil* costumes in the area is startling. All are embroidered in
the front with floral designs in brightly colored silk. The women's Tarahumara
outfit from Sonora features a brightly colored blouse and long, full skirt. The
Tarahumara women resemble nineteenth-century women from the American
West. These garments, with their rich color and fine weaving and embroidery,
are some of the most remarkable of Mexico's folk costumes. A person with
just a bit of knowledge about Mexican clothing may be able to tell where a
person in Mexico comes from by the folk clothes he or she wears.

TYPES OF FLY FIGHTERS*

Marge Tanner

One of the major annoyances here at the women's prison is flies. Situated as it   1
is in the middle of an agricultural zone where breeding sites for flies abound,
the prison attracts them by the millions. Inmates, even those who have seldom dealt with fly infestation, must learn to cope with the problem, especially at eating time, when the flies want to share our meals. In observing
what goes on at different tables in the dining hall, I have discovered that there
are three kinds of fly fighters: the shooers, the hiders, and the baiters.

The shooers are the most unimaginative. They wave their hands at the   2
flies, shooing them after they have landed, or by constant waving trying to
keep them from landing. This technique requires an almost constant movement, one which is contrary to the movements associated with eating and is
almost as difficult as patting one's head while rubbing one's stomach. At any
time one can look around the dining room and see the women waving their
hands and the files waving their wings as if they are all communicating. If so,
the flies have the last word.

The hiders, the second class, practice stealth, figuring that any human   3
being should be intelligent enough to hide food from a small-brained creature

like a fly. After using several napkins to enshroud food, the hiders, head bent forward to close space, scoop food from under the covering and "chow down." Unfortunately, the food often saturates the napkin, or flies manage to crawl under the covering. But overall, this technique is fairly successful and is probably the most popular.

The baiters, the third class, while being the most clever, are probably the most cynical. They have concluded that flies will succeed in some fashion. The baiters offer a self-serving compromise to the flies. Upon taking a seat at the table, they will immediately deposit a spoonful of food near the edge of the tray or even on the table itself. The next step is to use the hider's technique of covering the major portion of food. While flies swarm to the exposed portion—the bait—the baiters, often with a smug look of superiority, eat and then carry the bait away to the dump zone.

Although the baiting method is probably the most successful, it is used the least. Most women shoo flies or hide food as an expression of their good manners and dignity. If you believe that last statement, I have a very entertaining fly farm kit I am selling for only $29.95.

WRITER'S CHECKLIST

- Clearly define your subject (what you are classifying) and consider your purpose (to inform or to persuade).
- Classify your material on the basis of one principle. For example, if you classify community college students as vocational, academic, specialty, and serious, you would be mixing principles because the first three are based on main concerns and the last is based on attitude.
- Consider whether you need subclasses. If you do, clearly distinguish the different levels.
- Avoid an unimaginative pattern, such as "good-average-bad" and "fast-medium-slow."

WHAT IS A FAMILY?

Jean Seligman

In this paragraph from "Variations on a Theme," Jean Seligman points out the difficulty of defining the word family.

What's in a family? A mommy, a daddy, a couple of kids, and maybe a grandma, right? Well, yes, but that's not the whole picture anymore. The family tree of American society is sending forth a variety of new and fast-growing branches. Gay and lesbian couples (with or without children) and unmarried heterosexual couples are now commonplace. What's surprising is not so much that these offshoots of the main trunk are flourishing but that the public seems more and more willing to recognize them as families. [In 1990] the Massachusetts Mutual Life Insurance Co. asked 1,200 randomly selected adults to define the word *family*. Only 22 percent picked the legalistic definition. "A group of people related by blood, marriage, or adoption." Almost three quarters instead chose a much broader and more emotional description: "A group of people who love and care for each other." As usual, the American people are changing old perceptions much faster than the courts are. But in many parts of the country lawmakers are now finally catching up and validating the legitimacy of the nontraditional family.

Critical Thinking and Discussion

1. What kinds of "families" are mentioned in this paragraph?
2. What is more important to society, the legal definition or the emotional definition chosen by the majority? Explain.
3. Note that neither definition includes children specifically. How do you feel about that omission?

Reading-Related Writing

1. Write a piece discussing two specific "families," one an example of the legalistic definition and the other an example of the broader definition.

THE FAMILY AND ITS PARTS

Ian Robertson

Author and college professor Ian Robertson gives his definition of family with its necessary components.

What characteristics, then, are common to all family forms? First, the family consists of a group of people who are in some way related to one another. Second, its members live together for long periods. Third, the adults in the group assume responsibility for any offspring. And fourth, the members of the family form an economic unit—often for producing goods and services (as when all members share agricultural tasks) and always for consuming goods and services (such as food or housing). We may say, then, that the "family" is a relatively permanent group of people related by ancestry, marriage, or adoption, who live together, form an economic unit, and take care of their young. If this definition seems a little cumbersome, it is only because it has to include such a great variety of family forms.

Critical Thinking and Discussion

1. Is Robertson's definition mostly legalistic?
2. The author says the definition is by necessity perhaps "a little cumbersome . . . because it has to include such a great variety of forms." May it be said that a definition with this many necessary parts nevertheless excludes some varieties?
3. Relate this definition to the discussion in "What Is a Family?"

Reading-Related Writing

1. Discuss a particular family in terms of Robertson's definition.
2. Discuss an "unconventional" or "nonlegal" family in relation to this definition.

A TRADITIONAL CHINESE WIFE*

Ko-Mei Chaing

Ko-Mei Chaing has lived in the United States for more than ten years. She is married, works, and goes to college. As part of the transitional generation, the one with experiences in both the old-country way of life and the new-country way of life, she sees things she likes and does not like in both. Here she considers the role of the wife in the traditional Chinese family in which she was raised.

What is a traditional Chinese wife? A traditional Chinese wife has to abandon her original family, please her in-laws, and obey her husband. The wife in my generation can keep both her original family where she grows up and her new family, but a traditional wife has to keep distance from her original family. A traditional Chinese wife belongs to her husband's family totally, so that she is not allowed to visit her parents or her original family unless there is a special reason. Most wives in my generation don't live with their in-laws; nevertheless, a traditional Chinese wife has not only to live with her in-laws but also to take care of them and please them. In a big family, the parents-in-law are the decision makers and the power center of the family; thus, pleasing them is very important for a traditional Chinese wife. If she is lucky, her parents-in-law will like her; otherwise, her life will be miserable. My grandfather was good to his grandchildren, and we loved him, but he was very stern with my mother. If he didn't like the food she prepared, he would turn over the table, and wait for more food to be brought. A traditional Chinese wife has to obey her husband and his mother and father. There is no discussion or negotiation between husband and wife. Moreover, she has to serve him in every detail; for example, she has to adjust the water temperature and prepare clothes for her husband when he wants to take a shower. I have known many traditional Chinese wives in my mother's and grandmother's generations. I respect them but feel sad also, for their life is totally for others and not for themselves.

Critical Thinking and Discussion

1. Who are the members of the traditional Chinese family?
2. What is the ranking of these members?
3. Why does the author feel more fortunate than the mothers who preceded her?

Reading-Related Writing

1. Write a piece in which you discuss the contemporary marriage and the traditional marriage within your own culture or both types of marriage from a culture other than Chinese with which you are familiar.
2. Discuss the traditional Chinese marriage from the point of view of Chinese culture as you understand it (concern for ancestors, responsibility for family members, and so on).

ALL HAPPY CLANS ARE ALIKE

Jane Howard

Defining families in a broad sense to include both those of birth and invention, author and university professor Jane Howard reasons that we should be able to determine what makes good families good. In this passage from her book Families, *she presents and illustrates ten common characteristics that one can use to evaluate a family, and even to create a good one.*

Already each of us is born into one family not of our choosing. If we're going   1
to devise new ones, we might as well have the luxury of picking the members ourselves. Clever picking might result in new families whose benefits would

surpass or at least equal those of the old. As a member in reasonable standing of six or seven tribes in addition to the one I was born to, I have been trying to figure which characteristics are common to both kinds of families.

1. Good families have a chief, or a heroine, or a founder—someone around whom others cluster, whose achievements, as the Yiddish word has it, let them *kvell,* and whose example spurs them on to like feats. . . .

2. Good families have a switchboard operator—someone who cannot help but keep track of what all the others are up to, who plays Houston Mission Control to everyone else's Apollo. This role is assumed rather than assigned. The person who volunteers for it often has the instincts of an archivist, and feels driven to keep scrapbooks and photograph albums up to date, so that the clan can see proof of its own continuity.

3. Good families are much to all their members, but everything to none. Good families are fortresses with many windows and doors to the outer world. The blood clans I feel most drawn to were founded by parents who are nearly as devoted to what they do outside as they are to each other and their children. Their curiosity and passion are contagious. Everybody, where they live, is busy. Paint is spattered on eyeglasses. Mud lurks under fingernails. . . . Catcher's mitts, ballet slippers, overdue library books, and other signs of extrafamilial concerns are everywhere.

4. Good families are hospitable. Knowing that hosts need guests as much as guests need hosts, they are generous with honorary memberships for friends, whom they urge to come early and often and to stay late. Such clans exude a vivid sense of surrounding rings of relatives, neighbors, teachers, students, and godparents, any of whom at any time might break or slide into the inner circle. Inside that circle a wholesome, tacit emotional feudalism develops: you give me protection, I'll give you fealty. Such pacts begin with, but soon go far beyond, the jolly exchange of pie at Thanksgiving or cake on a birthday. They mean that you can ask me to supervise your children for the fortnight you will be in the hospital, and that however inconvenient this might be for me, I shall manage to do so. It means I can phone you on what for me is a dreary, wretched Sunday afternoon and for you is the eve of a deadline, knowing you will tell me to come right over, if only to watch you type. It means we need not dissemble. ("To yield to seeming," as Martin Buber wrote, "is man's essential cowardice, to resist it is his essential courage . . . one must at times pay dearly for life lived from the being, but it is never too dear.")

5. Good families deal squarely with direness. Pity the tribe that doesn't have, and cherish, at least one flamboyant eccentric. Pity too the one that supposes it can avoid for long the woes to which all flesh is heir. Lunacy, bankruptcy, suicide, and other unthinkable fates sooner or later afflict the noblest of clans with an undertow of gloom. Family life is a set of givens, someone once told me, and it takes courage to see certain givens as blessings

rather than as curses. It surely does. Contradictions and inconsistencies are givens, too. So is the battle against what the Oregon patriarch Kenneth Babbs calls malarkey. "There's always malarkey lurking, bubbles in the cesspool, fetid bubbles that pop and smell. But I don't put up with malarkey, between my stepkids and my natural ones or anywhere else in the family."

6. Good families prize their rituals. Nothing welds a family more than these. Rituals are vital especially for clans without histories, because they evoke a past, imply a future, and hint at continuity. No line in the seder service at Passover reassures more than the last: "Next year in Jerusalem!" A clan becomes more of a clan each time it gathers to observe a fixed ritual (Christmas, birthdays, Thanksgiving, and so on), grieves at a funeral (anyone may come to most funerals; those who do declare their tribalness), and devises a new rite of its own. Equinox breakfasts can be at least as welding as Memorial Day parades. Several of my colleagues and I used to meet for lunch every Pearl Harbor Day, preferably to eat some politically neutral fare like smorgasbord, to "forgive" our only ancestrally Japanese friend, Irene Kubota Neves. For that and other things we became, and remain, a sort of family.

"Rituals," a California friend of mine said, "aren't just externals and holidays. They are the performances of our lives. They are a kind of shorthand. They can't be decreed. My mother used to try to decree them. She'd make such a goddamn fuss over what we talked about at dinner, aiming at Topics of Common Interest, topics that celebrated our cohesion as a family. These performances were always hollow, because the phenomenology of the moment got sacrificed for the *idea* of the moment. Real rituals are discovered in retrospect. They emerge around constitutive moments, moments that only happen once, around whose memory meanings cluster. You don't choose those moments. They choose themselves." A lucky clan includes a born mythologizer, like my blood sister, who has the gift for apprehending such a moment when she sees it, and who cannot help but invent new rituals everywhere she goes.

7. Good families are affectionate. This of course is a matter of style. I know clans whose members greet each other with gingerly handshakes or, in what pass for kisses, with hurried brushes of jawbones, as if the object were to touch not the lips but the ears. I don't see how such people manage. "The tribe that does not hug," as someone who has been part of many *ad hoc* families recently wrote to me, "is no tribe at all. More and more I realize that everybody, regardless of age, needs to be hugged and comforted in a brotherly or sisterly way now and then. Preferably now."

8. Good families have a sense of place, which these days is not achieved easily. As Susanne Langer wrote in 1957, "Most people have no home that is a symbol of their childhood, not even a definite memory of one place to serve that purpose . . . all the old symbols are gone." Once I asked a roomful of supper guests if anyone felt a strong pull to any certain spot on the face of the

earth. Everyone was silent, except for a visitor from Bavaria. The rest of us seemed to know all too well what Walker Percy means in *The Moviegoer* when he tells of the "genie-soul of a place, which every place has or else is not a place [and which] wherever you go, you must meet and master or else be met and mastered." All that meeting and mastering saps plenty of strength. It also underscores our need for tribal bases of the sort which soaring real estate taxes and splintering families have made all but obsolete.

So what are we to do, those of us whose habit and pleasure and doom is our tendency, as a Georgia lady put it, to "fly off at every other whipstitch"? Think in terms of movable feasts, that's what. Live here, wherever here may be, as if we were going to belong here for the rest of our lives. Learn to hallow whatever ground we happen to stand on or land on. Like medieval knights who took their tapestries along on Crusades, like modern Afghanis with their yurts, we must pack such totems and icons as we can to make short-term quarters feel like home. Pillows, small rugs, watercolors can dispel much of the chilling anonymity of a motel room or sublet apartment. When we can, we should live in rooms with stoves or fireplaces or at least candlelight. The ancient saying is still true: Extinguished hearth, extinguished family. 10

Round tables help too, and as a friend of mine once put it, so do "too many comfortable chairs, with surfaces to put feet on, arranged so as to encourage a maximum of eye contact." Such rooms inspire good talk, of which good clans can never have enough. 11

9. Good families, not just the blood kind, find some way to connect with posterity. "To forge a link in the humble chain of being, encircling heirs to ancestors," as Michael Novak has written, "is to walk within a circle of magic as primitive as humans knew in caves." He is talking of course about babies, feeling them leap in wombs, giving them suck. Parenthood, however, is a state which some miss by chance and others by design, and a vocation to which not all are called. Some of us, like the novelist Richard P. Brickner, look on as others "name their children and their children in turn name their own lives, devising their own flags from their parents' cloth." What are we who lack children to do? Build houses? Plant trees? Write books or symphonies or laws? Perhaps, but even if we do these things, there should be children on the sidelines if not at the center of our lives. 12

It is a sadly impoverished tribe that does not allow access to, and make much of, some children. Not too much, of course; it has truly been said that never in history have so many educated people devoted so much attention to so few children. Attention, in excess, can turn to fawning, which isn't much better than neglect. Still, if we don't regularly see and talk to and laugh with people who can expect to outlive us by twenty years or so, we had better get busy and find some. 13

10. Good families also honor their elders. The wider the age range, the stronger the tribe. Jean-Paul Sartre and Margaret Mead, to name two spectac- 14

ularly confident former children, have both remarked on the central importance of grandparents in their own early lives. Grandparents are now in much
more abundant supply than they were a generation or two ago, when old age
was more rare. If actual grandparents are not at hand, no family should have
too hard a time finding substitute ones to whom to pay unfeigned homage.
The Soviet Union's enchantment with day-care centers, I have heard, stems at
least in part from the state's eagerness to keep children away from their
presumably subversive grandparents. Let that be a lesson to clans based on
interest as well as to those based on genes.

Vocabulary

exude (4)	fealty (4)	cohesion (7)
tacit (4)	eccentric (5)	tendency (10)
feudalism (4)	fetid (5)	subversive (14)

Critical Thinking and Discussion

1. Is Howard dealing with the idea of family in a traditional sense?
2. Using her implied definition of a family, do you believe it is possible to
   have a family without having a good family?
3. Using her standards for the good family, what is the difference between a
   good club (any mainly social organization) and a family?
4. What is the role of the mythologizer in a family?
5. What is the importance of children? of elders?
6. What can families do to enhance the sense of place when very little
   exists?

Reading-Related Writing

1. Write about your family or one that you know well in relation to these
   characteristics.
2. Write about the traditional family of a particular culture in relation to
   these characteristics.
3. Write a piece in which you rank the characteristics of Howard's definition
   of family in terms of their importance.
4. Assuming that some of these characteristics may be more prominent in
   certain families, come up with three or four classes of families, each
   noted primarily for one characteristic named by Howard (such as
   founder, switchboard operator, busy in every way, hospitable, eccentric-
   ity, rituals, affection, sense of place, children, elders).

TUNING IN TO THE MIXED MESSAGES CHILDREN GET

Howard Rosenburg

Satire holds ideas up to ridicule and pokes fun. Laughter is its proper response. Thus we laugh at many of our institutions, especially when they become dull, pompous, corrupt, or wicked. We may even be able to laugh at ourselves, on occasion. The family, with all its inconsistencies, posturing, and failures, as well as its beneficial, praiseworthy features, is a fit topic for satire. In these treatments, the weaknesses are exaggerated so we can see them as all the more ridiculous, and we howl gleefully. However, Howard Rosenburg, media critic for the Los Angeles Times, argues that the very young members of families may see satirical television shows and lose respect for family values.

> Bud Bundy: "Hey, Dad."
> Al Bundy: "Go away."
>
> —From "Married . . . With Children"

It's our nature to chemo-shoot one cancer at a time. Thus, with a laser beam   1
of criticism now being aimed at TV violence, scant attention is being directed
at other kinds of programming that potentially can harm kids and distort
their perceptions. For example: Parents, do you know where *your* children are
at 6 P.M. or 7 P.M.?

Bad-case scenario: They're in front of a television set watching reruns of   2
"Married . . . With Children," the half-hour sitcom whose first-run episodes
Fox has the good sense to withhold on Sundays until 9 P.M. in eastern and
western time zones, but whose syndicated oldies are available weeknights in
Los Angeles at kid-prime 6 and 7 on KTTV-TV Channel 11. In some other
cities, they even air in the afternoon.

At its best, "Married . . . With Children" is one of the funniest, cleverest,   3
tartest comedies on TV, and even when below form can be a real cliché-
crashing kick. Its cast is a grand howl, its humor refreshingly nasty, biting and
irreverent.

It's tailored to older minds, though, not the milk-and-cookie set. Because   4
the Fox prime-time schedule ends at 10 P.M., "Married . . . With Children" is
excusable at 9 P.M., although 9:30 would be even better. But imagine little
kiddies in the late afternoon or early evening, wide-eyed in front of reruns of
a series that spews raunchy sex jokes and exhibits attitudes about families
that are as cynical and pessimistic as "Father Knows Best" was corny, saccharine and hopelessly out of touch.

They are doing just that, and by the millions. The A.C. Nielsen Co. says 5
that "Married . . . With Children" reruns are not only the most popular after-
noon/early-evening fare nationally with kids ages 12 to 17, but also ranks
10th among children 2 to 11. Yes, 2 to 11.

"Married . . . With Children" as toddler television? Even station manag- 6
ers must be bright enough to perceive the danger of that. Traditionally, they
slough off the responsibility on parents, as if the United States were a familial
Camelot in which parents or other accountable parties were always present in
the home to guide or dictate what young children watch on television. The
fact is, parents frequently are not, and in the best interests of children, the
stations that acquire these syndicated programs and broadcast them for profit
on public airwaves should address that reality and not cower behind their
own "Father Knows Best" family fantasy.

On "Married . . . With Children," no one knows anything, and the 7
show's whooping studio audiences—sounding like people who even
"Arsenio" wouldn't let in—definitely like it that way. The Bundy household is
inhabited entirely by lazies. Al (Ed O'Neill) is a shoe salesman, Peg (Katey
Sagal) is a—her word—"housewife." They have two kids: the airheaded, promiscuous, futureless Kelly (Christina Applegate) and the manipulative Bud
(David Faustino), who's prepping for a career in extortion.

Throughout its six years, the show's comedic meat and potatoes have 8
been sex—primarily Peg's appetite and Al's distaste for it—and family dys-
function.

On a recent rerun, Kelly chastised herself for continuing to sneak boys 9
into the house rather than being more open: "I'm not 12 anymore." In the
same episode, Peg asked Al if he thought she was getting old. "How would I
know?" he replied. "I never look at you." Later, when Kelly decided to move
out and live with her boyfriend, Peg turned to Al: "Our baby's gone. Hold
me." He replied: "I didn't hold you when I conceived her. Why should I start
now?"

On another rerun, Peg joked about the sexy Kelly making a career of 10
being the "other woman." Kelly then revealed her techniques for seducing
other girls' boyfriends. In this episode, which made a farce of philandering,
Peg suspected Al of playing around, so Kelly and Bud suggested men *she*
should sleep with, leading to the inevitable jokes about Al's anatomy. Meanwhile, when Peg confronted Al with her suspicions about him stepping out
on her, he put her at ease: "Why go out for milk when you got a cow at
home?"

And on another rerun, Peg boxed herself into getting a job outside the 11
house to pay for a VCR she wanted, even though she loathed working—
"That's why I got married." With Peg at work, cooking for the kids fell to Al.
He toasted marshmallows.

Snide put-downs are the favored discourse of Al and Peg, a distinctive   12
homemaker who neither tends her home nor her kids, to say nothing of her
husband. On a rerun that found Al trying to fix the rooftop TV antenna in a
driving rain, Peg and her kids laughed at his futile SOS calls as he fell off his
ladder, landing with a crash.

You'll find some similarities here with ABC's "Roseanne" and especially   13
with Fox's "The Simpsons," two other prime-time series that pan for comedy
in the mainstream of blue-collar America. Yet even though the Conners of
"Roseanne" often argue and sling wisecracks, the quality that sees them
through hard times is the very family bond missing in "Married . . . With
Children." And although Al Bundy is Homer Simpson with a larger brain,
Homer at least is capable of occasional contriteness over his parental indifference, and Marge Simpson is a devoted, if not altogether successful, mother.

It's clear that co-creators Ron Leavitt and Michael Moye cooked up "Mar-   14
ried . . . With Children" as an adult-oriented antidote to the formulaic, sani-
tized sitcom families that have infected television practically since its
inception. And amen for both their effort and their results. "We always hated
the typical family on television," Leavitt has said. Hence, it's not the American
family but the traditional *TV family* that "Married . . . With Children" seeks
to demolish through humor. But to some, that's a rather fine distinction. And
though it may be oxymoronic to mention subtlety in connection with "Married . . . With Children," the above nuance is surely lost on the youngest of
the young crowd watching these reruns.

Instead, what they're likely seeing and hearing is that marriage and family   15
are for the garbage heap, and the loveless Bundys are powerless to make a
difference.

Despite the shrewd one-liners, it's a message of hopelessness that's   16
unsuitable for malleable young minds.

Vocabulary

cynical (4)   slough (6)   oxymoronic (14)
pessimistic (4)   manipulative (7)   nuance (14)
saccharine (4)   philandering (10)   malleable (16)

Critical Thinking and Discussion

1. In what way are the Bundys a family?
2. What aspects of family are being made fun of in "Married . . . With
   Children"?
3. When this show was being developed, one title considered was "We
   Aren't the Huxtables." How does each show ("Cosby" and "Married")
   exaggerate the qualities of a family unit, but in different directions?

4. What desirable quality does each member of the Bundy family lack?
5. Why does Rosenburg say that viewing this show may be harmful to children? Do you agree? Explain.
6. Assuming that some youngsters might be influenced by watching "Married . . . With Children," what type of youngster might they be, from what kind of family?

Reading-Related Writing

1. Pick a definition from Seligman's "What Is a Family?" or Richardson's "The Family and Its Parts" and apply it to the Bundy family.
2. Write a response to question 6 in Critical Thinking and Discussion.
3. Discuss the role of each character in "Married . . . With Children" in considerable detail.
4. Write about how the members of a particular culture might react to the show. Consider language, behavior, and family values in general.

MOTHERS, SONS, AND THE GANGS

Sue Horton

Two kinds of families often coexist antagonistically in contemporary society: the traditional family and the gang family. Many individuals outside the context of this social situation assume that gang culture is almost exclusively the product of impoverished and dysfunctional families. In this essay published in the Los Angeles Times, *investigative reporter Sue Horton presents three case studies showing that the issue of gangs at odds with traditional families is cross-cultural and exceedingly complicated.*

On the side of a market in East Los Angeles is a roughly done mural, painted 1 by gang members from the Lil' Valley Barrio. The untrained artists did the wall to honor homeboys who met violent deaths on the streets. Two blocks away, the same gang painted another mural, this one depicting the mothers of slain gang members. But, when earthquake repairs were made on the small store that held the mural, the painting was covered over. The mothers are forgotten.

To many mothers of gang members, all across Southern California, the 2 obliterated mural could be taken as an appropriate symbol of their lives. They are, they feel, almost invisible, ignored by many of the law-enforcement agencies and institutions set up to deal with their sons. These women feel isolated, frustrated and angry. "I am tired of people assuming I must be a bad person because my son is a Crip," says a mother who lives in South-Central L.A. "I love my son and have cared for him just like any other mother. Maybe I wasn't perfect, but what mother is?"

Lately, however, some of the officials most involved in dealing with local street gangs have come to realize that to blame a gang member's family and upbringing is to grossly oversimplify the problem. "There is no typical profile of a gang parent," says Jim Galipeau, a Los Angeles County probation officer who works exclusively with gang kids and their families in South-Central Los Angeles. "I have one mother who owns a 12-unit complex, and on the other end of the spectrum is a mom who's a cocaine addict and a prostitute. Mostly it's a one-parent family and the mom making the money, but there are working families with nice homes and gardeners. These parents just happen to live where the gangs are a way of life and their kids become involved." 3

In many parts of Southern California where street gangs flourish, drop-out rates from neighborhood high schools are as high as 35%. A significant proportion of the families in South-Central and East L.A. are living below the poverty level. Drug use and violent crime are rampant. And opportunities for jobs, education and recreation are limited. It's a setting, authorities say, that causes youths to turn to gangs regardless of their upbringing. "For a lot of these kids," says one LAPD officer, "the gang is about the only happening thing in the neighborhood." 4

Gangs and gang violence have become subjects of great interest and concern for all of Southern California. Law-enforcement agencies are expending enormous resources in their fight against gang-related crime. But, for the mothers of the targets of this law-enforcement effort, the problem is far more immediate than newspaper headlines and stories on TV news. The problem is family. 5

And now, some police departments are beginning to realize that mothers, instead of being viewed as part of the problem, should be enlisted to help search for solutions. 6

Capt. Jack Blair of the Pomona Police Department leads weekly gang-truce meetings attended by parents, gang members and local clergy. In the course of his year-long involvement with the Pomona program, he has become convinced that "parents are the key to [solving] the whole problem." At his meetings, and at other meetings of parents around the county, Blair believes that parents have begun to make a difference. "Once the parents unite and form groups, talking to each other and sharing information, that is threatening to the gang members. They want anonymity. They don't want their tactics or activities talked about with parents of rival gangs. When the moms are saying, 'Hey, don't go over to this neighborhood,' or 'I know that you went over to that neighborhood,' there is a certain amount of sport removed." 7

"Ours is not a program to turn your kid in. We don't ask parents to be 8 informants on their child. But the moms realize what an effect they can have on the kids," Blair says. "The kids may go out gang-banging at night, but eventually they have to go back home and eat the dinner their mom's prepared. Even though they might exhibit some of the machismo characteristics, there is still concern on how they are impacting their family."

"Just because you shoot someone," Galipeau adds, "it doesn't mean that 9 you don't love your mother."

Still, even as outsiders begin to recognize the contributions they can 10 make, mothers of gang members face constant fear and worry. They feel overwhelming guilt, asking themselves again and again where they've failed as parents. And they have to deal with the scorn of a society that holds them in some measure responsible for the actions of their sons.

Although these mothers of gang members live in divergent parts of the 11 city and come from a variety of cultures, they share similar pains. These are some of their stories.

Teresa Rodriguez

Fear: Her Son Lived and the Family Became the Target Teresa Rodriguez 12 spends her Friday nights cowering in a back bedroom of the tiny stucco house she shares with her husband and eight children in a west Pomona barrio. The living room, she knows from experience, is simply not safe.

During the past two years, most often on Fridays, Rodriguez's home has 13 been shot up half a dozen times, and one night recently when her husband came home late from work, someone shot at him. The family's car and house still bear bullet holes.

The problems all started two years ago, when Rodriguez's youngest son 14 was 13. Unbeknown to his mother, he had become a member of a small Pomona gang, Sur 13. One day when he and several other Sur 13 members were out walking, a car full of rival gang members passed by. "Which barrio are you from?" the other gang demanded to know. Most of the Sur 13 boys didn't answer; Rodriguez's son did. Upon hearing the hated neighborhood name spoken aloud, one of the boys in the car leaned out the window with a gun and pulled the trigger.

Rodriguez didn't know for several hours that her son had been shot. "His 15 friends took him to the hospital and left him there. They couldn't find the courage to tell me," she said recently through an interpreter. Finally, one of the neighborhood kids came to the door and told Rodriguez what had happened. She was stunned. Having come to the United States from Mexico in 1973, she was still timid and uncertain about the culture here. "I had no idea any of my sons was in a gang until that day," she said.

The bullet had lodged near the 13-year-old's heart but hadn't damaged 16
any internal organs. "The doctor told me we were very, very lucky," Rodriguez
recalls. Her son recovered, but Rodriguez's life was irreversibly changed.

Because the boy claimed his neighborhood with so much bravado on the 17
day he was shot, he has become a target for the rival gang, which now sees
the boy as Sur 13's most visible member. "Whenever there is a problem, they
come after him," his mother says. "The problem is no longer just on him; it is
on the house."

Immediately after the shooting, Rodriguez was too grateful that her son 18
was alive to reprimand him. But events soon prompted her to take action.
Shortly after the boy returned to school, Rodriguez was summoned by the
principal. Four members of the rival gang had been circling the campus all
day waiting for her son. The school couldn't take that sort of disruption, so
officials were asking the boy to leave and attend continuation school. "My
older son told me that if I didn't get [his brother] away from here, he'd be
killed," Rodriguez says. "He is looked on as a particular enemy now."

Rodriguez says she knew she would have to talk to the boy, as her 19
husband had always left rearing the children to her. But getting her son to
listen proved difficult. "I said to him, 'You're going to get killed,' but he just
said, 'I don't care.' He is very rebellious."

This year he is enrolled in a Pomona program for gang members who are 20
at risk in other schools. He continues to dress like and act the part of a Sur
13, although he no longer hangs out on the street. "I finally told him that if he
went out, I would send him to live in Mexico," Rodriguez says. "He doesn't
want that, so he stays inside."

The shooting, says Rodriguez, has had some positive effects. For one 21
thing, she acknowledged that all three of her older sons were in the gang.
"Looking back now, I remember that when they were 9 years old they started
wearing khakis and white T-shirts. They started coming home later and later,"
Rodriguez says. One son had a size 32 waist, but he had his mother buy him
size 42 pants. "I didn't know these were gang clothes. Now I do.

"My 16-year-old threw away his *cholo* clothes right when he heard about 22
his brother," she says. "He hasn't been with the gang since then. The two
older boys are very repentant, but it is hard to step away from their pasts."

Rodriguez has begun attending meetings of the Pomona chapter of Con- 23
cerned Parents, a group working to stop gang violence, and is hopeful for the
first time that something can be done to prevent recurrences of the kind of
gang activity that nearly killed her son. "Communication between parents,
police and the church is very important. Together we can solve the problem.
We can't do it alone."

Still, Rodriguez dreads Friday nights. On her front door, where a thick 24
board has replaced a window shot out by a gang, she has posted a small
picture of Jesus on the cross. "The only thing I can do about the shooting is

put it in his hands," she says, gesturing toward the picture. "He's the only one who can take care of me."

Maggie Garcia

Acceptance: Mean Streets, But the Neighborhood Is Still Everything A few blocks 25 from the Rodriguez house, in another Pomona barrio, Maggie Garcia doesn't really see her youngest son as a gang member. He is just, she says, very loyal to his friends and his neighborhood.

Loyalty to the Cherryville barrio in Pomona where she lives is something 26 Garcia understands completely: "I was raised in the house next door to the one in which I raised my kids. Two of my sisters and one of my brothers live in the neighborhood, too." Maggie Garcia's whole life, she says, is wrapped up in the few blocks radiating from her house. "Here in the neighborhood, it is family."

Garcia realizes that her youngest son has taken his feelings for his barrio 27 a little far on occasion. Last September, when the boy had just turned 14, he got into a fight at school. "He claimed his neighborhood, and the other boy claimed his neighborhood, and all of a sudden they are fighting for two gangs."

After the fight, he was expelled and sent to a local continuation school. 28 "The principal at his old school was upset because my son said, 'I'd die for my neighborhood.' If he'd said, 'I'd die for my country,' the principal probably would have given him a medal."

Garcia worried about her son at the continuation school. Because it drew 29 students from the whole Pomona school district, her son was in constant contact with boys from rival gangs. "One day, two boys from Twelfth Street [another Pomona gang] laid in wait for my son. He came home all bloody and with bruises," Garcia recalls. "I told him you're not going back to school. You could be killed."

Garcia knew that inter-neighborhood conflicts could be deadly in the 30 Pomona barrios: Three nephews and three of her nieces' boyfriends had been killed by rival gang members. She told her son that if he was out late with his cousins, he wasn't to walk home on the streets but should instead cut through neighbors' back yards. When he goes out the door, Garcia blesses him in hopes that God will protect him out on the streets. But there is only so much, she feels, that she can do. "I've tried to talk to him," she says. "Some people think I should forbid him from being with his friends, but that would be like his telling me, 'Mom, I don't want you hanging out with your best friends in this neighborhood.' It's such a small neighborhood, there are only a few boys my son has here. If he didn't hang out with them, he wouldn't have any friends."

"I see it this way," she says. "Nowadays you have to protect yourself as 31 much as possible, and the friends help protect. The Bible says when you are slapped you turn the other cheek, but you don't do that around here because they will shoot you if you're not looking. Children in any neighborhood have to be aware and have eyes in the back of their heads or they will be dead. They are streetwise. I've taught them to be that way. I feel that when a child is running with three or four of his friends it's better than being alone."

So instead of forbidding her son to associate with the gang, Garcia says, 32 she has taken a more moderate line. "I tell him you can live in the fire, but you don't have to let yourself get burned. You've got to learn to live outside, but when you see something about to go down, you have to get out of there."

In early August, it became apparent that Garcia's youngest son hadn't 33 absorbed the lessons his mother was trying to teach him. After coming home late one night, the boy went back out into the neighborhood. What happened next is in dispute, but in the end he was arrested and charged with an armed robbery that took place a few blocks from his house. Garcia insists that her son was simply in the wrong place at the wrong time. After being held at Los Padrinos Juvenile Hall in Downey, he was released into this mother's custody and is attending school through a Pomona program for gang members who are at risk in other schools. His case will be reviewed by a judge in December.

"My older son has gotten very angry at my younger son," Garcia says. "He 34 tells [his brother], 'You know, if they kill you, your friends will go to your Rosary and they'll go to your funeral. Then they'll have a party and forget you.' But my younger son doesn't see it that way. He sort of says, 'Here today, gone tomorrow—so what?'"

Gayle Thomas Kary

Death: Just When She Thought She'd Beaten the Odds   Fifteen-year-old Jamee 35 Kary hadn't been active in the Five Deuce Broadway Crips in recent months. But that didn't matter to a car full of the rival Blood gang members who spotted the boy crossing West 27th Street on the night of Sept. 10. The Bloods called the boy to their car. Words were exchanged. The Bloods began to drive off, but then stopped and got out of their car. Jamee tried to run, but he was shot in the face before he could reach cover. He died within minutes.

Gayle Thomas Kary had worried frantically about Jamee, her middle son, 36 for more than two years before his death. His problems, she feels, started four years ago when tight finances forced her to move from Long Beach to a family-owned house in South-Central Los Angeles half a block from the Harbor Freeway. In the old neighborhood, there had been so much for an adolescent boy to do. There were youth centers and year-round organized sports. In the new neighborhood, there was only the gang.

Because Jamee had a slight learning disability, school had always been 37 difficult for him, but he had always had friends. A charming boy with a quick smile and easy affability, Jamee fit right into the new neighborhood. By the time he was 13, he had fit right into the gang.

Kary could tell from her son's style of dress and friends that he had become a gang member. And she was very worried. A data-entry operator with a full-time job and a steady life style, Kary had always believed that if she set a good example and enforced limits, her sons would turn out well. Her oldest son, now 20, had always met his mother's expectations. But Jamee seemed torn. At home he was respectful and loving, but out on the streets, he seemed like a different boy. "He knew that he was loved at home," Kary says, sitting in the immaculate California bungalow she shares with her sons. "But he somehow felt the need to be out there with those boys and not be considered a wimp." 38

One day during the summer of 1986, when Jamee was 13, his mother found him cutting up soap to look like cocaine. Kary was horrified that the boy found the drug culture so appealing. Within weeks, she sent Jamee off to stay with his father, a Louisiana minister, hoping that a change of environment would divert Jamee from trouble. Three weeks later, his father sent him back, saying he couldn't control the boy. 39

Later that summer, Jamee stole his mother's car one evening. He was stopped by police for driving the wrong way on a one-way street. But the police just gave the boy a traffic citation and told him to lock up the car and go home. When Kary heard about the incident, she was outraged. She bundled Jamee into the car, drove to the police station, and asked the police there to arrest her son. "I needed help in dealing with my son, but they just said, 'There's nothing we can do,'" Kary says, a bitter sorrow apparent in her voice. 40

In the months that followed, Jamee was increasingly out of control. Kary had always expected her sons to abide by certain household rules if they wanted to live under her roof. Jamee was required to attend school and do his homework, to keep his room clean, to wash his clothes, to wash dishes on alternate days and to feed the dogs. It was not too much to ask, Kary felt. 41

Jamee, by the fall of his 14th year, felt differently. "Jamee started seeing these guys out there who were wearing expensive clothes and they didn't have to go to school or do chores or ask their parents for money," Kary recalls. Unwilling to meet his mother's demands, Jamee began running away from home for short periods of time to live with members of the Five Deuce Broadway Crips. By this time, his mother knew from other kids in the neighborhood, her son was also selling drugs. 42

During his times away from home, Kary tried to keep tabs on him. "I always knew where he was and that he was safe," Kary says. "He'd sneak over and try to get his brothers to get him a clean set of clothes." Eventually, Jamee would tire of life on the streets and return home. "He'd always promise to toe the line," Kary says. "He'd say he had changed. He knew my rules were the same." 43

When her son was at home, Kary tried to reason with him. "I told him 44 that kind of life could lead to no good," Kary says with tears in her eyes. "I told him that a fast life goes fast." She warned him, she says, that he could be arrested or killed. "He would just tell me he wouldn't get busted because he could run faster than the police. He told me nobody would kill him because he didn't do any bad drug deals."

In the spring of 1987, Jamee was arrested for possession of cocaine with 45 intent to sell. The arrest was a relief for his mother, who hoped that at last her son would be in the hands of people who could help him. But when the time came for Jamee's sentencing, Kary was once again disappointed. "They wanted to give him probation. The conditions were things like he had to be in by 10 and stop associating with gang members. I told them I'd been trying to get him to do those things and he wouldn't. There was no way he was going to do them now, either. I said I wouldn't take him," Kary recalls.

Instead, the court sentenced Jamee to juvenile hall and later to a youth 46 camp. After five months, Jamee returned home. At first he seemed to be less involved with the gang, but he soon returned to his old ways. There was just one difference now: Jamee had been assigned to probation officer Jim Galipeau, who seemed to really care about the boy. Galipeau also listened to Kary's concerns.

"I called Mr. Galipeau and said Jamee was in trouble again. He told me to 47 keep a record of what he was doing and when," Kary recalls. Thankful for something to do, Kary kept detailed notes on her son's transgressions, hoping to build a case for revoking Jamee's probation. But before she could do that, Galipeau had a heart-to-heart talk with her son. "Jamee told Mr. Galipeau he was tired of life on the streets," Kary says. "He got tired of the police swooping up the street and having to run and now knowing where he was going to sleep." At his probation officer's suggestion, Jamee agreed to request placement in a county-run youth facility to get away from his life in Los Angeles.

By last summer, Jamee was doing beautifully. "I knew I still had to take it 48 one day at a time," his mother says, "but he really seemed to have changed. It was like he was the child I used to know. He wouldn't even go up to Broadway [where the gang liked to hang out]. The friends he associated with were not gang members."

Jamee arrived home for his last weekend furlough on Friday, Sept. 9. On 49 Saturday evening, he asked his mother if he could go with a friend to pick up another fellow and get something to eat. She readily agreed. An hour and a half later, a neighbor came to the door with the news that Jamee had been shot on 27th Street.

Kary raced to the scene, where she saw police had cordoned off a large 50 area. "I saw that yellow police rope, and I knew right then my son was dead," Kary recalls. But police at the scene refused to let her see whether the victim was her son, and after pleading to no avail for information, Kary was finally persuaded to go home and wait. Several hours later, the police called and asked Kary's oldest son to go and identify photographs. Kary finally knew for sure. Her 15-year-old son was dead.

After Jamee's killing, Kary continued to learn what it was like to have a 51 gang member for a son. She wanted to have the funeral service at her own church, but neighbors dissuaded her. "They told me there was a rival gang over there. They said, 'You can't have it there or there'll be troubles,'" Kary says. She also realized with shock that colors, particularly Crip blue, had taken on a new meaning in her life. "All those years that blue stood for boys, and I couldn't let my boy wear blue at his funeral or have the programs printed in blue," Kary says. She had originally planned to wear her nicest dress to the services, but then she realized that it, too, was blue. "A friend told me, 'You can't wear that or you'll be sitting there looking the queen Crip mother,'" Kary says.

Kary worried about how the Five Deuce Broadways would behave at her 52 son's funeral. But that, she says, turned out to be a pleasant surprise. Several days after Jamee's death, some 20 of the gang's members came to Kary's house. While Jamee was alive, she had never allowed gang members in her house, but this once she decided to make an exception.

The young men who gathered in her living room were, she says, very 53 respectful. "They said that even though Jamee wasn't actively involved with them at the time, he was still a member of their family, and they wanted to offer financial support," Kary recalls. The boys contributed about $400 toward funeral costs.

"After they spoke," Kary says, "I said to them, 'I don't like what you do 54 out there on the streets, but I want to tell you something from my heart. You say Jamee was a member of your family. That makes you a member of my family, too, because Jamee was my son. I'm asking you a favor as family members. I don't want any colors at the funeral. I don't want rags, and I don't want trouble.'" To a person, Kary says, the young men honored her requests, and since the funeral they have been eager to help in any way they can.

In the aftermath of Jamee's death, Kary feels lost. Her youngest son, 11- 55 year-old Lewis, had decided just before his brother's death to go live with his father in Louisiana. "He did not want to be involved on the streets with the gangs and the colors and the drugs. He was scared. He didn't want to go to junior high school here," Kary recalls. While Kary supports Lewis' decision, she is lonely. "I feel so empty inside," she says. "I can't remember when I last felt my heart beat inside my chest. The only thing I can feel in my whole body is my head because it hurts all the time."

In her lowest moments, Kary takes some solace in a poem Jamee wrote 56 for her while he was incarcerated after his cocaine arrest. She included the poem, which Jamee had entitled "If You Only Knew," in the program for Jamee's funeral.

> I sit here on my bunk
> And don't know what to do
> My life just caught up in a mess
> Because I was a fool
> I sometimes wonder to myself
> With my heart just full of pain
> Boy when I get out of this place
> My life won't be the same
> I'm sorry for all the pain I caused
> For you as well as them
> I promise you, and I'll try my best
> To not do wrong again
> Every night and every day
> I always think of you
> I just sit here thinking but
> If you only knew
>
> Dedicated to my Mom
> I love you

Vocabulary

depicting (1)   rampant (3)   affability (37)
obliterated (2)   divergent (11)

Critical Thinking and Discussion

1. What generalizations can be made about families of gang members?
2. What exceptions are there to these generalizations?
3. In many parts of Southern California where street gangs flourish, what are the factors that discourage youngsters from living a nongang life?
4. Why do gang members object to their parents attending antidrug activities?
5. How do most gang members feel about their mother?
6. How has the family life of the Rodriguez family changed because of their son's gang activities?
7. What does Teresa Rodriguez see as a positive effect of her ordeal?
8. What attitude does Maggie Garcia have toward the idea of neighborhood and loyalty? What is your reaction to her view?
9. Why does Maggie Garcia not insist that her son drop out of the gang?

10. What different views on drugs are held by members of the Garcia family?
11. How did moving to a different neighborhood influence Jamee Kary, according to his mother?
12. What did Gayle Thomas Kary do to try to help her son?
13. What relationship did she have with her son's gang after he was killed?
14. Why was Kary surprised by the behavior of the gang after her son's death?

Reading-Related Writing

1. Compare and contrast the conventional family and the gang family in terms of three or more points such as security, companionship, recreation, tradition, and guidance.
2. Analyze either the conventional family or the gang family in terms of three or more of the points in question #1.
3. Write a character sketch of each of the three mothers, showing that although they are individuals, they have much in common. Discuss whether you think each is representative of a certain type of mothers of gang members.
4. Invent a conversation between the mother and son from one of the three case studies.
5. Discuss the threat of gangs to the stability of the conventional family. Include references to this essay.
6. Discuss gangs as a cross-cultural problem.

Collaborative Project

Role playing in alternating groups of concerned citizens (such as police, school, city, or church), interview students representing the three mothers about issues relevant to gangs and family: their personal experiences, their solutions, their attempts to help, their concerns, and their attitudes toward family life and gangs. If you are posing as a concerned citizen, prepare your questions thoroughly before the interview sessions; if you are acting as one of the mothers, read the material carefully in order to answer in character. Keep in mind that the author includes these two statements: "To blame a gang member's family and upbringing is to grossly oversimplify the problem"; and "Although these mothers of gang members live in divergent parts of the city and come from a variety of cultures, they share similar pains."

Individually or in groups, as directed by your instructor, write a report relating your experiences during these interviews and stating any conclusions you drew from them.

THREE GENERATIONS OF NATIVE AMERICAN WOMEN'S BIRTH EXPERIENCE

Joy Harjo

Joy Harjo, a Native American of Creek, Cherokee, and white ancestry, has written screenplays, three books of poetry, and numerous essays, all about her culture. She is a consultant for the National Indian Youth Council and the Native American Broadcasting Consortium, and a professor of creative writing at the University of New Mexico. Here she gives accounts of childbirth experienced by her mother, herself, and her daughter.

It was still dark when I awakened in the stuffed back room of my mother-in- 1 law's small rented house with what felt like hard cramps. At 17 years of age I had read everything I could from the Tahlequah Public Library about pregnancy and giving birth. But nothing prepared me for what was coming. I awakened my child's father and then ironed him a shirt before we walked the four blocks to the Indian hospital because we had no car and no money for a taxi. He had been working with another Cherokee artist silk-screening signs for specials at the supermarket and making $5 a day, and had to leave me alone at the hospital because he had to go to work. We didn't awaken his mother. She had to get up soon enough to fix breakfast for her daughter and granddaughter before leaving for her job at the nursing home. I knew my life was balanced at the edge of great, precarious change and I felt alone and cheated. Where was the circle of women to acknowledge and honor this birth?

It was still dark as we walked through the cold morning, under oaks that 2 symbolized the stubbornness and endurance of the Cherokee people who had made Tahlequah their capital in the new lands. I looked for handholds in the misty gray sky, for a voice announcing this impending miracle. I wanted to change everything; I wanted to go back to a place before childhood, before our tribe's removal to Oklahoma. What kind of life was I bringing this child into? I was a poor, mixed-blood woman heavy with a child who would suffer the struggle of poverty, the legacy of loss. For the second time in my life I felt the sharp tug of my own birth cord, still connected to my mother. I believe it never pulls away, until death, and even then it becomes a streak in the sky symbolizing that most important warrior road. In my teens I had fought my mother's weaknesses with all my might, and here I was at 17, becoming as my mother, who was in Tulsa, cooking breakfasts and preparing for the lunch shift at a factory cafeteria as I walked to the hospital to give birth. I should be with her; instead, I was far from her house, in the house of a mother-in-law who later would try to use witchcraft to destroy me.

After my son's father left me I was prepped for birth. This meant my pubic area was shaved completely and then I endured the humiliation of an enema, all at the hands of strangers. I was left alone in a room painted government green. An overwhelming antiseptic smell emphasized the sterility of the hospital, a hospital built because of the U.S. government's treaty and responsibility to provide health care to Indian people.

I intellectually understood the stages of labor, the place of transition, of birth—but it was difficult to bear the actuality of it, and to bear it alone. Yet in some ways I wasn't alone, for history surrounded me. It is with the birth of children that history is given form and voice. Birth is one of the most sacred acts we take part in and witness in our lives. But sacredness seemed to be far from my lonely labor room in the Indian hospital. I heard a woman screaming in the next room with her pain, and I wanted to comfort her. The nurse used her as a bad example to the rest of us who were struggling to keep our suffering silent.

The doctor was a military man who had signed on this watch not for the love of healing or out of awe at the miracle of birth, but to fulfill a contract for medical school payments. I was another statistic to him; he touched me as if he were moving equipment from one place to another. During my last visit I was given the option of being sterilized. He explained to me that the moment of birth was the best time to do it. I was handed the form but chose not to sign it, and am amazed now that I didn't think too much of it at the time. Later I would learn that many Indian women who weren't fluent in English signed, thinking it was a form giving consent for the doctor to deliver their babies. Others were sterilized without even the formality of signing. My light skin had probably saved me from such a fate. It wouldn't be the first time in my life.

When my son was finally born I had been deadened with a needle in my spine. He was shown to me—the incredible miracle nothing prepared me for—then taken from me in the name of medical progress. I fell asleep with the weight of chemicals and awoke yearning for the child I had suffered for, had anticipated in the months proceeding from this unexpected genesis when I was still 16 and a student at Indian school. I was not allowed to sit up or walk because of the possibility of paralysis (one of the drug's side effects), and when I finally got to hold him, the nurse stood guard as if I would hurt him. I felt enmeshed in a system in which the wisdom that had carried my people from generation to generation was ignored. In that place I felt ashamed I was an Indian woman. But I was also proud of what my body had accomplished despite the rape by the bureaucracy's machinery, and I got us out of there as soon as possible. My son would flourish on beans and fry bread, and on the dreams and stories we fed him.

My daughter was born four years later, while I was an art student at the 7
University of New Mexico. Since my son's birth I had waitressed, cleaned
hospital rooms, filled cars with gas (while wearing a miniskirt), worked as a
nursing assistant, and led dance classes at a health spa. I knew I didn't want
to cook and waitress all my life, as my mother had done. I had watched the
varicose veins grow branches on her legs, and as they grew, her zest for
dancing and sports dissolved into utter tiredness. She had been born with a
caul over her face, the sign of a gifted visionary.

My earliest memories are of my mother writing songs on an ancient 8
Underwood typewriter after she had washed and waxed the kitchen floor on
her hands and knees. She too had wanted something different for her life. She
had left an impoverished existence at age 17, bound for the big city of Tulsa.
She was shamed in a time in which to be even part Indian was to be an
outcast in the great U.S. system. Half her relatives were Cherokee full-bloods
from near Jay, Oklahoma, who for the most part had nothing to do with white
people. The other half were musically inclined "white trash" addicted to
country-western music and Holy Roller fervor. She thought she could disappear in the city; no one would know her family, where she came from. She
had dreams of singing and had once been offered a job singing on the radio
but turned it down because she was shy. Later one of her songs would be
stolen before she could copyright it and would make someone else rich. She
would quit writing songs. She and my father would divorce and she would be
forced to work for money to feed and clothe four children, all born within
two years of each other.

As a child growing up in Oklahoma, I liked to be told the story of my 9
birth. I would beg for it while my mother cleaned and ironed. "You almost
killed me," she would say. "We almost died." That I could kill my mother
filled me with remorse and shame. And I imagined the push-pull of my life,
which is a legacy I deal with even now when I am twice as old as my mother
was at my birth. I loved to hear the story of my warrior fight for my breath.
The way it was told, it had been my decision to live. When I got older, I
realized we were both nearly casualties of the system, the same system flourishing in the Indian hospital where later my son Phil would be born.

My parents felt lucky to have insurance, to be able to have their children 10
in the hospital. My father came from a fairly prominent Muscogee Creek
family. *His* mother was a full-blood who in the early 1920s got her degree in
art. She was a painter. She gave birth to him in a private hospital in Oklahoma City; at least that's what I think he told me before he died at age 53. It
was something of which they were proud.

This experience was much different from my mother's own birth. She and 11
five of her six brothers were born at home, with no medical assistance. The
only time a doctor was called was when someone was dying. When she was
born her mother named her Wynema, a Cherokee name my mother says

means beautiful woman, and Jewell, for a can of shortening stored in the room where she was born.

I wanted something different for my life, for my son, and for my daugh- 12 ter, who later was born in a university hospital in Albuquerque. It was a bright summer morning when she was ready to begin her journey. I still had no car, but I had enough money saved for a taxi for a ride to the hospital. She was born "naturally," without drugs. I could look out of the hospital window while I was in labor at the bluest sky in the world. Her father was present in the delivery room—though after her birth he disappeared on a drinking binge. I understood his despair, but did not agree with the painful means to describe it. A few days later Rainy Dawn was presented to the sun at her father's pueblo and given a name so that she will always be recognized as a part of the people, as a child of the sun.

That's not to say that my experience in the hospital reached perfection. 13 The clang of metal against metal in the delivery room had the effect of a tuning fork reverberating fear in my pelvis. After giving birth I held my daughter, but they took her from me for "processing." I refused to lie down to be wheeled to my room after giving birth: I wanted to walk out of there to find my daughter. We reached a compromise and I rode in a wheelchair. When we reached the room I stood up and walked to the nursery and demanded my daughter. I knew she needed me. That began my war with the nursery staff, who deemed me unknowledgeable because I was Indian and poor. Once again I felt the brushfire of shame, but I'd learned to put it out much more quickly, and I demanded early release so I could take care of my baby without the judgment of strangers.

I wanted something different for Rainy, and as she grew up I worked hard 14 to prove that I could make "something" of my life. I obtained two degrees as a single mother. I wrote poetry, screenplays, became a professor, and tried to live a life that would be a positive influence for both of my children. My work in this life has to do with reclaiming the memory stolen from our peoples when we were dispossessed from our lands east of the Mississippi; it has to do with restoring us. I am proud of our history, a history so powerful that it both destroyed my father and guarded him. It's a history that claims my mother as she lives not far from the place her mother was born, names her as she cooks in the cafeteria of a small college in Oklahoma.

When my daughter told me she was pregnant, I wasn't surprised. I had 15 known it before she did, or at least before she would admit it to me. I felt despair, as if nothing had changed or ever would. She had run away from Indian school with her boyfriend and they had been living in the streets of Gallup, a border town notorious for the suicides and deaths of Indian peoples. I brought her and her boyfriend with me because it was the only way I could bring her home. At age 16, she was fighting me just as I had so fiercely fought my mother. She was making the same mistakes. I felt as if everything I had accomplished had been in vain. Yet I felt strangely empowered, too, at this repetition of history, this continuance, by a new possibility of life and love, and I steadfastly stood by my daughter.

I had a university job, so I had insurance that covered my daughter. She 16 saw an obstetrician in town who was reputed to be one of the best. She had the choice of a birthing room. She had the finest care. Despite this, I once again battled with a system in which physicians are taught the art of healing by dissecting cadavers. My daughter went into labor a month early. We both knew intuitively the baby was ready, but how to explain that to a system in which numbers and statistics provide the base of understanding? My daughter would have her labor interrupted: her blood pressure would rise because of the drug given to her to stop the labor. She would be given an unneeded amniocentesis and would have her labor induced—after having it artificially stopped! I was warned that if I took her out of the hospital so her labor could occur naturally my insurance would cover nothing.

My daughter's induced labor was unnatural and difficult, monitored by 17 machines, not by touch. I was shocked. I felt as if I'd come full circle, as if I were watching my mother's labor and the struggle of my own birth. But I was there in the hospital room with her, as neither my mother had been for me, nor her mother for her. My daughter and I went through the labor and birth together.

And when Krista Rae was born she was born to her family. Her father was 18 there for her, as were both her grandmothers and my friend who had flown in to be with us. Her paternal great-grandparents and aunts and uncles had also arrived from the Navajo Reservation to honor her. Something *had* changed.

Four days later, I took my granddaughter to the Saguaro forest before 19 dawn and gave her the name I had dreamed for her just before her birth. Her name looks like clouds of mist settling around a sacred mountain as it begins to speak. A female ancestor approaches on a horse. We are all together.

Vocabulary

caul (7)   cadavers (16)
obstetrician (16)   amniocentesis (16)

Critical Thinking and Discussion

1. How are the generations of Harjo's family different? On what basis other than time can they be divided?
2. In what way is this essay optimistic?
3. What strains of pessimism do you find in this essay?
4. What does Harjo see as the key to improvement for Native American culture?

5. Argue for or against calling the three generations described here the old, the transitional, and the new.

Reading-Related Writing

1. Responding to question 5 above, summarize this long essay in a paper of division in which you specifically categorize the three generations and comment on their differences and progression, if any.
2. Write about two or three generations of birth experience in a culture other than Native American. Use specific examples.

AN AMERICAN DREAM

Rosemarie Santini

This is a story of generations—from the immigrants to the second generation to the third. With time has come prosperity, but the satisfaction is bittersweet for the oldest members of this extended family.

"Where are the children?" Ida Rinaldi asks as she breaks one egg after another 1 into a large mound of flour, first breaking each egg into a glass and inspecting it for any discoloration. It is a process learned in the old days, in the tenements on Thompson St., when the eggs were often bad and destroyed whatever they were put into. "My mother taught me how to do this," she says.

Resting on the tablecloth that covers her kitchen table is a large, wooden 2 board on which she begins to knead the mixture. On the counter nearby, other necessities for her Italian cuisine are in evidence: tomatoes, canned, of course, in Italia, tomato paste from the same country—very expensive—beef meats, and stale bread mixed in milk, all ready to be rolled into large meatballs. She enjoys her chores, part of a process which will take hours. She is preparing fettucine as her Neapolitan mother taught her. "Let's see, eight people, eight eggs," she counts with peasant logic.

It is hot in the kitchen this August day, and she puts her hand to her 3 forehead, smearing her tanned complexion with white flour. "Where are the children?" she asks again, although there is no one to answer.

At 67, Mrs. Rinaldi does not fit the popular picture of an Italian Mama. 4 She is chic, petite, and slender. The she wears the tight pants of the '70s, a shell blouse and tiny gypsy earrings. On the left finger of her right hand are a diamond engagement ring and a wedding band in an antique setting. They are not the original ones. In 1931 when she married, she was given no engagement ring and her wedding band was of plain silver.

Other things were different then, too. Now her house is a three-story ₅
brick-attached house in a lovely section in Queens. A backyard, a porch, a
lawn are her proud possessions. Her apartment on the second floor could be
featured in *The Sunday News* interior decorating pages. It is modern and sleek,
and the only signs of her Italian heritage are tiny Botticelli angels in antique
gold, which liven up the living room.

In 1931, her wedding home was an unheated, three-room tenement ₆
apartment in the Italian section of Greenwich Village. There, while working as
a dressmaker, she raised her family, keeping the small apartment spotless,
cooking on an old stove, cooling her groceries in an ice box; a living-room
couch was her children's bed. Enduring these hardships, Ida Rinaldi and her
husband worked and saved for the fulfillment of their American Dream, a
house of their own. Finally, when their daughter Kathleen married and had a
family, the Rinaldi-DeGiovanni clan moved from the tenements to the suburban splendor of Queens.

Here the brick houses all stand in a row, attached but separated by fence ₇
lines announcing ownership in this working-class neighborhood. Most owners, like the Rinaldi family, spent their life savings on the down payments.
Only the electrical wires, hanging like kite lines over the pretty streets, mar
the vista of this lovely neighborhood, an effect which the homeowners add to
by stringing up clothesline in the backyards, probably a hangover from tenement days. Although most houses have washer-dryers, old habits die hard,
and the Italians prefer their clothes bleached and dried in the sun, a custom
inherited from ancestors who washed clothes in the village brooks of Italy.

Other neighbors have planted tomatoes in their gardens, but not this ₈
family. In the Rinaldi house there is a *House Beautiful* quality of floors polished
almost too clean, of furniture oiled, of dustlessness, and in the duplex below,
where the DeGiovannis live, the same cleanliness dominates all.

The other dominating interest in this household is "What's for dinner?" ₉
Today, it is the egg fettucine specialty, hand-rolled, to be served with a thick
meat sauce. Mrs. Rinaldi explains that she is spending so much time on this
delicacy as a treat for the children, her two grandsons, teenagers Paul and
John, who were, of course, a major reason for the Rinaldi-DeGiovanni move
from Greenwich Village. But where are the children?

Kathleen DeGiovanni brings her mother the news. Her two sons have ₁₀
baseball games to play. After that, they are going to the DeGiovanni beach
club for a swim and a party.

Mrs. Rinaldi's eyes look sad. "What about the egg noodles?" she asks.   ₁₁

"Can we keep them?" her tall, brunette daughter suggests.   ₁₂

Sighing, the older woman cuts the dough carefully in strips, then carries ₁₃
the long, thin pasta into the extra bedroom. "Well, no one's using the extra
bedroom. We can lay them out here," she says, laying the pasta carefully on
the bed.

Afterwards, she pours a cup of espresso. "It's all changed," she says. 14
"When we first came here, our life was more centered in this house. It was the
'60s, and we were so glad to get out of the tenements. This seemed like a
good place for our grandchildren to play and grow up. Now, everyone is
going this way and that. I guess that's life."

She spoons three sugars into her tiny demitasse cup. "I hope it doesn't get 15
damp. Noodles are impossible to keep separate when it gets damp." As she sits,
her hands move with infinite patience and care, a habit from another era when
hands were important for darning, sewing, crocheting, knitting, making pasta.

Does she miss the old style of living in the Italian section of Greenwich 16
Village? "I loved it, but now everyone has either died or moved away. When I
walk down the streets, I don't know anyone." But weekly, she does walk down
the streets, riding the bus and subway into the city to have her hair done,
buying ricotta and mozzarella in the old cheese store across the street from
the church, the same store where she shopped as a young bride whenever she
could afford it. Once in a while, she runs into an old neighbor or friend who
tells her how terrible living in the Village is nowadays.

Sometimes she wonders whether her life has really improved, although 17
they have more room and more conveniences. Later, her daughter Kathleen
comments on this: "I grew up sleeping on a living-room couch. Here, my sons
have a bedroom to themselves. We moved into a brand-new area where
everyone was mostly Italian and mostly friendly. When the kinds were small,
I could leave them on the front lawn and not worry about them."

But the kids were no longer small, and Kathleen and her husband spend 18
most of their time working in the city, going to church and school meetings,
chauffeuring the boys to baseball games, grabbing a moment or two at the
beach club, where a swim, a game of tennis give them much pleasure, not
returning home until it is time to sleep.

The boys do not even mow the lawn nowadays, even though their 19
weekly allowance from their grandfather should influence them to do so.
Their major interests are sports, dancing, music, visiting more affluent neighborhoods, attending rock concerts, meeting new girls. John and Paul, 15 and
17, are tall, solid, muscular young men who say they want to live farther out
on Long Island, near the sea, in a house complete with a boat moored at a
dock, an office nearby in town, and lots and lots of privacy.

Dark-haired, studious Felix DeGiovanni agrees with his sons. "My par- 20
ents were immigrants, born in Europe. They didn't have any choice on how to
live when they arrived here. I had to compromise, too, and live in Queens,
instead of farther out, because I work in the city."

Although Mr. DeGiovanni likes suburban living, he feels that his boys 21
have been too much sheltered. "I learned all about life very young, on city
streets. I was working in the neighborhood pasta store after school when I
was 13. My kids will be put through college without having to work. They

have everything they need. They don't know how to take care of themselves, and I'm not sure that's good for them."

Mr. DeGiovanni earned his M.A. in engineering by going to night school 22 and working as a draftsman during the day. Because his children do not have to struggle, he feels they are not as mature as he was at their age. Also, he reiterates a familiar parental theme, questioning whether his sons have any respect for authority.

Grandfather Rinaldi agrees that life is very, very different from the time he 23 came over on a boat from Italy. "Then we worked hard and respected our parents and our family." White-haired, retired from the U.S. Post Office, Mr. Rinaldi sits on the porch in his rocking chair, pensively smoking his pipe as he watches the comings and goings in the neighborhood, talking about how different his life would have been if his parents were not immigrants.

If he had stayed in Italy, he might wander down to the town's square 24 where he would find the other older men sitting and pondering the past and would argue with them, raising his voice in melodramatic splendor. If he had remained in Greenwich Village, he might walk over to the private men's club where Italian men play bocce and pinochle and talk about politics. But in Queens there are only a few senior-citizen centers for this kind of social interchange, and Mr. Rinaldi says the people there are too old.

Still, he is happy that he has at last attained his idea of a successful life: a 25 house he owns out of what he considers the city, a safe place far removed from tenement living. Yet, there is a bittersweet element to his satisfaction, as if now he has everything, what does he really have?

"When we lived in Italy, I felt superior," he explains. "My parents were 26 respected. We lost all that when we came to America. For years, I couldn't speak the language properly. Other kids from the neighborhoods called me names. I had to fight a lot, and I didn't understand the ways of living here. It took me a long time to get accustomed to America. That's why I worked so hard to better myself. To get what I had dreamed of all these years."

What is this dream anyhow, and has it worked for these former city 27 dwellers in their effort for a better life? There is a lack of primitiveness here on these residential streets, so far from the tumultuous streets of their youth in the city . . . a sterility, almost a disease of cleanliness, where a speck of trash spills over onto their private thoughts and peaceful existence. Yet the neighborhood concepts which most of these former tenement dwellers grew up with are still in evidence. There are eyes in every second-story window, observing any stranger on the streets in minute detail, and visitors are associated with this house and that. There are pleasantries on the street, greeting of neighbors and friends.

Then, suddenly, the streets are empty. It is 5:30, dinner time in an Italian 28 working-class neighborhood. The men have walked or driven home from their jobs. The children have stopped playing. In the Rinaldi-DeGiovanni home, the beautiful homemade noodles lie on the bed in the guest bedroom, uncooked, waiting for the meat sauce and imported, expensive cheese.

In the kitchen on the top floor apartment, the Rinaldi grandparents are   29 eating vegetables in garlic oil with fresh Italian bread, waiting for the third generation of the family to be available from their busy life. This third generation is swimming in the beach-club pool, clowning with friends, listening to rock music, drinking soda pop, eating frankfurters, oblivious to the lifetime of dedication and hardship represented by the plates of rare and delicious fettucine in marvelous sauce that await them.

Critical Thinking and Discussion

1. Briefly characterize each of the three generations of the Rinaldi-DeGiovanni home.
2. Is this account of change pessimistic, optimistic, or neither?
3. How is this family's immigrant experience different from immigrant experiences you are familiar with?
4. The young in this family are now busy living their own lives. Do you think that as they mature they will be more concerned with family and with their roots?

Reading-Related Writing

1. Summarize the experiences, behavior, and attitudes of the three generations of the Rinaldi-DeGiovanni family.
2. Write about three generations in your own family or in another family you know well.
3. Assuming that the three generations of the Rinaldi-DeGiovanni family represent not only age differences but also differences imposed by comprehensive views of the immigrant, the transitional, and the assimilated, how are they like the separation of generations in families that have *not* recently immigrated?

THE EARTHQUAKE AT NEVADA STREET*

Michael Jimenez

Student Michael Jimenez remembers that before an earthquake, there were three types of families in his neighborhood—Latino, Asian, and white. They were separate entities; they always kept to themselves. Then the earthquake came.

My immediate neighborhood was a lot like many other middle-class neigh- 1
borhoods. We had white picket fences, green lawns, dogs in the back, and
racial tension. Certain behavior seemed to characterize each racial group. No
one expected that anything could bring us together.

Across the street was a park where every weekend morning, no matter 2
what the weather conditions, Asians ran. At six o'clock they circled the park
in uniform lines. From the houses that were still occupied, their neighbors
peered out suspiciously from the windows. As the morning melted away into
midday, no trace of the Asians was left. It was as if they had vanished from the
earth without a trickle of sweat to be found. Only then would the whites
occupy their portion of the day. The air would be filled with sounds of
yardwork, mainly lawnmowers severing off the crowns of little blades of
grass. After a hard day's work, the whites would drag out lawn chairs, plant
them next to their doorways, sit down, and sip beverages. Eyes again peered
out of windows distrustfully. As the sun slowly sank into the horizon, those
with a darker shade of skin claimed their time. Trumpets, accordion, and
guitars pounded out sounds from the porches of Latinos. Their conversations
could be heard in neighboring houses. Often they sang along with the music,
irritating everyone within a radius of a block. A third time, unfriendly eyes
peered out. The tension among the block's inhabitants was reaching its simmering point.

Then on a cold October day, without any notice, the earth shook back- 3
ward and forward, up and down. It terrified every living creature in Southern
California. The Asians bounded out of their houses. The whites rolled onto
their lawns. The Latinos trampled each other in their escape. Everyone scurried across the street to the park. Each family held tightly to its own tree as it
swung back and forth. People could hear a rumbling. Dogs howled and
jumped in desperation, and glass shattered on floors. After the shaking
ceased, family members slowly walked back into their houses, eyeballing each
other, frowning, mumbling insincere greetings.

Before the families had a chance to estimate their losses, the earth jolted 4
once more, returning the families to the park. For the remainder of the day,
short, violent shockwaves detained the families within the park perimeter for
fear that their houses would crumble. Night visited the families, and they
brought out barbecue grills and started fires for cooking and warmth. The
frowns suddenly turned into sympathetic sighs. The mumbling turned into
snorts of laughter, as family members recalled their own and others' gestures
and action in the heat of panic. Children whispered shyly, and grown-ups
grouped. Later into the night they talked as they had never talked before.

Currently, things seem to be working our for the inhabitants of Nevada 5
Avenue. The Asians are no longer the Asians, but the Trans and the Wongs.
The whites have become the Taylors and the Millers. The Latinos are now the

Jimenez and the Rivera families. Occasionally there are little disputes, but people of different races are more willing to listen to each other now.

Critical Thinking and Discussion

1. What seems to distinguish the cultural groups on Jimenez's block?
2. What seems to keep them apart?
3. Why didn't the first quake bring them together?
4. Is the neighborhood perfect now?
5. What is the message here?

Reading-Relating Writing

1. Write about a neighborhood you are familiar with in terms of its racial divisions.
2. Write about a neighborhood you are familiar with that was brought together by an extraordinary event.

Collaborative Learning

After dividing the class into small groups, follow these steps:

1. Discuss and set up a classification of families according to how they deal with problems. Each group will represent a type of family. These are some possible types: Father Knows Best (patriarchal), Mother Knows Best (matriarchal), Father or Mother Knows Best, Depending on the Problem (bureaucratic), Father, Mother, or Child Knows Best, Depending on the Problem (relativistic), The Whole Family Knows Best (democratic), No One Knows Best (anarchic). If you have students from different cultures in your class who believe that they can fairly represent typical ethnic family types for decision making, then you might instead use terms such as Traditional Chinese, Traditional Native American, and so on (but try to avoid flagrant stereotyping).
2. Decide on a problem that might occur and discuss how each of your family types would deal with that particular problem.
3. As groups, write simple scripts (at least indicating some of the content of the speaking parts) to show how the different families would deal with the issue.
4. Act out the scripts for the class.
5. Either as a group or as individuals, write a classification-and-division paper (classification for the types of families and division for the organization within a particular family) based on what you have learned from

developing ideas within your group and listening to what others have done.

Connections

1. Point out similarities and dissimilarities among the generations of Native Americans (Harjo) and Italian-Americans (Santini).
2. Examine "An American Dream," a family from a movie or from television, or any family with which you are familiar in terms of the family traits presented in "All Happy Clans Are Alike."

8

Culture: Blends and Clashes

All societies change as new ideas encounter the old. In the culturally diverse society, those encounters may represent vastly different perspectives, as shown in these blends and clashes. Richard Rodriguez writes poignantly of the private world inside his own home and the alien public world outside. In "Cultural Barriers and the Press to Americanize," Punjabi students deal with a new set of values and a new environment. Zora Neale Hurston discusses her lifelong conflict, which she largely ignored while she celebrated her own identity as an African-American, in "How It Feels to Be Colored Me." The Hispanic clash with Anglos is analyzed in "Anglo vs. Hispanic: Why?" and Spanish and English language blending is discussed and illustrated in "Spanglish." Amy Tan explores the resistance to cultural compromise and the destructiveness caused by lack of understanding in her autobiographical short story "Four Directions." Its title offers a fitting characterization for the many facets of cultural diversity.

WRITING STRATEGIES AND TECHNIQUES: COMPARISON AND CONTRAST

Comparison and contrast is a method of showing similarities and dissimilarities between subjects. *Comparison* is concerned with organizing and developing points of similarity; *contrast* has the same function for dissimilarity. In some instances a writing assignment may require that you cover only similarities or only dissimilarities. Occasionally, an instructor may ask you to separate one from the other. Usually, you will combine them within the larger design of your paragraph or essay. For convenience, the term *comparison* is often applied to both comparison and contrast, because both utilize the same techniques and are usually combined into one operation.

This chapter will help you deal with topics and choose strategies in writing comparison and contrast.

Generating Topics and Working with the 4 Ps

Comparison and contrast is basic to your thinking. In your daily activities, you consider similarities and dissimilarities between persons, things, concepts, political leaders, doctors, friends, instructors, schools, nations, classes, movies, and so on. You naturally turn to comparison and contrast to solve problems and make decisions in your affairs and in your writing. Because you have had so many comparative experiences, finding a topic to write about is likely to be only a matter of choosing from a great number of appealing ideas. Freewriting, brainstorming, and clustering will help you generate topics that are especially workable and appropriate for particular assignments.

Many college writing assignments will specify a topic or ask you to choose one from a list. Regardless of the source of your topic, the procedure for developing your ideas by comparison and contrast is the same. That procedure can be appropriately called the "4 Ps": *purpose, points, pattern,* and *presentation.*

Purpose

Two kinds of purposes exist: informative and persuasive.

Informative   If you want to explain something about a topic by showing each subject in relationship with the other, then your purpose will be informative. For example, you might be comparing two composers, Beethoven and Mozart. Both were musical geniuses, so you might decide that it would be senseless to argue that the work of one is superior to the other. Instead, you choose to reveal interesting information about both by showing them in relation to each other. The emphasis of your writing would be on insights into their characteristics, heightened by these characteristics' being placed alongside each other.

Persuasive   If you want to show that one actor, one movie, one writer, one president, one product, or one idea is better than another, your purpose will be persuasive. It will take shape as you write, beginning with emphasis in the topic sentence or thesis and being reinforced by repetition throughout your paper, in each case indicating that one side is superior.

Let's say for sake of an extended illustration that you are taking a course in twentieth-century European history and you are asked to write about two leaders. You have always been fascinated by the dictators Mussolini and Hitler, and you decide to pursue that as a topic. In freewriting, you discover that you know quite a bit about the two leaders. By brainstorming you come up with some specific information about the two.

Who?   Mussolini and Hitler.
What?   fascist leaders, racists—with Hitler being more extreme
Where?   in Italy and Germany, respectively
When?   the decade before and during World War II
Why?   greed, morals, possible psychological problems, with Hitler being more extreme
How?   setting up totalitarian states

You tentatively decide that your purpose will be to persuade readers that, although both men were fascists, Hitler was more extreme in all important respects. If you need more information, you will have to consult your textbooks, your lecture notes, or sources in the library.

Points

The points are the ideas that will be applied somewhat equally to both sides of your comparison and contrast. They begin to emerge in freewriting, take on more precision in brainstorming, acquire a main position in further brainstorming, and assume the major part of the framework in the outline.

Especially when writing on an assigned topic based on lectures and reading, you will able to decide on these points quickly. The subject material itself may dictate the points. For example, if you were comparing the federal governments of the United States and Great Britain, you would probably use these three points: executive, legislative, and judicial.

Using Clustering as a Technique for Finding Points   If you need to search for points (ideas that will be applied to both sides in your comparative study), clustering can serve you well. You might want to try this approach:

Step 1: Begin your first cluster on the left side of a page in which you double-bubble the side of the comparison you know better, and then to the right of that add bubbles for points based on your tentative purpose. For the second bubble in each chain, add a particular fact about the point.

Step 2: Repeat Step 1 for the second cluster. Draw this one on the right side of the page, and develop the bubbles to the left, making the ideas parallel to those in the first cluster.

Step 3: Add other divisions as they occur to you.

Step 4: Select the divisions that will serve you best in developing your tentative thesis or topic sentence, and connect those points from the two sides with double lines.

See Figure 8.1 for an example of a cluster on the Mussolini-Hitler topic.

Figure 8.1 Sample Cluster on the Mussolini-Hitler Topic

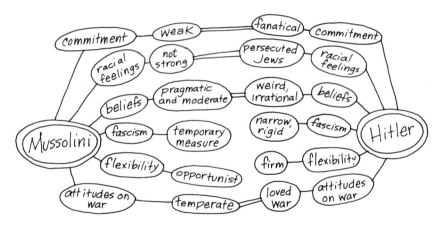

With this much organized information, you are ready to decide if you wish to modify the tentative topic sentence or thesis that has directed your use of the first three strategies. In this instance, the information supports your controlling idea.

TOPIC SENTENCE OR THESIS: Although Mussolini and Hitler were both fascist dictators, they were also significantly different, and Hitler was more extreme.

At this time you have a purpose and points. The final preparation stage will help you select and develop a pattern for your comparison.

Pattern

Now you will choose between two basic patterns of organization: (1) subject by subject (opposing) or (2) point by point (alternating). In long papers you may mix them, but in the shorter pieces associated with most college assignments, you will almost certainly select one and make it your basic organizational plan.

In comparison and contrast, the outline works especially well in indicating relationships and sequence. As with most other writing forms we have worked with, the sequence of a comparison-and-contrast essay can be based on time, space, or emphasis. Emphasis is the most likely order.

The following illustrations will show you the two patterns as they are applied to both the paragraph (on the left) and the essay (on the right).

In the *subject-by-subject* approach, organize your material around the subjects—the sides of the comparative study, as shown in Figure 8.2.

Figure 8.2 Subject-by-Subject Organization

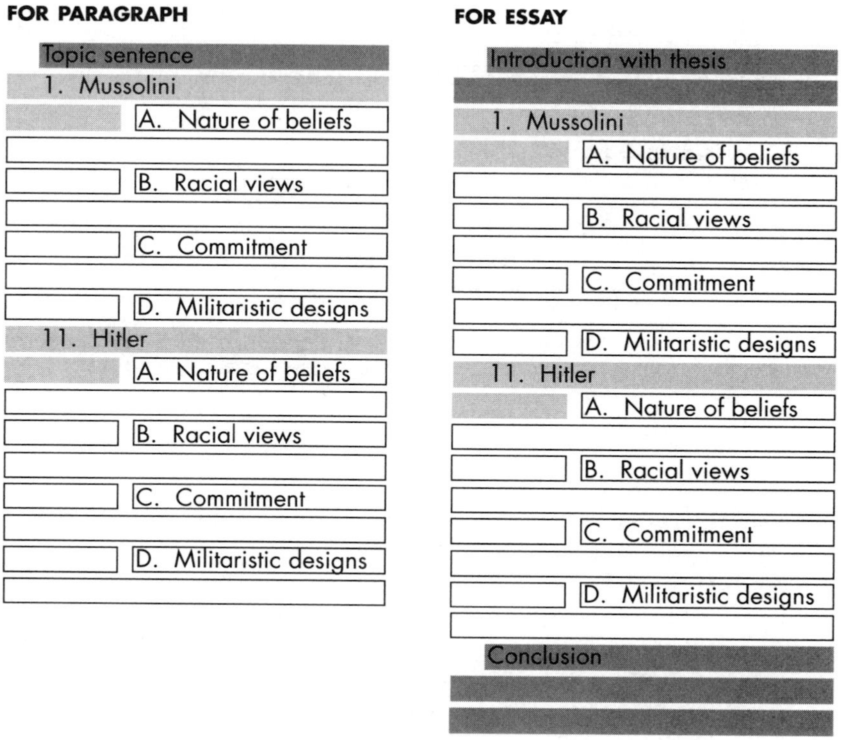

FOR PARAGRAPH

Topic sentence
1. Mussolini
   A. Nature of beliefs
   B. Racial views
   C. Commitment
   D. Militaristic designs
11. Hitler
   A. Nature of beliefs
   B. Racial views
   C. Commitment
   D. Militaristic designs

FOR ESSAY

Introduction with thesis

1. Mussolini
   A. Nature of beliefs
   B. Racial views
   C. Commitment
   D. Militaristic designs
11. Hitler
   A. Nature of beliefs
   B. Racial views
   C. Commitment
   D. Militaristic designs

Conclusion

In the *point-by-point* approach, organize your paper mainly around the points that you will apply to the two subjects as shown in Figure 8.3.

Figure 8.3   Point-by-Point Organization

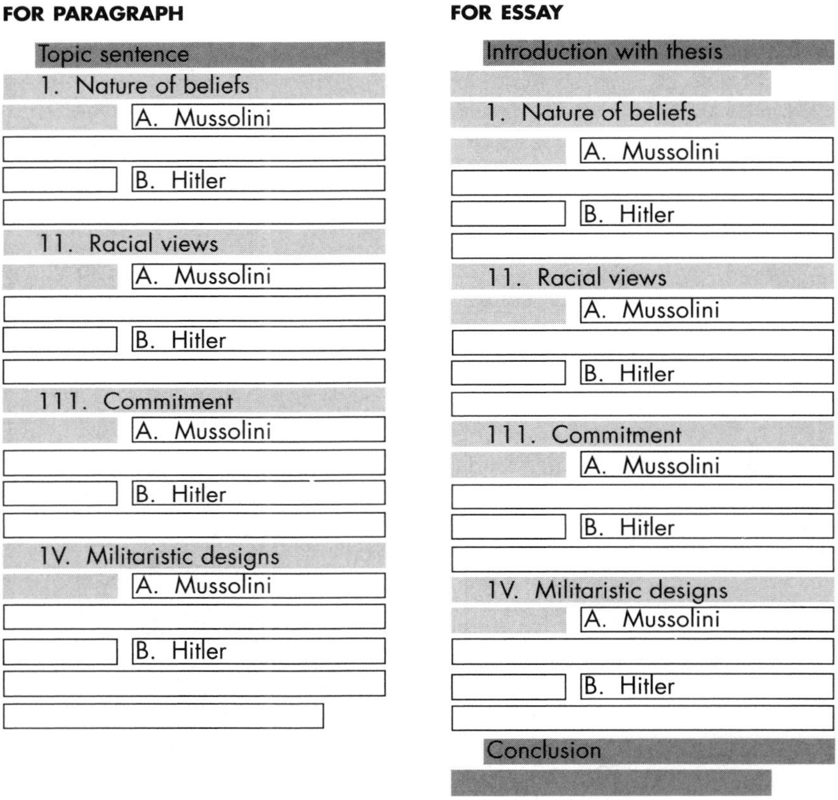

FOR PARAGRAPH

> Topic sentence
>
> 1. Nature of beliefs
>   - A. Mussolini
>   - B. Hitler
> 11. Racial views
>   - A. Mussolini
>   - B. Hitler
> 111. Commitment
>   - A. Mussolini
>   - B. Hitler
> 1V. Militaristic designs
>   - A. Mussolini
>   - B. Hitler

FOR ESSAY

> Introduction with thesis
>
> 1. Nature of beliefs
>   - A. Mussolini
>   - B. Hitler
> 11. Racial views
>   - A. Mussolini
>   - B. Hitler
> 111. Commitment
>   - A. Mussolini
>   - B. Hitler
> 1V. Militaristic designs
>   - A. Mussolini
>   - B. Hitler
>
> Conclusion

Presentation

The two patterns of organization—subject by subject and point by point—are equally valid, and each has its strengths for presentation of ideas.

As shown in Figure 8.2, the subject-by-subject pattern presents material in large blocks, which means the reader can see a body of material that is complete. However, if the body of material is complex, the reader has the burden of remembering ideas in going from one part to the next. Parallel development of ideas and cross-references in the second portion of the paragraph or essay can often offset that potential problem.

The point-by-point pattern shown in Figure 8.3 provides an immediate and direct relationship of points to subject. Therefore, it is especially useful in arguing that one side is superior to the other, in dealing with complex topics, and in working with longer compositions. But because of its direct applications, if development is not sufficient, it can appear mechanical and monotonous. You can avoid that appearance by developing each idea thoroughly.

Of the two patterns of development, the point-by-point is used more frequently in college writing assignments in both the paragraph and the essay forms.

In the following examples, the topic of Mussolini and Hitler is presented first in the final draft stage of the paragraph form and then in the essay form. Note that the paragraph (often, as here, the essay in miniature) is expanded into an essay by developing the topic sentence, the supporting points, and the restated topic sentence into separate paragraphs: introduction, middle paragraph, middle paragraph, middle paragraph, middle paragraph, and conclusion. Although both the paragraph and the essay make good observations and illustrate the use of pattern for presentation, for this topic the full essay would probably be more suitable in fulfilling the writer's purpose. Both the paragraph and the essay use a point-by-point arrangement.

Here is the paragraph:

topic sentence	Hitler and Mussolini have often been thought of as twin dictators, but there was considerable difference between the two men and their regimes, and Hitler was more extreme. Both
point 1: beliefs	were fascists; however, the intensity of their beliefs varied. Until he fell under the influence of Hitler, Mussolini had
transition	tended to be pragmatic and often moderate. Hitler, *on the contrary,* carved out a series of weird, nihilistic goals near the beginning of his career and held to them unswervingly. Racism
point 2: racism	is justly associated with all fascism at that time, and, therefore,
transition	Mussolini is implicated. It should be pointed out, however, that the blatant racism by the Italians occurred after Mussolini's deep association with Hitler. *But* Hitler had held racist views from the beginning of his political career, and it was a main
point 3: commitment	motive in the Nazi movement. Their degree of commitment to act also varied. Mussolini merely talked and strutted for the
transition	most part. He had few fixed doctrines and increasingly accommodated himself to circumstances. *But* Hitler meant every bit of his bellicosity, and was willing to wage the most frightful
point 4: militaristic designs	war of all time. A study of their involvement in that war, however, reveals striking dissimilarities. Italian fascism was com-
transition	paratively restrained and conservative until the Nazi example spurred it to new activity. *In contrast,* the radical and dynamic

pace of Hitler hardly flagged from January 1933 to April 1945. In the process, anti-Semitism, concentration camps, and total war produced a febrile and sadistic nightmare without any parallel in the Italian experience. Though both were fascists, history shows them to be different in all of these respects, and in each one Hitler was more radical.

restated topic sentence

Here is the essay:

introduction with thesis

Hitler and Mussolini have often been thought of as twin 1 dictators, but there were considerable differences between the two men and their regimes, and Hitler was more extreme. These differences become apparent when one considers the nature of their beliefs, their racial views, their commitment, and their militaristic designs.

topic sentence

(middle paragraph)

Both were fascists; however, the intensity of their beliefs 2 varied. Until he fell under the influence of Hitler, Mussolini had tended to be pragmatic and often moderate. Though Italian fascism coined the concept of "totalitarianism," it allowed some nonfascist elements to enjoy partial liberty and never achieved a true totalitarian state. Hitler, on the contrary, carved out a series of weird, nihilistic goals near the beginning of his career and held to them unswervingly. Though he often showed a fine sense of tactics and timing, he was not so pragmatic and adjustable as Mussolini, but was bent on fixed, narrow ends. He was sexually perverted and his mind betrayed the marks of severe compulsive neurosis and emotional instability, conceiving irrational hatreds and enthusiasms of a thoroughly demonic nature which he was determined to see through to the end.

topic sentence

(middle paragraph)

Racism is justly associated with all fascism at that time, 3 and, therefore, Mussolini, along with Hitler, is implicated. It should be pointed out, however, that the blatant racism by the Italians occurred after Mussolini's deep association with Hitler. Prior to that, for many years there had been no racial doctrine in Italian fascist ideology. But Hitler had held racist views from the beginning of his political career, and it was a main motive in the Nazi movement. To resolve the "Jewish problem," he eventually slaughtered at least five million people.

topic sentence

(middle paragraph)

Their degree of commitment to act also varied. From a 4 distance toward the end of the war, they may have seemed quite similar, but over the span of their reigns, they were different. Mussolini merely talked and strutted for the most part. He had few fixed doctrines and increasingly accommodated himself to circumstances. But Hitler meant every bit of his bellicosity, and was willing to wage the most frightful war of all time.

topic sentence

(middle paragraph)

A study of their involvement in that war, however, reveals 5
striking dissimilarities. Italian fascism was comparatively
restrained and conservative until the Nazi example spurred it
to new activity. Mussolini talked of a militaristic policy, while
he followed a more temperate course in practice and kept the
peace for thirteen years, knowing that Italy could not gain from
a major war. In contrast, the radical and dynamic pace of Hitler
hardly flagged from January 1933 to April 1945. In the process, anti-Semitism, concentration camps, and total war produced a febrile and sadistic nightmare without any parallel in
the Italian experience.

conclusion

Thus, though both were fascists, history shows them to be 6
different in both ideas and action. Only at the end of their
relationship, when Mussolini succumbed to Hitler's domina-
tion, do the two leaders appear as twin dictators, but beneath
those appearances it is Hitler who is the pure true believer, the
fascist dictator.

The following student-written paragraph and essay illustrate effective
uses of comparison and contrast.

VIETNAMESE WOMEN IN VIETNAM AND IN THE UNITED STATES*

Thung Tran

Fleeing from communism, many Vietnamese have left Vietnam to resettle
with their families in the United States. Here they have discovered that American culture is very different from Vietnamese culture, especially for women in
the home. As a young child, a Vietnamese woman in Vietnam is educated in
Confucian theories: "Obey your father as a child, and your husband when
you get married." In Vietnam the woman's role is that of childbearer and
housekeeper. She has to be a good wife, a good mother, and a good daughter-
in-law, if she wants to be happy. She is the first to rise and the last to go to
bed in a household that includes her husband and his parents. She will
seldom make decisions, and she will always be obedient. She expects that her
husband will support the family financially and that he and her in-laws will
direct the family. But in American society, family relationships are different. A
wife is likely to work outside the family, and because she provides part of the
financial support, she expects her husband to share some of the work in
raising the children, keeping the house, and maintaining a relationship with
the in-laws, who will probably live in a separate house. In America, the

Vietnamese wife will probably have more freedom in the home and more responsibility outside the home.

FAMILIES: STREET AND PRISON

Jodie Monroe

thesis

When I say that all parts of ordinary society also exist in 1 a women's prison, people sometimes say, "What about families?" The answer is easy. Yes, even families. And prison families even have all the parts that "street" families do. Although most inmates are not and will not be involved in prison families, I've been in two, and I've observed dozens of them from up close. I know all about the parents, the children and relatives, and the activities. I even know about the broken families.

topic sentence

Whether the family is conventional or prison, the 2 parents set the tone. In conventional families, it's the male and female, from Ward and June Cleaver, to Cliff and Claire Huxtable, to Roseanne and Dan Conners. We know the TV families well; the parents hold things together and solve problems. In the prison, it's a strong lesbian couple that attracts a family arrangement. Usually one member has the masculine image and the other has the feminine. Sometimes the authority is shared, but as with TV families, the male figure is usually dominant. One family in our unit now has a dominant father figure called "Daddy Wabash" (who likes to play "Wabash Cannonball" on her harmonica), and "Mama Catalina" (who frequently wears a bathing suit for underwear).

topic sentence

Offspring have their family needs, regardless of 3 where they are. In TV families, like most others, kids are busy growing up. They want to be independent, but they want their comforts and nurturing. They need guidance and protection, even from themselves. Wherever they are, families also enjoy the sense of having an extended family with aunts, uncles, cousins, and grandparents. The prison "children" are the same in almost all respects. They want the security they once had in a family or simply the security that others had and they didn't when they were growing up in dysfunctional families, foster homes, and juvenile halls. Cricket and Loco are two such prison children. It so happens that they are young and both products of foster homes and juvenile halls, but not all prison children are young; they just need to be willing subordinates to a couple in a family arrangement. Cricket and Loco are not sexually involved with anyone, but that can vary, too. Daddy Wabash and Mama Catalina boss their children around, but they also protect them from some of the strong-arming that goes on out on the yard, and they provide them with birthday parties, family conferences, and special family meals and get-togethers. The extended family is likely to have some cousins, aunts and uncles, and sometimes grandparents who will attend meetings periodically and be around to satisfy their own special needs and provide services. In return, children such as Cricket and Loco clean their parents' cells and bring them special presents. This being summer, one will sometimes see Cricket and Loco bring ice water to the family meetings and use swatters to keep flies away from their parents. People are commonly called "Mama" and "Daddy" and "Daughter" and so on. Sometimes drugs and prison wine (called "hootch") are part of family life.

topic sentence   These days families everywhere break up in record 4 number. More than half the regular marriages will end in divorce. When that occurs the family may be divided and members will join other families. The prison situation is not so different. The parent couple, such as Daddy Wabash and Mama Catalina, may break up (over drugs, infidelity, or basic incompatibility), one parent may get sent to a different prison, or one parent may be paroled. When that occurs, the remaining parent may take on a new partner, even someone else from the family, and the family will continue. Or the family may just disintegrate. The Daddy Wabash and Mama Catalina family is stable because the parents have been together for a long time, and they are both lifers who do not have bad problems with drugs.

This family is only one of numerous families active 5 now. If there is any trend at this prison, it is for the new inmates to be part of established gangs with street connections instead of being members of prison families. From my point of view, that makes prison a worse place to live. The breakdown of the American family weakens society no matter where it happens.

WRITER'S CHECKLIST

- Purpose: At some point during the exploration of your topic, define your purpose clearly, answering these questions:

  Am I writing a work that is mainly comparison, mainly contrast, or balanced?
  Is my main purpose to explain or to persuade?

- Points

  List your points of comparison and contrast, perhaps in your clustering.
  Eliminate irrelevant points.

- Pattern

  Select the subject-by-subject or the point-by-point pattern after considering your topic and planned treatment. The point-by-point is usually preferred. Only in long papers is there likely to be a mixture of patterns.
  Compose an outline reflecting the pattern you select.

- Presentation

  Be sure to give somewhat equal treatment to each application of a point to the subject. Attention to each part of the outline will usually ensure balanced development.
  Use transitional words and phrases to indicate comparison and contrast and to establish coherence.
  Note that the paragraph should have a carefully stated topic sentence; the essay should have a clear thesis and each developmental paragraph should have a topic sentence broad enough to embrace its content.

PUBLIC AND PRIVATE

Richard Rodriguez

Every person has a public life and a private life, and the character of each is colored by a variety of cultural forces. If the family in the United States includes parents born in Mexico, then the public life may be conducted mainly in English and the private life mainly in Spanish. In this passage from "Private Language, Public Language," Rodriguez says cultural contrast is natural and even complementary.

For me there were none of the gradations between public and private society so normal to a maturing child. Outside the house was public society; inside the house was private. Just opening or closing the screen door behind me was an important experience. I'd rarely leave home all alone or without reluctance. Walking down the sidewalk, under the canopy of tall trees, I'd warily notice the—suddenly—silent neighborhood kids who stood warily watching me. Nervously, I'd arrive at the grocery store to hear there the sounds of the *gringo*—foreign to me—reminding me that in this world so big, I was a foreigner. But then I'd return. Walking back toward our house, climbing the steps from the sidewalk, when the front door was open in summer, I'd hear voices beyond the screen door talking in Spanish. For a second or two, I'd stay, linger there, listening. Smiling, I'd hear my mother call out, saying in Spanish (words), "Is that you, Richard?" all the while her sounds would assure me: *You are home now; come closer; inside. With us.*

Critical Thinking and Discussion

1. What is the topic sentence of this paragraph?
2. What sounds especially remind Rodriguez of the separation between private or public society?
3. What part of the house separates public and private society?
4. Is the pattern used in this paragraph point by point or subject by subject?

Reading-Related Writing

1. Write a comparative study of a similar experience you or someone you know has had.
2. Write about the gap that sometimes occurred between generations, classes, or genders as you were growing up.

ETHNIC SPACE INVADERS

Sandra Tsing Loh

When you are talking to another person, how close do you typically stand? Do people sometimes encroach on your space? Of course, the space you need may depend on your mood, your psychological state, the immediate noise levels, and so on, but it just may be something else: Sandra Tsing Loh says it may be a matter of cultural preference.

Ethnicity has a lot to do with our basic tendencies toward the use of personal space. Misunderstandings are most likely to occur because of the different requirements of different populations, according to the large and growing body of social research that is now decades old. People who live in high-contact cultures—including Mediterranean, Latin American and Middle Eastern countries—typically stand about a foot apart when they interact, face each other directly, and engage in lots of eye contact and touching. At the noncontact end of the continuum are North European cultures, where people stand farther apart and try to avoid accidental touching in social or business settings. . . . While Middle Easterners may want to smell and touch whomever they're interacting with, visually oriented Americans are more concerned with being able to see the person clearly. Ultimately, Americans fall somewhere in between the "contact" and "noncontact" ethnic groups (appropriate for a melting-pot society), generally standing two feet apart—or sitting four to five feet apart—during social conversations. And hyphenated Americans seem to space themselves between their two cultures. "It appears that Hispanics do use less space than Anglos when interacting," says Rutgers University professor of psychology John R. Aiello, Ph.D., in the *Handbook of Environmental Psychology.* Dr. Aiello also reports that, on average, African-Americans stand farther apart when conversing than Anglo-Americans do.

Critical Thinking and Discussion

1. What is meant by "high-contact" cultures?
2. Why do Americans fall somewhere in between the contact and noncontact societies?
3. Why do you think African-Americans stand farther apart when conversing than Anglo-Americans do?

Reading-Related Writing

1. Do a study in which you experiment with different conversational distances with people from various cultural groups. Write a paper about

these examples that will tend to confirm or contradict the ideas in this paragraph.
2. Write a piece in which you discuss people you know from different cultural groups who have different space requirements.
3. Do space requirements differ depending on the region of the United States a person comes from (West, South, East) or on whether he or she is from an urban, suburban, or rural setting? Experiment and write a report.

ON KISSING ASIANS IN PUBLIC*

Karen Tran Baker

Marriage within a culture is a series of confrontations and compromises; marriage between cultures compounds those problems. At the core of any good marriage is love and affection, but the appropriateness of place and occasion for displays of love and affection may vary greatly. Karen Tran Baker offers her Asian view of American kissing.

When an Asian-American marries an American, it's not just two people getting married; it's two cultures. As a Vietnamese immigrant, I married an American and discovered that both my husband and I had adjustments to make. We married for love, and we are still in love. Our love is the same deep down, but our expression of it differs somewhat. As for Americans, the majority seem to have no problem in showing affection for each other, whether in private or public. When my husband comes home, he wants to kiss me right there even if it is in front of the whole family. In public, he may take my hand, or sometimes even kiss me in a place as open as a restaurant. Although I am flattered by his affection and I know it is genuine, which makes me feel affectionate in return, I am sometimes self-conscious and uncomfortable. In my culture, expressions of emotion such as kissing, touching, and hugging are done behind closed doors. In my twenty-nine years, I don't recall the last time I hugged my parents, though I am with them frequently for all kinds of occasions. And I have never seen my parents hold hands or hug one another. I don't want my husband to stop showing his affection in public, because it is his way, but I do wish I could stop feeling embarrassed when he bends over and gives me a big kiss in Burger King.

Critical Thinking and Discussion

1. How are "private and public" at the center of Baker's concern?
2. Does she love her husband less because of the timing and occasion of his kisses?

3. Is she more concerned about his behavior or hers? How do you react to her feelings about her husband's behavior?
4. What other cultures are similar to hers regarding public and private displays of affection? What other cultures are similar, and perhaps even more demonstrative, than her husband's? Do these attitudes also vary, depending on the generation and the region from which a person comes?

Reading-Related Writing

1. Write about your own attitudes toward the private and public displays of affection in terms of your cultural background.
2. Write about your observations regarding the display of affection (hugging, kissing, touching) within families of different cultures.

SPANGLISH

Janice Castro, with Dan Cook and Cristina Garcia

When people of two cultures and two languages come together, the most natural of blends is that of language. In the United States, that idea has been explored extensively by linguists, who have documented just how the migration of people from different regions to states such as California has resulted in the blending of dialects. For example, in California a person may give a Southern pronunciation to the word apricot *("ā pri cot" rather than "ap ri cot") and a Northern pronunciation to the word* blouse *("blous" rather than "blouz"). Phrases also get mixed. As shown in the following essay, the same occurs with Spanish and English.*

In Manhattan a first-grader greets her visiting grandparents, happily 1 exclaiming, "Come here, *siéntate!*" Her bemused grandfather, who does not speak Spanish, nevertheless knows she is asking him to sit down. A Miami personnel officer understands what a job applicant means when he says, "*Quiero un* part time." Nor do drivers miss a beat reading a billboard alongside a Los Angeles street advertising CERVEZA—SIX-PACK!

This free-form blend of Spanish and English, known as Spanglish, is 2 common linguistic currency wherever concentrations of Hispanic Americans are found in the U.S. In Los Angeles, where 55% of the city's 3 million inhabitants speak Spanish, Spanglish is as much a part of daily life as sunglasses. Unlike the broken-English efforts of earlier immigrants from Europe, Asia and other regions, Spanglish has become a widely accepted conversational mode used casually—even playfully—by Spanish-speaking immigrants and native-born Americans alike.

Consisting of one part Hispanicized English, one part Americanized ₃
Spanish and more than a little fractured syntax, Spanglish is a bit like a Robin
Williams comedy routine: a crackling line of cross-cultural patter straight
from the melting pot. Often it enters Anglo homes and families through the
children, who pick it up at school or at play with their young Hispanic
contemporaries. In other cases, it comes from watching TV; many an Anglo
child watching *Sesame Street* has learned *uno dos tres* almost as quickly as one
two three.

Spanglish takes a variety of forms, from the Southern California Anglos ₄
who bid farewell with the utterly silly "*hasta la* bye-bye" to the Cuban-
American drivers in Miami who *parquean* their *carros*. Some Spanglish sentences are mostly Spanish, with a quick detour for an English word or two. A
Latino friend may cut short a conversation by glancing at his watch and
excusing himself with the explanation that he must "*ir al* supermarket."

Many of the English words transplanted in this way are simply handier ₅
than their Spanish counterparts. No matter how distasteful the subject, for
example, it is still easier to say "income tax" than *impuesto sobre la renta*. At
the same time, many Spanish-speaking immigrants have adopted such terms
as VCR, microwave and dishwasher for what they view as largely American
phenomena. Still other English words convey a cultural context that is not
implicit in the Spanish. A friend who invites you to *lonche* most likely has in
mind the brisk American custom of "doing lunch" rather than the languorous
afternoon break traditionally implied by *almuerzo*.

Mainstream Americans exposed to similar hybrids of German, Chinese or ₆
Hindi might be mystified. But even Anglos who speak little or no Spanish are
somewhat familiar with Spanglish. Living among them, for one thing, are 19
million Hispanics. In addition, more American high school and university
students sign up for Spanish than for any other foreign language.

Only in the past ten years, though, has Spanglish begun to turn into a ₇
national slang. Its popularity has grown with the explosive increases in U.S.
immigration from Latin American countries. English has increasingly collided
with Spanish in retail stores, offices and classrooms, in pop music and on
street corners. Anglos whose ancestors picked up such Spanish words as
rancho, bronco, tornado and *incommunicado,* for instance, now freely use such
Spanish words as *gracias, bueno, amigo* and *por favor.*

Among Latinos, Spanglish conversations often flow easily from Spanish ₈
into several sentences of English and back.

Spanglish is a sort of code for Latinos: the speakers know Spanish, but ₉
their hybrid language reflects the American culture in which they live. Many
lean to shorter, clipped phrases in place of the longer, more graceful expressions their parents used. Says Leonel de la Cuesta, an assistant professor of
modern languages at Florida International University in Miami: "In the U.S.,
time is money, and that is showing up in Spanglish as an economy of

language." Conversational examples: *taipiar* (type) and *winshi-wiper* (windshield wiper) replace *escribir a maquina* and *limpiaparabrisas*.

Major advertisers, eager to tap the estimated $134 billion in spending 10
power wielded by Spanish-speaking Americans, have ventured into Spanglish to promote their products. In some cases, attempts to sprinkle Spanish through commercials have produced embarrassing gaffes. A Braniff airlines ad that sought to tell Spanish-speaking audiences they could settle back *en* (in) luxuriant *cuero* (leather) seats, for example, inadvertently said they could fly without clothes (*encuero*). A fractured translation of the Miller Lite slogan told readers the beer was "Filling, and less delicious." Similar blunders are often made by Anglos trying to impress Spanish-speaking pals. But if Latinos are amused by mangled Spanglish, they also recognize these goofs as a sort of friendly acceptance. As they might put it, *no problema*.

Critical Thinking and Discussion

1. Why do people change and blend languages?
2. How do such changes occur?
3. Why are mistakes tolerated so easily, according to the author?

Reading-Related Writing

1. If you are from a region in which Spanglish is spoken, do your own comparative study of Spanglish and your native language, complete with your comments on causes, occasions for usage, and reactions to the blends.
2. Write about a blend of other languages or about a blend of dialects by people from different parts of the country (for example, Southern dialect with another in California).
3. Write about a blend of class dialects that occurs because of the influence of music and movies (rap, reggae, and so on). Give specific examples.
4. Apply the idea of blending to another aspect of culture, such as dress, home furnishings, diets, or behavior.

CULTURAL BARRIERS AND THE PRESS TO AMERICANIZE

Margaret A. Gibson

For most people, moving from one country to another involves much more than geography; it involves culture, with a whole configuration of behavior. In this excerpt from a sociological study, Punjabi students are in a new world, the United States, and they must deal with ways that are alien to their experiences.

All Punjabi students were faced with conflicting sets of expectations regarding 1 appropriate behavior, one set applicable to their Punjabi world and the other to the world of school. At home, for example, Punjabi young people learned to defer to their elders and to remain respectfully quiet in their presence. When Punjabis first entered American schools, whether as small children or teenagers, they were reluctant to speak in class except to respond with factual information to a teacher's direct question. Punjabi students were especially uncomfortable with the American technique of "brainstorming," one elementary teacher observed, and fell silent when expected to express their own ideas. High school teachers made similar observations. " 'I don't know,' is their answer almost before the question is asked," one English teacher responded, when asked if Punjabi students participated in class discussions. It was rare, said another, for Punjabi girls "to be outgoing enough to initiate conversation in class." Part of the difficulty stemmed from the coeducational nature of American high schools.

In Punjab villages teenage boys and girls traditionally avoid conversation 2 with one another and even eye contact. In Indian schools, girls are not faced with the necessity of mixing with boys or speaking up in their presence. Classroom interaction is structured differently and, in most cases, secondary schooling is segregated by sex. At Valleyside High the Punjabi girls, including those born in America, participated only with great reluctance in coeducational activities, especially those that appeared competitive, such as physical education classes. They did not wish to draw attention to themselves in the presence of the opposite sex.

Just talking to boys could pose difficulty, particularly for the newer arriv- 3 als: "A family that has just come over gets really upset if they see their [teenage] daughter talking to some guy," one student explained. Even for the American-educated students informal conversation between the sexes did not always come easily: "When I came here [to the high school] from eighth grade and saw girls talking to guys I though, 'Oh my God, what are you doing?' I had never thought of myself doing that. And if a guy came I'd go the other way." Most Punjabi girls did talk to boys at school, we discovered, but not in front of their parents. One student explained in an interview.

Interviewer: Does it bother your parents if you just speak to fellow stu- 4 dents who are guys?

Girl: A lot of guys . . . come by [my house]and say "Hi, how are you?" I 5 tell them not to stop [by] . . . because my mom and dad would get mad. They say, "Okay, we understand." I talk to guys here at school, and if my parents were to find out they would probably kick me out of school.

Interviewer: Just for chatting with them?   6

Girl: They are afraid . . . the guy might start liking me.   7

Interviewer: How do they feel about your making friends with American 8
girls?

Girl: They don't say anything about that, just as long as I stay away from 9
boys and going out on dates.

Interviewer: So you can mix with all kinds of girls?   10

Girl: Yes . . . I enjoy talking to everybody. I even like to talk to boys. I've 11
always been shy, but I enjoy talking to them. . . . If you don't talk to people
they might say, "She thinks she's too good." I don't consider myself too good
to talk to anybody. I think everybody is equal.

Interviewer: It must be awfully hard on the girls when they know their 12
parents would really get upset.

Girl: Just about every girl here [at the high school] talks to everybody. If 13
their parents were to be with them, they would have to face the other way. It's
like in India. You hardly can look at anybody at all.

Punjabi students had learned to behave one way at home, another at 14
school, but even in school the separation between the sexes remained. In
sharp contrast to Valleysider social patterns, Punjabi boys and girls were
never seen walking or sitting together. In group meetings, such as a get-
together of the Asian Club, girls and boys sat separately. Most girls also
refrained from speaking up in these sorts of gatherings, not, they said,
because they felt incompetent to do so, but because it was their way of
showing respect for the opposite sex.

Coeducational schooling posed the most obvious difficulties for Punjabis, 15
but the constant attention given to preparing young people to go off on their
own and to make decisions in accordance with individual rather than family
wishes provided equal cause for tension. The entire high school curriculum
carried an implicit emphasis on teaching students that they had both the
responsibility and the right to make decisions independent of their elders'
views. So strong was the individualist orientation that it had become formal-
ized in a social studies course titled "On Your Own." This course or one
similar to it was required for graduation.

In this class students learned how to rent an apartment, get married, plan 16
the family budget, and even arrange a funeral—all on their own. Punjabi
students were distinctly uncomfortable with this class, which from start to
finish presumed white, middle-class values. Lessons dealing with marriage
and family life, always taught from a Western point of view, were embarrassing to Punjabi adolescents, as were units dealing with contraception, abor-
tion, and divorce, particularly in the coeducational setting of the American
classroom. Outside of class Punjabi girls were teased by Punjabi boys for
having to pair off with members of the opposite sex for some of their assign-

ments, in accordance with the teacher's instructions. In spite of their discomfort with this and many other class assignments, however, the girls reported that "whatever the teacher says, we have to do."

Even some Valleysider parents expressed concern about the heavy 17 emphasis by school personnel on independent decision making for young people. The high school, they felt, was undercutting parental authority, teaching students, for example, not to believe something just because "your parents believe it." Some objected to the message that at age eighteen the child, then legally an adult, could "do as he pleases, at school, at home, or any place else, and the parents don't have anything to say about it." Those Valleysiders who wished the schools would do more to support parental authority were also those who reinforced the legitimacy of school authority. In this respect, some Valleysider parents sounded very much like their Punjabi counterparts.

Most Punjabi students in time learned to juggle the different demands 18 and expectations of home and school. There were occasions, however, when Punjabi girls resisted complying with class requirements, even at the risk of losing credit. Physical education raised the most difficult problems. Two years of physical education were mandatory for high school graduation. Students received full credit if they attended class regularly, changed into gym clothes (short shorts and shirt), and made a reasonable effort to do what was asked of them. Although requirements seemed straightforward to Valleyside teachers, for many of the Punjabi girls in the senior sample they were simply beyond the pale. "Our children cannot change for sports," said one Punjabi parent; "this is against our culture." Almost no Punjabi parents wanted their daughters to expose their legs in the presence of boys or men. Some girls wore street clothes to class until they realized they would fail. Then they changed to sweat pants, no matter the temperature. . . .

Quite a few Punjabi parents were opposed to all sports for adolescent 19 girls, especially if they were expected to run around in the presence of boys or men. In Punjab villages, only little girls played outside. An older girl, one man pointed out, would be seen "walking with her head low." Right or wrong, he concluded, Punjabi parents wanted the same from their daughters in Valleyside. . . .

In spite of all the pressures and counterpressures, Punjabi students made 20 every effort to meet the demands of the formal curriculum, only rarely refusing to comply with a teacher's demands or school regulations, and then only in matters perceived to affect family and community honor. This was true even though Punjabi students often found the values of the classroom incompatible with those advocated by their parents. The easy give and take between the sexes and between students and teachers, the emphasis on individual decision making and on asserting one's own ideas, and the underlying assumption that majority-group norms should prevail were examples of home-school discontinuities with which all Punjabi students had to contend and with which, in fact, they were successfully contending, by working out a multicultural modus vivendi.

Punjabis did not view compliance with school rules or doing what one 21
must to succeed academically as symbols of majority-group conformity, and they rewarded those who excelled in school. Diligence in matters academic and the acceptance of school authority were not equated, in the Punjabi view, with "acting white" or "like the Americans." Furthermore, although Punjabi teenagers condemned peers who acted "like whites," they enjoyed American burgers, wore designer jeans, and, if they could possibly manage it, zoomed down a highway standing on the seat in an open Trans Am.

Vocabulary

Punjabi (1)　　　　　defer (1)
applicable (1)　　　 modus vivendi (20)

Critical Thinking and Discussion

1. Is this more a study of comparison or contrast?
2. What is the thesis?
3. Is there much difference between Punjabi students in elementary school and in high school?
4. What cultural norms condition the Punjabi students to behave as they do?
5. How do Punjabi students sometimes compromise between home and school values?
6. How do Punjabi students and parents typically react to lessons based on "white, middle-class values"?
7. How do the Punjabi students feel about becoming Americanized, and what aspects of American culture do they readily accept?

Reading-Related Writing

1. Write about any cultural differences you have experienced between your family and your community or school.
2. Write about a cultural group within your school that has had to make special adjustments because of a conflict of values.
3. Write a piece in which you agree or disagree with the way Valleyside High has handled the problem of conflict of values relating to the Punjabis. Consider writing this statement from the point of view of a typical Punjabi parent.
4. Draw up a set of guidelines to regulate conflicts in a school with a multicultural makeup. Include the guidelines in a piece about the need to be considerate of diversity within the larger American culture.

HOW IT FEELS TO BE COLORED ME

Zora Neale Hurston

Zora Neale Hurston (1903–1960) was born into a highly segregated society, yet she heroically refused to be overwhelmed and silenced by prejudice. After completing her formal education at Howard University, Barnard College, and Columbia University, she went on to edit a collection of black folklore, Mules and Men, *and to write numerous essays, short stories, poems, novels, and her autobiography,* Dust Tracks on a Road. *This essay was written when she was twenty-five.*

I am colored but I offer nothing in the way of extenuating circumstances   1
except the fact that I am the only Negro in the United States whose grandfather on the mother's side was *not* an Indian chief.

I remember the very day that I became colored. Up to my thirteenth year   2
I lived in the little Negro town of Eatonville, Florida. It is exclusively a
colored town. The only white people I knew passed through the town going
to or coming from Orlando. The native whites rode dusty horses, the Northern tourists chugged down the sandy village road in automobiles. The town
knew the Southerners and never stopped cane chewing when they passed.
But the Northerners were something else again. They were peered at cautiously from behind curtains by the timid. The more venturesome would
come out on the porch to watch them go past and got just as much pleasure
out of the tourists as the tourists got out of the village.

The front porch might seem a daring place for the rest of the town, but it   3
was a gallery seat for me. My favorite place was atop the gate-post. Pro-
scenium box for a born first-nighter. Not only did I enjoy the show, but I
didn't mind the actors knowing that I liked it. I usually spoke to them in
passing. I'd wave at them and when they returned my salute, I would say
something like this: "Howdy-do-well-I-thank-you-where-you-goin'?" Usually
automobile or horse paused at this, and after a queer exchange of compli-
ments, I would probably "go a piece of the way" with them, as we say in
farthest Florida. If one of my family happened to come to the front in time to
see me, of course negotiations would be rudely broken off. But even so, it is
clear that I was the first "welcome-to-our-state" Floridian, and I hope the
Miami Chamber of Commerce will please take notice.

During this period, white people differed from colored to me only in that   4
they rode through town and never lived there. They liked to hear me "speak
pieces" and sing and wanted to see me dance the parse-me-la, and gave me
generously of their small silver for doing these things, which seemed strange
to me for I wanted to do them so much that I needed bribing to stop. Only

they didn't know it. The colored people gave no dimes. They deplored any joyful tendencies in me, but I was their Zora nevertheless. I belonged to them, to the nearby hotels, to the county—everybody's Zora.

But changes came in the family when I was thirteen, and I was sent to 5 school in Jacksonville. I left Eatonville, the town of the oleanders, as Zora. When I disembarked from the river-boat at Jacksonville, she was no more. It seemed that I had suffered a sea change. I was not Zora of Orange County any more. I was now a little colored girl. I found it out in certain ways. In my heart as well as in the mirror, I became a fast brown—warranted not to rub nor run.

But I am not tragically colored. There is no great sorrow dammed up in 6 my soul, nor lurking behind my eyes. I do not mind at all. I do not belong to the sobbing school of Negrohood who hold that nature somehow has given them a lowdown dirty deal and whose feelings are all hurt about it. Even in the helter-skelter skirmish that is my life, I have seen that the world is to the strong regardless of a little pigmentation more or less. No, I do not weep at the world—I am too busy sharpening my oyster knife.

Someone is always at my elbow reminding me that I am the granddaugh- 7 ter of slaves. It fails to register depression with me. Slavery is sixty years in the past. The operation was successful and the patient is doing well, thank you. The terrible struggle that made me an American out of a potential slave said, "On the line!" The Reconstruction said "Get set!"; and the generation before said "Go!" I am off to a flying start and I must not halt in the stretch to look behind and weep. Slavery is the price I paid for civilization, and the choice was not with me. It is a bully adventure and worth all that I have paid through my ancestors for it. No one on earth ever had a greater chance for glory. The world to be won and nothing to be lost. It is thrilling to think—to know that for any act of mine, I shall get twice as much praise or twice as much blame. It is quite exciting to hold the center of the national stage, with the spectators not knowing whether to laugh or to weep.

The position of my white neighbor is much more difficult. No brown 8 specter pulls up a chair beside me when I sit down to eat. No dark ghost thrusts its leg against mine in bed. The game of keeping what one has is never so exciting as the game of getting.

I do not always feel colored. Even now I often achieve the unconscious 9 Zora of Eatonville before the Hegira. I feel most colored when I am thrown against a sharp white background.

For instance at Barnard. "Beside the waters of the Hudson" I feel my race. 10 Among the thousand white persons, I am a dark rock surged upon, and overswept, but through it all, I remain myself. When covered by the waters, I am; and the ebb but reveals me again.

Sometimes it is the other way around. A white person is set down in our 11 midst, but the contrast is just as sharp for me. For instance, when I sit in the drafty basement that is The New World Cabaret with a white person, my color comes. We enter chatting about any little nothing that we have in common and are seated by the jazz waiters. In the abrupt way that jazz orchestras have, this one plunges into a number. It loses no time in circumlocutions, but gets right down to business. It constricts the thorax and splits the heart with its tempo and narcotic harmonies. This orchestra grows rambunctious, rears on its hind legs and attacks the tonal veil with primitive fury, rending it, clawing it until it breaks through to the jungle beyond. I follow those heathen—follow them exultingly. I dance wildly inside myself; I yell within, I whoop; I shake my assegai above my head, I hurl it true to the mark *yeeeeooww!* I am in the jungle and living in the jungle way. My face is painted red and yellow and my body is painted blue. My pulse is throbbing like a war drum. I want to slaughter something—give pain, give death to what, I do not know. But the piece ends. The men of the orchestra wipe their lips and rest their fingers. I creep back slowly to the veneer we call civilization with the last tone and find the white friend sitting motionless in his seat, smoking calmly.

"Good music they have here," he remarks, drumming the table with his 12 fingertips.

Music. The great blobs of purple and red emotion have not touched him. 13 He has only heard what I felt. He is far away and I see him but dimly across the ocean and the continent that have fallen between us. He is so pale with his whiteness then and I am *so* colored.

At certain times I have no race, I am *me*. When I set my hat at a certain 14 angle and saunter down Seventh Avenue, Harlem City, feeling as snooty as the lions in front of the Forty-Second Street Library, for instance. So far as my feelings are concerned, Peggy Hopkins Joyce on the Boule Mich with her gorgeous raiment, stately carriage, knees knocking together in a most aristocratic manner, has nothing on me. The cosmic Zora emerges. I belong to no race nor time. I am the eternal feminine with its string of beads.

I have no separate feeling about being an American citizen and colored. I 15 am merely a fragment of the Great Soul that surges within the boundaries. My country, right or wrong.

Sometimes, I feel discriminated against, but it does not make me angry. It 16 merely astonishes me. How *can* any deny themselves the pleasure of my company? It's beyond me.

But in the main, I feel like a brown bag of miscellany propped against a 17 wall. Against a wall in company with other bags, white, red and yellow. Pour out the contents, and there is discovered a jumble of small things priceless and worthless. A first-water diamond, an empty spool, bits of broken glass, lengths of string, a key to a door long since crumbled away, a rusty knife-blade, old shoes saved for a road that never was and never will be, a nail bent under the weight of things too heavy for any nail, a dried flower or two still a little fragrant. In your hand is the brown bag. On the ground before you is the jumble it held—so much like the jumble in the bags, could they be emptied, that all might be dumped in a single heap and the bags refilled without altering the content of any greatly. A bit of colored glass more or less would not matter. Perhaps that is how the Great Stuffer of Bags filled them in the first place—who knows?

Critical Thinking and Discussion

1. When and why does Hurston become aware of her color?
2. Why does she not bemoan her color?
3. Why does she feel it is exciting to be "colored"?
4. What does she say is the difference between the experience of the blacks and the whites who listen to jazz?
5. When does she feel she has no race?
6. Why does being discriminated against not make her angry?
7. Explain the meaning of the last paragraph.

Reading-Related Writing

1. Using this essay as a model, write a piece about your own culture.
2. If you disagree with the author, write a comparison and contrast statement about what you feel is the proper response to some of the issues she brings up.
3. Write a comparative study about your own experiences before and after you became aware of racial identify and the way different groups are treated.

LIVING IN TWO WORLDS

Marcus Mabry

Coming from a poor family in New Jersey, Marcus Mabry encountered a very different part of society at Stanford University, a prestigious and expensive private school across the continent. Returning home made him all the more aware of the disparity between rich and poor, black and white. This essay was published in Newsweek on Campus.

A round, green cardboard sign hangs from a string proclaiming, "We built a proud new feeling," the slogan of a local supermarket. It is a souvenir from one of my brother's last jobs. In addition to being a bagger, he's worked at a fast-food restaurant, a gas station, a garage and a textile factory. Now, in the icy clutches of the Northeastern winter, he is unemployed. He will soon be a father. He is 19 years old.

In mid-December I was at Stanford, among the palm trees and weighty 2 chore of academe. And all I wanted to do was get out. I joined the rest of the undergrads in a chorus of excitement, singing the praises of Christmas break. No classes, no midterms, no finals . . . and no freshmen! (I'm a resident assistant.) Awesome! I was looking forward to escaping. I never gave a thought to what I was escaping to.

Once I got home to New Jersey, reality returned. My dreaded freshmen 3 had been replaced by unemployed relatives; badgering professors had been replaced by hard-working single mothers, and cold classrooms by dilapidated bedrooms and kitchens. The room in which the "proud new feeling" sign hung contained the belongings of myself, my mom and my brother. But for these two weeks it was mine. They slept downstairs on couches.

Most students who travel between the universes of poverty and affluence 4 during breaks experience similar conditions, as well as the guilt, the helplessness and, sometimes, the embarrassment associated with them. Our friends are willing to listen, but most of them are unable to imagine the pain of the impoverished lives that we see every six months. Each time I return home I feel further away from the realities of poverty in America and more ashamed that they are allowed to persist. What frightens me most is not that the American socioeconomic system permits poverty to continue, but that by participating in that system I share some of the blame.

Last year I lived in an on-campus apartment, with a (relatively) modern 5 bathroom, kitchen and two bedrooms. Using summer earnings, I added some expensive prints, a potted palm and some other plants, making the place look like the more-than-humble abode of a New York City Yuppie. I gave dinner parties, even a *soirée française*.

For my roommate, a doctor's son, this kind of life was nothing extraordi- 6 nary. But my mom was struggling to provide a life for herself and my brother. In addition to working 24-hour-a-day cases as a practical nurse, she was trying to ensure that my brother would graduate from high school and have a decent life. She knew that she had to compete for his attention with drugs and other potentially dangerous things that can look attractive to a young man when he sees no better future.

Living in my grandmother's house this Christmas break restored all the 7 forgotten, and the never acknowledged, guilt. I had gone to boarding school on a full scholarship since the ninth grade, so being away from poverty was not new. But my own growing affluence has increased my distance. My friends say that I should not feel guilty: what could I do substantially for my family at this age, they ask. Even though I know that education is the right thing to do, I can't help but feel, sometimes, that I have it too good. There is no reason that I deserve security and warmth, while my brother has to cope with potential unemployment and prejudice. I, too, encounter prejudice, but it is softened by my status as a student in an affluent and intellectual community.

More than my sense of guilt, my sense of helplessness increases each time 8 I return home. As my success leads me further away for longer periods of time, poverty becomes harder to conceptualize and feels that much more oppressive when I visit with it. The first night of break, I lay in our bedroom, on a couch that let out into a bed that took up the whole room, except for a space heater. It was a little hard to sleep because the springs from the couch stuck through at inconvenient spots. But it would have been impossible to sleep anyway because of the groans coming from my grandmother's room next door. Only in her early 60s, she suffers from many chronic diseases and couldn't help but moan, then pray aloud, then moan, then pray aloud.

This wrenching of my heart was interrupted by the 3 A.M. entry of a 9 relative who had been allowed to stay at the house despite rowdy behavior and threats toward the family in the past. As he came into the house, he slammed the door, and his heavy steps shook the second floor as he stomped into my grandmother's room to take his place, at the foot of her bed. There he slept, without blankets on a bare mattress. This was the first night. Later in the vacation, a Christmas turkey and a Christmas ham were stolen from my aunt's refrigerator on Christmas Eve. We think the thief was a relative. My mom and I decided not to exchange gifts that year because it just didn't seem festive.

A few days after New Year's I returned to California. The Northeast was 10 soon hit by a blizzard. They were there, and I was here. That was the way it had to be, for now. I haven't forgotten; the ache of knowing their suffering is always there. It has to be kept deep down, or I can't find the logic in studying and partying while people, my people, are being killed by poverty. Ironically, success drives me away from those I most want to help by getting an education.

Somewhere in the midst of all that misery, my family has built within me, 11 "a proud feeling." As I travel between the two worlds it becomes harder to remember just how proud I should be—not just because of where I have come from and where I am going, but because of where they are. The fact that they survive in the world in which they live is something to be very proud of, indeed. It inspires within me a sense of tenacity and accomplishment that I hope every college graduate will someday possess.

Vocabulary

academe (2)	affluence (3)	ironically (10)
badgering (3)	socioeconomic (4)	tenacity (11)
dilapidated (3)	*soirée française* (5)	

Critical Thinking and Discussion

1. What is the thesis of this essay?
2. What is the purpose of this comparative study? Is Mabry only showing differences or is he making a point—for instance, about one standard of life having a higher quality?
3. What are the main points used for comparison?
4. Does poverty make people more considerate of others in the same condition?
5. How does Mabry draw strength from contemplating the misery of his family?

Reading-Related Writing

1. Write about a similar situation in which you or someone you know has had significant experiences in two contrasting environments. The two situations might be home and work, home and school, your home and the home of a friend, your home and the home of a relative, your home in this country and the home you had in another country. Consider using points such as physical surroundings, behavior of people, attitudes of others, and your attitude.

ANGLO VS. HISPANIC: WHY?

Arthur L. Campa

Arthur L. Campa (1905–1978), professor and chairperson of the Department of Modern Languages at Denver University, served as cultural attaché at numerous United States embassies and wrote widely about cultural matters. Here he points out how two cultures often find it difficult to understand each other and make accommodations.

The cultural differences between Hispanic and Anglo-American people have 1
been dwelt upon by so many writers that we should all be well informed about the values of both. But audiences are usually of the same persuasion as the speakers, and those who consult published works are for the most part specialists looking for affirmation of what they believe. So, let us consider the same subject, exploring briefly some of the basic cultural differences that cause conflict in the Southwest, where Hispanic and Anglo-American cultures meet.

   Cultural differences are implicit in the conceptual content of the lan- 2
guages of these two civilizations, and their value systems stem from a long

series of historical circumstances. Therefore, it may be well to consider some of the English and Spanish cultural configurations before these Europeans set foot on American soil. English culture was basically insular, geographically and ideologically; was more integrated on the whole, except for some strong theological differences; and was particularly zealous of its racial purity. Spanish culture was peninsular, a geographical circumstance that made it a catch-all of Mediterranean, central European and north African peoples. The composite nature of the population produced a marked regionalism that prevented close integration, except for religion, and led to a strong sense of individualism. These differences were reflected in the colonizing enterprise of the two cultures. The English isolated themselves from the Indians physically and culturally; the Spanish, who had strong notions about *pureza de sangre* [purity of blood] among the nobility, were not collectively averse to adding one more strain to their racial cocktail. Cortés led the way by siring the first *mestizo* in North America, and the rest of the conquistadores followed suit. The ultimate products of these two orientations meet today in the Southwest.

Anglo-American culture was absolutist at the onset; that is, all the domi- 3 nant values were considered identical for all, regardless of time and place. Such values as justice, charity, honesty were considered the superior social order for all men and were later embodied in the American Constitution. The Spaniard brought with him a relativistic viewpoint and saw fewer moral implications in man's actions. Values were looked upon as the result of social and economic conditions.

The motives that brought Spaniards and Englishmen to America also 4 differed. The former came on an enterprise of discovery, searching for a new route to India initially, and later for new lands to conquer, the fountain of youth, minerals, the Seven Cities of Cíbola and, in the case of the missionaries, new souls to win for the Kingdom of Heaven. The English came to escape religious persecution, and once having found a haven, they settled down to cultivate the soil and establish their homes. Since the Spaniards were not seeking a refuge or running away from anything, they continued their explorations and circled the globe 25 years after the discovery of the New World.

This peripatetic tendency of the Spaniard may be accounted for in part 5 by the fact that he was the product of an equestrian culture. Men on foot do not venture far into the unknown. It was almost a century after the landing on Plymouth Rock that Governor Alexander Spotswood of Virginia crossed the Blue Ridge Mountains, and it was not until the nineteenth century that the Anglo-Americans began to move west of the Mississippi.

The Spaniard's equestrian role meant that he was not close to the soil, as 6 was the Anglo-American pioneer, who tilled the land and built the greatest agricultural industry in history. The Spaniard cultivated the land only when he had Indians available to do it for him. The uses to which the horse was put also varied. The Spanish horse was essentially a mount, while the more robust

English horse was used in cultivating the soil. It is therefore not surprising that the viewpoints of these two cultures should differ when we consider that the pioneer is looking at the world at the level of his eyes while the *caballero* [horseman] is looking beyond and down at the rest of the world.

One of the most commonly quoted, and often misinterpreted, character-   7 istics of Hispanic peoples is the deeply ingrained individualism in all walks of life. Hispanic individualism is a revolt against the incursion of collectivity, strongly asserted when it is felt that the ego is being fenced in. This attitude leads to a deficiency in those social qualities based on collective standards, an attitude that Hispanos do not consider negative because it manifests a measure of resistance to standardization in order to achieve a measure of individual freedom. Naturally, such an attitude has no *reglas fijas* [fixed rules].

Anglo-Americans who achieve a measure of success and security through   8 institutional guidance not only do not mind a few fixed rules but demand them. The lack of a concerted plan of action, whether in business or in politics, appears unreasonable to Anglo-Americans. They have a sense of individualism, but they achieve it through action and self-determination. Spanish individualism is based on feeling, on something that is the result not of rules and collective standards but of a person's momentary, emotional reaction. And it is subject to change when the mood changes. In contrast to Spanish emotional individualism, the Anglo-American strives for objectivity when choosing a course of action or making a decision.

The Southwestern Hispanos voiced strong objections to the lack of cour-   9 tesy of the Anglo-Americans when they first met them in the early days of the Santa Fe trade. The same accusation is leveled at the *Americanos* today in many quarters of the Hispanic world. Some of this results from their different conceptions of polite behavior. Here too one can say that the Spanish have no *reglas fijas* because for them courtesy is simply an expression of the way one person feels toward another. To some they extend the hand, to some they bow and for the more *íntimos* there is the well-known *abrazo*. The concepts of "good or bad" or "right or wrong" in polite behavior are moral considerations of an absolutist culture.

Another cultural contrast appears in the way both cultures share part of   10 their material substance with others. The pragmatic Anglo-American contributes regularly to such institutions as the Red Cross, the United Fund and a myriad of associations. He also establishes foundations and quite often leaves millions to such institutions. The Hispano prefers to give his contribution directly to the recipient so he can see the person he is helping.

A century of association has inevitably acculturated both Hispanos and   11 Anglo-Americans to some extent, but there still persist a number of culture traits that neither group has relinquished altogether. Nothing is more disquieting to an Anglo-American who believes that time is money than the time perspective of Hispanos. They usually refer to this attitude as the "*mañana* psychology." Actually, it is more of a "today psychology," because Hispanos cultivate the present to the exclusion of the future; because the latter has not arrived yet, it is not a reality. They are reluctant to relinquish the present, so they hold on to it until it becomes the past. To an Hispano, nine is nine until it is ten, so when he arrives at nine-thirty, he jubilantly exclaims: "*¡Justo!*" [right on time]. This may be why the clock is slowed down to a walk in Spanish while in English it runs. In the United States, our future-oriented civilization plans our lives so far in advance that the present loses its meaning. January magazine issues are out in December; 1973 cars have been out since October; cemetery plots and even funeral arrangements are bought on the installment plan. To a person engrossed in living today the very idea of planning his funeral sounds like the tolling of the bells.

It is a natural corollary that a person who is present oriented should be   12
compensated by being good at improvising. An Anglo-American is told in advance to prepare for an "impromptu speech," but an Hispano usually can improvise a speech because "*Nosotros lo improvisamos todo*" [we improvise everything].

Another source of cultural conflict arises from the difference between   13
being and *doing*. Even when trying to be individualistic, the Anglo-American achieves it by what he does. Today's young generation decided to be themselves, to get away from standardization, so they let their hair grow, wore ragged clothes and even went barefoot in order to be different from the Establishment. As a result they all ended up doing the same things and created another stereotype. The freedom enjoyed by the individuality of *being* makes it unnecessary for Hispanos to strive to be different.

In 1963 a team of psychologists from the University of Guadalajara in   14
Mexico and the University of Michigan compared 74 upper-middle-class students from each university. Individualism and personalism were found to be central values for the Mexican students. This was explained by saying that a Mexican's value as a person lies in his *being* rather than, as is the case of the Anglo-Americans, in concrete accomplishments. Efficiency and accomplishments are derived characteristics that do not affect worthiness in the Mexican, whereas in the American it is equated with success, a value of highest priority in the American culture. Hispanic people disassociate themselves from material things or from actions that may impugn a person's sense of being, but the Anglo-Americans shows great concern for material things and assumes responsibility for his actions. This is expressed in the language of each culture. In Spanish one says, "*Se me cayó la taza*" [the cup fell away from me] instead of "I dropped the cup."

In English, one speaks of money, cash and all related transactions with   15
frankness because material things of this high order do not trouble Anglo-Americans. In Spanish such materialistic concepts are circumvented by referring to cash as *efectivo* [effective] and when buying or selling as something *al*

contado [counted out], and when without it by saying *No tengo fondos* [I have no funds]. This disassociation from material things is what produces *sobriedad* [sobriety] in the Spaniard according to Miguel de Unamuno, but in the Southwest the disassociation from materialism leads to *dejadez* [lassitude] and *desprendimiento* [disinterestedness]. A man may lose his life defending his honor but is unconcerned about the lack of material things. *Desprendimiento* causes a man to spend his last cent on a friend, which when added to lack of concern for the future may mean that tomorrow he will eat beans as a result of today's binge.

The implicit differences in words that appear to be identical in meaning 16 are astonishing. Versatile is a compliment in English and an insult in Spanish. An Hispano student who is told to apologize cannot do it, because the word doesn't exist in Spanish. *Apología* means words in praise of a person. The Anglo-American either apologizes, which is a form of retraction abhorrent in Spanish, or compromises, another concept foreign to Hispanic culture. *Compromiso* means a date, not a compromise. In colonial Mexico City, two hidalgos once entered a narrow street from opposite sides, and when they could not go around, they sat in their coaches for three days until the viceroy ordered them to back out. All this because they could not work out a compromise.

It was that way then and to some extent now. Many of today's conflicts 17 in the Southwest have their roots in polarized cultural differences, which need not be irreconcilable when approached with mutual respect and understanding.

Vocabulary

implicit (2)	*mestizo* (2)	incursion (7)
conceptual (2)	conquistadores (2)	*abrazo* (9)
configuration (2)	peripatetic (5)	circumvented (15)
zealous (2)	equestrian (5)	hidalgo (16)

Critical Thinking and Discussion

1. The points for Campa's comparative study of Hispanic- and Anglo-Americans include historical circumstances for values, integration, absolutism, motives for coming to America, need for laws, concepts of polite behavior, charity, time, being and doing, and word and meaning differences. Add subdivisions to those points.
2. Is Campa's purpose to give information about each side or to show that one side is superior? How does the last paragraph give you an answer?
3. What kind of evidence does he give to support each point?

4. Is the treatment of the two sides balanced, or is one discussed in more detail? If you believe one is presented with more emphasis, why might the author have done that?

Reading-Related Writing

1. Take one of the smaller points such as "polite behavior" among Anglos and Hispanics (or any groups) and develop it, using your own examples.
2. Using this essay as a model or partial model, write about the differences between other groups such as Chinese-Americans and Euro-Americans, Korean-Americans and African-Americans, or Native Americans and Euro-Americans.
3. This essay was written about twenty years ago. Are Campa's views still valid? Discuss your own reactions in detail.
4. How deeply ingrained are the attitudes he discusses? Write an essay in which you discuss the extent to which Hispanics may change after living in the United States for more than one generation and perhaps inter-marrying with other cultural groups. Give some examples from your own experience or from what you have read.

FOUR DIRECTIONS

Amy Tan

This story comes from The Joy Luck Club, *Amy Tan's book on which an acclaimed film of the same name is based. The plot of this story deals with the differences between generations and cultures and the difficulties of communication and understanding.*

After much thought, I came up with a brilliant plan. I concocted a way for   1
Rich to meet my mother and win her over. In fact, I arranged it so my mother would want to cook a meal especially for him. I had some help from Auntie Suyuan. Auntie Su was my mother's friend from way back. They were very close, which meant they were ceaselessly tormenting each other with boasts and secrets. And I gave Auntie Su a secret to boast about.

After walking through North Beach one Sunday, I suggested to Rich that   2
we stop by for a surprise visit to my Auntie Su and Uncle Canning. They lived on Leavenworth, just a few blocks west of my mother's apartment. It was late afternoon, just in time to catch Auntie Su preparing Sunday dinner.

"Stay! Stay!" she had insisted.   3

"No, no. It's just that we were walking by," I said.   4

"Already cooked enough for you. See? One soup, four dishes. You don't   5
eat it, only have to throw it away. Wasted!"

How could we refuse? Three days later, Auntie Suyuan had a thank-you   6
letter from Rich and me. "Rich said it was the best Chinese food he has ever
tasted," I wrote.

And the next day, my mother called me, to invite me to a belated birth-   7
day dinner for my father. My brother Vincent was bringing his girlfriend, Lisa
Lum. I could bring a friend, too.

I knew she would do this, because cooking was how my mother expressed   8
her love, her pride, her power, her proof that she knew more than Auntie Su.
"Just be sure to tell her later than her cooking was the best you ever tasted,
that is was far better than Auntie Su's," I told Rich. "Believe me."

The night of the dinner, I sat in the kitchen watching her cook, waiting   9
for the right moment to tell her about our marriage plans, that we had
decided to get married next July, about seven months away. She was chopping
eggplant into wedges, chattering at the same time about Auntie Suyuan: "She
can only cook looking at a recipe. My instructions are in my fingers. I know
what secret ingredients to put in just by using my nose!" And she was slicing
with such a ferocity, seemingly inattentive to her sharp cleaver, that I was
afraid her fingertips would become one of the ingredients of the red-cooked
eggplant and shredded pork dish.

I was hoping she would say something first about Rich. I had seen her   10
expression when she opened the door, her forced smile as she scrutinized him
from head to toe, checking her appraisal of him against that already given to
her by Auntie Suyuan. I tried to anticipate what criticisms she would have.

Richard was not only *not* Chinese, he was a few years younger than I was.   11
And unfortunately, he looked much younger with his curly red hair, smooth
pale skin, and the splash of orange freckles across his nose. He was a bit on
the short side, compactly built. In his dark business suits, he looked nice but
easily forgettable, like somebody's nephew at a funeral. Which was why I
didn't notice him the first year we worked together at the firm. But my
mother noticed everything.

"So what do you think of Rich?" I finally asked, holding my breath.   12

She tossed the eggplant in the hot oil and it made a loud, angry hissing   13
sound. "So many spots on his face," she said.

I could feel the pinpricks on my back. "They're freckles. Freckles are   14
good luck, you know," I said a bit too heatedly in trying to raise my voice
above the din of the kitchen.

"Oh?" she said innocently.   15

"Yes, the more spots the better. Everybody knows that."   16

She considered this a moment and then smiled and spoke in Chinese: 17
"Maybe this is true. When you were young, you got the chicken pox. So many
spots, you had to stay home for ten days. So lucky, you thought."

I couldn't save Rich in the kitchen. And I couldn't save him later at the 18
dinner table.

He had brought a bottle of French wine, something he did not know my 19
parents could not appreciate. My parents did not even own wineglasses. And
then he also made the mistake of drinking not one but two frosted glasses
full, while everybody else had a half-inch "just for taste."

When I offered Rich a fork, he insisted on using the slippery ivory chop- 20
sticks. He held them splayed like the knock-kneed legs of an ostrich while
picking up a large chunk of sauce-coated eggplant. Halfway between his plate
and his open mouth, the chunk fell on his crisp white shirt and then slid into
his crotch. It took several minutes to get Shoshana to stop shrieking with
laughter.

And then he had helped himself to big portions of the shrimp and snow 21
peas, not realizing he should have taken only a polite spoonful, until everybody had had a morsel.

He had declined the sautéed new greens, the tender and expensive leaves 22
of bean plants plucked before the sprouts turn into beans. And Shoshana
refused to eat them also, pointing to Rich: "He didn't eat them! He didn't eat
them!"

He thought he was being polite by refusing seconds, when he should 23
have followed my father's example, who made a big show of taking small
portions of seconds, thirds, and even fourths, always saying he could not
resist another bite of something or other, and then groaning that he was so
full he thought he would burst.

But the worst was when Rich criticized my mother's cooking, and he 24
didn't even know what he had done. As is the Chinese cook's custom, my
mother always made disparaging remarks about her own cooking. That night
she chose to direct it toward her famous steamed pork and preserved vegetable dish, which she always served with special pride.

"Ai! This dish not salty enough, no flavor," she complained, after tasting a 25
small bite. "It is too bad to eat."

This was our family's cue to eat some and proclaim it the best she had 26
ever made. But before we could do so, Rich said, "You know, all it needs is a
little soy sauce." And he proceeded to pour a riverful of the salty black stuff
on the platter, right before my mother's horrified eyes.

And even though I was hoping throughout the dinner that my mother 27
would somehow see Rich's kindness, his sense of humor and boyish charm, I
knew he had failed miserably in her eyes.

Rich obviously had had a different opinion on how the evening had 28
gone. When we got home that night, after we put Shoshana to bed, he said

modestly, "Well, I think we hit it off *A-o-kay*." He had the look of a dalmatian, panting, loyal, waiting to be petted.

"Uh-hmm," I said. I was putting on an old nightgown, a hint that I was 29 not feeling amorous. I was still shuddering, remembering how Rich had firmly shaken both my parents' hands with that same easy familiarity he used with nervous new clients. "Linda, Tim," he said, "we'll see you again soon, I'm sure." My parents' names are Lindo and Tin Jong, and nobody, except a few older family friends, ever calls them by their first names.

"So what did she say when you told her?" And I knew he was referring to 30 our getting married. I had told Rich earlier that I would tell my mother first and let her break the news to my father.

"I never had a chance," I said, which was true. How could I have told my 31 mother I was getting married, when at every possible moment we were alone, she seemed to remark on how much expensive wine Rich liked to drink, or how pale and ill he looked, or how sad Shoshana seemed to be.

Rich was smiling. "How long does it take to say, Mom, Dad, I'm getting 32 married?"

"You don't understand. You don't understand my mother." 33

Rich shook his head. "Whew! You can say that again. Her English was *so* 34 bad. You know, when she was talking about that dead guy showing up on *Dynasty*, I thought she was talking about something that happened in China a long time ago."

Critical Thinking and Discussion

1. "Scripting" means planning something so that the people involved do as you want them to do without their knowing what is happening. To what extent did the narrator script the meeting between Rich and her family?
2. In what ways does Rich differ from the narrator's family?
3. In what ways does Rich fall short of her expectations?
4. What is the difference between the way the narrator sees Rich and the way her parents see him?
5. Why didn't she anticipate the problems and simply tell him how to behave?

Reading-Related Writing

1. Write about an occasion when you have introduced someone special to your family and discovered that the encounter did not meet your expectations.

2. Write a comparative study of two family members (such as your spouse and your parent, your parents, a sibling's spouse and you) who come from different cultural backgrounds.
3. Pose as Rich and write about the encounter with the narrator's parents from his point of view.
4. Discuss what he will have to do if he is to become an integral part of this family. Explain how the narrator can and should help.
5. What is the meaning of this short story? Consider what the narrator was trying to do, what happened, and what is likely to occur in the future.

CHINESE PARENTS AND AMERICAN PARENTS*

Cipher Wong

Student Cipher Wong grew up in a traditional Chinese family, which has attitudes different from those of the typical American family toward raising children, specifically when it comes to the idea of responsibility.

According to an old Chinese saying, "No matter how ogreish the tiger, it 1 would never hurt its own baby." Another saying holds that "there are no bad parents." We Chinese are brought up with the idea that parents are good. Therefore, I never doubt the love my parents feel for me. However, now that I am in the United States, I can see that different cultures have different ways of expressing love.

The Chinese way is very protective and directive. Chinese parents 2 express their love by caring about what their children are becoming. They seldom say "I love you" to their children because within our traditional culture it would be embarrassing and undignified to do so. They also don't have to say they are sorry, because everything they do is right ("There are no bad parents"). They want their children to be well educated so that they will be successful as adults. For example, my niece is only six years old, but after she does her school work each day, she must study music with the piano and violin for two hours. Then she practices tennis and ballet. Her parents believe that some day she will be appreciative.

The American parents I know treat their children differently. They are 3 more open with them, and they are more democratic. They say to their children, "I love you," and they give them many choices about work and study. They try to teach their children to distinguish right from wrong and to be their own master. Thus, in most cases, the American children have greater opportunities to be what they wish, and they are more likely to be more individualistic than Chinese. They are guided but not coerced. They can be whatever they want to be instead of what their parents want them to be. And they are more responsible for their own successes and failures. For example, my parents want me to be an accountant, and I am becoming one, though I can make more money at my current job of loan officer. Typically, an American student would not have the parental pressure I have.

All of these observations still remind me of that Chinese saying, "There are no bad parents." With the exception of some who are irresponsible, troubled, or mean spirited, I believe that the saying is true: parents do what they think is best for their children. But there are certainly different ways of parenting. 4

Critical Thinking and Discussion

1. What is the purpose of this comparison and contrast, to inform or to convince?
2. What are the main points in Wong's study?
3. Does he seem to express a preference for one type of family?
4. Do you think Wong will embrace the traditional Chinese family attitudes or the typical American ones when he has his own family?

Reading-Related Writing

1. Write a comparative study of parental values that are different for cultural, generational, or regional reasons.
2. Write a comparative study of behavior and attitudes of children of parents from different cultures or regions.

Collaborative Learning

1. In small groups, use some of the points considered in "Anglo vs. Hispanic: Why?" (values, historical background, motives, concepts of polite behavior, attitudes toward time, charity, laws, views on being and doing) to analyze other pairings (such as Anglo versus Chinese, Anglo versus African-American, Anglo versus Native American, Hispanic versus African-American). Then write a group report, followed by oral reports to the class. In the end, individuals could write their own evaluations of the differences.
2. Form small groups to study each of several pieces in this chapter. Each group will concentrate on a single piece. First, select and discuss a piece. Next, select and coach a group member to impersonate the author of the piece in a class presentation. Presenters should first exchange ideas about cultural blends and clashes (the ideas coming mainly from the pieces) and then answer questions from nonpresenters.

Finally, as a group, write about the idea of blends or clashes, using as support examples from the readings in this chapter.

Connections

1. Write an essay about the blending of cultures. Use evidence from at least three readings in this chapter.
2. Write an essay about cultural clashes. Use evidence from at least three readings in this chapter.
3. Use at least three points from "Anglo vs. Hispanic: Why?" (see question 1 in "Collaborative Projects" above) to write a comparative study of two readings in this chapter.

9

Types and Stereotypes

Look carefully beneath the distortion of a stereotype and find a type. Look carefully beneath a type and find an individual. Typing, as defined in this chapter, means grouping according to one or more common characteristics such as gender, race, and age. Having accurate information about types may enable us to be sensitive to cultural diversity within our society. Stereotyping at best oversimplifies and exaggerates. At worst, it misrepresents and even damages groups and individuals by perpetuating misinformation.

Many of the selections in this chapter are concerned with such stereotyping. Judith Ortiz Cofer writes about the myth of the Latin woman. Jack G. Shaheen contrasts the image of the Arab as presented in the media with the Arabs he knows. Bel Kaufman celebrates, rather than laments, old age and reminds us that there, too, stereotyping misrepresents and demeans, for, as she says, "none of us is a statistic. Each is individual and unique, with untapped potential and unexplored possibilities."

WRITING STRATEGIES AND TECHNIQUES: DEFINITION

Definition is a method of identifying and making the meaning of a term clear. By defining, you answer the question What is the meaning of

293

this? In establishing the meaning, you put limits on the term in the form of characteristics that distinguish it from other entities. For example, in the sentence that follows, the writer defines *incursion:*

> The German *incursion,* a sudden, hostile invasion into Polish territory, was the beginning of World War II.

Here, the writer places limits on *incursion.* It is a certain kind of movement into another's territory that is characterized as being a "sudden hostile invasion." It differs from a visit, a migration to settle land, and even an invasion that is not sudden and, in some cases, not hostile.

Most definitions, like the one in the example sentence, are short, usually a synonymous word, a phrase, or a sentence. Some definitions, however, are a paragraph or an entire essay covering several pages. The short definition is called a *simple definition;* the longer one (a paragraph or essay) is known as an *extended definition.*

Extended Definition

An *extended definition* is the organization and development of the meaning of a term. It may be a paragraph or two or even an entire essay in length. Terms like *socialism, school spirit, correct English, democracy, power, personality, symbolism, prejudice, conformity, ethnocentrism,* and *affluent society* cannot be defined adequately for most assignments with just a synonym or a few lines of explanation. As with other forms of discourse, we are concerned with the purpose, techniques for development, and the organization of extended definitions.

Purpose

The definition can be used as a subordinate part of any one of the other forms of discourse, and it can be the main thrust of the paragraph or essay. Regardless of its stature within the framework of a piece of writing, it will attempt mainly to persuade or inform. Especially when subordinated to the patterns of argumentation, comparison and contrast, and causes and effects, the definition will serve to persuade. Terms such as *discrimination, racism, sexist,* and *punishment* almost always deal with attitudes in a persuasive manner. As always, determine your purpose at the outset and match it with an appropriate tone for the anticipated audience.

Techniques for Development

Definitions can take many forms. In a simple definition, terms can be defined in various ways—by synonyms, direct and indirect explanation, and analytical or formal definitions. They can also be defined by *etymol-*

ogy, the history of the term. For example, the dictionary definition of *indigenous* gives *indigena,* meaning "native" in Latin, as the origin of the word. Another example is *hypocrite,* which once meant "actor" (*hypokrites*) in Greek. A hypocrite, in other words, is a person pretending to be someone else. The history of a word may be of no use in an extended definition because the meaning has changed so drastically, or it may be strikingly useful because it is colorful and incisive. Etymology as a technique for defining is simply one of several to be considered.

Among the more common techniques for defining are the forms of discourse we have worked with in previous chapters. One useful approach is to consider each of the forms as part of your writing of the extended definition. For a particular term, some forms will be more useful than others, and you will naturally use the material that best fulfills your purpose.

Each of the following questions takes an aspect of a form of discourse and directs it toward definition.

- Narration
  Can I tell an anecdote or story to define this subject (such as *jerk, humanitarian, patriot*)? This form may overlap with description and exemplification.
- Description
  Can I describe this subject (such as *a whale* or *the moon*)?
- Exemplification
  Can I give examples of this subject (such as naming individuals to provide examples of *actors, diplomats, comics, satirists,* or *racists*)?
- Functional Analysis or Division
  Can I divide this subject into parts (for example, the parts of a *heart, cell,* or *carburetor*)?
- Process Analysis
  Can I define this subject (such as *lasagna, tornado, hurricane, blood pressure,* or any number of scientific processes) by describing how to make it or how it occurs? (Common to the methodology of communicating in science, this approach is sometimes called the "operational definition.")
- Analysis by Causes and Effects
  Can I define this subject (such as *a flood, a drought, a riot,* or *a cancer*) by its causes or effects?
- Classification
  Can I group this subject (such as kinds of *families, cultures, religions, governments*) into classes?
- Comparison and Contrast
  Can I define this subject (such as *extremist* or *patriot*) by explaining what it is similar to and different from? If you are defining *orangutan* to a person who has never heard of one but is familiar with the gorilla,

then you could make comparison-and-contrast statements. If you want to define *patriot,* then you might want to stress what it is not (the contrast, also called negation) before you explain what it is: a patriot is not a one-dimensional flag waver, not someone who hates "foreigners" because America is always right and always best.

When writing, you can easily incorporate a consideration of these forms into your clustering by adding words to designate the forms of discourse at the first extension of bubbles from the double-bubbled subject to be defined. Figure 9.1 shows an example.

Figure 9.1 Sample Completed Bubble Cluster on Development Techniques

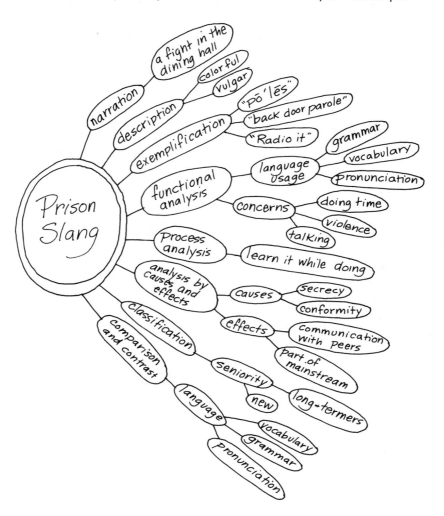

Order

The organization of your extended definition is likely to be one of emphasis, but it may be space or time, depending on the subject material. You
may use one form of discourse for the overall pattern; if so, then you
would employ the principles of organization discussed in previous chapters. Freewriting, brainstorming, and in particular, clustering will provide
you with material. Refine the focus of your ideas into a topic sentence or
thesis, and write an outline to establish the sequence. As you write drafts
and revise, you may go back to modify parts of the writing, especially the
outlining.

Introduction and Development

The three most common ways of introducing an extended definition are
discussing why it is important to define the word, why it is difficult to
define the word, and how the word is often misused.

   Development, whether in the form of sentences for the paragraph or
of paragraphs for the essay, is likely to represent one or more of the forms
of discourse: narration, description, exposition (with its own subdivisions), and argumentation.

   The following student-written paragraph and essay illustrate effective
uses of definition.

PRISON SLANG

Jeri Linda White

topic sentence and basic definition   Prison slang is like other slang in that it is language that
is used in a special way for special reasons. Like conven-
tional slang, some words have unusual, nonstandard
meanings, and some words are invented. Most slang is
used by people who want to conform to group language
customs. In prison it is used both by people who don't
want others to know what they are talking about and by
those who are seeking group identify. As a variety of
more basic definition   language it is like a dialect because it is just part of the
culture of that group. Prison slang covers many areas,
classification   but it especially reflects prisoners' concerns: violence,
talking, and reputation. The very idea of violence is
examples follow   strangely muted by the terms used to discuss brutal acts.
If a person is attacked by a group of people who throw a

blanket over her head before they beat her, she is said to be the recipient of a "blanket party" given by a "rat pack." If she "caught a cold" or they "took her wind," she died. They may have killed her with a sharp instrument called a "shank" or a "shiv." Perhaps she didn't know there was a "raven" (contract) out on her; she thought they were only "putting on a floor show" (pretending) or "selling wolf tickets" (bluffing). She should have listened to their talk more carefully. They said she had "snitched them off" (informed), and her friend had "pulled her coat" (told her something she should know), but then a cop came by and she said, "Radio it, dog-face it, dummy up" (all meaning "shut up"), and then she "put it on hold" (filed it away for future use). That was her mistake because the woman out to get her was a "die hard, hard core, cold piece" (each meaning "career criminal"), who was a "hog" (enforcer), "dancer" (fighter), and a "jive bitch" (agitator). These are only a few of the hundreds of slang words used by women behind bars. They are part of prison life.

MODERN WIFE*

Marie Maxwell

The modern woman, according to dozens of magazine   1
articles, is a super being of incredible organization, patience, wisdom, and grooming. She is never cross with loved ones and never too tired for a game with her children. She wouldn't think of throwing a frozen dinner into the oven and calling it supper. She even has the courage (and the cleaning skills) to own a white carpet. She is a being apart, and I could never quite measure up. I believed that, until I recently decided there were far more women like me than there were Wonder Women.

thesis

The ideal woman featured in the magazines has a   2
lovely home, a handsome husband, and children who at all times appear to have just stepped from the pages of a clothing catalog. Her house is always clean and ready for drop-in guests, and should these guests arrive at supper

time, so much the better. My reality is a single-parent home. I have a son whom I suspect is color-blind, judging from some of his outfits. Often when I return home from work, I must step carefully to avoid the assortment of books, clothes, and toys strewn from one room to the next. Unexpected company better not show up! As for feeding uninvited guests—they had better have an invitation if they expect to be fed.

Unlike me, the women in the articles always seem to have such glamorous and exciting jobs. Most of them receive six-figure incomes and love their jobs (oops!) *careers*. They are fashion designers, doctors, or managers on their way up the corporate ladder. Every working day is another fascinating challenge to anticipate. I sigh wistfully as I read, and I think how dull my secretarial duties are by comparison. I've received two promotions in eight years—hardly a mercurial rise to the top. I generally enjoy my job; it pays the bills and a little bit more, and it has enough variety to prevent abysmal boredom. It's just that I feel somehow shamed by the way I earn my living after reading an article about the "new woman."

Most magazine writers choose as a subject a woman who has also returned to school, in addition to everything else she does. It depresses me to read that she has usually earned a 3.80 grade point average, seemingly effortlessly. Her family cheers her on and never seems to mind the time that school and homework demand from her. Even more disheartening is that her family members report with pride that she was able to make those grades without depriving them of their normal family life. That certainly hasn't been my experience. Algebra, for example, demanded so much of my time and energy that bitter words and sarcasm were routine. When I was married, my husband was supportive only as long as my classes didn't disrupt his life.

Some modern women may indeed be just as they are described in the magazines, but I feel certain that there are many more just like me. My wish would be to have a writer showcase a woman, if not with feet of clay, at least shuffling her way artlessly through a cluttered life and, at times, barely coping. I might not admire her, but I wouldn't feel inadequate, and I'm certain I could identify with her. In fact, I think I would like her.

WRITER'S CHECKLIST

- At the outset, determine your purpose as either persuasive or informative.
- Match your tone to the purpose of the writing.
- Use clustering to consider the other forms of discourse as sources of information for your definition.
- Use an outline to establish the sequence in your main points of development.
- Don't overlook word derivation, synonyms, direct explanations, indirect explanations.
- Avoid *is where* and *is when* circular definitions, and the use of more difficult words in the definition than the one being defined.
- For the extended formal or analytic definition, specify the term, class, and characteristic(s). Example: Capitalism is an economic system characterized by investment of money, private ownership, and free enterprise.
- Consider these ways of introducing a definition: with a question, with a statement of what it is not, with a statement of what it originally meant, or with a discussion of why a clear definition is important. You may use a combination of these ways or all of them before you continue with your definition.
- Whether you will personalize a definition depends on your purpose and your audience. Your instructor may ask you to write about a word within the context of your experience or to write about it from a detached, clinical viewpoint.

TALKING LIKE A LADY

Francine Frank and Frank Anshen

We've all heard that women like to talk. Is that a good generalization, or is this another myth?

Perhaps the most common stereotype about women's speech is that women talk a lot. If we take "a lot" to mean more than men, we are faced with the surprising fact that there seems to be no study which supports this belief, while there are several which show just the opposite. One such study, by Otto Sonder, Jr., is particularly interesting. Sonder organized discussion groups which included women and men and assigned them specific topics. The discussions were recorded and transcribed, but in the transcripts, the participants were identified only by letters, as A, B, etc. Panels of judges who tried to identify the sex of each speaker from these transcripts were correct about fifty-five percent of the time, a result which is better than chance, but not overwhelmingly so. Closer examination of the data, however, reveals some interesting facts. A word count of the recorded discussions showed a clear tendency for the men who participated in the study to utter more words than the women. In other words, men, on the average, actually talked more than did women. Even more interesting is the fact that individuals of either sex who talked a lot were more likely to be judged as males, while taciturn individuals of either sex were more likely to be identified as females. Not only does this study suggest that men are more talkative, it also suggests that the judges "knew" this fact and used it to make judgments about the sexual identify of unknown speakers. Although, consciously, they would probably subscribe to the cultural stereotype of the talkative woman, their judgments show that they knew that the real situation is the direct opposite of the stereotype.

Critical Thinking and Discussion

1. Precisely what is the stereotype and what is the truth about women's speech?
2. Is this surprising to you?
3. To what extent were the judges in Sonder's study familiar with the truth?

Reading-Related Writing

1. Write about other stereotypes relating to women, such as gossiping, superficiality, and emotionalism. Base your conclusions on your experiences or on an experiment or special study you do.

DISABLEDNESS AS A VIOLATION OF THE IDEAL

Nancy Mairs

Why are people bothered by the idea of being disabled? Is it only the matter of inconvenience that is the burden of the disabled? Or is it that we cannot stand imperfection?

Because I hate being crippled, I sometimes hate myself for being a cripple. Over the years I have come to expect—even accept—attacks of violent self-loathing. Luckily, in general our society no longer connects deformity and disease directly with evil (though a charismatic once told me that I have MS because a devil is in me) and so I'm allowed to move largely at will, even among small children. But I'm not sure that this revision of attitude has been

particularly helpful. Physical imperfection, even freed of moral disapprobation, still defies and violates the ideal, especially for women, whose confinement in their bodies as objects of desire is far from over. Each age, of course,
has its ideal, and I doubt that ours is any better or worse than any other.
Today's ideal woman, who lives on the glossy pages of dozens of magazines,
seems to be between the ages of eighteen and twenty-five; her hair has body,
her teeth flash white, her breath smells minty, her underarms are dry; she has
a career but is still a fabulous cook, especially of meals that take less than
twenty minutes to prepare; she does not ordinarily appear to have a husband
or children; she is trim and deeply tanned; she jogs, swims, plays tennis, rides
a bicycle, sails, but does not bowl; she travels widely, even to out-of-the-way
places like Finland and Samoa, always in the company of the ideal man, who
possesses a nearly identical set of characteristics. There are a few exceptions.
Though usually white and often blonde, she may be black, Hispanic, Asian,
or Native American, so long as she is unusually sleek. She may be old,
provided she is selling a laxative or is Lauren Bacall. If she is selling a deter-
gent, she may be married and have a flock of strikingly messy children. But
she is never a cripple.

Vocabulary

disapprobation

Critical Thinking and Discussion

1. From what is the image of the idealized woman derived, according to
   Mairs?
2. What are the main characteristics of the idealized woman?
3. According to Mairs, why is being a "cripple" held in low regard?

Reading-Related Writing

1. Write about others who may suffer from comparison with the idealized
   woman or the idealized man. Consider race, appearance, or social class.

GEORGIA ON MY MIND

Ray Jenkins

*What was it like to be a white Southerner in the not-too-distant Old
South? Ray Jenkins knows. As you read this selection, anticipate a read-*

*ing-related writing topic asking you to indicate what it is like to live in
your neighborhood or the neighborhood where your parents grew up.*

Unless a man has picked cotton all day in August; has sat in an outhouse in   1
20 degrees in January and passed this time of necessity by reading last year's
Sears Roebuck catalogue; has eaten a possum and liked it; has castrated a live
pig with a dull pocket knife and has wrung a chicken's neck with his own
hands; has learned at least a few chords on a fiddle and guitar; has tried to
lure a sharecropper's daughter into the woods for mischievous purposes; has
watched a man who had succeeded in doing just that have his sins washed
away in the Blood of the Lamb in a baptism in a muddy creek; has been
kicked by a mean milch cow and kicked her back; has drunk busthead likker
knowing full well it might kill him; has wished the next day it had killed him;
has watched a neighbor's house burn down; has drawn a knife on an adver-
sary in fear and anger; has half-soled his one pair of shoes with a tire repair
kit; has gone into a deep dark well to get out a dead chicken that had fallen
in; has waited beside a dusty road in the midday heat, hoping the R.F.D.
postman would bring some long-coveted item ordered from the catalogue;
has been in close quarters with a snake; has, in thirsty desperation, drunk
water that worked alive with mosquito larvae called wiggletails; has eaten
sardines out of a can with a stick; has killed a cat just for the hell of it; has felt
like a [black] was mistreated but was afraid to say so; has stepped in the
droppings of a chicken and not really cared; has been cheated by someone he
worked hard for; has gone to bed at sundown because he could no longer
endure the crushing isolation; has ridden a bareback mule three miles to visit
a pretty girl who waited in a clean, flimsy cotton dress—unless he has done
these things, then he cannot understand what it was like in my South.

It is a definition, I hasten to add, which conveys neither superiority nor   2
inferiority; it is morally neutral. It is just that my experience was different
from that of my children.

Critical Reading and Discussion

1. Is the purpose of this selection mainly to persuade or to inform?
2. What form of discourse (narration, description, exemplification (examples), process analysis, cause and effect, classification, or comparison and
   contrast) is used more than others in this piece?
3. Is it possible to give a one-sentence definition of the subject of this piece?

Reading-Related Writing

1. Jenkins defines *traditional rural, white Southerner* by listing the unique
   and colorful experiences of that kind of person. By listing his or her

experiences, define a dweller in a project, barrio, shantytown, homeless shelter, prison, juvenile hall, migrant worker camp, reservation, or refugee camp.

2. Define yourself or someone you know by using Jenkins's pattern. Observe that the first paragraph contains only one sentence and that the word *has* follows each semicolon.

REFUGEE*

Kathy Silavong

Using the pattern from "Georgia on My Mind" by Ray Jenkins, student Kathy Silavong shows what it was like being a refugee.

Unless you have been picked up by strangers who helped you across a river at 1 the border; have seen dead bodies buried one after the other; have watched a man stab his enemy in the chest with a dull pocket knife; have lived in a concentration camp and waited desperately to leave; have been separated from your mother; have been in a coma while suffering from severe anemia and malaria; have received blood transfusions from a father who risked his life to supply what you needed to live; have emigrated to the United States and thought it was heaven; have had to communicate with people who don't know any of your language; have struggled to finish high school and also college; have been befriended by strangers; have not understood jokes but laughed out loud anyway; and have been taken advantage of but was afraid to say so; then you will not know what is was like to be a Vietnam War refugee.

It is a definition, I hasten to add, which conveys neither superiority nor 2 inferiority; it is a deadly dream, and it is my past—and, as memory, my present.

Critical Thinking and Discussion

1. Does Silavong use Jenkins's form in an inventive or in a derivative (copying) way?
2. Has this form limited her creativity?

Reading-Related Writing

1. Use the same form to write about your experience or the experience of someone you know.

2. As an option, use Jenkins's form as a preliminary exercise (much like freewriting) and then convert it into a conventional piece of writing.

WE WEAR THE MASK

Paul Laurence Dunbar

Paul Laurence Dunbar (1872–1906) was the first black poet to achieve popularity and critical distinction. Known mainly during his lifetime for the poems he wrote in black folk dialect, he is now read for his expression in standard English. This poem goes directly to the heart of the ideal of stereotyping. The person who is stereotyped may be forced to behave according to the expectations of those in power, but behind that mask of behavior is a human being not unlike all other human beings.

> We wear the mask that grins and lies,
> It hides our cheeks and shades our eyes,—
> This debt we pay to human guile;
> With torn and bleeding hearts we smile,
> 5 And mouth with myriad subtleties.
>
> Why should the world be over-wise,
> In counting all our tears and sighs?
> Nay, let them only see us, while
>   We wear the mask.
>
> We smile, but, O great Christ, our
> 10   cries
> To thee from tortured souls arise.
> We sing, but oh the clay is vile
> Beneath our feet, and long the mile;
> But let the world dream otherwise,
> 15   We wear the mask.

Critical Thinking and Discussion

1. What does the word *mask* mean in this poem?
2. What is the difference between the mask and the reality?
3. Why did African-Americans of Dunbar's time wear the mask?
4. Do oppressed people still wear the mask?
5. Why do people wear masks?

Reading-Related Writing

1. Write about how we all wear masks and how people who are persecuted wear a special kind of mask.
2. Write about a specific cultural group that seems to wear a mask.
3. Relate this poem to Tantranon-Saur's essay "What's Behind the 'Asian Mask'?"
4. Relate this poem to any other reading in this chapter, explaining how the mentally ill, Native Americans, modern women, people of mixed race, or others wear the mask.

THE BEAUTY OF BEING A LATE BLOOMER

Bel Kaufman

A teacher and writer, Bel Kaufman is best known for her novel about public education, Up the Down Staircase *(1965). Here she writes about old age, the stage of life that is often dreaded or regarded as a time of doing nothing but waiting for death. Kaufman explains how it can and should be a period of excitement and great productivity—if only people would stop believing in their own stereotypes.*

I see them everywhere—attractive, well-groomed, fit and energetic, women   1
no longer young, often alone, involved in living and doing, pursuing hobbies, jobs, careers or causes. It's hard to tell their age; they are referred to as "older women."

Older than who? Older than what? This euphemism, like "women in   2
their later years," or "senior citizens" (as opposed to junior citizens?) sounds apologetic. I much prefer the French "la belle age," or the phrase bestowed upon me in Israel by an interviewer: "Bel Kaufman, in the best of her years."

I'll buy that. For mine have certainly been the best of years after I turned   3
50. I was a late bloomer. I was 50-plus when I gathered the courage to scramble out of a deteriorated marriage and found myself for the first time entirely on my own. I was 50-plus when I wrote my first novel—a best seller. I was 50-plus when I discovered a new career of public speaking. And I was 50-plus when I formed a totally satisfying relationship with a man.

Not that I spent my earlier years lolling on a chaise lounge, munching   4
chocolates. I taught school, brought up two children, published an occasional story or light verse, but balancing for many years on the tightrope of a perilous marriage did not lend itself to creativity. Nor to independence. Nor to a

sense of identity. I knew how to be a daughter, a wife, a mother; I did not know how to be *me*.

Now I do. I have learned a simple, powerful lesson: I learned to say NO. 5 What a heady, liberating sound that can be! I do not have to be loved by everyone; I can risk disapproval. I can trust my opinions. I have profited from my mistakes—and they were lulus! With each small success my confidence grew. And with my children's independence came my own. I no longer do what I *have* to do; I now do what I *want* to do.

I am one of the lucky ones: I have options. 6

Many don't. Statistics are scary and realities are grim for women over 50 7 who are poor, powerless and alone. They are not welcome in the job market or at the social dinner table, and they are losers in the competitive mating arena.

Yet it can also be a time of rich fulfillment, even innovation. A time to 8 take that first lesson in playing the piano, flying a plane, mastering the word processor. A time of sexual freedom, with no need for contraception and no invasion of hard-won privacy. A time for new joys: grandchildren.

In 19th century novels, the elderly spinster turned out to be 28; the old 9 woman—40. The average life-span at the turn of the century was 47. Today women live some 30 years longer, are much healthier and have greater opportunities in fields closed to them in the past.

You've gone a long way, baby—but at the same time, baby, it's cold 10 outside.

In her recent book *A Lesser Life: The Myth of Women's Liberation in* 11 *America,* Sylvia Ann Hewlett claims that women are worse off than they used to be. They have lost the guarantees of marriage as a source of security, yet failed to improve their earning power. In 1939 they earned 63 cents to a man's dollar for the same work; in 1985—64 cents. Single women over 65 are the fastest growing and the most impoverished segment of our population. "Poverty is feminine," says Jane Seskin, author of "Living Alone" and coordinator of Women's Issues at the National Council of Jewish Women. And Victoria Secunda, in her book, "By Youth Possessed: The Denial of Age in America," speaks eloquently of women who are disenfranchised because of the "tyranny of youth" in our culture.

Since women live on an average nine years longer than men and there are 12 five widows to every widower, the problem is loneliness. Who was it who told of coming home one evening, opening her door with her key, and saying: "Hello, my furniture!"?

In my novel, "Love, Etc.," which was published in 1979, I describe "the 13 legion of lonely women huddled together against the weather . . . who had to unlearn marriage and learn to live alone . . . " and I quote their sad ads, discreetly tucked away on back pages of magazines: "50, look 40, considered attractive, seeking sincere, financially secure man interested in culture and permanence . . . "

But I also make another point in that book: Passionate, physical, lyrical 14 love is not preempted only by the young. The lovers in my story are a man and a woman in their mid-50s.

Untrained in a career, mate gone, children flown, the woman today can 15 find support groups in recently sprung up networks of women and in organizations such as Resources for Midlife and Older Women, Inc., the Clairol Scholarship Program and many others. But I think that sometimes it may be just one woman, one foul-weather friend who has suffered and survived, who serves as her telephone life-line.

Now young women are smarter; whatever their plans for marriage, they 16 prepare themselves for a career. There is hope for the future: The latest statistics reported by the U.S. Labor Department in March 1986 are that women today hold the majority of professional jobs. There are more female psychologists, statisticians, editors and reporters than men, although the earning gap between men and women still exists.

But none of us is a statistic. Each is individual and unique, with 17 untapped potential and unexplored possibilities. We have role models who defy statistics; mature women successful in the arts, sciences, politics, industry and communications, who spell out what may be possible for others.

I am constantly impressed by the ingenuity of women over 50 who have 18 been able to translate their interests, talents or skills into paying jobs or careers. Among my friends, a well-known writer of children's books and a world traveler to unusual and exotic places has just started a newsletter: The Privileged Traveler.

Another friend, when she turned 50, made a list of her priorities. One 19 was music. She picked up the phone, called the Metropolitan Opera, and asked: "What can I do for you?" This led to a job, which led to another—and now she is director of cultural events for the Statue of Liberty Centennial.

A successful psychologist, who more than 20 years ago was the best 20 secretary I ever had, subsequently went back to college and graduate school, at the same time doing all kinds of odd jobs, including crocheting hats for dogs, which she sold for $3 each. It took her 11 years to get her doctorate, but at last she made it.

A friend who had never signed a check, suddenly widowed, went to 21 school to learn money management. Another studied computers and found a lucrative job. Another made of her modest apartment an art gallery and began to sell paintings on commission.

"Life Begins at Forty" was a daring title for a book published years ago. 22 Today life begins at 50, 60, and yes, 70. If health lasts, this is truly a time for a "new beginning"—a phrase I had always found redundant, like "free gift" or "rich millionaire," but which is apt for a fresh start of a new, uncharted phase of life. The woman can say: "It's *my* turn now!" She has gone through the early years of uncertainty and confusion, overcome obstacles and disappointments; she has learned who she is and earned what she wants.

When I was young, a weekend was forever, and tomorrow—someplace 23
in the dim future. Now my tomorrow is today. I have no time to waste on preliminaries of living.

It's good to be young, but as a friend puts it, "It's hard to maintain it." 24
Youth is temporary. Growth is constant.

I spoke of role models, whose success is highly visible. But there are 25
thousands upon thousands of women, unknown, unhonored and unsung, who are succeeding too, in growing older with wisdom reaped from who knows what past pain?

Time was when a woman's age was her secret, and her prerogative was 26
not to reveal it. On questionnaires and applications she would coyly put down "21-plus." Today, I hope she writes "51-plus" with pride, because she deserves it. She is a non-dropout. She has passed difficult tests. She is still learning. As a teacher, I give the woman of 50-plus a large, bold A-plus.

Vocabulary

euphemism (2)	innovation (8)	preempted (14)
deteriorated (3)	disenfranchised (11)	prerogative (26)

Critical Thinking and Discussion

1. What did Kaufman do before she turned fifty? How did those experiences help her later?
2. What is the main lesson she learned upon turning fifty?
3. What disadvantages do women over fifty have?
4. What advantages do women over fifty have?
5. How should statistics be regarded?
6. What is the importance of a role model?
7. What is the stereotype and what is the reality of women beyond fifty?

Reading-Related Writing

1. Write about the stereotype and the reality of a woman beyond fifty, using your own examples.
2. Write about the stereotype and the reality of a man beyond fifty.
3. Write about the stereotype and the reality of men or women over fifty in a specific immigrant group with traditional values.

THE MYTH OF THE LATIN WOMAN: I JUST MET A GIRL NAMED MARIA

Judith Ortiz Cofer

Born in Puerto Rico in 1952, Judith Ortiz Cofer moved with her parents to New Jersey where she learned a new language and new culture while in elementary school. Now a poet and university professor, she writes poignantly about her experiences trying to embrace two cultures with different customs and different languages.

On a bus trip to London from Oxford University where I was earning some 1 graduate credits one summer, a young man, obviously fresh from a pub, spotted me and as if struck by inspiration went down on his knees in the aisle. With both hands over his heart he broke into an Irish tenor's rendition of "Maria" from *West Side Story.* My politely amused fellow passengers gave his lovely voice the round of gentle applause it deserved. Though I was not quite as amused, I managed my version of an English smile: no show of teeth, no extreme contortions of the facial muscles—I was at this time of my life practicing reserve and cool. Oh, that British control, how I coveted it. But "Maria" had followed me to London, reminding me of a prime fact of my life: you can leave the island, master the English language, and travel as far as you can, but if you are a Latina, especially one like me who so obviously belongs to Rita Moreno's gene pool, the island travels with you.

This is sometimes a very good thing—it may win you that extra minute 2 of someone's attention. But with some people, the same things can make *you* an island—not a tropical paradise but an Alcatraz, a place nobody wants to visit. As a Puerto Rican girl living in the United States and wanting like most children to "belong," I resented the stereotype that my Hispanic appearance called forth from many people I met.

Growing up in a large urban center in New Jersey during the 1960s, I 3 suffered from what I think of as "cultural schizophrenia." Our life was designed by my parents as a microcosm of their *casas* on the island. We spoke in Spanish, ate Puerto Rican food bought at the *bodega,* and practiced strict Catholicism at a church that allotted us a one-hour slot each week for mass, performed in Spanish by a Chinese priest trained as a missionary for Latin America.

As a girl I was kept under strict surveillance by my parents, since my 4 virtue and modesty were, by their cultural equation, the same as their honor. As a teenager I was lectured constantly on how to behave as a proper *señorita.* But it was a conflicting message I received, since the Puerto Rican mothers also encouraged their daughters to look and act like women and to dress in clothes our Anglo friends and their mothers found too "mature" and flashy. The difference was, and is, cultural, yet I often felt humiliated when I appeared at an American friend's party wearing a dress more suitable to a semi-formal than to a playroom birthday celebration. At Puerto Rican festivities, neither the music nor the colors we wore could be too loud.

I remember Career Day in our high school, when teachers told us to come dressed as if for a job interview. It quickly became obvious that to the Puerto Rican girls "dressing up" meant wearing their mother's ornate jewelry and clothing, more appropriate (by mainstream standards) for the company Christmas party than as daily office attire. That morning I had agonized in front of my closet, trying to figure out what a "career girl" would wear. I knew how to dress for school (at the Catholic school I attended, we all wore uniforms), I knew how to dress for Sunday mass, and I knew what dresses to wear for parties at my relatives' homes. Though I do not recall the precise details of my Career Day outfit, it must have been a composite of these choices. But I remember a comment my friend (an Italian American) made in later years that coalesced my impressions of that day. She said that at the business school she was attending, the Puerto Rican girls always stood out for wearing "everything at once." She meant, of course, too much jewelry, too many accessories. On that day at school we were simply made the negative models by the nuns, who were themselves not credible fashion experts to any of us. But it was painfully obvious to me that to the others, in their tailored skirts and silk blouses, we must have seemed "hopeless" and "vulgar." Though I now know that most adolescents feel out of step much of the time, I also know that for the Puerto Rican girls of my generation that sense was intensified. The way our teachers and classmates looked at us that day in school was just a taste of the cultural clash that awaited us in the real world, where prospective employers and men on the street would often misinterpret our tight skirts and jingling bracelets as a "come-on."

Mixed cultural signals have perpetuated certain stereotypes—for example, that of the Hispanic woman as the "hot tamale" or sexual firebrand. It is a one-dimensional view that the media have found easy to promote. In their special vocabulary, advertisers have designated "sizzling" and "smoldering" as the adjectives of choice for describing not only the foods but also the women of Latin America. From conversations in my house I recall hearing about the harassment that Puerto Rican women endured in factories where the "bossmen" talked to them as if sexual innuendo was all they understood, and worse, often gave them the choice of submitting to their advances or being fired.

It is custom, however, not chromosomes, that leads us to choose scarlet over pale pink. As young girls, it was our mothers who influenced our decisions about clothes and colors—mothers who had grown up on a tropical island where the natural environment was a riot of primary colors, where showing your skin was one way to keep cool as well as to look sexy. Most important of all, on the island, women perhaps felt freer to dress and move more provocatively since, in most cases, they were protected by the traditions, mores, and laws of a Spanish/Catholic system of morality and machismo whose main rule was: *You may look at my sister, but if you touch her I will kill you.* The extended family and church structure could provide a young woman with a circle of safety in her small pueblo on the island, if a man "wronged" a girl, everyone would close in to save her family honor.

My mother has told me about dressing in her best party clothes on ₈ Saturday nights and going to the town's plaza to promenade with her girlfriends in front of the boys they liked. The males were thus given an opportunity to admire the women and to express their admiration in the form of *piropos:* erotically charged street poems they composed on the spot. (I have myself been subjected to a few *piropos* while visiting the island, and they can be outrageous, although custom dictates that they must never cross into obscenity.) This ritual, as I understand it, also entails a show of studied indifference on the woman's part; if she is "decent," she must not acknowledge the man's impassioned words. So I do understand how things can be lost in translation. When a Puerto Rican girl dressed in her idea of what is attractive meets a man from the mainstream culture who has been trained to react to certain types of clothing as a sexual signal, a clash is likely to take place. I remember the boy who took me to my first formal dance leaning over to plant a sloppy, over-eager kiss painfully on my mouth; when I didn't respond with sufficient passion, he remarked resentfully: "I thought you Latin girls were supposed to mature early," as if I were expected to *ripen* like a fruit or vegetable, not just grow into womanhood like other girls.

It is surprising to my professional friends that even today some people, ₉ including those who should know better, still put others "in their place." It happened to me most recently during a stay at a classy metropolitan hotel favored by young professional couples for weddings. Late one evening after the theater, as I walked toward my room with a colleague (a woman with whom I was coordinating an arts program), a middle-aged man in a tuxedo, with a young girl in satin and lace on his arm, stepped directly into our path. With his champagne glass extended toward me, he exclaimed "Evita!"[1]

Our way blocked, my companion and I listened as the man half-recited, ₁₀ half-bellowed "Don't Cry for Me, Argentina." When he finished, the young girls said: "How about a round of applause for my daddy?" We complied, hoping this would bring the silly spectacle to a close. I was becoming aware that our little group was attracting the attention of the other guests. "Daddy" must have perceived this too, and he once more barred the way as we tried to walk past him. He began to shout-sing a ditty to the tune of "La Bamba"— except the lyrics were about a girl named Maria whose exploits rhymed with

---

[1]A musical about Eva Duarte de Peron, the former first lady of Argentina.

her name and gonorrhea. The girl kept saying "Oh, Daddy" and looking at me with pleading eyes. She wanted me to laugh along with the others. My companion and I stood silently waiting for the man to end his offensive song. When he finished, I looked not at him but at his daughter. I advised her calmly never to ask her father what he had done in the army. Then I walked between them and to my room. My friend complemented me on my cool handling of the situation, but I confessed that I had really wanted to push the jerk into the swimming pool. This same man—probably a corporate executive, well-educated, even worldly by most standards—would not have been likely to regale an Anglo woman with a dirty song in public. He might have checked his impulse by assuming that she could be somebody's wife or mother, or at least *somebody* who might take offense. But, to him, I was just an Evita or a Maria: merely a character in his cartoon-populated universe.

Another facet of the myth of the Latin woman in the United States is the 11 menial, the domestic—Maria the housemaid or countergirl. It's true that work as domestics, as waitresses, and in factories is all that's available to women with little English and few skills. But the myth of the Hispanic menial—the funny maid, mispronouncing words and cooking up a spicy storm in a shiny California kitchen—has been perpetuated by the media in the same way that "Mammy" from *Gone with the Wind* became America's idea of the black woman for generations. Since I do not wear my diplomas around my neck for all to see, I have on occasion been sent to that "kitchen" where some think I obviously belong.

One incident has stayed with me, though I recognize it as a minor 12 offense. My first public poetry reading took place in Miami, at a restaurant where a luncheon was being held before the event. I was nervous and excited as I walked in with notebook in hand. An older woman motioned me to her table, and thinking (foolish me) that she wanted me to autograph a copy of my newly published slender volume of verse, I went over. She ordered a cup of coffee from me, assuming that I was the waitress. (Easy enough to mistake my poems for menus, I suppose.) I know it wasn't an intentional act of cruelty. Yet of all the good things that happened later, I remember that scene most clearly, because it reminded me of what I had to overcome before anyone would take me seriously. In retrospect I understand that my anger gave my reading fire. In fact, I have almost always taken any doubt in my abilities as a challenge, the result most often being the satisfaction of winning a convert, of seeing the cold, appraising eyes warm to my words, the body language change, the smile that indicates I have opened some avenue for communication. So that day as I read, I looked directly at that woman. Her lowered eyes told me she was embarrassed at her faux pas, and when I willed her to look up at me, she graciously allowed me to punish her with my full attention. We shook hands at the end of the reading and I never saw her again. She has probably forgotten the entire incident, but maybe not.

Yet I am one of the lucky ones. There are thousands of Latinas without 13
the privilege of an education or the entrees into society that I have. For them
life is a constant struggle against the misconceptions perpetuated by the myth
of the Latina. My goal is to try to replace the old stereotypes with a much
more interesting set of realities. Every time I give a reading, I hope the stories
I tell, the dreams and fears I examine in my work, can achieve some universal
truth that will get my audience past the particulars of my skin color, my
accent, or my clothes.

I once wrote a poem in which I called all Latinas "God's brown daugh- 14
ters." This poem is really a prayer of sorts, offered upward, but also, through
the human-to-human channel of art, outward. It is a prayer for communication and for respect. In it, Latin women pray "in Spanish to an Anglo God /
with a Jewish heritage," and they are "fervently hoping / that if not omni-
potent / at least He be bilingual."

Vocabulary

coveted (1) surveillance (4) regale (10)
microcosm (3) composite (5) facet (11)
casas (3) innuendo (6) faux pas (12)
bodega (3)

Critical Thinking and Discussion

1. What is the stereotype of the Latin woman? Does it have more than one
   part?
2. How are Latin women sometimes victimized at work because of stereotypes?
3. Why do women feel freer to dress as they do in Puerto Rico?
4. Explain what Ortiz Cofer means in paragraph 8 when she says, "So I do
   understand how things can be lost in translation."
5. How does she typically handle situations involving being stereotypes?
   During those unpleasant encounters, what is the difference between her
   controlled behavior and her impulses?

Reading-Related Writing

1. Write about an experience that you have had or someone you know has
   had involving stereotyping.
2. Write about a time when you may have been guilty of stereotyping someone else.

THE MEDIA'S IMAGE OF THE ARAB

Jack G. Shaheen

As a professor of communications at the University of Illinois, Jack G. Shaheen knows the power of the media in establishing images of cultural groups. His studies and personal experiences show him that Arabs are almost always presented in a negative light, especially in television and the cinema. The impact of these misrepresentations on the Arab-American population is devastating. This essay was first published in Newsweek.

America's bogeyman is the Arab. Until the nightly news brought us TV pictures of Palestinian boys being punched and beaten, almost all portraits of Arabs seen in America were dangerously threatening. Arabs were either billionaires or bombers—rarely victims. They were hardly ever seen as ordinary people practicing law, driving taxis, singing lullabies or healing the sick. Though TV news may portray them more sympathetically now, the absence of positive media images nurtures suspicion and stereotype. As an Arab-American, I have found that ugly caricatures have had an enduring impact on my family.

I was sheltered from prejudicial portraits at first. My parents came from Lebanon in the 1920s; they met and married in America. Our home in the steel city of Clairton, Pa., was a center for ethnic sharing—black, white, Jew and gentile. There was only one major source of media images then, at the State movie theater where I was lucky enough to get a part-time job as an usher. But in the late 1940s, Westerns and war movies were popular, not Middle Eastern dramas. Memories of World War II were fresh, and the screen heavies were the Japanese and the Germans. True to the cliché of the times, the only good Indian was a dead Indian. But when I mimicked or mocked the bad guys, my mother cautioned me. She explained that stereotypes blur our vision and corrupt the imagination. "Have compassion for all people, Jackie," she said. "This way, you'll learn to experience the joy of accepting people as they are, and not as they appear in films. Stereotypes hurt."

Mother was right. I can remember the Saturday afternoon when my son, Michael, who was seven, and my daughter, Michele, six, suddenly called out: "Daddy, Daddy, they've got some bad Arabs on TV." They were watching that great American morality play, TV wrestling. Akbar the Great, who liked to hear the cracking of bones, and Abdullah the Butcher, a dirty fighter who liked to inflict pain, were pinning their foes with "camel locks." From that day on, I knew I had to try to neutralize the media caricatures.

It hasn't been easy. With my children, I have watched animated heroes 4
Heckle and Jeckle pull the rug from under "Ali Boo-Boo, the Desert Rat," and
Laverne and Shirley stop "Sheik Ha-Mean-Ie" from conquering "the U.S. and
the world." I have read comic books like the "Fantastic Four" and "G.I. Combat" whose characters have sketched Arabs as "lowlifes" and "human hyenas."
Negative stereotypes were everywhere. A dictionary informed my youngsters
that an Arab is a "vagabond, drifter, hobo and vagrant." Whatever happened,
my wife wondered, to Aladdin's good genie?

To a child, the world is simple: good versus evil. But my children and 5
others with Arab roots grew up without ever having seen a humane Arab on
the silver screen, someone to pattern their lives after. Is it easier for a camel to
go through the eye of a needle than for a screen Arab to appear as a genuine
human being?

Hollywood producers must have an instant Ali Baba kit that contains 6
scimitars, veils, sunglasses and such Arab clothing as *chadors* and *kufiyahs*. In
the mythical "Ay-rabland," oil wells, tents, mosques, goats and shepherds
prevail. Between the sand dunes, the camera focuses on a mock-up of a palace
from "Arabian Nights"—or a military air base. Recent movies suggest that
Americans are at war with Arabs, forgetting the fact that out of 21 Arab
nations, America is friendly with 19 of them. And in "Wanted Dead or Alive,"
a movie that starred Gene Simmons, the leader of the rock group Kiss, the
war comes home when an Arab terrorist comes to the United States dressed as
a rabbi and, among other things, conspires with Arab-Americans to poison
the people of Los Angeles. The movie was released last year.

The Arab remains American culture's favorite whipping boy. In his 7
memoirs, Terrel Bell, Ronald Reagan's first secretary of education, writes
about an "apparent bias among mid-level, right-wing staffers at the White
House" who dismissed Arabs as "sand niggers." Sadly, the racial slurs continue. At a recent teacher's conference, I met a woman from Sioux Falls, S.D.,
who told me about the persistence of discrimination. She was in the process
of adopting a baby when an agency staffer warned her that the infant had a
problem. When she asked whether the child was mentally ill, or physically
handicapped, there was silence. Finally, the worker said: "The baby is
Jordanian."

To me, the Arab demon of today is much like the Jewish demon of 8
yesterday. We deplore the false portrait of Jews as a swarthy menace. Yet a
similar portrait has been accepted and transferred to another group of
Semites—the Arabs. Print and broadcast journalists have started to challenge
this stereotype. They are now revealing more humane images of Palestinian
Arabs, a people who traditionally suffered from the myth that Palestinian
equals terrorist. Others could follow that lead and retire the stereotypical Arab
to a media Valhalla.

It would be a step in the right direction if movie and TV producers 9 developed characters modeled after real-life Arab-Americans. We could then see a White House correspondent like Helen Thomas, whose father came from Lebanon, in "The Golden Girls," a heart surgeon patterned after Dr. Michael DeBakey on "St. Elsewhere," or a Syrian-American playing tournament chess like Yasser Seirawan, the Seattle grandmaster.

Politicians, too should speak out against the cardboard caricatures. They 10 should refer to Arabs as friends, not just as moderates. And religious leaders could state that Islam like Christianity and Judaism maintains that all mankind is one family in the care of God. When all imagemakers rightfully begin to treat Arabs and all other minorities with respect and dignity, we may begin to unlearn our prejudices.

Vocabulary

bogeyman (1)   *chadors* (6)   Semite (8)
caricatures (3)   *kufiyahs* (6)   Valhalla (8)
vagabond (4)   mythical (6)   moderates (10)
scimitars (6)

Critical Thinking and Discussion

1. Why did Shaheen not experience Arab stereotyping in his youth?
2. How did he initially feel about stereotyping?
3. What is the importance of media role models for children?
4. Is anti-Arab sentiment also reflected in American Foreign policy? Explain.
5. In what way is this article optimistic?
6. What are Shaheen's suggestions for correcting the problem of stereotyping Arabs?

Reading-Related Writing

1. Write about Arab stereotyping you have encountered in the media and elsewhere.
2. Write about the stereotyping of any other cultural group in the media.
3. What is the proper response when one hears a joke, a slur, or other racially demeaning expression? Should one confront the person with his or her prejudice, remain silent, or what? Write a piece in which you give some examples of how you have observed people handling that kind of situation.

WHAT'S BEHIND THE "ASIAN MASK"?

Alexandra Tantranon-Saur

Speaking from behind the Asian mask, Alexandra Tantranon-Saur invites us to go beyond the stereotypes that have long falsified the character of Asians and to try to understand their behavior and values from their point of view. This essay defines especially by explaining in clear detail how people can understand another culture.

First the "yellow peril," now the "model minority"—most of you know 1
enough to scoff at these racist stereotypes. Some are beginning to know the
violence and sorrow visited upon the Asian and Pacific peoples in this country by ordinary white people blinded by stereotypes, and mourn and rage
with us as we demand justice.

But there is yet another layer to penetrate, a layer of seemingly innocuous 2
assumptions, that clouds your vision of us, and confuses your attempts to
find, work with, experience us. You see us wearing masks; we see you imagin-
ing we should prefer your cultures to ours! Let's take a look at this "Asian
mask."

Asian/Pacific people are quiet. Asian/Pacific people are not quiet! Certainly 3
in this area[1] most of us have had a chance to visit one Chinatown or another;
is it quiet? Lots of Chinese, especially the older immigrants, walking on the
streets having loud and musical conversations with each other. Chinese working-class women waiting tables and shouting to each other and the cooks.
Pushing their carts of dim sum through the aisles, tempting the weekend
brunch crowd with *"Ha gow! Shui mei! Cha-shu bow!"*[2] For the Chinese, as for
many other peoples, the issue of speaking quietly versus loudly is a class
issue.

And as for the volume of spoken words—no one can tell me Asian/Pacific 4
people don't say much. My mother, sister and I outtalk my non-Asian father
hands down. My Asian/Pacific friends can outtalk me. Go into the Thai Buddhist temple during service. The monks have to chant over the microphone;
everyone else is talking. In language class, the children talk and the teachers
talk louder.

Don't get me wrong; I'm sure there are some quiet Asian/Pacific people. 5
I've heard there are. (Even I occasionally like to be quiet.) I just don't know any.

So why does it appear to non-Asian/Pacific people (and in fact to many 6
Asian/Pacific Americans as well) that we are quiet? A closer look at some
common Asian/Pacific-American conversational habits may surprise you.

[1] The San Francisco Bay area.
[2] Different types of Chinese hors d'oeuvres. (Ed.)

The *pause*. I learned the proper way to speak was to leave pauses in   7
between thoughts and even sentences. We sculpt the flow of our words
with silences; spaces for thinking, reflecting, relaxing. Get together with
people who talk like this, hold your tongue, and you'll see how comfortably
a conversation goes. You can think with pauses! You can see that, from a
purely mechanical point of view, most people who speak without pauses
will be constantly interrupting us; and while we wait for the longer pause
which signals that the speaker has finished a thought and that the next
speaker may start, the non-Asian/Pacific people will talk on and on, marvel-
ing that they have found such a good listener who seems to have nothing
to say.

But this is more than just a mechanical speech pattern. I was taught, and   8
I observe this in other Asian/Pacific Americans, to be constantly aware of the
attention level of my listener, in fact to monitor and nurture it. The *pause* is
part of this. If someone else immediately grabs the moment of silence, then
that person must not have been listening with much attention, right? In fact,
they may have been waiting desperately to get a chance to unload. So of
course they should get the attention if they're that desperate.

The pause is also often lengthened into the *question pause*. That is: from   9
time to time it is good to stop in the middle and see if a listener asks, "What
else? Say more!" This is a useful check to see if they are listening and interested. If they don't ask, why continue to talk?

In addition to monitoring the attention level in our listener, the *start-off*   10
question is the most clear example of actively building our listener's attention
level. You all know this one. I want to tell you what I think about the World
Bank (we have been talking about canoeing), so I ask you what *you* think
about the World Bank. Why don't I just start out on the World Bank? Well,
why should I assume that you'll be able to listen to that? First I check, and I
listen to you, and by the time you have gotten whatever you need to off your
chest, you will probably realize that you want to know what *I* think about the
World Bank.

You may notice another attention-maintaining technique we use in con-   11
versations. It is the frequent *sorry's* you hear. If you find this irritating, it's no
wonder—you probably think we are apologizing! Many people were apparently raised to think that "I'm sorry" is an admission of guilt or statement of
contriteness or self-denigration. I'm sorry, it's not true. It simply means, "no
offense intended by what I have to say to you." It means, "listen to me
knowing that you are not being personally attacked"; it means, "listen atten-
tively with an open mind."

You will notice that my behavior is based on the assumption that I pay   12
better attention to others than do non-Asian/Pacific people. Can this be true?
In the sense of having the habit of thinking about others in uncomfortable
situations, it is true. How can this happen, that we pay better attention?

Part of this is a survival technique, not unique to Asian/Pacific Ameri- 13
cans: the experience of an oppressed people is that we have to pay more
attention to the feelings of our oppressors than vice versa. Everyone knows
this one—how much time do we spend talking about the boss? We know the
boss's habits, preferences, moods, irrationalities—we have to! But the boss is
unlikely to know ours. The same thing happens between people of color and
white people.

But the primary reason that Asian/Pacific people pay more attention to 14
others has to do with the principles of cooperation and exchange, which form
the basis of our societies and cultures. Consider typical Asian/Pacific group
behavior:

Asian/Pacific people have a pattern of going last ("invisibility"). If you could 15
be a fly on my shoulder in an Asian/Pacific group, you would notice the
conversational customs I mentioned above. If you look also at how the group
attention flows from subject to subject, you would see that our number one
priority is to take care of the group as a whole. You will notice us attending to
business matters first. We will rarely risk the integrity of the group by presenting "personal" needs or demands before all the group needs are taken care
of. This cooperative behavior functions quite well in the Asian/Pacific context.

Let me tell you a story illustrating what often happens in the mixed 16
context. In a group dealing with issues of internalized racism, we first separated into our "racial" groups (Asian/Pacific, African, European, Latino/a[3, 4]
with a list of questions to answer and two lists to make and present to the
larger group. The schedule allowed forty-five minutes total for presentations.
Back in the larger group, we Asians made our presentation first, and for the
most part simply read through the two lists. That took about five minutes.
The African group was next. They had decided not to do the assigned questions and lists, and instead made up four different lists, and presented them,
each member of the group speaking several times. That took about twenty
minutes. It was important for the African group to make the exercise useful
by changing it as needed, and to express to the group the feelings that had
come up for them. The schedule would just have to give. It was important
to us to make sure things moved along as planned (i.e., time-wise and
assignment-wise); instead of changing the assignment and schedule, we
would wait with our feelings.

Both fine approaches. But again, simply the mechanics of mixing the two 17
approaches means that, without thoughtful intervention, our personal needs
will come last, if at all. If others are unaware of our approach, and are
carrying around "quiet/unemotional Asian" stereotypes of us, it may never

---

[3]We unfortunately had no Native American group.
[4]These terms are not inclusive or descriptive enough. African Americans, Latinos, and Latinas
are working hard to find names that define themselves accurately and respectfully.

occur to them to ask us, after everything else is done, "Well, what about *your* feelings?"

Asian/Pacific people are "nice" and "polite." These so-called Asian traits are 18 praised by those who would like to keep us in line (teachers and employers, for example) and damned by our loving supporters who wish we would assimilate to Western-style bumper-car social interactions. I'm sorry, folks (see above), but I just have to complain about labeling being "nice" and "polite" as a problem. Why don't we use the right words? Gracious and hospitable. Cultural strengths which help us maintain the functioning and integrity of our families and groups. It sure never stopped us from making war on each other, exploiting each other, defending ourselves, or making revolution! The problem is not the behavior itself; it is the inability to choose another behavior when more appropriate. Obviously *that* has nothing to do with being Asian or Pacific, but rather with the experience of being immigrant minorities and being murdered in large numbers.

A variation on this is *Asian/Pacific people don't show their feelings.* Just like 19 anyone else, we will laugh, cry, rage, shiver, and melt with love, as soon as we get enough loving attention. And, just like anyone else, our feelings are written all over our faces and bodies. Not seeing how we express it is part of the "they all look the same to me" syndrome. "But what if someone always has the same look on their face?" you say. Put on your thinking cap! What does it mean if your friend has the same feelings frozen into her face all the time she's around you? That's a rather eloquent message, I would say. "But she can't/won't tell me what she's feeling!" Nope, we sure do resist translating for you, don't we?

Asian/Pacific people need assertiveness training. It sure might look like that 20 to someone accustomed to bumper-car social interactions. But welcome, ye weary bumper cars, to another cultural setting. Interactions between Asian/Pacific people are based to a great extent upon cooperation and exchange. Consider the group behavior—cooperation before individualism. Consider the *start-off question*—I give you attention first, then you offer it back to me. Exchange is an important cultural principle. A non-Asian/Pacific American was counseling an Indian woman on a decision she needed to make. The conversation went something like this:

"After all, who's the most important?" 21

"My mother." 22

"Wrong!" 23

"My father?" 24

"No!" 25

"My sister??" 26

"*You* are!" 27

"???" 28

In the Indian social system, you make someone else the most important; 29 watch out for their welfare, make decisions based on their needs. *You* get to be the most important for someone else; you have someone thinking about *your* needs. You give and you get, and it all evens out.

Several Japanese and Japanese-American customs also illustrate this exchange principle. You don't split up the bill at a restaurant; you treat your friends, knowing that the next time they will treat you back. People pay attention to each other through *exchange of appreciations*. The woman who has spent three days preparing a feast offers it to her guests with "This isn't much, but please help yourselves." This is a signal for the guests to express their appreciation of her. They respond without rancor, because they, too, will get validated by the same mechanism. This extends to speaking about the children—"My daughter, she isn't very good at that." "But she's so good at these other things. You have a fine daughter!" Of course, sometimes it is important that you let someone know what you can do. In that case, your friend speaks for you. You never have to toot your own horn.

This is not to say that people don't get squished by these rules. The Japanese have a saying, "The nail that stands above the others will get hammered down to the same level." The historical lack of natural resources required cooperation and discouraged individualism, there having been no excess to cover the risks of individual mistakes. Now the Japanese are far beyond survival level, and the cultural survival techniques have not been discarded. But within the cultural context, the exchange principle functions well.

What's a friend to do? How can you put your new-found insights into action? These suggestions and exercises will not only bring you closer to us, but will also challenge you to act clearly and decisively in groups and one-to-one relationships.

1. Take responsibility for equal time-sharing, especially in mixed groups.
2. Notice and deal with the feelings that come up for you when there is silence in a conversation. There is often desperation behind the habit of filling every second with words. An appreciation of silence will allow you to awarely encourage us to break the silence when we choose.
3. Notice when Asian/Pacific people are not talking. Assume that when we are not talking, you are interrupting us. It will become obvious what to do. Also, don't assume we are finished when we stop talking. It may be a *thinking pause* or a *question pause,* instead of an *end-of-thought pause.* It is perfectly acceptable to simply ask if we are finished.
4. Don't try to assist us by taking the perspective that we should change our behavior, but rather that we need to have more choices. Remember the exchange principle. We need to deal with the hurt we experience when other people don't come through on the exchange, but instead simply take from us. Encourage us to have the highest expectations of our allies, to require your attention, in fact to demand it, instead of always giving it first and waiting for it to be offered back.

5. Talk and listen Asian/Pacific-style with us. Practice recognizing and using the various *pauses*.

6. Remember that our "politeness," "apologies," etcetera, are not necessarily forms of self-invalidation. In European-American culture, these habits are often also considered to be signs of the weakness of the female. In this way, acting out sexism/internalized sexism by wishing us to give up our "weak" habits can turn out to be racist. Don't buy it! These are women's cultural strengths as well as Asian/Pacific cultural strengths.

7. Remember that, just like anyone else, we will express and release the full range of emotions as soon as we get enough caring attention. And, just like anyone else, our feelings are written all over our faces and bodies. We will do you the favor of not translating. Trust your thinking, make lots of mistakes, and pretty soon you'll be able not only to translate, but to think and see Asian/Pacific-style, too.

Vocabulary

innocuous (2)
contriteness (11)
self-denigration (11)

Critical Thinking and Discussion

1. What does Tantranon-Saur mean by saying that "speaking quietly versus loudly is a class issue"?
2. How is the pause in conversation used by Asian/Pacific Americans?
3. What is the function of the question pause?
4. When is "I'm sorry" not an apology?
5. How does the author compare our knowing the boss with Asian/Pacific Americans knowing Americans?
6. How do Asian/Pacifics rank group needs and personal feelings?
7. Are Asian/Pacific Americans nicer or more polite than others?
8. How do Asian/Pacific Americans regard individualism?
9. What can one do to better understand an Asian/Pacific American?

Reading-Related Writing

1. Discuss the stereotype and the reality presented in this essay.
2. Discuss another cultural group with attention to the stereotype, the reality, and suggestions for improving relationships with that group.
3. Try the strategies Tantranon-Saur offers at the end of her essay with a group of Asian/Pacific Americans and report on the results. Explain what you have learned.

4. Assuming that Asian-Americans are not all the same, interview Asian/Pacific Americans from different countries, determine if they are in agreement on the points made in this essay, and write a report on your findings.

IT HURTS LIKE CRAZY

James Willwerth

Writing in Time *(1993), James Willwerth points out that victims of mental illness have more to deal with than just the debilitating conditions of their disorder. He says that in movies, in advertising, even in political rhetoric, the offhanded portrayals of the mentally ill add to the pain.*

DC comics Superman editor Mike Carlin, hoping to boost newsstand sales, 1 declares that "an escapee from a cosmic lunatic asylum" named Doomsday will murder the Man of Steel. The state of Pennsylvania touts itself as a place for "multiple personalities" to suggest it has much to offer tourists. A character on "Roseanne" argues that only "murderers, psychos and schizos" can beat a lie-detector test. On election eve, Ross Perot tells a cheering crowd, "We're all crazy again now! We got buses lined up outside to take you back to the insane asylum."

At a time of growing sensitivity to racist and sexist language, no such 2 caution governs the use of the vocabulary of mental illness, whether as a metaphor, a plot device or a put-down. "There is hardly a moment when we turn on television or read newspapers that we don't see violent stereotypes or hear bad jokes at the expense of the mentally ill," says Nora Weinerth, cofounder of the National Stigma Clearinghouse, which organizes protests against prejudicial images of mental illness in the media. "When children are told that a superhero will be killed by someone who is mentally ill, it stigmatizes us." Backed by research showing that mental illness is biological in origin—like cancer or heart disease—patients and advocates are gearing up a national antidefamation campaign.

With the help of the New York State Alliance for the Mentally Ill, 3 Weinerth and New York City activist Jean Arnold set up the clearinghouse operation in January 1990. Its efforts reflect more than concerns over hurt feelings or political correctness. A stream of negative images, advocates argue, makes it harder for recovering patients to find work, obtain housing or participate fully in society. "We're not language police," concludes Arnold. "We don't expect the word *crazy* to disappear. But we're hoping for the day when these stereotypes are as unacceptable as racist and sexist remarks."

The stigma borne by present-day patients "is harder to live with than the   4 illness itself," laments Joanne Verbannic, a Michigan grandmother employed at the Ford Motor Credit Co., who at age 25 had paranoid schizophrenia diagnosed. "Every time I read about a 'paranoid killer' or hear on TV that the weather will be 'schizophrenic,' I feel like someone has put a knife in me."

Experts who work with the mentally ill are especially concerned about   5 the misinformation spread by the jokes and casual use of medical terms. When *Time* uses the word *schizophrenic* to describe internal conflict within the Republican Party, the metaphor perpetuates a misunderstanding, as does a *New York Times* article describing the hyena's laughlike calls as "psychotic in pitch." Schizophrenia, a brain disorder whose symptoms can include hearing voices, has nothing to do with multiple or "split" personalities. Psychotic refers to a period of severe, treatable and often terrifying disorientation.

The label *psychotic killer,* a favorite of headline writers and Hollywood   6 producers, reinforces an inaccurate link between mental illness and violence. According to recent studies, slightly more than 11 percent of the mentally ill are prone to violence, roughly the same percentage as in the general population. In reality, most mentally ill patients are withdrawn, frightened and passive. For 25 years, researchers at the University of Pennsylvania's Annenberg School for Communication tracked television portrayals of the mentally ill in prime time: more than 72 percent of the characters were portrayed as violent.

Activists have directed much of their fire at Madison Avenue. In late   7 1991, the communications giant GTE ran an ad featuring a man who was "temporarily insane" because he heard strange voices on his non-GTE system. The New York State Lottery game Crazy 8s last year had an ad showing a "typical" customer bragging that he was "crazy, nuts. I'm out of control." Ads have run recently for "psycho" sunglasses and "Skitzocolor" T shirts.

Some of the protests have been successful. Former First Lady Rosalynn   8 Carter, a leading mental-health advocate, persuaded one North Carolina company to pull ads featuring cans of peanuts in straitjackets promoting a product line called Certifiably Nuts. One of her annual mental-health-policy symposiums at Emory University's Carter Center was devoted entirely to stigma issues. "We are all concerned about stigma," she says. "It holds back progress in the whole field."

Deere & Co. listened to protests and pulled catalog ads for a "schizo-   9 phrenic" power mower, putting in its place a public service ad that read, "The most shocking thing about mental illness is how little people understand about it." Wordstar took "loony bin," "bobby hatch" and "funny farm" out of its thesaurus list of synonyms for "institution."

But such victories are sporadic at best. Last spring a Manhattan and New 10
Jersey discount clothier named Daffy's ran an ad showing a straitjacket with
the caption, "If you're paying over $100 for a dress shirt, may we suggest a
jacket to go with it?" Protesters picketed a store, wrote letters and petitioned
the New York City Commission on Human Rights. A Daffy's spokesperson
insisted that the ad was humorous and called the protest unfair.

The stigma is even being passed on to the next generation. DC Comics 11
insists that Superman's killer was never meant to be portrayed as mentally ill,
but another of its comics features a character named Shade. "Greetings from
the mental states of America," said one of its early promotion circulars,
"where every citizen has the right to remain deranged!"

Vocabulary

metaphor (2)   perpetuates (5)   portrayals (6)
stigmatizes (2)   psychotic (5)   symposiums (8)
advocates (2)   schizophrenia (5)   sporadic (10)
antidefamation (2)   prone (6)

Critical Thinking and Discussion

1. What are the effects of stereotyping the mentally ill?
2. What is meant by the statement "The stigma borne by present-day
   patients 'is harder to live with than the [mental] illness itself' "?
3. What misinformation about the mentally ill is spread by jokes and casual
   use of medical terms?
4. Are the mentally ill more prone to violence than others?
5. What protests against this stereotyping have been successful?
6. Are most protests successful or not? Explain by referring to the article
   and to your own experience.

Reading-Related Writing

1. Do your own study by asking individuals to define the word *schizophrenia* and then writing about their responses in relation to the correct
   definition provided in this article.
2. Write about the stereotyping or casual use of other terms such as *paranoid, manic,* and *depression* that also label types of mental illness.
3. You may have noticed that professionals in mental health and their
   patients often use the word *crazy.* Write a piece in which you discuss why
   they do that and what the effects of their diction are.

NAME POWER

Ferdinand M. de Leon and Sally Macdonald

"Is it African American *or is it* black? *Should we use* Latino, Hispanic, *or* Hispanic American? Native American *or* American
Indian? *What about* white? *What about* Asian American? *Then
comes the underlying question that—depending on who does the asking
and what spurred the question—can inspire understanding or provoke
outrage:* "Why can't we all just be Americans?"

All these many years after the nation's wrenching confrontations over civil 1
rights, you can still hear the clenched fist in Rick Olguin's voice as he
declares, "I am a Chicano." And the firm resolve in Maxine Chan's as she
corrects someone who has just called her an Oriental, "I am *not* a rug." And
the calm certainty in Nona Brazier's as she talks about abandoned labels and
concludes, "I will *always* refer to myself as an African American." Few things
are as fundamental as what we call ourselves.

The labels we use affect how others perceive us and how we see our- 2
selves; they shape how we see others and how we want to be seen by them;
they are used by those in power to define the rest even as they struggle to
define themselves. They shape who we are.

Little wonder then, that when the names we have always used for our- 3
selves and for others start to change, as they are doing, we feel a tremor down
the spine of our collective national consciousness. Is it *African American* or is
it *black*? Should we use *Hispanic* or *Latino*? *Native American* or *American
Indian*? What about *white*? What about *Asian American*? Then comes the
underlying question that—depending on who does the asking and what
spurred the question—can inspire understanding or provoke outrage: "Why
can't we all just be Americans?"

'Language Is Political'

Today, more of us than ever come from somewhere else. More of us than ever 4
have brown or black skins, not white ones. More of us than ever are demand-
ing that the names people call us are respectful ones, ones we have chosen to
best describe ourselves. "Language is political," says Guadalupe Friaz, an
assistant professor of ethnic studies at the University of Washington. "When
we talk about language we're talking about the relationships between people,
and what people call each other reflects whatever tension and anxiety that
society is going through." We've fought for power among ourselves for
generations, and words have been a frequent weapon. We sling epithets that

bruise as much as bricks and police batons. Nicknames for whole groups of people slide from slang to slur, gathering the power to maim psychologically. Some labels retain for generations the power to call up a host of stereotypes that dig and slice and kill the spirit. But sometimes the group at the receiving end of that abuse reclaims a label, like "black," effectively changing it from a negative term to a positive and proud one. "Change is constant," Friaz says. "Group relationships always change, so of course terminology is going to change. As people of color we don't have power, and we haven't had the power to name." But that, too, is changing.

Black or African American?

In 1967, Larry Gossett stopped using *Negro* and became *black*. Today, he's 5
African American. Gossett, executive director of the Central Area Motivation Program, was then involved in the civil-rights struggle, and the switch came as the black-power and black-pride movement gained steam. "We were defining black as beautiful and not as something ugly," Gossett says. "It had a profound inspirational impact on the youth of the '60s." The new label was a rejection of the labels imposed by whites and the labels of his parents' generation—a radical reclaiming of a word that had been viewed as a slur. "It was revolutionary and emotionally wrenching because we had parents saying, 'We've been Negroes and coloreds all our lives. Why are you calling yourselves black?' " Gossett says. "Black, in America and in the English language, had such a negative connotation that it scared our parents."

The changes in the labels used by or for African Americans over the 6
course of the country's history reflect the struggles between the dominant culture and other groups. For centuries, negro—in the lower case—was the accepted label. But after Reconstruction there was a push by black leaders and the black press to give dignity to the name by capitalizing it—an effort that took 50 years. In the 1900s, "colored" competed with Negro as the preferred group name, and it lives on today in the name of the National Association for the Advancement of Colored People, founded in 1910. Afro-American was first proposed in 1880, but it didn't catch on. Eventually Negro emerged as the preferred name, surviving until the late 1960s, when it was rejected by younger black people because of its associations with slavery.

Three years ago, Gossett decided it was time for him to make another 7
switch—this time to African American. "How you refer to yourselves as a people has social, historical and cultural significance," Gossett says. "I'm from the current school of thought which says that African American comes closest to describing who we are as a people." The change is rooted in the political growth of the African-American community, Gossett says, and was also prompted in part by a sense of identification with Africa—especially the struggles of black South Africans. For Gossett, it was again the reclaiming of a

word that had been tarnished. Today Gossett uses *African American* and *black* interchangeably, but he believes *African American* will prevail. Although most people still use black, many community leaders agree.

For Nona Brazier, the switch to African American happened further back. 8 Like Gossett, Brazier used *black* as a reaction to her parents' use of *Negro*. But by the end of the 1960s, she had started to use *African American*. "I often refer to black folks and the black community, but I never refer to myself as a black American," says Brazier, who is co-owner of Northwest Recovery Systems, a recycling firm. Brazier's preference for *African American* is rooted in her direct ties to Africa. She has a business in Nigeria and feels an attachment to the land from which her ancestors came. "The fact that I refer to myself as an African American reflects my time," Brazier says. "It's based on myself, my life and times, and even if other labels emerge, I will always refer to myself as an African American." "It doesn't matter what others call you, but it's very important what you call yourself."

Native Americans or American Indians?

As every child learns in grade school, Christopher Columbus sailed the ocean 9 blue to find India, and when he arrived in the New World, he mistakenly named the people Indians. Yet the name survives today. And to Joseph Brown, a Lakota elder who has worked with the homeless and street kids, Indian is just fine. "The word *Indian* identifies us," Brown says. "*Indian* covers a lot. A lot of Indians don't like to be called Indian because they're trying to be white men and they're prejudiced against themselves."

But for others, especially those who are younger, Native American is the 10 preferred label because it rejects the tragic historical associations that the word *Indian* carries. "The idea of calling people Native Americans appeals to me because we are native—more so than any other group," says Allethia Allen, an assistant professor of social work at the UW. "I would prefer that because the name *Indian* comes from Columbus."

Others say there are no right or wrong choices. "I think the majority feels 11 comfortable with the word *Indian*," says Cecil James, a resource-management worker for the Yakima fisheries. "Each individual has their own definition of how they want to be called. When I talk in public, I identify myself as an Indian of the Yakima Nation, but it should be up to each person to decide." Allen, who is half Native American and part black and white, says she hasn't eliminated *Indian* from her own vocabulary. "People tend to do what the majority does," Allen says. "But people are getting much more distinctive about what they say about their heritage and their customs and very, very identified with their bloodline."

While there seems to be no overwhelming majority for using either 12 *Indian* or *Native American*, most agree that using tribal affiliations is usually preferred. "Traditionally, among Native Americans, we identified each other by our tribal affiliation, and very often people greet each other that way," says Allen, who is Mohawk and Mohican. "To me, the more clearly a person is described in terms of heritage, the better it is." Robert Eaglestaff, the principal of American Indian Heritage School in Seattle says: "Most Indian tribes describe themselves as The People or human beings. The Lakotas, my tribe, means the friendly people. The others are labels, and I take labels for what they're worth—with a grain of salt. But I know who I am."

What About Asian Americans?

Not long ago, Ron Chew, director of the Wing Luke Museum in Seattle's 13 International District, was interviewing an elderly woman in Sequim about some of the Chinese people who settled on the Olympic Peninsula in the early days. She described them as Chinamen. "I didn't correct her," he says. "She grew up in another era and was frozen in time. Maybe in her time and her place that was not a derogatory term. But language evolves. What might be appropriate at one time might not be at another." *Chinaman* is not OK anymore, and neither is *Oriental*, although it's a term still used by some older Asians and many whites. "*Oriental* has a negative connotation," says Maxine Chan, a Chinese American who works with the community for the Seattle Police Department. "It's very much the Fu Manchu, Suzy Wong thing. It speaks about the 'yellow peril,' and the 'yellow horde.' If someone calls me that, I just say I'm not a rug."

While *Asian American* is all right, most people of Asian heritage would 14 rather be identified by the country of their origin. "Asian Americans need to be divided into Japanese Americans or Chinese Americans or Korean Americans—just because they want to be," says Setsuko Buckley, a Japanese language teacher and multicultural education expert at Western Washington University in Bellingham. "Even Southeast Asians are different from each other—Vietnamese, Thai, Cambodian—and they should have the option of being called what they want."

Tomie Rogers, a UW medical student, says she's "half Japanese, half 15 Swedish-Irish." When she was younger, new friends often thought—based on her almond-shaped eyes and tall stature—she must be Native American. "I don't really take offense to whatever people call me," she says. "I don't really have much ethnic feeling, and I don't even know how I'm listed as a student. I often mark the 'other' box."

Being considered Asian poses a problem for some Filipinos and Pacific 16 Islanders: They aren't from the Asian continent and feel they shouldn't be put in that category. Many Filipinos have the Catholic religion, Spanish surnames and some cultural vestiges of their colonial days. "Our biggest problem in the

Filipino community, besides economics, is an identity crisis," says Fred Cordova, a historian, author and manager of the UW information-services office. "We've never had a chance to identify ourselves. The majority of our community here is made up of immigrants now, and they're very different from the ones who have been here a long time."

Most of the Asian and Latino groups are trying to deal with the chaos 17
created by large waves of immigrants in recent years. As each new group begins to settle itself in the United States, another new group comes pouring in. Many never come to think of themselves as full-fledged U.S. citizens, and neither do their children. They continue to use the ethnic label arrived with, identifying themselves as, say, Chinese—not Chinese American. "A lot of us just don't put on the American tag," says Chew. "For most of us, it's understood that we're here, and for some, particularly the older generation, when they say American, they mean white."

Hispanic, Latino or Chicano?

Like Asians, people whose ethnic roots are in Latin America most often iden- 18
tify themselves by the country of their forebears—Mexican American, Cuban American. If they have to be inclusive, they'll be Latino. Even that is "an umbrella term that will suffer the same complications" with age as the other broad ethnic identifications, says the UW's Guadalupe Friaz. "If you have to have a broad term, it's OK. At least it's not Eurocentric."

If Lorenzo Alvarado is given the choice of Hispanic to mark on a docu- 19
ment, he'll say that's what he is. But when he marks the box that way, he feels he's losing his real heritage somehow. "I may be in America, but I'm a Mexican," says the Kent School District math teacher. Hispanic—a tag made up by census workers to identify Latin Americans, Caribbean Islanders and Spaniards—is considered by most of those it would describe as too broad, irritatingly bureaucratic or just plain unacceptable. "My understanding is there is no place called Hispanica," says Eduardo Diaz, a social-service administrator. "I think it's degrading to be called something that doesn't exist. Even Latino is a misnomer. We don't speak Latin."

Friaz calls herself a Chicana, a term—like a raised fist of defiance—that 20
gathered power during the antiwar and civil-rights movements. Although the term has lost some of its punch, many baby boomers who called themselves Chicanos (or Chicana, the feminine form) in their youth still do today. For some Mexican Americans, the term became a survival tool to replace *Mexican,* which had become tainted with racism, says Rick Olguin, a UW ethnic-studies assistant professor. Now *Mexican* is back in favor.

Javier Almaya, a native Colombian who has been in the United States for 21
10 years, is reasonably comfortable calling himself a Latino. But, like many

Latin Americans, he considers himself a mestizo—a mixture of European and Indian ancestry. It's a term that's used widely in Central and South America but isn't readily recognized in this country.

Such complexity is the rule in discussions of ethnic labels for Latinos. 22 Consider the employees of Diaz's Seattle office: Diaz is the assistant manager of the King County Guardian Ad Litem program, a court advocacy program for children. A Puerto Rican who grew up in the Bronx in New York City, he says he feels degraded if he's called a Hispanic. But Cathy Ortiz, the office's support staff supervisor, whose grandparents still live in Mexicali, Baja California, says although *Hispanic* is OK with her, she'd rather be called an American of Mexican descent. And Rita Amaro, an office worker, is a third-generation Mexican American who says people can call her Latina, although the word reminds her of "kind of an island, like Puerto Rico or Cuba."

Minority, Non-White or People of Color?

When whites were clearly the dominant group in this country, it was easy to 23 divide the population into majority and minority. Not the most sensitive division, but a handy one for whites that reflected the existing power dynamics and neatly summed up who had the power and numbers and who didn't. But as whites lose their numerical dominance, and non-white immigrants continue to come into the country, the racial makeup of the nation becomes even more complex. The balance is shifting. At the current rate of growth, the groups we consider minorities will collectively become the majority in this country in about 2050, according to recent projections by the Population Reference Bureau, a non-profit Washington, D.C., agency that studies demographic trends. The bureau based its projection on 1990 census figures.

There has long been a debate over what to call people who aren't white. 24 In 1962, in *The Negro History Bulletin,* Eldridge Cleaver wrote of the term *non-white*: "The very words that we use indicate that we have set a premium on the Caucasian ideal of beauty. When discussing interratial relations, we speak of 'white people' and 'non-white people.' Notice that that particular choice of words gives precedence to 'white people' . . . making them a center—a standard—to which "non-white" bears a negative relation. Notice the different connotation when we turn around and say "colored" and 'non-colored' or 'black' or 'non-black.' "

These days much of the discussion centers on the phrase "people of 25 color," an alternative that has emerged in recent years. It has generated strong reactions—but so far little consensus among those to whom the phrase would be applied. "I don't like the term 'people of color,' " says Almaya, a health educator with the AIDS Prevention Project. "It doesn't give us any definition. It could be a person from Colombia or a person from Samoa, and they don't really have anything in common at all." But Olguin likes the phrase and argues that it was significantly different from the now discredited "colored people." "It's viewing it from the top instead of the bottom," he says. " 'Colored people' says 'inferior,' and to be a colored person is to define a people by their color. But people of color are persons with other attributes."

But the changes won't come easily, and those who would claim the power 26 to name themselves—and do away with long-entrenched labels—should expect resistance, says UW Professor Haig Bosmajian, whose book *The Language of Oppression* explores the power of language. Bosmajian says opposition usually comes from two groups: those who need to be persuaded that there is a problem, and those who have a psychological stake in maintaining their power and not acquiescing to the new labels. "It's more than etiquette, it's power," he says.

White, Caucasian or Euro-American?

White people don't tend to think much about what they're called. Since 27 they're already the majority, they see no need to label themselves. "I don't think of it the way a black person would call himself black," says Nick Wilson, a Metro bus driver. "I think my grandparents were Irish, but I don't really even know. The only thing I can tell you about one of my grandfathers is that he was from Texas. Come to think of it, he was a Texan."

"I don't think about it at all," says Jerry Edwards, a Seattle yacht broker. 28 "And I guess that's as much an indication of the situation as anything. "It points out how privileged we are compared to other racial groups." When pressed to make a choice between *white* and *Caucasian,* Edwards dislikes both. "*Caucasian* is too antiseptic somehow, and *white* is too racial."

"It's easy in America to be white," says Pier van den Berghe, a UW sociol- 29 ogy and anthropology professor. "It's easy for whites to forget they're white. But it's impossible for blacks to forget they're black." When van den Berghe is asked to check a box with his ethnic background, he marks 'Other' or 'African American.' He's white, but he can do that, he says, because he was born in South Africa. In the Southwest, whites are used to being called Anglos. But *Anglo,* introduced by Mexicans, means English. And many whites point out that England is not their homeland. Many white people dislike being called Caucasian. Van den Berghe calls it "a pseudo-ethnic label" and he finds it "profoundly objectionable." Most modern scholars no longer use racial divisions. Genetically, people are people, and any differences between them only skin deep. Friaz, the UW ethnic-studies professor, calls whites Euro-Americans, a term many whites consider contrived and unnecessary and in some cases erroneous.

Friaz believes whites should start their own discussion of heritage. 30 "Everyone has an ethnicity," she says. "Euro-Americans have to start seeing themselves as ethnics. Most Euro-Americans are not proud of who they are. I ask my white students about their ethnicity and they say, 'I guess I'm American.' They say it in an apologetic way." This denial of cultural background is something that wasn't widely seen until World War I, Friaz says. Until then, most whites sent their children to language schools after their regular classes to preserve their culture. But with the onset of the war, becoming "American" meant proving your loyalty by rejecting all ties to other lands. "This is one of the few countries in the world that is willfully ignorant—which is a worse kind of ignorance," says the UW's Olguin. "In the rest of the world it's a virtue to speak different languages. Here if you speak three languages you're trilingual, and if you speak two languages you're bilingual, and if you speak one language, you're American."

Why Can't We All Just Be Americans?

It seems like a simple enough question, but it can be fraught with insensitiv- 31
ity and misunderstanding, depending on who hears it and who asks. At best, it's a naive, idealistic attempt to say, "Why can't we quit categorizing each other?" If we call each other the same thing, it insists, other differences will dissolve. But Friaz and some other people of color hear the question this way: "Why do you have to keep emphasizing your ethnicity, your color? Why can't *you* be white like *us*?" Those questions release a flood of perceived insensitivities: Why don't you adopt white values, white culture? Why don't you dress in Western styles, eat Western foods? Why press universities to offer ethnic studies in a curriculum served perfectly well by the study of Western culture? To many, whites and people of color alike, the questions are a sign of a new imagery. The melting pot is now an ethnic salad.

The simplistic solution is to cut ethnic roots. "The day we can just call 32
ourselves Americans comes after the day that we can figure out what we call each other," Olguin says. "After centuries of antagonism, it's naive to think that we can just forget all of that." "God, if we *could* all just be Americans," says Cordova. "But there is such a thing as reality, and it's borne out by the acts of the past weeks. There is racism in this country. As long as we have to call ourselves something, I'm proud to be a Filipino American. What you call yourself, hell, that's up to you."

Cecilia Concepcion Alvarez, an artist, believes the white majority and the 33
society it dominates eye the immigrating cultures with suspicion because the country has never been racially homogenous. Some whites fear—singly and collectively, consciously or not—giving any other culture or its people even a sliver of power. Minorities sometimes fear losing their personal identity to a nameless mass. "We have to talk about that. We can't just dismiss it," says Alvarez. "A lot of people have been dismissed in the past. It's not cultural; it's not even necessarily genetics. It's human, and the discussion has to be how we can get together."

So how do we get together? One way is to recognize and respect each 34 other's identity, rather than insist everyone adopt the same identify. Nona Brazier argues that clinging to separate labels does not necessarily detract from the idea of a united people. "One of the best things about this country is the variety," she says. "I think people need to accentuate the American, but people also need to accentuate the love of their history and culture."

The UW's Bosmajian offers the following anecdote: During the late 35 1960s, at a panel discussion on the Vietnam War, one of the panelists used the phrase "our colored boys," a phrase that Bosmajian points out is triply offensive. The phrase erected a wall that divided the participants along racial lines and blocked further communication. "You're not going to change race relations by changing the language," Bosmajian says. "You're not going to get jobs by changing the language. But changing the language is one of the steps that has to be taken. . . . At least we'd be talking to each other."

Critical Thinking and Discussion

1. What power do names have as weapons?
2. Once a name has an implied meaning, can it ever be changed? If so, give an example.
3. What changes in labels have African-Americans undergone?
4. How important is tribal affiliation to Native Americans?
5. Why do most people of Asian-American heritage prefer a label other than *Asian-American?*
6. What are some of the name preferences of people with ethnic roots in Latin America?
7. What are the problems with the labels *white, Caucasian, Anglo,* and *Euro-American?*

Reading-Related Writing

1. Discuss the ethnic label you prefer for yourself and explain why others are inappropriate or less desirable.
2. Write a piece explaining why you use the labels you do for the main groups mentioned in this essay.

I DON'T SOUND BLACK*

Lourdes Morrow

Student Lourdes Morrow feels that she has blended characteristics of two cultures—Puerto Rican and African-American. Yet she is often

*questioned and looked on with some suspicion by her friends when she
talks about her heritage.*

Growing up was a struggle for me. Like others I wanted to be proud of who I   1
was racially, but in the society where I lived everyone seemed to be either
black or white. As for me, my father is Puerto Rican and my mother is black. I
didn't fit into any box that people tried to put me in. If I'd said I was black,
people would have seen me as a certain kind of person; if I'd said Puerto
Rican, people would have seen me as something else. But living mainly
among blacks, when I said I was mixed, people questioned me. As a result it
was difficult doing what I wanted to do: grow up proud of the two parts of
my heritage.

When I was a little girl, I did not have to worry about my identify. All I   2
did was play and eat. But once in junior high school, I discovered that finding
and proclaiming my identify was very important. When my friends, who were
mostly black, asked me what culture I claimed, I would say Puerto Rican and
black. This would lead to an argument. My friends would tell me that Puerto
Rican was not a race and that I was trying to deny being black, which was not
true. All I was doing was acknowledging both cultures.

I still feel that way. I suppose I like the Puerto Rican culture because that's   3
what I was introduced to initially. My first language was Spanish, and all of
the foods I ate during my childhood were Puerto Rican food. For example, I
grew up eating rice, beans, fried green bananas, and flan. I also learned to
appreciate Latin music, such as salsa, mergenge, and bolero. The foods, customs, and music from my childhood are all special to me, and I would never
deny them.

My introduction to black culture of the American variety came later, and   4
I like it equally well. The majority of my friends are black, and I enjoy their
company very much. In a sense they were my teachers. I now find myself
attracted to black music and to foods such as greens, chitlins, cornbread, and
grits. I can relate to and appreciate black music such as rap, blues, and funk. I
have discovered and cultivated the blackness in me, and I am very proud to
claim and express it.

What frustrates me the most, even now, is that black people sometimes   5
judge me by saying I am not black enough because I'm not hip enough to
black slang or black culture. They sometimes say I "don't sound black." They
don't take into consideration where my parents came from. Although my
mother is black and through her I did experience my African roots, neither of
my parents spoke English when I was born.

The way I have dealt with my being biracial is by learning more about   6
both cultures. I have been doing this by reading books, taking classes in
college, and speaking to family members and friends about each culture. But
what has helped me the most is accepting myself and not letting people's

comments or criticism define or limit me. I am proud of who I am racially—
Puerto Rican and black in a culture called American. And I am an individual.

Critical Thinking and Discussion

1. What is the thesis of Morrow's essay?
2. What methods does she use in defining herself?
3. How has she learned about her cultural diversity?
4. What is the effect of the last sentence?

Reading-Related Writing

1. Most Americans are of mixed heritage. If you are, write about yourself in terms of your heritage and what you like about your dual or multiple roots.
2. Write about someone else who is biracial or bicultural, discussing the characteristics the person associates with different parts of his or her heritage.
3. Culture can also be defined by region (East, West, South, North, Midwest, Southwest, Northwest, etc.), class (upper, middle, lower), or area (urban, suburban, rural). Write about yourself as a member of these types of cultures, explaining what you have inherited, discovered and learned to appreciate.

Collaborative Learning

1. In groups, enumerate the stereotypes featured in this chapter and complete these tasks:

   - Decide which stereotypes are the most obvious (blatant) and which are the most subtle.
   - Decide what steps can be taken to reduce or eliminate the use of these stereotypes or to offset their effects.
   - Make an oral presentation of your findings to the entire class.
   - Participate in a class discussion that compares and contrasts the group findings.
   - Complete a written report of your findings.

Connections

1. Write an essay in which you define stereotyping by giving examples and by discussing causes and effects. Use examples and conclusions from at least four readings from this chapter.

10

Discrimination:
Playing the Exclusion Game

One of the basic dictionary definitions of *discriminate* is "to distinguish differences accurately." The definition that we usually intend carries a full social connotation: "to judge individuals favorably or unfavorably on the basis of the group, category, or class of which they are part rather than on the basis of their merit." *Unfavorably* is likely to be the operative word, and the group is likely to be their race, but, of course, there are other areas of very harmful discrimination.

The range of discrimination covered in this chapter is extensive. Betty Friedan discusses the exclusion and misrepresentation of those over sixty-five. Karen Peterson invites you to walk in the shoes of someone who is overweight. Patty Fischer says "women have begun to fight" in rape cases. Jesse Jackson points out the danger of misplaced loyalty in protecting wrongdoing in one's own race. Sucheng Chan explains what it is like being a short, Chinese, female, physically disabled person. Richard Worsnop examines stereotyping in the use of Indian names for sports teams. In some of the most famous lines in American poetry, Paul Laurence Dunbar reminds us that the caged bird does not sing because it is happy. Michael Holguin writes poignantly of the homophobia that surfaces in the home, at church, and in society generally, so that a gay youngster may grow up convinced he's wicked, and may even discriminate against himself.

WRITING STRATEGIES AND TECHNIQUES: PERSUASION

If you are writing a piece that has a thesis (an assertion), you are trying to convince your audience of its validity. That is *persuasion*. It is a much broader term than *argument*. You may, for example, be stating that exercise is good for most people. You would probably not expect your audience to disagree with that assertion, though the members of your audience may not be exercising enough for their good health. Your intent might be to move them to action—to exercise. Or you might be trying to promote a product, such as wholesome bread, to people who eat unwholesome bread. In those cases, persuasion is there, but argument is absent because no contrary view exists.

Although persuasion can exist without argumentation, all argumentation is by its very nature persuasive. *Argumentation* begins with a debatable issue and attempts to persuade an audience. It differs from pure exposition, which attempts to explain, though in trying to convince an audience that an assertion is valid, exposition can also be regarded as persuasive. Similarly, argumentation differs from narration and description. But it may use any of these other forms of discourse in developing its ideas; therefore, it can be regarded as the most complex form. Because persuasion, in its broadest sense, can be presented in various patterns of thesis and support and because argumentation has a traditional pattern, argumentation will be featured in the remainder of this discussion.

Specifically, an argument may begin with a controversy or disagreement. A friend may say that Martin Luther King, Jr., was a better civil rights leader than Malcolm X. You disagree, stating your reasons for your view, refuting some of your friend's points, and perhaps accepting others. Spirited discussion ensues. Most arguments are that simple. However, in college writing assignments and in other situations, you will be expected to write out an argument in a systematic fashion designed to appeal to your audience's sense of reason and often, in a fair manner, to your audience's emotions. And you will be expected to examine the arguments of others. Argumentation as a form of discourse is the essence of critical thought.

Argumentation requires that you think clearly, organize your points skillfully, present your side honestly, cogently, and logically, and, if advantageous to your viewpoint, refute your opponent's claims. Opinions and generalizations must be supported with relevant evidence: facts, testimony, and valid reasons. You must control your biases and prejudices, omit any emotional and vehement outbursts, and discard any trivial, irrelevant, and false claims if you are to command the respect of your audience.

Purpose

The purpose of your persuasion or argumentation will be to win the members of the audience to your view or modify their views.

The Problem and Your Proposition

The *proposition* (the main point or thesis) should be a clear, concise statement of your position on a problem that is subject to argument. Good propositions are statements of policy, value, or belief. A *question of policy* calls for action by the reader. The writer of the proposition "The United States should not give military aid to Central American countries" advocates action in relation to diplomatic problems between the United States and Central American countries. A *question of value or belief* calls for acceptance by the reader. The proposition "Future historians will praise the Clinton administration's program on environmental protection" implies that the writer, within the context of divided opinion, will offer proof to try to persuade the reader to accept the writer's view.

Your Audience

Your audience may be uninformed, informed, biased, hostile, receptive, apathetic, sympathetic, empathetic—any one, a combination, or something else. The point is that you should be intensely concerned about who will read your composition. If your readers are likely to be uninformed about the social and historical background of the issue, then you need to set the issue in its context. The discussion of the background should lead to the problem for which you have a proposition or solution. If your readers are likely to be biased or even hostile to your view, take special care to refute the opposing view in a thoughtful, incisive way that does not further antagonize them. If your readers are already receptive and perhaps even sympathetic, and you wish to move them to action, then you might appeal to their conscience and the need for commitment.

Components of Your Paper

All arguments will include a *proposition* and *support* (the evidence or the reasons for a view being valid). In addition to those components, you may want to include *definitions, background,* and *refutation.* Always take care to define terms that may be obscure or ambiguous. Arguments often break down or are misguided because terms are left undefined. For example, terms such as *liberal* and *conservative* mean different things to different people and should be defined within the specific context. The need for background and the extent of that background will depend on the knowledge of the audience. Refutation is a common feature in argumentation because you usually have to show that the other side is wrong in order to advance your own view. However, given a sympathetic audience that needs only to be moved, refutation may be unnecessary.

Organizational Plan

You can organize your composition of argumentation in various ways. You may wish to start with a brief introduction such as a short history of the controversy, an analysis of the situation, policy, problem, or plan, or a condition that is the source of disagreement. You may start by presenting your case, saving the statement of the main issue for your conclusion. You may state the main issue, refute your opponent's claims, and then follow with a confirmation of your position. You may present your case and follow with a refutation of your opponent's case. You may also use any of the methods that have proved effective in the organization and development of the other kinds of discourse, especially exposition. Below are some possible patterns.

- main issue—support
- main issue—refutation—support
- main issue—support—refutation

There are, of course, other variants, and there are also several methods of developing the material within each pattern. You may organize the supporting facts by comparison, one side at a time or one issue at a time (present an issue favoring your position, then refute one of your opponent's claims). You may develop the argument (or persuasive writing, in a broader sense) by a method such as cause and effect, contrast, or a combination of methods.

Appropriate Kinds of Evidence

In order to appeal to those with different viewpoints, you must prove your claims are valid. Your proof must consist of evidence and sound reasons forcefully and logically interwoven into an effective pattern of organization and development. Supporting the individual issues, then, is the most important part of writing a good argument.

What kinds of evidence make up proof?

First, you can offer facts. Martin Luther King, Jr., was killed in Memphis, Tennessee, on April 4, 1968. Because an event that has happened is true and can be verified, this statement about King is a fact. But that James Earl Ray acted alone in killing King is to some a questionable fact. That King was the greatest of all civil rights leaders is also opinion because it cannot be verified.

Some facts are readily accepted because they are general knowledge—you and your reader know them to be true, because they can be or have been verified. Other "facts" are based on personal observation and are often reported in various publications. You should always be concerned about the reliability of the source for both the information you use and that used by those with other viewpoints.

Second, you can cite examples. Keep in mind that you must present a sufficient number of examples and that the examples must be relevant.

Third, you can present statistics. Statistics, as defined in *Webster's New World Dictionary,* are facts and data of a numerical kind that are classified and tabulated in order to present significant information about a given subject.

Avoid presenting a long list of figures; select statistics carefully and relate them to things familiar to your reader. The millions of dollars spent on a war in a single week, for example, become more comprehensible when expressed in terms of what the money would purchase in education, highways, or urban renewal.

To test the validity of statistics, either yours or your opponent's, ask: Who gathered them? Under what conditions? For what purpose? How are they used?

Fourth, you can cite evidence from, and opinions of, authorities. Most readers accept facts from recognized, reliable sources—governmental publications, standard reference works, and books and periodicals published by established firms. In addition, they will accept evidence and opinions from individuals who, because of their knowledge and experience, are recognized as experts.

In using authoritative sources as proof, keep these points in mind:

- Select authorities who are generally recognized as experts in their field.
- Use authorities who qualify in the field pertinent to your argument.
- Select authorities whose views are not biased.
- Try to use several authorities.
- Identify the authority's credentials clearly in the essay.

The following student-written paragraph and essay illustrate effective uses of persuasion.

NO HABLA ESPAÑOL

David Camacho

topic sentence

Being a recognizable racial type has been at times confusing for me and has led to a peculiar type of discrimination. I grew up in a middle-class neighborhood in which there were few immigrants from any country. My mother is white and my father is Hispanic, but because my features are definitely Hispanic, I'm often expected to identify with Hispanic groups exclusively. My father's great-grandparents came from Mexico; my mother's grandparents came from Ireland. At home we have foods from each culture, and we celebrate Cinco de Mayo and St. Patrick's Day. When we visit with my Hispanic grandparents, my father sometimes speaks to them in Spanish. Some of my Hispanic relatives tease me about not speaking Spanish, but they're never mean in doing so. I have some vocabulary and grammar in Spanish, but I don't speak it fluently. Perhaps I

support

should have learned. Maybe my father should have taught me Spanish. When I am working as a salesperson in a large department store, Hispanic people approach me and ask questions in Spanish. When I say I don't speak Spanish, I may get a comment on my lack

support

of ethnic pride or on my parents' irresponsibility. On the other cultural side, many non-Hispanic customers assume I'm a recent immigrant and will not understand the use of certain products I sell. Actually I want to learn more about my Irish and Mexican heritage, and am doing so, but I would like to make my studies because I want to, not because I have an obligation to do so. As for the Mexican side, I even intend to take a college class in Spanish next semester. There are practical reasons for everyone in California to learn more than one language, and Spanish is the language spoken by the cultural group that will be in the majority here in a few decades. So what do I want? I want to be treated not as a Hispanic, not even as an Irish-Hispanic-American, and certainly not as a cultural traitor, but as an individual.

WHAT IF I'M OVERWEIGHT AND NOT JOLLY?*

Karen Peterson

proposition

Society as a whole views being fat as unacceptable. *This 1 stereotype has devastating psychological effects.* Society is taught to believe that people who are fat are unhealthy, unhappy, low in self-esteem, unmotivated, and lazy.

support

I don't agree with this view; to me society is really 2 misjudging people. I am overweight, but I do not fit the stereotype. I am in great health. I am subject to the same emotions as those of a thin person. As far as having low self-esteem, for me that couldn't be farther from the truth. I have always liked myself and have been secure in who I am. With regard to being unmotivated and lazy, I go to school full-time (17 semester units), and I take care of a household of four. In my opinion, I make the White Tornado look sluggish by comparison.

support

The fashion industry, which is also dictated to by 3 society, has long ignored the "full figure." When I was growing up, it was difficult to find fashionable, stylish clothing that fit me. Most clothing manufacturers designed clothes for the "model" figure, even though the world's population isn't all models. I often found myself going from store to store, discovering that the only place that carried my size was called something like Coleman Tents R Us. This may seem funny, but for a person like me, it can be traumatic.

support

The media contribute to stereotyping by promoting 4 the idea that in order to be beautiful, happy, healthy, and loved, a person must be thin. They promote this concept by showing thin people exclusively when they advertise cosmetics, clothing, cards, and alcohol. Only thin people are seen enjoying themselves on vacations. It's no wonder that fat people feel overwhelmed and defeated, when this is the image they continually see on virtually every television commercial, billboard, magazine cover, and movie. These concepts and images create extreme pressure to conform. For instance, Oprah Winfrey was subjected to pressure and ridicule when one diet didn't work. She failed to fit the media's image. But she was still the same person. Surely a person is worth more than an image, heavy or light. Like her, I'm worth more than a perfect image.

support

The worst offender of social stereotyping of fat peo- 5
ple is the health-and-fitness industry. No other industry can do more psychological and physical damage while making a bundle of money by exploiting fat people. With all the fad diets, quick-weight-loss pills, "miracle" fat creams, and exercise weight-loss videos, it is no wonder that fat people don't know whom to believe, which weight-loss guru to follow, or simply how to lose weight successfully and safely. All of the marketed diets and solutions seem to place great emphasis on being fit and healthy. Yet in reality, many are detrimental. For most of my life, I have tried a variety of these so-called get-thin-quick regimens. The outcome at first was always great, but they fail to help me maintain the new, thin look. What resulted is commonly known as the yo-yo syndrome. I lost weight, but once I stopped dieting, the old habit and pounds returned, sometimes accompanied by even *more* pounds.

restatement of
main idea

People really need to accept others for the way they 6
are and not put so much emphasis on how they look. Stereotyping of any form is, in my opinion, demeaning—mentally, physically, and spiritually. To assume that an individual is any less of a human being because of his or her weight is pure ignorance. It tends to get in the way of good friendships, relationships, communication, understanding, and compassion. A human being is a human being regardless of size.

WRITER'S CHECKLIST

- State the problem and your proposition.
- Consider your audience.
- Determine the components of your paper, such as definitions, background, and refutation.
- Decide on your organizational plan. The main patterns are these:
  main issue—support
  main issue—refutation—support
  main issue—support—refutation

- Consider the most commonly used pattern as presented here:

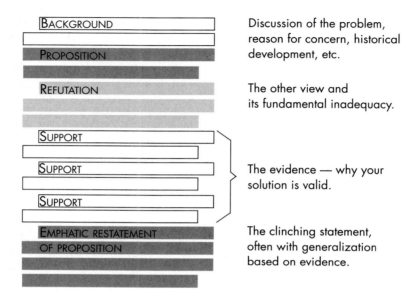

BACKGROUND	Discussion of the problem, reason for concern, historical development, etc.
PROPOSITION	
REFUTATION	The other view and its fundamental inadequacy.
SUPPORT	
SUPPORT	The evidence — why your solution is valid.
SUPPORT	
EMPHATIC RESTATEMENT OF PROPOSITION	The clinching statement, often with generalization based on evidence.

- Select the appropriate kinds of evidence, such as the following, to use with your explanations:
  facts
  examples
  statistics
  data from and opinions of authorities

A SHACK OF MISERY

Raymond Barrio

This descriptive passage, used as argument, comes from The Plum Pickers, *a novel about Hispanic-American migrant workers. Here Manuel, a farm worker, looks around his "shack of misery" and considers each detail. He naturally asks, What is such a shack good for?*

Manuel studied the whorls in the woodwork whirling slowly, revealed in   1
the faint crepuscular light penetrating his shack. His cot was a slab of half-
inch plywood board twenty-two inches wide and eight feet long, the width of
the shack, supported by two two-by-four beams butted up against the wall at

both ends beneath the side window. The shack itself was eight by twelve by seven feet high. Its roof had a slight pitch. The rain stains in the ceiling planks revealed the ease with which the rain penetrated. Except for two small panes of glass exposed near the top, most of the window at the opposite end was boarded up. A single, old, paint-encrusted door was the only entry. No curtains. No interior paneling. Just a shack. A shack of misery. He found he was able to admire and appreciate the simplicity and the strength of the construction. He counted the upright studs, level, two feet apart, the double joists across the top supporting the roof. Cracks and knotholes aplenty, in the wall siding, let in bright chinks of light during the day and welcome wisps of clear fresh air at night. The rough planking of the siding was stained dark. The floor was only partly covered with odd sections of plywood. Some of the rough planking below was exposed, revealing cracks leading down to the cool black earth beneath. A small thick table was firmly studded to a portion of the wall opposite the door. A few small pieces of clear lumber stood bunched together, unsung, unused, unhurried, in the far corner. An overhead shelf, supported from the ceiling by a small extending perpendicular arm, containing some boxes of left-over chemicals and fertilizers, completed the furnishings in his temporary abode.

It was habitable.   2

He could raise his family it it.   3

If they were rabbits.   4

Vocabulary

crepuscular (1)
perpendicular (1)

Critical Thinking and Discussion

1. What is the dominant impression that implies argument?
2. Is the order based mainly on time or space (direction)?
3. What would be the effect of this passage if the last line were not included?
4. How could Manuel develop admiration for the shack?

Reading-Related Writing

1. Describe a place in which you lived that you would not have wanted to bring your family to.
2. Pose as a government inspector of housing for migratory workers, and using Manuel's details, explain why the shack is unsatisfactory.

3. Pose as an unscrupulous farm manager who is writing about the conditions of the shack. He could be filing the report for the government or advertising for workers.

A BUILDING IN UPPER HARLEM

Claude Brown

It is a building. It was a home. People lived in it. It is owned. But you wouldn't want to live there; neither did the people who lived there. And you wouldn't want to own it. But if you live in New York, maybe you are part owner. Notice how the author describes it as "this building" as if he is trying to keep it at a distance, for it is a danger to us all. But he, nevertheless, conducts a tour—because we need to know.

There is a building in upper Harlem on a shabby side street with several other buildings that resemble it in both appearance and condition. "This building" is in an advanced state of deterioration; only cold water runs through the water pipes, the rats here are as large as cats. The saving grace of this building might very well be the erratic patterns of the varied and brilliant colors of the graffiti which adorn it internally and externally from basement to roof. This building has no electricity in the apartments, but the electricity in the hallway lamp fixtures is still on. Some of the apartments have garbage piled up in them five feet high and that makes opening the door a very difficult task for those whose nasal passages are sufficiently insensitive to permit entry. In some of the apartments and on the rooftop, the garbage and assorted debris are piled only one or two feet high, and the trash has been there so long that plant life has generated. The most rapid tour possible through this building will necessitate boiling oneself in a hot tub of strong disinfectant for a couple of hours, and even then this astonishingly formidable breed of lice will continue to make its presence felt throughout a long itchy night. This building is adjacent to a fully occupied tenement whose inhabitants are families, some of which include several children. This building has a few steps missing from the staircase above the second floor and there are no lightbulbs in the hallway; it's a very unsafe place for trespassers, even during the day. This building's last family of tenants was emancipated several weeks ago; they hit the numbers and moved to the Bronx, shouting, "Free at last, free at last; thank God for the number man." Prior to their liberation, the "last family" had lived a most unusual existence. Somebody had to be at home at all times to protect the family's second-hand-hot television from becoming a third-hand-hot television; there were too many junkies in and out who used the vacant apartments to stash their loot until they could "down" it and who also used some of the apartments for sleeping and as "shooting galleries." For protection, the last family had a large, vicious German shepherd. This dog was needed for the rats as well as the junkies. A cat would be no help at all. The sight of the rats in this building would give any cat smaller than a mountain lion instant heart failure. The last family considered itself fortunate, despite the many unpleasant, unhealthy and unsafe aspects of its residence. "We ain't paid no rent in two years. I guess the city just forgot that we was here or they was just too embarrassed to ask for it," said the head of the last family. This building has holes in the wall large enough for a man to walk through two adjacent apartments. This building has holes in the ceilings on the fourth and fifth floors, and when it rains, the rain settles on the floor of a fourth-story apartment. This building is not unique, there are many others like it in the ghettos of New York City; and like many others . . . this building is owned by the City of New York.

Critical Thinking and Discussion

1. What is the dominant impression that suggests argument?
2. What are the uses of the building and who and what are its inhabitants?
3. What sense does the author mainly appeal to?
4. Is the organization based mainly on time or space?
5. What does the author do to make the tone (attitude toward his subject material and the way he presents it to the reader) and purpose clearly persuasive?

Reading-Related Writing

1. Use this paragraph as a pattern to write about an apartment building or project that you think should be renovated or demolished.

THE FOUNTAIN OF AGE

Betty Friedan

Best known for her revolutionary book The Feminine Mystique *(1963) and her leadership in the women's movement, Betty Friedan has embraced a crusade to eliminate discrimination against older people by dispelling misinformation and eliminating legal barriers. This excerpt is from her most recent book,* The Second Stage *(1993).*

Why the increased emphasis by professional age experts and the media 1
on the nursing home as the locus of age when, in fact, more than 95% of
those over 65 continue to live in the community? Why the preoccupation
with senility, Alzheimer's disease, when less than 5% of people over 65 will
suffer it? Why the persistent image of the aged as "sick" and "helpless," as a
burden on our hospitals and health-care system, when, in fact, people over 65
are less likely than those who are younger to suffer from the acute illnesses
that require hospitalization? Why the persistent image of those over 65 as
sexless when research shows people capable of sex until 90, if they are
healthy and not shamed out of seeking or otherwise deprived of sex partners?
Why don't most people know that current research shows some *positive*
changes in certain mental abilities, as well as muscular, sexual and immune
processes, that can compensate for age-related declines?

What are we doing to ourselves—and to our society—by denying age? 2
(Peter Pan and Dorian Gray found it hell staying "forever young.") Is there
some serious foreclosure of human fulfillment, forfeiture of values, in that
definition of age as "problem"? In fact, the more we seek the perpetual fountain of youth and go on denying age, defining age itself as "problem," that
"problem" will only get worse. For we will never know what we could be, and
we will not organize in our maturity to break through the barriers that keep
us from using our evolving gifts in society, or demand the structures we need
to nourish them.

Critical Thinking and Discussion

1. What is Friedan's principal support, and how effective is it?
2. As she refutes charges, what positive characteristics does she reveal?
3. Who loses when people over sixty-five are misrepresented?

Reading-Related Writing

1. Friedan uses statistics and statements to refute commonly held beliefs.
   Use some examples from your own experiences to argue the same points.

SYMPATHY

Paul Laurence Dunbar

*In his poem "Sympathy," Paul Laurence Dunbar writes one of the most
haunting lines in American literature: "I know why the caged bird*

sings." About sixty years after he penned that line, Maya Angelou selected it as the theme and title for a book about her own African-American experience.

I know what the caged bird feels, alas!
When the sun is bright on the upland
slopes;
When the wind stirs soft through the
springing grass
And the river flows like a stream of glass;
5 When the first bird sings and the first bud
opes.
And the faint perfume from its chalice
steals—
I know what the caged bird feels!

I know why the caged bird beats his wing
Till its blood is red on the cruel bars;
10 For he must fly back to his perch and cling
When he fain would be on the bough
a-swing;
And a pain still throbs in the old, old scars
And they pulse again with a keener sting—
I know why he beats his wing!

15 I know why the caged bird sings, ah me,
When his wing is bruised and his bosom
sore,—
When he beats his bars and would be
free;
It is not a carol of joy or glee,
But a prayer that he sends from his heart's
deep core,
20 But a plea, that upward to Heaven he flings—
I know why the caged bird sings!

Critical Thinking and Discussion

1. What does the caged bird feel?
2. Why does the caged bird beat his wing?
3. Why does the caged bird sing?
4. How do these three points relate to the experience of an oppressed people?

Reading-Related Writing

1. Use one of the lines from this poem or a combination of them as a discussion point or points and write a paragraph or essay.

WALK IN MY FULL-FIGURE SHOES*

Karen Peterson

Working with the basic idea of identifying with those with different experiences, student Karen Peterson asks you to walk in her shoes. Peterson is a hardworking, highly competent, witty student. She says that she has experienced all of the things you are going to read about, but now she has accepted herself for what she is—a proud and beautiful woman with a lot of confidence, intelligence, sensitivity, and self-fulfillment, who happens to be overweight. This paragraph is a reworking of the exemplary essay at the beginning of this chapter, and utilizes the pattern used by Ray Jenkins in "Georgia on My Mind" in the previous chapter.

If you have never experienced being called bubbles, two-ton Tessie, chunky, or plump; if you have never walked into a store and been told, "We don't carry your size"; if you have never experienced being left out of a trip to the beach by a group of your peers; if you have never been the last one chosen for a team and then sent to right field; if you have never been rejected by a friend who was becoming popular with the "in" crowd; if you have never been laughed at when you sat in a tiny chair; if you have never dreamed of being a cheerleader or a homecoming queen; if you have never cried yourself to sleep and wished for a fairy godmother to transform your body; if you have never been treated as if you were invisible and wished you really were; if you have never been made to feel unlovable by those who are unworthy of your love; if you have never forced yourself to laugh at a joke about weight and wanted the teller punished; if you have never tried, succeeded with, and then crashed every diet ever invented; if you have never known the pain of those things, then you have never been fat. Fat is only a word, not a human being. Fat cannot feel, need, or want as I have and as I still do.

Critical Thinking and Discussion

1. According to Peterson, is the stigma of being overweight more severe for the young or the mature?
2. Is there anything positive about being overweight?

3. In what way does she make her points specific?
4. Who might and should do something to offset the problems of the over-weight person?
5. Some of Peterson's most hurtful experiences occurred in childhood. Should schools and other agencies take some steps to alleviate the pains of the overweight through education? Or is what she describes something that is part of growing up because "kids will be kids" and we all have a tough time in childhood?

Reading-Related Writing

1. Write about your own experience in growing up different from peers in some way, using either the "walk in my shoes" pattern or a more conventional approach.
2. Peterson now says that despite all these hurtful experiences, she grew up with considerable happiness because her family, especially her mother, offered her much love and comfort. Role-play her mother and write about what her mother would tell her; include some dialogue if you like.

THE INJUSTICE SYSTEM: WOMEN HAVE BEGUN TO FIGHT

Patty Fisher

Writing for the San Jose Mercury News, *Patty Fisher discusses the prejudice against women who file rape charges. Her sources are wide and diverse: statistics, authoritative statements by prosecutors, news accounts, testimonials, and personal observations.*

They called it "Brock's problem." Sen. Brock Adams, a respected Democrat, was known to make sexual advances toward young women assistants. For years, his staff and close friends protected him, even after a woman told police he had drugged and molested her in his Washington apartment.   1

Then, the *Seattle Times* printed allegations from eight unnamed women that Adams raped, fondled, drugged or sexually harassed them over a period of 20 years. Before the day was over, Adams abruptly withdrew from his race for re-election.   2

So clean, so neat. No criminal charges, no trial, no witnesses. Just like that, the man's career is over, his reputation is shattered.   3

Vigilante justice, certainly. But if you believe the women's stories—and I   4
do—it is justice nonetheless. And if you understand how the official justice
system fails in cases of crimes against women, you see why women long ago
abandoned the courts and began to fight against rape, spouse abuse and
sexual harassment with whatever tools they could find.

The FBI has estimated that only one in 10 cases of rape is reported to the   5
police. Why don't women report these crimes? Some are afraid. Some are
ashamed. All too many have learned that the system serves the interests of
men and puts women victims on trial.

Cookie Ridolfi, a professor at Santa Clara University law school, worked   6
for eight years as a public defender in Philadelphia. In most of the criminal
cases she tried, her client was at a disadvantage, even though the burden of
proof was on the prosecution.

"There is enormous bias against the defendant simply because he was   7
arrested," she said. "Juries assume that he must have done something wrong."

Except in rape.   8

In a rape trial, the defense attorney has the edge. Instead of assuming the   9
defendant is guilty, the jury assumes the victim either provoked the attack or
made it up. "I can't think of one other criminal offense where the victim is
blamed so routinely," she said.

It might be difficult for a man to see a situation short of Kafka in which   10
he, as an innocent victim, is blamed for the crime in court. But imagine this
scenario:

A man is robbed at gunpoint. At the trial, he positively identifies the   11
defendant as the one who followed him into a parking garage late at night
and robbed him. The prosecution produces the man's credit cards and wedding ring, which were found on the defendant.

An open and shut case.   12

Until the defense attorney goes to work. The alleged victim, he says, is a   13
liberal, guilt-ridden yuppie with a history of giving to homeless shelters. He
spotted the defendant on the street, saw that he hadn't eaten all day and gave
him his valuables. Only later, when he had to explain to his wife about his
missing wedding ring, did he make up the story about being robbed.

The defense attorney points out inconsistencies in the victim's story: Why   14
did he go into the garage alone that night when he knew it might be dangerous? Why didn't he leave his car and take a cab home? Why did he wear an
expensive suit and flashy diamond ring unless he wanted to draw attention to
his wealth? Why didn't he scream, fight or try to run away instead of docilely
handing over his money?

There were no witnesses. There's plenty of room for reasonable doubt.   15
The jury returns a verdict of not guilty.

Preposterous? Only because juries don't assume that people give away 16
their money and then lie about it later. But juries do assume that women have
sex and then lie about it, file rape charges, lie to prosecutors and convince
them to go to court.

Rape is a problem for the justice system in part because it is a unique 17
crime. The act of sexual intercourse can be love or it can be rape, depending upon whether both parties consent to it. So the prosecution in a rape
trial must prove the woman did not consent. That is difficult if the victim
knew the rapist, which usually is the case; if there were no witnesses, which
is nearly always the case; or if there are no bruises or other signs of
struggle.

If the rapist had a gun or knife, if there was a group of assailants, or if the 18
woman decided it was fruitless to struggle, the case comes down to her word
against his. And traditionally, juries believe him and not her.

In ancient times, when women were regarded as the property of first 19
their fathers and then their husbands, "consent" had nothing to do with rape.
A man who deflowered a virgin not his wife was guilty of rape. He was
ordered to marry the girl and pay her father the equivalent of what an intact
virgin would have brought on the marriage market.

There was no such thing as rape of a married woman. If attacked, she 20
was expected to fight to the death rather than give up her precious virtue
(and her husband's good name). If she was unfortunate enough to live
through the attack, she was guilty of adultery.

How far have we come? Only within the past 20 years have rape shield 21
laws barred a victim's past sexual relations from being introduced as evidence
in a rape trial. It remains more difficult to convict a man of raping a divorced
woman than an "innocent" one.

Rape is not the only crime in which the system fails to treat women fairly. 22
Wife beating wasn't even a crime until the 1800s. Today it is estimated that
between 2 million and 6 million women are battered each year in this country
by their husbands or boyfriends. Often their attempts to get protection from
the justice system fail. And when they fight back and kill their abusers, the
courts treat them more harshly than they do men who kill their wives or
girlfriends.

According to statistics compiled by the National Clearinghouse for Bat- 23
tered Women, the average prison sentence for abusive men who kill their
mates is two to six years. The average sentence for women who kill abusive
men is 15 years.

Apparently juries make allowances for the remorseful man who kills in a 24
momentary fit of rage, but not for the woman who pulls a gun on an unarmed
man who has beaten her senseless for years and threatened to kill her.

Without the justice system to protect them, women have found ways to 25
protect themselves. They taught their daughters to be "good" and follow the
rules:

Never talk to strangers. Never walk alone at night. Never wear revealing 26
clothes. Never let a boy kiss you on the first date.

But even "nice" girls get raped. In a San Jose courtroom recently, a man 27
who confessed to raping more than 20 women said he attacked a Japanese
exchange student because he thought she was flirting with him at a bus stop.
"We stared at each other for a second," Gregory Smith told the jury. He
apparently interpreted that one second as an invitation to follow her off the
bus, drag her into a school playground, brutally rape and murder her.

Never look at strangers. Never take buses. Never leave the house. Of course 28
there's always the chance you will be raped at home. Better get married so you'll
have a man around to protect you.

Since Susan Brownmiller's landmark book on rape, *Against Our Will: Men,* 29
Women and Rape, was published in 1975, women have recognized that fighting
violence against women means more than avoiding dark alleys. Brownmiller
dispelled the myth that women are better off if they submit to rapists. More
women are taking self-defense classes and carrying guns. And they are fighting
to change the system, through the courts, Congress and state legislatures.

Yet changing laws is only the first step in reforming the system. We have 30
to change attitudes. One attitude we have to change is the notion that when it
comes to sex, "no" means "yes."

Men didn't make up the notion that "no" means "yes." Those parents who 31
taught their daughters to be "good" fostered it. For generations, they raised
girls to believe that only bad girls have sexual feelings. Consenting to sex or,
heaven forbid, initiating it would be acknowledging "bad" feelings. What a
way to mess with a normal adolescent's already fragile self-esteem.

For generations girls dealt with this dilemma by denying their sex drive. 32
That was easy enough. Their boyfriends were willing to take all the necessary
action, so the girls could feign resistance as a way of experimenting with sex
without taking responsibility for it, without being bad girls.

Of course, once girls forfeited their integrity on the question of consent, 33
it was difficult to get it back. Once boys got the word that "no" sometimes
meant "yes," it was open season on resisting females.

Imagine a society in which when a woman says "no," a man stops. One 34
man I spoke with suggested that in such a society there would be a lot less sex
and a steep drop in the birth rate. I doubt it. I think that if men backed off
from women who said no, more women would say yes.

It's hard to change 3,000 years of attitudes, but parents and teachers, 35
judges and lawmakers can help. We start by teaching little boys to respect the
feelings—and words—of little girls. And what do we teach little girls?

I have two young daughters, and I want to protect them from harm just 36
as my parents wanted to protect me. But the days are long gone when girls
went directly from their father's house to their husband's.

I hope I can teach my daughters more than just how to avoid being alone 37
with a man in an elevator. They will study karate as well as ballet. I want
them to understand their own strength, the importance of knees and elbows,
the power of a well-placed kick.

I want them to understand the difference between "no" and "yes." While 38
I'll probably preach the virtue of "no," I hope I won't lead them to think that
there is something wrong with them if they have sexual feelings.

I'll teach them that the justice system can be unjust. They should use the 39
system, but not trust it, and work to reform it.

A woman was telling me about being raped many years ago. She was 40
young and naive, she said. He invited her to a party at his mother's fancy
apartment. When they got there she realized she was the party. The apartment was deserted. He showed her a gun and told her to do as he said.
She did.

She saw no point in calling the police. He was wealthy, she had gone 41
there on her own, he hadn't injured her. But she told the story to a friend, a
man, who was furious. He had some vague mob connections. He offered to
fix the guy for her. She declined.

"I figured somehow it was sort of my fault. I didn't think he deserved to 42
die."

Today, she says, she wishes she had told her friend to go ahead. "What 43
that man did to me was a crime."

Vigilante justice. It's not the best way, but sometimes it's the only way.　44

Vocabulary

allegations (2)　　　docilely (14)
Kafka (10)　　　　　remorseful (24)

Critical Thinking and Discussion

1. How does paragraph 4 carry the thesis of this essay and prepare you for
   the last paragraph?
2. Is the reference to "ancient times" in paragraphs 19 and 20 an effective
   one, or would you prefer more specific information?
3. To what other crime against women can the crime of rape be compared?
4. In what way have men been conditioned to believe that "no" means
   "yes"?
5. How does the author justify vigilante justice?

Reading-Related Writing

1. Apply Fisher's ideas to a well-known case such as the Kennedy-Smith case, the Bobbitt case, or the Simpson case.
2. Develop an argument for or against the idea of vigilante justice in certain cases. Use this essay for source material.

AIN'T I A WOMAN?

Sojourner Truth

When Sojourner Truth made this speech in 1852, women had virtually no political rights. Men argued that men were more intelligent than women, that even Jesus Christ had not spoken for women's political rights, and that women's inadequacies started with Eve. Truth didn't need any preparation; she used her considerable intelligence and humor to refute their arguments, but it would be almost eighty years before women would gain greater political rights.

Well, children, where there is so much racket there must be something out of 1 kilter. I think that 'twixt the negroes of the South and the women at the North, all talking about rights, the white men will be in a fix pretty soon. But what's all this here talking about?

That man over there says women need to be helped into carriages, and 2 lifted over ditches, and to have the best place everywhere. Nobody ever helps me into carriages, or over mud-puddles, or gives me any best place. And ain't I a woman? Look at me! Look at my arm! I have ploughed and planted, and gathered into barns, and no man could head me! And ain't I a woman? I could work as much and eat as much as a man—when I could get it—and bear the lash as well! And ain't I a woman? I have borne thirteen children, and seen most sold off to slavery, and when I cried out with my mother's grief, none but Jesus heard me! And ain't I a woman?

Then they talk about this thing in the head; what's this they call it? 3 [Intellect, someone whispers.] That's it, honey. What's that got to do with women's rights or negro's rights? If my cup won't hold but a pint, and yours holds a quart, wouldn't you be mean not to let me have my little half-measure full?

Then that little man in black there, he says women can't have as much 4 rights as men, 'cause Christ wasn't a woman! Where did your Christ come from? Where did your Christ come from? From God and a woman! Man had nothing to do with Him.

If the first woman God ever made was strong enough to turn the world 5
upside down all alone, these women together ought to be able to turn it back,
and get it right side up again! And now they is asking to do it, the men better
let them.

Obliged to you for hearing me, and now old Sojourner ain't got nothing 6
more to say.

Critical Thinking and Discussion

1. This speech was given in response to a specific situation, but it is well
   organized. Show how it fits the basic framework for argumentation: thesis, support, refutation.
2. Discuss the main method Truth uses for emphasis.
3. Why would people interested in the slavery issue also be interested in
   women's rights?
4. Discuss how she blends logic and humor.

Reading-Related Writing

1. Convert this speech into a conventional essay of argumentation.
2. Use the same type of approach to write a similar piece about another
   topic—for example, "Ain't I A Native American?"

TEAMS WITH INDIAN NAMES

Richard Worsnop

*Teams are now named for colors at Dartmouth ("Big Green") and
Stanford ("Cardinal"), and no longer for Indians. But not all teams
agree to change, hence the "Chiefs," the "Braves," the "Redskins," and
even the "Savages." In this essay first published in 1992, Richard Worsnop relates the naming of teams to stereotyping and explains why
Native Americans are rightfully offended.*

Why have teams with Indian names stirred such anger among Native 1
Americans?

Many sports fans profess bafflement over Native Americans' claims that 2
Indian team names are demeaning and should be changed. If fans even think
about team names, they probably view them as no more than handy identification tags—and may even believe the names flatter Indians by linking them
to skilled athletes.

Native Americans say this rationale completely misses the point. Appro-   3
priating Indian names and paraphernalia for sports use, they explain, is
always offensive and sometimes blatantly racist. A particular sore point is the
feathered headdress often worn by fans and team mascots. Andrea Nott, a
community activist in Naperville, Ill., notes that Indians regard feathers as
sacred symbols that must be earned before they can be worn. "It's analogous,"
she says, "to somebody dressing up as the pope, going out on the field,
waving a cross and performing a mock communion."

Suzan Shown Harjo, president of the nonprofit Morning Star Founda-   4
tion, in Washington, D.C., which promotes traditional Native American culture, goes further. She feels "very strongly" that Indian names for sports
teams, such as Chippewas, Braves, Apaches and Chiefs, lower the self-esteem
of Native American teenagers and thus contribute to their high suicide rate.
Possibly as damaging, she says, is the stereotype of the drunken Indian passed
out in the gutter, an image that may have especially dire consequences for
young Indians. Realizing they have little chance of following in the footsteps
of professional athletes, youths may emulate the other role model, she says.

Many high schools and colleges have bowed to the argument that por-   5
traying Indians as one-dimensional warrior figures robs them of their dignity.
In the early 1970s, for example, Dartmouth College and Stanford University
responded to protests by changing their nicknames. More recently, St. John's
University in New York City retired its ersatz Indian mascot, replacing him
with a costumed student who looks "like a lion," says a school spokesman.

Five teams in major U.S. professional sports leagues have Indian   6
names—baseball's Atlanta Braves and Cleveland Indians, football's Kansas
City Chiefs and Washington Redskins and hockey's Chicago Blackhawks.
None plan to change its name or logo, though some have quietly discarded
Indian trappings of doubtful authenticity.

The Redskins marching band, for example, no longer struts to the beat of   7
tom-toms; the cheerleading Redskinetts stopped wearing squaw wigs with
feathered headbands years ago; and the team's fight song has been pared of its
more offensive wording. ("Scalp 'em, swamp 'em . . . we want heap more.")
Similarly, the Chiefs bade farewell to the Indian-costumed mascot who
patrolled Arrowhead Stadium's sidelines on horseback.

But that's as far as the five pro teams are now prepared to go, as millions   8
of sports fans recently learned: The appearance of the Braves in the 1991
World Series and the Redskins in this year's Super Bowl gave angry Native
Americans a double-barreled opportunity to beam their protest message to a
nationwide audience.

At the Series, the Braves came under fire not only for their name but also   9
for their fans' behavior. Braves rooters bellowed an Indian "war chant" popu-
larized at Florida State University (the "Seminoles") while brandishing foam-
rubber tomahawks. The "tomahawk chop" quickly became a focal point of
Indians' ire.

At the Super Bowl, the name Redskins was sufficient to fuel demonstra- 10
tors' anger. "There is no more derogatory name" in professional sports, Harjo
says. Two Redskins stalwarts, linebacker André Collins and defensive end
Charles Mann, told a TV interviewer before the game that the team's name
should be changed. "It doesn't matter whether I personally find it derogatory
or not," said Mann. "If they say it bothers them, then that's good enough
for me."

However, team owner Jack Kent Cooke has said he won't budge. "The 11
name was never intended to offend anyone," a Redskins policy statement
declares. "Over the long history of the Washington Redskins, the name has
reflected positive attributes of the American Indian such as dedication, courage and pride."

The four other pro teams with Indian names have taken similar positions. 12
"Why would any team adopt a name it didn't hold the highest respect for?"
says Bob Moore, public relations director for the Kansas City Chiefs. He adds
that "Sports teams are the last place to look for people who are mistreating
minorities . . . In some instances [they are] the highest-paid employees."

Bob DiBiasio, the Cleveland Indians' vice president for public relations, 13
acknowledges that some people bristle at the team's logo, a cartoon of a grinning Indian. "But we haven't been under any pressure to change it," he says.

The Atlanta Braves, like the Redskins, obviously can make no such claim. 14
Still, club President Stan Kasten says the team has no plans to change its
name or logo, nor to issue any statements that might prolong the controversy.
Does that mean the debate will just die down of its own accord? "Probably
not," Kasten concedes.

The debate seems likely to drag on, if for no other reason than the news 15
media and politicians have chimed in. In February, *The Oregonian,* in Port-
land, Ore., became the first major U.S. daily to banish team nicknames offensive to Native Americans. WTOP-AM, an all-news radio station in
Washington, D.C., followed suit with a similar policy. WTOP's proscribed list
even includes the University of Notre Dame's Fighting Irish. And sportswriter
Dave Kindred of *The Sporting News* has pledged not to mention Indian team
names in his future columns for the weekly tabloid.

Possibly discerning a vote-getting issue, elected officials are also begin- 16
ning to speak out. William P. Lightfoot, Jr., a member of the Washington,
D.C., City Council, introduced a Redskins name-change resolution on March
3. The proposal, which is still in committee, would not have the force of law
if passed. In Missouri, meanwhile, state Rep. Vernon Thompson of Kansas
City has introduced a bill that would prod the Chiefs to discourage fan
behavior offensive to Native Americans. The bill was recently approved in
committee and sent on to the General Assembly for possible action this year.

For those who find the Indian-name question overblown, Harjo offers a 17
passionate argument. "It's not a peripheral issue at all," she insists. "It underlies many of our other concerns." Eliminating Indian team names will help

erase ethnic stereotypes, she says, making it easier for Americans to see Indians as individuals.

Vocabulary

appropriating (3)	ersatz (5)	derogatory (10)
blatantly (3)	authenticity (6)	banish (15)
analogous(3)	brandishing (9)	peripheral (17)
emulate (4)		

Critical Thinking and Discussion

1. In what way is the use of Indian names and paraphernalia a mocking act?
2. How are young Native Americans affected by negative stereotyping?
3. What encouraging changes have occurred in response to protests about the stereotyping of Native Americans?
4. What arguments against change are offered by the owners of sports clubs with Indian names?
5. In what way is the "Fighting Irish" used by the University of Notre Dame offensive? Might the name Minnesota Vikings also be regarded as offensive?
6. What does Suzan Shown Harjo say is the most important concern of the protest movement?

Reading-Related Writing

1. Many elementary, junior high, and high schools use Indian and other ethnic nicknames. Some of those schools are populated mainly by members of the named group. Is is possible for the use of ethnic nicknames to be positive? Discuss this issue by using some specific examples.
2. Write about a particular school or athletic club that uses an Indian nickname, discussing how different uses of the term (in logos, advertising, cheers, promotional items, ceremonies, and so on) give different dimensions to the stereotype.

END THE SILENCE
THAT IS KILLING OUR CHILDREN

Jesse Jackson

In this newspaper column written in 1993, prominent African-American civil rights leader Jesse Jackson says it's time to break the code of silence:

"We cannot let alienation from authority and misplaced loyalty protect those who are destroying our neighborhoods."

Four-year-old Launice Janae Smith was too young to know better. Lively and innocent, she thought she could play in a public playground in Washington, D.C. Now she is dead, her life cut short by a stray bullet fired into a crowd at a pick-up football game. The gunman was involved in a drug shootout. 1

Her short life and sudden death cannot be forgotten. Let us see her as an angel, a messenger dispatched to warn us of our misbegotten ways. Backs have been turned too long. Shame has bred silence too long. The guns and drugs have become an urban plague that is consuming our young. 2

The conspiracy of silence must end. A few weeks ago, I asked youngsters in Miami what they would do if they saw drugs and guns in someone's locker in school, "I'd stay away from that person," was the common reply. Then, I asked what they would do if they saw a hood, a white sheet and a rope in someone's locker. "I'd tell it. That sounds like the Klan and the Klan kills people. I'd tell it." 3

Yet, more young black men die each year from guns than the total who died from lynching by the Klan. Our sense of loyalty, of solidarity is misplaced. If the killers were white, surely the young would report them to the police. But when blacks kill blacks, the young resist snitching to a police force that too often doesn't seem to care much anyway. 4

Recent testimony by some renegade New York City police officers who profit from the drug trade and official corruption, may horrify the innocent, but it merely confirms what too many urban residents have come to expect. But alienation from authorities cannot be allowed to make the black community into a silent protector of those who kill brothers and sisters. The silence that protects these killers is not solidarity. It is betrayal. We have got to tell it—just as we would if they were with the Klan. 5

The neighborhood where Launice Smith was murdered is the deadliest in Washington, if not the nation. Thirty-two people have been murdered this year within a square mile of where she was shot. At her funeral, when I asked who there had lost family members to the drug war, 50 people came forward. 6

It is time for a new civil-rights struggle to take back our neighborhoods. Yes, it's true that this horrible plague has external sources. As gang members in Los Angeles' Nickerson Gardens have told me, drugs are now grown in the city. Guns are not made there. But the agents of death are homegrown. They live in the neighborhood. They are young, black and proud. But they are killing our children and must be stopped. 7

We must end the silence. It is not disloyal to the race to tell it. The killers will burn the race up unless those in the neighborhood tell it and stop it. 8

For many urban African-Americans and Latinos, this is a terrible time. The politics of malign neglect have become bipartisan. Our cities are 9 hemorrhaging, but there is no urban policy. Racism abounds, but the President has nothing to say on civil rights. No assistant attorney general for civil rights has been nominated to head a department that is demoralized and in disarray. The moribund Equal Employment Opportunity Commission lacks both director and direction.

But we must look inward if we are to go forward. The scourge of race and 10
poverty will not be addressed unless we regain the moral center. And we cannot do so unless we come together to address the killing, to stop the spread of drugs and guns, the black-on-black crime that is terrorizing our children.

As always, the victims and most vulnerable must be the first to act. We 11
need to establish neighborhood preschool programs, to offer alternatives to jail in churches and community groups, to provide mentoring to the young, to set up job and scholarship programs.

At the same time, we must end the silence and stop providing sanctuary 12
for those who prey on our young. It simply cannot be any more acceptable for blacks to kill blacks than it was for the Klan to do so. We have got to tell it.

Critical Thinking and Discussion

1. Jesse Jackson writes of violence and says there is something that can be done by the individual. What is it?
2. In what way can a person's failure to act make him or her one of the causes?
3. Under what circumstances will some people "tell it"?
4. How does Jackson use the word *betrayal* in a different way?
5. Is there any chance that people will respond to Jackson and change their behavior? If not now, under what conditions might they change? What would have to happen for people to change their view on "telling"?

Reading-Related Writing

1. Write about why you think most people accept or reject Jackson's statement "The silence that protects these killers is not solidarity. It is betrayal. We have got to tell it." You might also give your own reasons for accepting or rejecting it.
2. Write about an incident (something bad happening and no one telling, out of a sense of loyalty) that illustrates the ideas (causes and effects) discussed by Jackson.
3. Discuss the idea that fear is as important as solidarity or loyalty as a reason for not "telling it."

YOU'RE SHORT, BESIDES!

Sucheng Chan

For people who are handicapped, the way they look at themselves is as important as the way others look at them. One's self-image is often derived from the way others react. Those reactions may vary from culture to culture, and a person who moves from one culture to another may have a lot of sorting out to do. In this case the cultures are Chinese and American, and the subject, Sucheng Chan, who contracted polio when she was four, has dealt with pain and disability all her life. Today, as a university professor and author, she can reflect on her experience with considerable insight and even humor.

When asked to write about being a physically handicapped Asian American 1 woman, I considered it an insult. After all, my accomplishments are many, yet I was not asked to write about any of them. Is being handicapped the most salient feature about me? The fact that it might be in the eyes of others made me decide to write the essay as requested. I realized that the way I think about myself may differ considerably from the way others perceive me. And maybe that's what being physically handicapped is all about.

I was stricken simultaneously with pneumonia and polio at the age of 2 four. Uncertain whether I had polio of the lungs, seven of the eight doctors who attended me—all practitioners of Western medicine—told my parents they should not feel optimistic about my survival. A Chinese fortune teller my mother consulted also gave a grim prognosis, but for an entirely different reason: I had been stricken because my name was offensive to the gods. My grandmother had named me "grandchild of wisdom," a name that the fortune teller said was too presumptuous for a girl. So he advised my parents to change my name to "chaste virgin." All these pessimistic predictions notwithstanding, I hung onto life, if only by a thread. For three years, my body was periodically pierced with electric shocks as the muscles of my legs atrophied. Before my illness, I had been an active, rambunctious, precocious, and very curious child. Being confined to bed was thus a mental agony as great as my physical pain. Living in war-torn China, I received little medical attention; physical therapy was unheard of. But I was determined to walk. So one day, when I was six or seven, I instructed my mother to set up two rows of chairs to face each other so that I could use them as I would parallel bars. I attempted to walk by holding my body up and moving it forward with my arms while dragging my legs along behind. Each time I fell, my mother gasped, but I badgered her until she let me try again. After four nonambulatory years, I finally walked once more by pressing my hands against my thighs so my knees wouldn't buckle.

My father had been away from home during most of those years 3 because of the war. When he returned, I had to confront the guilt he felt about my condition. In many East Asian cultures, there is a strong folk belief that a person's physical state in this life is a reflection of how morally or sinfully he or she lived in previous lives. Furthermore, because of the tendency to view the family as a single unit, it is believed that the fate of one member can be caused by the behavior of another. Some of my father's relatives told him that my illness had doubtless been caused by the wild carousing he did in his youth. A well-meaning but somewhat simple man, my father believed them.

Throughout my childhood, he sometimes apologized to me for having to 4 suffer retribution for his former bad behavior. This upset me; it was bad enough that I had to deal with the anguish of not being able to walk, but to have to assuage his guilt as well, was a real burden! In other ways, my father was very good to me. He took me out often, carrying me on his shoulders or back, to give me fresh air and sunshine. He did this until I was too large and heavy for him to carry. And ever since I can remember, he has told me that I am pretty.

After getting over her anxieties about my constant falls, my mother 5 decided to send me to school. I had already learned to read some words of Chinese at the age of three by asking my parents to teach me the sounds and meaning of various characters in the daily newspaper. But between the ages of four and eight, I received no education since just staying alive was a full-time job. Much to her chagrin, my mother found no school in Shanghai, where we lived at the time, which would accept me as a student. Finally, as a last resort, she approached the American School, which agreed to enroll me only if my family kept an *amah* (a servant who takes care of children) by my side at all times. The tuition at the school was twenty U.S. dollars per month—a huge sum of money during those years of runaway inflation in China—and payable only in U.S. dollars. My family afforded the high cost of tuition and the expense of employing a full-time *amah* for less than a year.

We left China as the Communist forces swept across the country in 6 victory. We found an apartment in Hong Kong across the street from a school run by Seventh-Day Adventists. By that time I could walk a little, so the principal was persuaded to accept me. An *amah* now had to take care of me only during recess when my classmates might easily knock me over as they ran about the playground.

After a year and a half in Hong Kong, we moved to Malaysia, where my 7 father's family had lived for four generations. There I learned to swim in the lovely warm waters of the tropics and fell in love with the sea. On land I was a cripple; in the ocean I could move with the grace of a fish. I liked the freedom of being in the water so much that many years later, when I was a graduate student in Hawaii, I became greatly enamored with a man just because he called me a "Polynesian water nymph."

As my overall health improved, my mother became less anxious about all 8
aspects of my life. She did everything possible to enable me to lead as normal
a life as possible. I remember how once some of her colleagues in the high
school where she taught criticized her for letting me wear short skirts. They
felt my legs should not be exposed to public view. My mother's response was,
"All girls her age wear short skirts, so why shouldn't she?"

The years in Malaysia were the happiest of my childhood, even though I 9
was constantly fending off children who ran after me calling, *"Baikah! Baikah!"*
("Cripple! Cripple!" in the Hokkien dialect commonly spoken in Malaysia).
The taunts of children mattered little because I was a star pupil. I won one
award after another for general scholarship as well as for art and public
speaking. Whenever the school had important visitors my teacher always
called on me to recite in front of the class.

A significant event that marked me indelibly occurred when I was twelve. 10
That year my school held a music recital and I was one of the students chosen
to play the piano. I managed to get up the steps to the stage without any
problem, but as I walked across the stage, I fell. Out of the audience, a voice
said loudly and clearly, "Ayah! A *baikah* shouldn't be allowed to perform in
public." I got up before anyone could get on stage to help me and, with tears
streaming uncontrollably down my face, I rushed to the piano and began to
play. Beethoven's "Für Elise" had never been played so fiendishly fast before or
since, but I managed to finish the whole piece. That I managed to do so made
me feel really strong. I never again feared ridicule.

In later years I was reminded of this experience from time to time. Dur- 11
ing my fourth year as an assistant professor at the University of California at
Berkeley, I won a distinguished teaching award. Some weeks later I ran into a
former professor who congratulated me enthusiastically. But I said to him,
"You know what? I became a distinguished teacher by *limping* across the stage
of Dwinelle 155!" (Dwinelle 155 is a large, cold, classroom that most colleagues of mine hate to teach in.) I was rude not because I lacked gracious-
ness but because this man, who had told me that my dissertation was the
finest piece of work he had read in fifteen years, had nevertheless advised me
to eschew a teaching career.

"Why?" I asked. 12

"Your leg . . . " he responded. 13

"What about my leg?" I said, puzzled. 14

"Well, how would you feel standing in front of a large lecture class?" 15

"If it makes any difference, I want you to know I've won a number of 16
speech contests in my life, and I am not the least bit self-conscious about
speaking in front of large audiences. . . . Look, why don't you write me a
letter of recommendation to tell people how brilliant I am, and let *me* worry
about my leg!"

This incident is worth recounting only because it illustrates a dilemma 17
that handicapped persons face frequently: those who care about us sometimes

get so protective that they unwittingly limit our growth. This former professor of mine had been one of my greatest supporters for two decades. Time after time, he had written glowing letters of recommendation on my behalf. He had spoken as he did because he thought he had my best interests at heart; he thought that if I got a desk job rather than one that required me to be a visible, public person, I would be spared the misery of being stared at.

Americans, for the most part, do not believe as Asians do that physically 18 handicapped persons are morally flawed. But they are equally inept at interacting with those of us who are not able-bodied. Cultural differences in the perception and treatment of handicapped people are most clearly expressed by adults. Children, regardless of where they are, tend to be openly curious about people who do not look "normal." Adults in Asia have no hesitation in asking visibly handicapped people what is wrong with them, often expressing their sympathy with looks of pity, whereas adults in the United States try desperately to be polite by pretending not to notice.

One interesting response I often elicited from people in Asia but have 19 never encountered in America is the attempt to link my physical condition to the state of my soul. Many a time while living and traveling in Asia people would ask me what religion I belonged to. I would tell them that my mother is a devout Buddhist, that my father was baptized a Catholic but has never practiced Catholicism, and that I am an agnostic. Upon hearing this, people would try strenuously to convert me to their religion so that whichever God they believe in could bless me. If I would only attend this church or that temple regularly, they urged, I would surely get cured. Catholics and Buddhists alike have pressed religious medallions into my palm, telling me if I would wear these, the relevant deity or saint would make me well. Once while visiting the tomb of Muhammad Ali Jinnah in Karachi, Pakistan, an old Muslim, after finishing his evening prayers, spotted me, gestured toward my legs, raised his arms heavenward, and began a new round of prayers, apparently on my behalf.

In the United States adults who try to act "civilized" toward handicapped 20 people by pretending they don't notice anything unusual sometimes end up ignoring handicapped people completely. In the first few months I lived in this country, I was struck by the fact that whenever children asked me what was the matter with my leg, their adult companions would hurriedly shush them up, furtively look at me, mumble apologies, and rush their children away. After a few months of such encounters, I decided it was my responsibility to educate these people. So I would say to the flustered adults, "It's okay, let the kid ask." Turning to the child, I would say, "When I was a little girl, no bigger than you are, I became sick with something called polio. The muscles of my leg shrank up and I couldn't walk very well. You're much luckier than I am because now you can get a vaccine to make sure you never get my disease. So don't cry when your mommy takes you to get a polio vaccine, okay?" Some adults and their little companions I talked to this way were glad to be rescued from embarrassment; others thought I was strange.

Americans have another way of covering up their uneasiness: they become jovially patronizing. Sometimes when people spot my crutch, they ask if I've had a skiing accident. When I answer that unfortunately it is something less glamorous than that they say, "I bet you *could* ski if you put your mind to it!" Alternately, at parties where people dance, men who ask me to dance with them get almost belligerent when I decline their invitation. They say, "Of course you can dance if you *want* to!" Some have given me pep talks about how if I would only develop the right mental attitude, I would have more fun in life.

Different cultural attitudes toward handicapped persons came out clearly during my wedding. My father-in-law, as solid a representative of middle America as could be found, had no qualms about objecting to the marriage on racial grounds, but he could bring himself to comment on my handicap only indirectly. He wondered why his son, who had dated numerous high school and college beauty queens, couldn't marry one of them instead of me. My mother-in-law, a devout Christian, did not share her husband's prejudices, but she worried aloud about whether I could have children. Some Chinese friends of my parents, on the other hand, said that I was lucky to have found such a noble man, one who would marry me despite my handicap. I, for my part, appeared in church in a white lace wedding dress I had designed and made myself—a miniskirt!

How Asian Americans treat me with respect to my handicap tells me a great deal about their degree of acculturation. Recent immigrants behave just like Asians in Asia; those who have been here longer or who grew up in the United States behave more like their white counterparts. I have not encountered any distinctly Asian American pattern of response. What makes the experience of Asian American handicapped people unique is the duality of responses we elicit.

Regardless of racial or cultural background, most handicapped people have to learn to find a balance between the desire to attain physical independence and the need to take care of ourselves by not overtaxing our bodies. In my case, I've had to learn to accept the fact that leading an active life has its price. Between the ages of eight and eighteen, I walked without using crutches or braces but the effort caused my right leg to become badly misaligned. Soon after I came to the United States, I had a series of operations to straighten out the bones of my right leg; afterwards though my leg looked straighter and presumably better, I could no longer walk on my own. Initially my doctors fitted me with a brace, but I found wearing one cumbersome and soon gave it up. I could move around much more easily—and more important, faster—by using one crutch. One orthopedist after another warned me that using a single crutch was a bad practice. They were right. Over the years my spine developed a double-S curve and for the last twenty years I have suffered from severe, chronic back pains, which neither conventional physical therapy nor a lighter work load can eliminate.

The only thing that helps my backaches is a good massage, but the 25 soothing effect lasts no more than a day or two. Massages are expensive, especially when one needs them three times a week. So I found a job that pays better, but at which I have to work longer hours, consequently increasing the physical strain on my body—a sort of vicious circle. When I was in my thirties, my doctors told me that if I kept leading the strenuous life I did, I would be in a wheelchair by the time I was forty. They were right on target: I bought myself a wheelchair when I was forty-one. But being the incorrigible character that I am, I use it only when I am *not* in a hurry!

It is a good thing, however, that I am too busy to think much about my 26 handicap or my backaches because pain can physically debilitate as well as cause depression. And there are days when my spirits get rather low. What has helped me is realizing that being handicapped is akin to growing old at an accelerated rate. The contradiction I experience is that often my mind races along as though I'm only twenty while my body feels about sixty. But fifteen or twenty years hence, unlike my peers who will have to cope with aging for the first time, I shall be full of cheer because I will have already fought, and I hope won, that battle long ago.

Beyond learning how to be physically independent and, for some of us, 27 living with chronic pain or other kinds of discomfort, the most difficult thing a handicapped person has to deal with, especially during puberty and early adulthood, is relating to potential sexual partners. Because American culture places so much emphasis on physical attractiveness, a person with a shriveled limb, or a tilt to the head, or the inability to speak clearly, experiences great uncertainty—indeed trauma—when interacting with someone to whom he or she is attracted. My problem was that I was not only physically handicapped, small, and short, but worse, I also wore glasses and was smarter than all the boys I knew! Alas, an insurmountable combination. Yet somehow I have managed to have intimate relationships, all of them with extraordinary men. Not surprisingly, there have also been countless men who broke my heart— men who enjoyed my company "as a friend," but who never found the courage to date or make love with me, although I am sure my experience in this regard is no different from that of many able-bodied persons.

The day came when my backaches got in the way of having an active sex 28 life. Surprisingly that development was liberating because I stopped worrying about being attractive to men. No matter how headstrong I had been, I, like most women of my generation, had had the desire to be alluring to men ingrained into me. And that longing had always worked like a brake on my behavior. When what men think of me ceased to be compelling, I gained greater freedom to be myself.

I've often wondered if I would have been a different person had I not ²⁹ been physically handicapped. I really don't know, though there is no question that being handicapped has marked me. But at the same time I usually do not *feel* handicapped—and consequently, I do not *act* handicapped. People are therefore less likely to treat me as a handicapped person. There is no doubt, however, that the lives of my parents, sister, husband, other family members, and some close friends have been affected by my physical condition. They have had to learn not to hide me away at home, not to feel embarrassed by how I look or react to people who say silly things to me, and not to resent me for the extra demands my condition makes on them. Perhaps the hardest thing for those who live with handicapped people is to know when and how to offer help. There are no guidelines applicable to all situations. My advice is, when in doubt, ask, but ask in a way that does not smack of pity or embarrassment. Most important, please don't talk to us as though we are children.

So, has being physically handicapped been a handicap? It all depends on ³⁰ one's attitude. Some years ago, I told a friend that I had once said to an affirmative action compliance officer (somewhat sardonically since I do not believe in the head count approach to affirmative action) that the institution which employs me is triply lucky because it can count me as non-white, female and handicapped. He responded, "Why don't you tell them to count you four times? . . . Remember, you're short, besides!"

Vocabulary

prognosis (2)	indelibly (10)	orthopedist (24)
nonambulatory (2)	agnostic (19)	incorrigible (25)
retribution (4)	patronizing (21)	debilitate (26)
chagrin (5)	acculturation (23)	sardonically (30)
nymph (7)		

Critical Thinking and Discussion

1. How does Chan look at herself and how do others look at her?
2. How was she treated by Chinese and Americans?
3. Do you think the different treatment by the two cultures is typical, or have the differences been mainly because of specific circumstances? Would different generations also react differently—for example, second- and third-generation immigrants?
4. Is there a difference between her private self and her public self?

Reading-Related Writing

1. Chan did something that was not expected of her in her culture, both as a woman and as a person with a handicap. Write about yourself or

someone you know who exceeded expectations within a particular culture (for instance, as a female, as a member of a certain class, as one with a handicap, as one who got off to a bad start, as one from a certain part of the country, or as one of a certain race). Concentrate on a particular moment or on particular moments for your narrative account.

2. Discuss the different attitudes of those from the Chinese culture and from the American culture. How valid are Chan's observations? See discussion question 3.

SOMEONE IS LISTENING*

Michael Holguin

Student Michael Holguin grew up with shame and guilt because he knew he was wicked. His belief was implanted and reinforced by all institutions he encountered—family, church, school, government. It was wrong in every sense to be sexually attracted to people of the same gender. Therefore, he knew he must keep his mortal sin a secret.

In today's society there is a form of child abuse that not even Oprah talks   1
about. Unlike some other forms of abuse, it knows no limitations—no ethnic, no religious, no educational, and no socioeconomic boundaries. Lives are destroyed by parents who act in fear and ignorance. Dreams are shattered by the cruel and hurtful words of friends. Every day, hundreds of gay youths hide in their rooms and cry from pain caused by the mean and careless behavior of those who claim to love them.

In a Judeo-Christian society it is common for families to attend church   2
with their children. The pastor in many of these churches stands at the podium and announces, "Homosexuals are an abomination unto the Lord." The church walls shake from the resounding "Amen" from the congregation. The pastor continues, "Homosexuals are sick. Perverted. They are a danger to our children." In agreement the congregation once more says, "Amen." I know how this feels. As a gay person, I recall the pain of many such Sundays during my childhood. I prayed extra hard for God's cure before someone would find out my secret and embarrass me and my family, because I remembered what had happened to Jason the year before. So I kept answering the altar call every Sunday when the unwanted feeling wouldn't go away. The fear of rejection and eternal damnation made me too terrified to confide in anyone or to ask for help. After all, my parents seemed to tell me I deserved such a fate every time they said, "Amen."

Every day became more difficult to endure. I faced the jokes in the locker 3
room. Even my best friend told some, and sometimes, to keep from being
discovered, I told some. At this point, how much self-esteem could I have
had? I cringed when my coach urged us to "kick those faggots' asses" but I
still kicked. Yet every day my feelings were denied. My health teacher told us,
"Someday you will all grow up and get married and have children." I couldn't
understand why I had no such desire. I would turn on the television, and
there would be a cop show on. This week's criminal was a gay child molester
. . . again. I think "Baretta" had the same story the week before. I changed the
station to "Barney Miller," where there was an old man wearing a polyester
jumpsuit and a silk scarf around his neck, and talking with a lisp. Couldn't
they drop the lisp just once? I wonder. I cringe, thinking this is my inevitable
fate, my curse.

By the time I reached my teen years, I'd heard and seen so much negativ- 4
ity toward my "condition" that my life became plagued with constant fears. I
became afraid of rejection. I knew my Christian family would think I was
sick, perverted, and dangerous to children. Dad would be disappointed, even
though I had six brothers to carry on the family name. Mom would not want
me around because she'd worry about what to tell Grandma and Grandpa.
My brother would pretend he didn't know me at school.

My fears were reinforced by close-up examples. Once I had a friend 5
named Daniel, who was the son of a local preacher. I don't know where
Daniel got the nerve at the age of twelve to tell his parents he was gay, but
that's what he did. It was also at the age of twelve that his father put him out
on the street after all the beatings failed to cure him. Daniel managed to stay
alive on the streets as a prostitute. He's in prison now, dying of AIDS. The fear
of rejection was real.

I learned how to fit in out of fear of humiliation but especially out of fear 6
of physical abuse. I had seen Daniel's father and brothers beat him up almost
daily. An even earlier memory from when I was very young involved a boy
named Terry, who everyone knew was different. Some kids had figured Terry
out. One day behind the school, way out in the field, four kids beat Terry up.
Kicking and slugging him as he fell to the ground, they called out "Sissy" and
"Queer" as they swung at him. We had only heard the word *queer* from the
older boys, and no one was sure what it meant exactly. We hadn't encountered the word *faggot* yet. I suppose I didn't like Terry much either, but I felt
bad as I watched in terror, knowing that the next time it could be me that
they considered "different."

After years of living with low self-esteem, a battered self-image, and a 7
secret life, one's psyche tends to give out. The highest rate of teen suicide is
among gay youths. In a recent five-year study, it was determined that fear of
rejection was the number one cause of suicide among gay teenagers. After
losing the loving environment of friends and families, many gays turn to other

means of comfort. Drug and alcohol abuse is high among gays. Many turn to multiple lovers, looking for acceptance and emotional support. The result of this has been the devastating spread of AIDS. With nowhere to go, suicide often seems to be the only option. My friend Billy, when visiting his younger sister at his mother's home, would have to stay on the front porch and talk through the screen door at his mother's request. Last February, at the age of 19, Billy drove up to the mountains and there took his own life. Before he died he wrote on the hood of his car, "God, help me." I recall my own suicide attempt, which was the result of my inability to deal with a life-style everyone close to me was unable to accept. It was only my self-acceptance that eventually saved me from being a statistic.

When planning a family, people should ask themselves, "Will I love my   8 children for who they are, or will I love them only if they're what I want them to be?" If people answer the latter, they shouldn't be parents. The same kind of thing might be said for others who are responsible for helping children develop. Abuse comes in many forms, and ignorance and self-centeredness are usually its foundation. Parents, preachers, teachers, clergy, friends—please be cautious of what you say. The children are listening.

Critical Thinking and Discussion

1. What are the sources of abuse of gay youth?
2. Why does this kind of abuse go largely unreported?
3. What is Holguin's main support?
4. How did he survive?

Reading-Related Writing

1. Write a piece in which you advocate some specific kind of education that would alleviate this problem in schools.
2. Pretend that you are a sympathetic parent of a gay child and explain how you would help your child to cope with attitudes in society.
3. Discuss this problem from a lesbian perspective. Is it essentially the same or different in significant respects?

Collaborative Learning

1. Form into small groups. Then select one piece of writing from this chapter for each group and develop an argument in the style used by Sojourner Truth in "Ain't I a Woman?" Examples of titles: "Ain't I an Arab?" "Ain't I an Old Person?" "Ain't I a Hispanic Woman?" "Ain't I Gay?"
2. Form into small groups. Then select one piece of writing from this chapter for each group and, using Karen Peterson's "Walk in My Full-Figure

Shoes" as a model, develop a piece based on information from the subject passage. In effect, this exercise becomes role-playing through writing.

Connections

1. Do either of numbers 1 and 2 above as an individual assignment.
2. Most of the groups discussed in this chapter are presented as victims of society. Pick one or more essays and discuss what the particular group (women, those past 65, gays, minorities) can do to go beyond the idea of victimization and improve its lot (for instance, promote group unity, educate themselves and others, refuse to be bullied, fight back, and so on).

11

America: What Is It?
What Should It Be?

Throughout this book, you have encountered views expressed by writers of remarkably different backgrounds and cultures. No doubt you formed opinions as you read, discussed, and wrote about the issues raised. The selections in this final chapter invite you to consider and respond to some fundamental questions: What is America? What *should* America be? Is there such a person as an American any more? Does the diversity of America make our nation stronger?

Several selections in this chapter, including those by Shelby Foote, Jack Chen, Itabari Njeri, and Ishmael Reed, discuss the metaphor of America as a melting pot. Is this metaphor still useful? Or do we need a new one to take us, as Njeri suggests, "beyond the melting pot"?

A larger question, both sides of which are examined by Sharon Bernstein, Ishmael Reed, and Arthur Schlesinger, Jr., is whether increased ethnic pride is a benefit or a detriment to America as a whole. If ethnic chauvinism erupts into violence or forces the individual into a "cult of ethnicity," to quote Schlesinger, how does America prosper? Is it time for America to adopt a new collective identity to replace our identification with the Puritans and what Reed calls their "strange and paranoid attitudes toward those different" from themselves?

And should we, as Ji-Yeon Mary Yuhfill suggests, examine America's history more critically, measuring "the reasons for the inconsistencies between the ideals of the U.S. and the social realities"? Should we dispense with the metaphors, as Richard Rodriguez suggests, and start accepting the mutual assimilation that America's cultures impress upon one another? Should we begin to pay more attention to what Rodriguez points out as "the deepest separation between us," the one that "derives not from race or ethnicity but from class"?

MELTING POT

Shelby Foote

Noted Civil War historian Shelby Foote is more concerned with what comes out of the pot rather than what goes into it. To him the recipe is less important than the food on the plate.

Teaching that America is a melting pot of all kinds of cultures takes care of each culture. I'm from the Mississippi Delta, which God knows is the melting pot of melting pots, but we thought of ourselves as having the purest American blood. There were Chinese, Syrians, Italians, Jews from all over doing their best to appear to be native-born Americans. That's changed a lot. Now they realize the value of what they've been trying to shed. It should always be kept in mind that we are a diverse strand of peoples. But to break it down into what the Hungarians contributed, what the Russians contributed, the English, Irish and Germans contributed, I'm not sure that's a good idea. Are you willing to dilute the pure stream of history in order to investigate all the creeks that run into it?

Critical Reading and Discussion

1. How has Foote's background contributed to his thinking on the idea of the "melting pot"?
2. What comparison, stated in the form of a question, does he offer for the historian?

Reading-Related Writing

1. Discuss how we can or cannot easily keep in mind "that we are a diverse strand of peoples" by using Foote's version of history according to the "melting pot" theory.

DUMP THE MELTING POT

Jack Chen

Although the "melting pot" concept was once an unchallenged idea, it is now regarded by some as harmful to the development of the country generally and democracy specifically.

America is one of the most ethnically and culturally pluralistic countries in the world. Seeking national unity, national leaders and the dominant public opinion once held that America could be forged into some kind of homogeneous all-American alloy by a process of more or less pressured fusing of its diverse elements and expulsion of "unassimilable" entities. That "melting pot" concept is now rejected by Chinese Americans and other ethnic groups as a guide to national policy. In fact, it is harmful in this day and age. National cohesion can now only come about by a frank recognition of America's pluralism and a voluntary joint effort to legitimize cultural democracy and diversity. Only in this way can the full economic and cultural potential of the nation's last remaining Chinatowns and its Chinese communities be developed and the special aptitudes of its Chinese American and all other citizens be fostered for the good of themselves and their families and of the nation and all its parts. Cultural democracy among ethnic groups will strengthen their political unity.

Critical Thinking and Discussion

1. What is the topic sentence of this paragraph?
2. On what would Chen develop national cohesion?
3. How would he define cultural democracy?

Reading-Related Writing

1. Evaluate Chen's view within the framework of your own experience, referring to ethnic communities and individuals you are familiar with.

FROM THE MELTING POT TO THE GENE-POOL MIXING BOWL

Itabari Njeri

One way of stirring the "melting pot" is by marrying interracially. And the children of interracial marriages may marry children of other interracial marriages, and. . . .

Potentially the most significant phenomenon in the next decades will be the emergence of the multiracial population. In the United States, interracial marriages tripled from 310,000 in 1970 to 956,000 in 1988. An estimated 1 to 2 million children have been born to interracial couples since about 1970, according to an expert on multiracial children. And early reports show an increase in the number of people who called themselves "multiracial" or "biracial" on the 1990 census, according to the U.S. Census Bureau. The discussion generated by this new multiethnic generation is going to stimulate a decades-long debate—one that may force Americans to confront the myths that surround race and ethnicity in the United States. What the coming multicultural, polyethnic, pluralistic—unarguably diverse—America will be no one knows for certain. There are no models anywhere for what is happening here. America is the experiment and California is the first on-line lab.

Critical Thinking and Discussion

1. Why may the emergence of the multiracial population be the most significant phenomenon in the next decades?
2. Why is California said to be serving as a lab for experiment?

Reading-Related Writing

1. This paragraph comes from an essay entitled "Beyond the Melting Pot." Use evidence from this paragraph and from your own experience to discuss the appropriateness of the added reference to a gene-pool mixing bowl in the title given to this paragraph.

CAN ETHNIC PRIDE PROMOTE VIOLENCE?

Sharon Bernstein

In an effort to build ethnic pride, school systems have implemented various cultural programs. Among the results have been acts of violence. What went wrong? This passage is from an article by reporter Sharon Bernstein that appeared in the Los Angeles Times.

Even students, searching for reasons why violence erupted recently at North Hollywood High School and other campuses in the Los Angeles Unified School District, suggested that some youngsters have misunderstood lessons about ethnic pride, developing ethnic chauvinism instead. "They teach you that you have to identify with your own group," said Karina Escalante, a senior at Cleveland High School in Reseda, where African-American and

Latino students clashed last year [1991]. She said students receive conflicting messages that teach them pride in their ethnic identities but not how those identities can and should mesh with others in society. "They tell you to keep with your own. Then they tell you to go out and mix. They should have a program that says: 'Yes, you should identify yourself but then you have to go out and mix.' " Educators in the Los Angeles district say they are particularly troubled and point to the violence that broke out in October [1992] between African-American and Latino students at North Hollywood and Hamilton high schools.

Critical Thinking and Discussion

1. What were the intentions of the schools' lessons?
2. What conflicting messages did some of the students feel they received?
3. What does this paragraph imply should be taught?

Reading-Related Writing

1. Describe your likely feelings for your own cultural group and others if you were attending a program that was celebrating your cultural heritage. Be specific.
2. Describe your likely feelings for your own cultural group if you were attending a program that was celebrating the heritage of another cultural group. Be specific.
3. Write a piece in which you present an ideal school program on the value of ethnic diversity.

AMERICA: THE MULTICULTURAL SOCIETY

Ishmael Reed

Born and educated in New York, writer and teacher Ishmael Reed now lives in Oakland, California, and knows the territory between those two locations. To him it is multicultural territory. He sees a blend and a mix. When he came across a newspaper article about the cultural mix at a gathering in New York City, he was not surprised. He is merely reminded of what he has witnessed, as reported here in a section from his book Writin' Is Fightin' *(1988).*

At the annual Lower East Side Jewish Festival yesterday, a Chinese woman ate a pizza slice in front of Ty Thuan Duc's Vietnamese grocery store. Beside her a Spanish-speaking family patronized a cart with two signs: "Italian Ices" and "Kosher by Rabbi Alper." And after the pastrami ran out, everybody ate knishes.

New York Times, June 23, 1983

On the day before Memorial Day, 1983, a poet called me to describe a city he 1 had just visited. He said that one section included mosques, built by the Islamic people who dwelled there. Attending his reading, he said, were large numbers of Hispanic people, forty thousand of whom lived in the same city. He was not talking about a fabled city located in some mysterious region of the world. The city he'd visited was Detroit.

A few months before, as I was leaving Houston, Texas, I heard it 2 announced on the radio that Texas's largest minority was Mexican-American, and though a foundation recently issued a report critical of bilingual education, the taped voice used to guide the passengers on the air trams connecting terminals in Dallas Airport is in both Spanish and English. If the trend continues, a day will come when it will be difficult to travel through some sections of the country without hearing commands in both English and Spanish; after all, for some western states, Spanish was the first written language and the Spanish style lives on in the western way of life.

Shortly after my Texas trip, I sat in an auditorium located on the campus 3 of the University of Wisconsin at Milwaukee as a Yale professor—whose original work on the influence of African cultures upon those of the Americas has led to his ostracism from some monocultural intellectual circles—walked up and down the aisle, like an old-time southern evangelist, dancing and drumming the top of the lectern, illustrating his points before some serious Afro-American intellectuals and artists who cheered and applauded his performance and his mastery of information. The professor was "white." After his lecture, he joined a group of Milwaukeeans in a conversation. All of the participants spoke Yoruban, though only the professor had ever traveled to Africa.

One of the artists told me that his paintings, which included African and 4 Afro-American mythological symbols and imagery, were hanging in the local McDonald's restaurant. The next day I went to McDonald's and snapped pictures of smiling youngsters eating hamburgers below paintings that could grace the walls of any of the country's leading museums. The manager of the local McDonald's said, "I don't know what you boys are doing, but I like it," as he commissioned the local painters to exhibit in his restaurant.

Such blurring of cultural styles occurs in everyday life in the United States 5 to a greater extent than anyone can imagine and is probably more prevalent than the sensational conflict between people of different backgrounds that is played up and often encouraged by the media. The result is what the Yale Professor, Robert Thompson, referred to as a cultural bouillabaisse, yet members of the nation's present educational and cultural Elect still cling to the notion that the United States belongs to some vaguely defined entity they refer to as "Western civilization," by which they mean, presumably, a civilization created by the people of Europe, as if Europe can be viewed in monolithic terms. Is Beethoven's Ninth Symphony, which includes Turkish marches, a part of Western civilization, or the late nineteenth- and twentieth-century French paintings, whose creators were influenced by Japanese art? And what of the cubists, through whom the influence of African art changed modern painting, or the surrealists, who were so impressed with the art of the Pacific Northwest Indians that, in their map of North America, Alaska dwarfs the lower forty-eight in size?

Are the Russians, who are often criticized for their adoption of "Western" 6 ways by Tsarist dissidents in exile, members of Western civilization? And what of the millions of Europeans who have black African and Asian ancestry, black Africans having occupied several countries for hundreds of years? Are these "Europeans" members of Western civilization, or the Hungarians, who originated across the Urals[1] in a place called Greater Hungary, or the Irish, who came from the Iberian Peninsula?

Even the notion that North America is part of Western civilization 7 because our "system of government" is derived from Europe is being challenged by Native American historians who say that the founding fathers, Benjamin Franklin especially, were actually influenced by the system of government that had been adopted by the Iroquois hundreds of years prior to the arrival of large numbers of Europeans.

Western civilization, then, becomes another confusing category like 8 Third World, or Judeo-Christian culture, as man attempts to impose his small-screen view of political and cultural reality upon a complex world. Our most publicized novelist recently said that Western civilization was the greatest achievement of mankind, an attitude that flourishes on the street level as scribbles in public restrooms: "White Power," "Niggers and Spics Suck," or "Hitler was a prophet," the latter being the most telling, for wasn't Adolph Hitler the archetypal monoculturalist who, in his pigheaded arrogance, believed that one way and one blood was so pure that it had to be protected from alien strains at all costs? Where did such an attitude, which has caused so much misery and depression in our national life, which has tainted even our noblest achievements, begin? An attitude that caused the incarceration of Japanese-American citizens during World War II, the persecution of Chicanos and Chinese-Americans, the near-extermination of the Indians, and the murder and lynchings of thousands of Afro-Americans.

Virtuous, hardworking, pious, even though they occasionally would 9 wander off after some fancy clothes, or rendezvous in the woods with the

---

[1]Mountain system in Russia, traditional boundary between Europe and Asia.

town prostitute, the Puritans are idealized in our schoolbooks as "a hardy band" of no-nonsense patriarchs whose discipline razed the forest and brought order to the New World (a term that annoys Native American historians). Industrious, responsible, it was their "Yankee ingenuity" and practicality that created the work ethic. They were simple folk who produced a number of good poets, and they set the tone for the American writing style, of lean and spare lines, long before Hemingway. They worshiped in churches whose colors blended in with the New England snow, churches with simple structures and ornate lecterns.

The Puritans were a daring lot, but they had a mean streak. They hated 10 the theater and banned Christmas. They punished people in a cruel and inhuman manner. They killed children who disobeyed their parents. When they came in contact with those whom they considered heathens or aliens, they behaved in such a bizarre and irrational manner that this chapter in the American history comes down to us as a late-movie horror film. They exterminated the Indians, who taught them how to survive in a world unknown to them, and their encounter with the calypso culture of Barbados resulted in what the tourist guide in Salem's Witches' House refers to as the Witchcraft Hysteria.

The Puritan legacy of hard work and meticulous accounting led to the 11 establishment of a great industrial society; it is no wonder that the American industrial revolution began in Lowell, Massachusetts, but there was the other side, the strange and paranoid attitudes toward those different from the Elect.

The cultural attitudes of that early Elect continue to be voiced in every- 12 day life in the United States: the president of a distinguished university, writing a letter to the *Times*, belittling the study of African civilizations; the television network that promoted its show on the Vatican art with the boast that this art represented "the finest achievements of the human spirit." A modern up-tempo state of complex rhythms that depends upon contacts with an international community can no longer behave as if it dwelled in a "Zion Wilderness" surrounded by beasts and pagans.

When I heard a schoolteacher warn the other night about the invasion of 13 the American educational system by foreign curriculums, I wanted to yell at the television set, "Lady, they're already here." It has already begun because the world is here. The world has been arriving at these shores for at least ten thousand years from Europe, Africa, and Asia. In the late nineteenth and early twentieth centuries, large numbers of Europeans arrived, adding their cultures to those of the European, African, and Asian settlers who were already here, and recently millions have been entering the country from South America and the Caribbean, making Yale professor Bob Thompson's bouillabaisse richer and thicker.

One of our most visionary politicians said that he envisioned a time 14 when the United States could become the brain of the world, by which he meant the repository of all of the latest advanced information systems. I thought of that remark when an enterprising poet friend of mine called to say that he had just sold a poem to a computer magazine and that the editors were delighted to get it because they didn't carry fiction or poetry. Is that the kind of world we desire? A humdrum homogeneous world of all brains and no heart, no fiction, no poetry; a world of robots with human attendants bereft of imagination, of culture? Or does North America deserve a more exciting destiny? To become a place where the cultures of the world criss-cross. This is possible because the United States is unique in the world: The world is here.

Vocabulary

ostracism (3)	cubists (5)	ornate (9)
mythological (4)	surrealists (5)	calypso (10)
prevalent (5)	dissidents (6)	meticulous (10)
entity (5)	archetypal (8)	paranoid (11)
monolithic (5)	patriarchs (9)	bouillabaisse (13)

Critical Thinking and Discussion

1. What sentence in paragraph 5 states Reed's thesis?
2. How does he use the first four paragraphs that lead to the thesis?
3. To Reed, American society suggests mixture rather than purity in terms of both culture and race. What mixtures does he refer to both in North America and in Europe? (See paragraphs 5–13.)
4. How and why do some people refuse to acknowledge America as a multicultural society?
5. What is Reed's attitude (reflected in his tone) toward the idea of multiculturalism?
6. He suggests that a blending of cultures has already occurred ("blurring," paragraph 5, sentence 1). Is this a manifestation of the "melting pot" process, or not?

Reading-Related Writing

1. Give evidence from your own studies and observations to support Reed's thesis or a slight modification of his thesis.
2. Evaluate his use of evidence in a specific area, such as the Puritan influence in America.
3. Discuss whether Reed approves of the "blurring of cultural styles" and whether you do. Explain in detail why you agree or disagree with him.

THE CULT OF ETHNICITY, GOOD AND BAD

Arthur Schlesinger, Jr.

Historian, professor, Pulitzer Prize-winning writer, and adviser to President Kennedy, Arthur Schlesinger, Jr., is no ivory-tower intellectual who writes from a social and historical distance. One of the many topics that interests him is what he calls "the cult of ethnicity." His message in this essay, written in early 1991, is cautionary, placing him at odds with most other writers in this chapter.

The history of the world has been in great part the history of the mixing of 1 peoples. Modern communication and transport accelerate mass migrations from one continent to another. Ethnic and racial diversity is more than ever a salient fact of the age.

But what happens when people of different origins, speaking different 2 languages and professing different religions, inhabit the same locality and live under the same political sovereignty? Ethnic and racial conflict—far more than ideological conflict—is the explosive problem of our times.

On every side today ethnicity is breaking up nations. The Soviet Union, 3 India, Yugoslavia, Ethiopia, are all in crisis. Ethnic tensions disturb and divide Sri Lanka, Burma, Indonesia, Iraq, Cyprus, Nigeria, Angola, Lebanon, Guyana, Trinidad—you name it. Even nations as stable and civilized as Britain and France, Belgium and Spain, face growing ethnic troubles. Is there any large multiethnic state that can be made to work?

The answer to that question has been, until recently, the United States. 4 "No other nation," Margaret Thatcher[1] has said, "has so successfully combined people of different races and nations within a single culture." How have Americans succeeded in pulling off this almost unprecedented trick?

We have always been a multiethnic country. Hector St. John de Crève- 5 coeur, who came from France in the 18th century, marveled at the astonishing diversity of the settlers —"a mixture of English, Scotch, Irish, French, Dutch, Germans and Swedes . . . this promiscuous breed." He propounded a famous question: "What then is the American, this new man?" And he gave a famous answer: "Here individuals of all nations are melted into a new race of men." *E pluribus unum.*

The United States escaped the divisiveness of a multiethnic society by a 6 brilliant solution: the creation of a brand-new national identity. The point of America was not to preserve old cultures but to forge a new, *American* culture. "By an intermixture with our people," President George Washington told Vice President John Adams, immigrants will "get assimilated to our customs,

[1] Thatcher is a former British prime minister.

measures, and laws; in a word, soon become one people." This was the ideal that a century later Israel Zangwill crystallized in the title of his popular 1908 play *The Melting Pot*. And no institution was more potent in molding Crèvecoeur's "promiscuous breed" into Washington's "one people" than the American public school.

The new American nationality was inescapably English in language, 7 ideas, and institutions. The pot did not melt everybody, not even all the white immigrants: deeply bred racism put black Americans, yellow Americans, red Americans, and brown Americans well outside the pale. Still, the infusion of other stocks, even of nonwhite stocks, and the experience of the New World reconfigured the British legacy and made the United States, as we all know, a very different country from Britain.

In the 20th century, new immigration laws altered the composition of the 8 American people, and a cult of ethnicity erupted both among non-Anglo whites and among nonwhite minorities. This had many healthy consequences. The American culture at last began to give shamefully overdue recognition to the achievements of groups subordinated and spurned during the high noon of Anglo dominance, and it began to acknowledge the great swirling world beyond Europe. Americans acquired a more complex and invigorating sense of their world—and of themselves.

But, pressed too far, the cult of ethnicity has unhealthy consequences. It 9 gives rise, for example, to the conception of the United States as a nation composed not of individuals making their own choices but of inviolable ethnic and racial groups. It rejects the historic American goals of assimilation and integration. And, in an excess of zeal, well-intentioned people seek to transform our system of education from a means of creating "one people" into a means of promoting, celebrating and perpetuating separate ethnic origins and identities. The balance is shifting from *unum* to *pluribus*.

That is the issue that lies behind the hullabaloo over "multiculturalism" 10 and "political correctness," the attack on the "Eurocentric" curriculum, and the rise of the notion that history and literature should be taught not as disciplines but as therapies whose function is to raise minority self-esteem. Group separatism crystallizes the differences, magnifies tensions, intensifies hostilities. Europe—the unique source of the liberating ideas of democracy, civil liberties and human rights—is portrayed as the root of all evil, and non-European cultures, their own many crimes deleted, are presented as the means of redemption.

I don't want to sound apocalyptic about these developments. Education 11 is always in ferment, and a good thing too. The situation in our universities, I am confident, will soon right itself. But the impact of separatist pressures on our public schools is more troubling. If a Kleagle of the Ku Klux Klan wanted to use the schools to disable and handicap black Americans, he could hardly come up with anything more effective than the "Afrocentric" curriculum. And if separatist tendencies go unchecked, the result can only be the fragmentation, resegregation and tribalization of American life.

I remain optimistic. My impression is that the historic forces driving 12 toward "one people" have not lost their power. The eruption of ethnicity is, I believe, a rather superficial enthusiasm stirred by romantic ideologues on the one hand and by unscrupulous con men on the other: self-appointed spokesmen whose claim to represent their minority groups is carelessly accepted by the media. Most American-born members of minority groups, white or nonwhite, see themselves primarily as Americans rather than primarily as members of one or another ethnic group. A notable indicator today is the rate of intermarriage across ethnic lines, across religious lines, even (increasingly) across racial lines. "We Americans," said Theodore Roosevelt, "are children of the crucible."

The growing diversity of the American population makes the quest for 13 unifying ideals and a common culture all the more urgent. In a world savagely rent by ethnic and racial antagonisms, the United States must continue as an example of how a highly differentiated society holds itself together.

Critical Thinking and Discussion

1. How did America escape the divisiveness of a multiethnic society?
2. Did the melting pot melt all? Explain.
3. In what way has the cult of ethnicity been good?
4. In what way has the cult of ethnicity gone too far?
5. Why is Schlesinger optimistic?

Reading-Related Writing

1. Write a piece in which you agree or disagree with Schlesinger.
2. Assuming that there is some validity in what he says about group separatism crystallizing differences, write a piece in which you explain that concept and discuss what should be done.

LET'S TELL THE STORY OF ALL AMERICA'S CULTURES

Ji-Yeon Mary Yuhfill

Her surname offers a good introduction to the ideas of Ji-Yeon Mary Yuhfill. Ji-Yeon is Korean. Mary is American. Yuhfill is a combination of her surname (Yuh) and the last syllable of her husband's former name (Highfill). His married name is also Yuhfill. As a Korean-American student of American history with a specialty in immigration, she has long been interested in both the way our country has developed and how its history has been taught. Her title for this essay states her view and the thesis.

I grew up hearing, seeing and almost believing that America was white— albeit with a little black tinged here and there—and that white was best. 1

The white people were everywhere in my 1970s Chicago childhood: Founding Fathers, Lewis and Clark, Lincoln, Daniel Boone, Carnegie, presidents, explorers and industrialists galore. The only black people were slaves. The only Indians were scalpers. 2

I never heard one word about how Benjamin Franklin was so impressed by the Iroquois federation of nations that he adapted that model into our system of state and federal government. Or that the Indian tribes were systematically betrayed and massacred by a greedy young nation that stole their land and called it the United States. 3

I never heard one word about how Asian immigrants were among the first to turn California's desert into fields of plenty. Or about Chinese immigrant Ah Bing, who bred the cherry now on sale in groceries across the nation. Or that plantation owners in Hawaii imported labor from China, Japan, Korea and the Philippines to work the sugar cane fields. I never learned that Asian immigrants were the only immigrants denied U.S. citizenship, even though they served honorably in World War I. All the immigrants in my textbook were white. 4

I never learned about Frederick Douglass, the runaway slave who became a leading abolitionist and statesman, or about black scholar W.E.B. Du Bois. I never learned that black people rose up in arms against slavery. Nat Turner wasn't one of the heroes in my childhood history class. 5

I never learned that the American Southwest and California were already settled by Mexicans when they were annexed after the Mexican-American War. I never learned that Mexico once had a problem keeping land-hungry white men on the U.S. side of the border. 6

So when other children called me a slant-eyed chink and told me to go back where I came from, I was ready to believe that I wasn't really an American because I wasn't white. 7

America's bittersweet legacy of struggling and failing and getting another step closer to democratic ideals of liberty and equality and justice for all wasn't for the likes of me, an immigrant child from Korea. The history books said so. 8

Well, the history books were wrong. 9

Educators around the country are finally realizing what I realized as a 10
teenager in the library, looking up the history I wasn't getting in school.
America is a multicultural nation, composed of many people with varying
histories and varying traditions who have little in common except their
humanity, a belief in democracy and a desire for freedom.

America changed them, but they changed America too. 11

A committee of scholars and teachers gathered by the New York State 12
Department of Education recognizes this in their recent report, "One Nation,
Many Peoples: A Declaration of Cultural Interdependence."

They recommend that public schools provide a "multicultural education, 13
anchored to the shared principles of a liberal democracy."

What that means, according to the report, is recognizing that America 14
was shaped and continues to be shaped by people of diverse backgrounds. It
calls for students to be taught that history is an ongoing process of discovery
and interpretation of the past, and that there is more than one way of viewing
the world.

Thus, the westward migration of white Americans is not just a heroic 15
settling of an untamed wild, but also the conquest of indigenous peoples.
Immigrants were not just white, but Asian as well. Blacks were not merely
passive slaves freed by northern whites, but active fighters for their own
liberation.

In particular, according to the report, the curriculum should help children 16
"to assess critically the reasons for the inconsistencies between the ideals of the
U.S. and social realities. It should provide information and intellectual tools
that can permit them to contribute to bringing reality closer to the ideals."

In other words, show children the good with the bad, and give them the 17
skills to help improve their country. What could be more patriotic?

Several dissenting members of the New York committee publicly worry 18
that America will splinter into ethnic fragments if this multicultural curriculum is adopted. They argue that the committee's report puts the focus on
ethnicity at the expense of national unity.

But downplaying ethnicity will not bolster national unity. The history of 19
America is the story of how and why people from all over the world came to
the United States, and how in struggling to make a better life for themselves,
they changed each other, they changed the country, and they all came to call
themselves Americans.

E pluribus unum. Out of many, one. 20

This is why I, with my Korean background, and my childhood tor- 21
mentors, with their lost-in-the-mist-of-time European backgrounds, are all
Americans.

It is the unique beauty of this country. It is high time we let all our 22
children gaze upon it.

Critical Thinking and Discussion

1. What kind of support does Yuhfill rely on primarily?
2. How does she think history should be taught?
3. What aspect of critical thinking becomes important in her approach to teaching American history?
4. Why is she optimistic about America's future?

Reading-Related Writing

1. Write a piece in which you agree or disagree with Yuhfill.
2. Compare her views with those of Schlesinger in the preceding essay.

SLOUCHING TOWARDS LOS ANGELES

Richard Rodriguez

Editor at Pacific News Service, author of several books including Days of Obligation, *and television commentator, Richard Rodriguez has his supporters and detractors within the Hispanic community. Some say that, as a perceptive social critic and brilliant writer, he merely describes what is happening. Others dislike him because of his message that ethnic assimilation is natural and inevitable; still others say he has lost his ethnic ties. Here, he says that a new kind of person is being born, a product of all the tumultuous mixing of cultures, and that person is, as he writes, "slouching towards Los Angeles" to claim position as the new American citizen.*

In the aftermath of last year's riot and looting, the commonplace about Los 1
Angeles has it that the city is melting, melting under a cloudless sky. On the contrary, it seems that a city—a new Los Angeles—is forming. The city famous as a collection of separate suburbs is no more. For people in suburbs realize now that they are not so far away from neighborhoods of poverty. Blacks are very much aware of Asians. Latinos are aware of blacks. Los Angeles is not dying; a new metropolitan idea is being born.

I have been traveling recently across America, visiting colleges and mak- 2
ing happy-talk appearances on morning television. On airplanes and in classrooms, I have been hearing Americans say—what they say in Los Angeles—that the country doesn't exist any more.

So what else is new? Americans have always said that. We Americans 3
have never believed in ourselves in the plural. What, traditionally, we share as

Americans is the belief that we share nothing in common at all. Who is more American, after all, than today's brown and black neo-nationalist in Los Angeles?

America is a Puritan country, Protestant-baptized. We believe in individu- 4
alism, are suspicious of the crowd. As Americans we trust diversity, not uniformity. We trust the space between us more than we like any notion of an American melting pot.

In a century less secular than our own, 19th-century Americans more 5
easily recognized the Protestant character of this country. Today, we speak of "Asians and Latinos." The 19th century spoke of Catholics and Jews.

When the Irish started coming to this country in the early 19th century, 6
America's fear was a theological one. War was brewing with Mexico. Nativists worried that the Irish would join with the Mexicans—their fellow Catholics—and overturn the Protestant state. Which was not a bad argument, except for the fact that it ignored the reality of America and the influence of America.

America exists. One hundred and fifty years after America feared the 7
Irish, Patrick J. Buchanan wonders if we can't, after all, erect a wall between San Diego and Tijuana.

Today, there is something called "multiculturalism" in the classroom, and 8
our teachers speak of our diversity. We celebrate "our friends" the Guatemalans.

In fact, our friends the Guatemalans are converting to the Mormon 9
church. And our friends the Guatemalans are working as nannies in Beverly Hills and teaching the children of 90210 how to ask and say thank you in Spanish. In fact, people influence one another, lives change, cultures mix.

Our teachers used to be able to tell us this. Our teachers used to be able 10
to pose the possibility of a national culture—a line connecting Thomas Jefferson, the slave owner, to Malcolm X. Our teachers used to be able to tell us why all of us speak Black English. Or how the Mexican farm workers in Delano were related to the Yiddish-speaking grandmothers who worked the sweatshops of the lower East Side. America may not have wanted to listen. But our teachers used to insist that there was something called an American culture, a common history.

We are without a sense of ourselves entire. In the classrooms of America, 11
I heard no term more often in recent weeks than multiculturalism. All over America, in identical hotels, there are weekend conferences for business executives on multiculturalism. The same experts fly from one city to the next to say the same thing: We live in a multicultural America.

What any immigrant kid could tell you for free, on the other hand, is that 12
America exists. There is a culture. There is a shared accent, a shared defiance of authority, a shared skepticism about community. There is a stance, a common impatience at the fast-food counter. Moreover, though the executives at

the multicultural seminar do not want to hear it, the deepest separation between us derives not from race or ethnicity but from class. To put matters bluntly, the black executive at Pac Bell or ARCO has more in common culturally with her white colleague than she does with the gang kids in South-Central.

White middle-class kids in Santa Barbara know this. They are infatuated 13 with lower-class black style. Ghetto talk, gesture, dress. The suburban kids see in the lower-class black their opposite. As Americans, the suburban kids are infatuated with the defiance of black toughs, with their swagger. Today's rapper is the new Huck Finn. Of course, the white kids want to imitate these outsiders and challenge authority—it is a most American thing to do.

Aficionados of multiculturalism, meanwhile, give us metaphors like the 14 mosaic.

America is a mosaic, they say. Or America is a rainbow. Or America is a 15 shopping bag, separate but equal, blah blah. The deeper truth is that people have souls. People meet, they argue, they flirt, they fight, they compete, they have children, they divorce, they remarry, they bewilder themselves.

The 19th-century schools were supposed to Anglicize immigrant chil 16 dren, dip them into the melting pot. But assimilation is reciprocal. The immigrant kids ended up changing American English. There are thousands of foreign words on the American tongue—Swedish, German, Italian, Yiddish.

One hundred years later, the descendants of Central American Indians 17 are becoming evangelical Protestants. At the same time, blond animal-rights activists in Orange County are becoming the new pantheists—California's new tribe of Indians—proclaiming the equality of all living things.

Among the prominent Latina leaders in this country, most have Jewish 18 husbands. Some of the best writers of American English are the great grandchildren of slaves. I know Mexican Indians from Oaxaca who are trilingual, speak their native Indian tongue, speak Spanish, speak English. They trespass borders. They live six months in Fresno, six months in Oaxaca. They deal with two currencies and several centuries. They are multicultural the way we are all becoming multicultural, people of many societies.

Oh, but I know some poor Mexican gang kids in Boyle Heights. They are 19 tatooed and they have guns and some of the littlest of them have killed. They live, bounded by four blocks, unable to find their way across town to the beaches. They do not know UCLA. What I want to tell them is to leave their four blocks and confront the city. Leave the tribe behind. Make friends with black kids. Find out what Vietnamese kids are like. Go to a museum. Become an Indian explorer. Belong to the city. Go to a library.

The library! Here in San Francisco there is a fund-raising campaign for a 20 new main library. There are separate fund-raising drives by Asians, by Filipinos, by gays and lesbians, by Latinos, by African-Americans. Which tribe do you belong to?

Every mother tells men—her husband, her sons—what men cannot 21 quite believe: Birth is traumatic. It is messy, it is slimy, it is painful beyond pain. There is blood. Birth begins with a scream.

I tell you, Los Angeles is being born. A city is forming within the terror 22 and suspicion and fear that people have of one another. As an outsider, I can sense the city forming. People in Los Angeles are preoccupied with one another, cannot forget one another. You have lost your suburban innocence. It is better this way, I think. Better not to like one another than not to know the stranger exists.

Vocabulary

secular (5)   infatuated (13)   traumatic (21)
skepticism (12)   reciprocal (16)

Critical Thinking and Discussion

1. What is the new metropolitan idea that is being born?
2. According to Rodriguez, what are the characteristics of American culture?
3. Why are white youth infatuated with black rappers?
4. What is the difference between the "melting pot" and assimilation concepts?

Reading-Related Writing

1. Write a piece in which you agree or disagree with Rodriguez; give your reasons, referring directly to his essay, and perhaps to other selections in this chapter.

Collaborative Learning

1. This activity works best in an atmosphere in which no one feels defensive or endangered—what has been called a "safe house for discussion." One doesn't create this atmosphere because of the fear of facing controversy, but because this activity is designed to be informative, not argumentative. It is based on the principle that we have worked with throughout the book—that when we study other cultures, we will recognize the great commonality of human experience and that the understanding of another culture will make us more tolerant and more appreciative of diversity.

   Adjust this procedure as necessary to fit the needs and circumstances of the class. For example, students may use sources from this book rather than the library, or they may mix sources.

(a) The class will be divided into small groups.

(b) Each group will concentrate on a cultural group (such as Hispanic-American, Asian-American, African-American, Native American).

(c) Each group will direct each of its members to prepare a written paper and a brief oral report.

- The intent will be to present nonconfrontational information about cultural groups.
- The aspects will vary from group to group but might include some of these: language, attitudes toward family, values, philosophy, art, music, food, celebrations, contributions to American society, and games.
- Students will use the library for research.

(d) Each group will meet several times to ensure that its members give a fairly comprehensive coverage of the cultural group.

(e) Each student will then present an oral report, respond to questions from the class, and submit a written report.

(f) After the oral reports are finished, the class will have a meal of ethnic and regional foods. Each group will be responsible for representative foods for a buffet table. Music and dancing are optional. Dress should reflect cultural diversity.

2. Form into small groups. Acting independently, each group should think ahead to the year 2050 and give reports on multiculturalism at that time. Consider topics such as families, government, language use, business, fashion, food, religion, military service, and the media. Incorporate comments on ideas and attitudes expressed in readings from this chapter (saying that the ideas were, in retrospect, either valid or invalid). You may want to include subjects not covered explicitly in these readings: the functionally handicapped, sexual preferences, gender rights, and age (the young or the old) rights. Individually write about a single aspect of your project, or collectively prepare a larger report.

3. Prepare a census form for your class or school. Several possibilities are open to you. You could establish committees to decide on labels for racial and cultural groups; you would have to decide whether you want a broad or narrow list. You could complete the census in your class. Write about a single aspect of your project.

4. Simulate a school-board meeting in a community that is becoming multicultural. Select five board members who will represent views that might be held in certain districts, such as those that are fearful, angry, compassionate, thoughtful, prejudiced, and unbiased. Have teachers, parents, students, and other citizens address the board on how to improve the school program in ways that will fairly represent different races while not inflaming passions; these presentations could be the product of collaborative work. Consider courses, programs, speakers, library materials, and

connections with other communities, and refer to some of the ideas discussed in the paragraphs and essays in this chapter.

Connections

1. Referring to two or more of the readings, explain what is happening— and what *should* happen—as this country incorporates more cultures. In other words, do you favor the idea of the melting pot, assimilation, separateness with coexistence, or some other concept?
2. Using the title of this chapter, "America: What Is It? What *Should* It Be?" write your own essay. Consider referring to selections in this and other chapters.

APPENDIX: A BRIEF GUIDE
TO THE RESEARCH PAPER

Although specific aims and methods may vary from one research activity to another, most library research tasks will depend on these basic steps:

1. **Choose a subject and then narrow and focus it until it becomes a topic you can investigate thoroughly and write about convincingly.** The narrowing and focusing will indicate what you will do with the subject (treatment).

   Example of subject: child abuse

   Example of subject and treatment (thesis):

   ```
   For the survivors, child abuse is more than the momentary
   pain and humiliation of a blow or an insult or even a
   sexual attack; it is a lifelong trauma.
   ```

   (For multicultural topics see writing suggestions at the end of Chapters 2–11, especially Chapter 11, pp. 393–395.)

2. **Determine which style of documentation is appropriate for this piece of research writing, and familiarize yourself with the conventions for preparing a bibliography or list of works cited and for documenting sources.** The documentation style used here is MLA (Modern Language Association).

3. **Use the resources in your college library, such as indexes, card catalogs, and electronic files, to identify books, articles, and other materials pertaining to your topic.**

Using the Library

Although some research topics require interviews, surveys, or the study of documents in off-campus archives, the center for most academic research is the college library. There you will find *primary sources* (examples of the actual subjects being investigated, such as literary works, letters, and the texts of speeches and interviews); *secondary sources* (biographies, scholarly books and monographs, periodical articles, and other works about the subject); and the various reference tools needed to identify and obtain these sources.

If your library uses a computerized indexing system, you can obtain lists of probable sources by going to the computer terminal and typing in a user code plus an author, title, or subject description. Libraries differ in the systems offered. The following material pertains to the noncomputerized library system. Always work with the best system available and obtain help from librarians.

The Library Catalog

One indispensable research tool is the card catalog or its equivalent, the computer catalog, which indexes all the books and bound periodicals in the library's collection. The catalog is usually divided into three sections: (1) an author file, which contains entries for all books arranged alphabetically by author; (2) a title file, which consists of entries for all books and bound periodicals arranged alphabetically; and (3) a subject file, which includes entries for all books arranged alphabetically by subject. The entries in this catalog provide several kinds of information that will aid you in your research:

1. A Library of Congress or Dewey Decimal system call number that indicates the exact location of the work in the library.

2. Author, title, and publication data for the book.

3. Brief notes about the book's contents.

4. Cross-references to other headings under which each book is listed. Figures A.1 through A.3 show examples of the three types of cards.

Figure A.1   Author Card

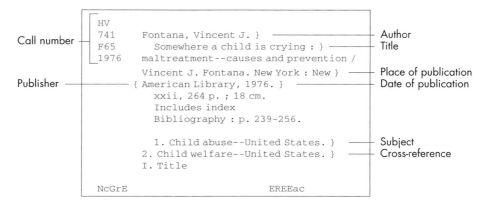

Periodical Indexes and Bibliographies

Although the subject headings of the library catalog and articles in encyclopedias and other such reference works will enable you to compile a partial bibliography on books on your topic, you will have to look elsewhere for bibliographical information about books that are not mentioned in these sources and for articles and reviews published in popular magazines, scholarly journals, and newspapers.

Figure A.2 Title Card

```
                    Somewhere a child is crying
    HV
    741     Fontana, Vincent J.
    F65          Somewhere a child is crying :
    1976    maltreatment--causes and prevention /
            Vincent J. Fontana. New York : New
            American Library, 1976.
                 xxii, 264 p. ; 18 cm.
                 Includes index
                 Bibliography : p. 239-256.

                 1. Child abuse--United States.
                 2. Child welfare--United States.

    NcGrE                               EREEtc
```

Figure A.3 Subject Card

```
                    CHILD ABUSE--UNITED STATES
    HV
    741     Fontana, Vincent J.
    F65          Somewhere a child is crying :
    1976    maltreatment--causes and prevention /
            Vincent J. Fontana. New York : New
            American Library, 1976.
                 xxii, 264 p. ; 18 cm.
                 Includes index
                 Bibliography : p. 239-256.

                 1. Child abuse--United States.
                 2. Child welfare--United States.

    NcGrE                               EREEsc
```

Indexes to Articles and Reviews in Popular Magazines

Book Review Digest. 1905– .

Nineteenth Century Reader's Guide to Periodical Literature. 1890–1899.

Poole's Index to Periodical Literature. 1802–1906.

Reader's Guide to Periodical Literature. 1900– .

How to Use the *Reader's Guide to Periodical Literature*

This is an index to about 185 popular U.S. magazines, representing the important scientific and humanistic subject fields.

Look up your topic alphabetically. If you are unable to find the topic you are looking for, ask for assistance from a reference librarian. The items listed under each subject heading are titles of magazine articles. If the title is not explanatory, it is followed by a short clarification in brackets.

After the title, these items follow:

Author (if available), last name, first initial

Abbreviated description of article features (see page headed "Abbreviations")

Title of magazine, sometimes abbreviated (see page headed "Abbreviations of Periodicals Indexed")

Volume Number (if any)

Page number(s)

Date

Figure A.4 labels the various parts of a *Reader's Guide* entry.

Figure A.4   Explanation of an Entry

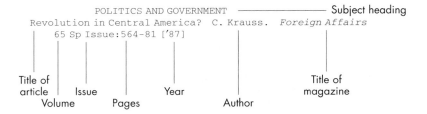

4. **Compile a preliminary bibliography of the sources referred to above, following the documentation style appropriate to your discipline.** The same style will be used later for the Works Cited page(s) at the end of your paper.

Books

The usual order is author, title of book, place of publication, publisher, and date of publication.

- A Book by One Author

  Adeler, Thomas L. *In a New York Minute*. New York: Harper, 1990.

- A Book by Two or More Authors
  To cite a book with two or three authors, list them in the sequence they appear on the title page, giving the first author's name in reverse order. If there are more than three authors, cite only the name of the person listed first on the title page and use the abbreviation *et al.* (Latin for "and others") in place of the other authors' names.

  Berry, Mary Frances, and John W. Blassingame. *Long Memory: The Black Experience in America*. New York: Oxford UP, 1981.
  Danziger, James N., et al. *Computers and Politics: High Technology in American Local Governments*. New York: Columbia UP, 1982.

- A Book with a Corporate Author

  Detroit Commission on the Renaissance. *Toward the Future*. Detroit: Wolverine, 1989.

Articles in Periodicals

The usual pattern for citing articles in periodicals is as follows: author's name followed by a period; title of article followed by a period; name of periodical, volume number, and date followed by a colon; and inclusive page numbers followed by a period. If no author is given, cite the title first and alphabetize the title.

- Article in a Weekly or Biweekly Magazine

  "How to Stop Crib Deaths." *Newsweek* 6 August 1993: 79.

- Article in a Monthly or Bimonthly Magazine

  Browne, Malcolm W. "Locking Out the Hackers: There Are Ways to Keep Trespassers Out of Computer Systems." *Discover* November 1993: 30-40.

- Newspaper Article

      Gregory, Tina. "When All Else Fails." Philadelphia
        Inquirer 2 April 1990: C12.

A Work in an Anthology

Give the author and title of the work you are citing. Then cite the title of the anthology. After the title, give the name of the editor or translator, preceded by the abbreviation "Ed." or "Trans." Follow with city, publisher, and date. Skip two spaces and cite the inclusive page numbers.

      Hull, John D. "A Boy and His Gun." Celebrating Diversity.
        Ed. Lee Brandon. Lexington: D. C. Heath and Company,
        1995. 196-198.

An Article in an Encyclopedia

      Schmitt, Barton D., and C. Henry Kempe. "Child Abuse."
        The Encyclopedia Americana. International ed. 1990.

A Personal Interview

      Thomas, Carolyn. Personal interview. 5 January 1993.

Government Publications

Usually the writer of a government publication is not named, so treat the issuing government agency as the author. Abbreviations are acceptable if they are clear. Most federal publications come from the Government Printing Office (GPO) in Washington, D.C.

      United States. Dept. of Transportation. National Highway
        Traffic Safety Admin. Driver Licensing Laws Annotated
        1980. Washington: GPO, 1980.

Citations from the *Congressional Record* require only a date and page number.

      Congressional Record. 11 September 1992: 12019-24.

5. **Locate, read, and take notes on the sources listed in the preliminary bibliography.** Your notes will be composed of quotation, summary, your commentary (in brackets), or a combination.

```
                                    Physical Abuse-definition ──── Topic
                                                                   division
Author ──────┤ Chase                                    p. 1 ──── Location in
                                                                   source
             │ "Child abuse is the deliberate and willful injury of a
Quoted ──────┤ child by a caretaker─hitting, beating with a belt,
material       . . . , burning with cigarettes . . . , hog-tying,
             │ or torturing [sexual abuse not mentioned here]."    ──── Omissions
                                                                   ──── Editorial
Summary ─────┤ All of these acts have long-range harmful effects.       comment
```

6. **Develop a thesis statement and an outline or some other tentative organizational plan based on the evidence you have accumulated.**

```
                        Outline
Thesis Statement: For the survivors, child abuse is more
than the momentary pain and humiliation of a blow or an
insult or even a sexual attack; it is a lifelong trauma.

Introduction
    I.   Types of child abusers
         A.   People who take pleasure in inflicting pain on
              others
         B.   People who have difficulty coping with stress
         C.   People with various types of personality
              problems
         D.   People who were themselves abused children
   II.   Typical victims of child abuse
         A.   Infants
         B.   School-age children
  III.   Major forms of child abuse and their effects on the
         victim
         A.   Physical abuse
              1.   Definition
              2.   Effects
         B.   Emotional abuse
              1.   Definition
              2.   Effects
         C.   Sexual abuse
              1.   Definition
              2.   Effects
         D.   Neglect
              1.   Definition
              2.   Effects
Conclusion
```

7. **Present results and conclusions in systematic, accurately documented written form, usually with these parts: cover page; thesis and topic outline; text with documentation; and a list of works cited.**

Basic Documentation

Documenting sources for papers based on textbook or library material is quite simple. Any idea borrowed, whether it is quoted, paraphrased, or summarized, should be documented. Borrowing words or ideas without giving credit to the originators constitutes plagiarism.

The three basic forms for giving credit are:

- If you state the author's name in introducing the quotation or idea, give only the page number: (45).

- If you do not state the author's name in introducing the quotation or idea, give the author's name and a page number: (Rivera 45).

- If the author has written more than one piece cited in your paper, also give a title or a shortened form of the title: (Rivera, The Land 45).

Examples of documenting a quotation by an author mentioned only once in the Works Cited section are:

- Using the author's name to introduce:

   Suzanne Britt says that ''neat people are bums and clods at heart'' (285).

- Not using the author's name to introduce:

   Another author says that ''neat people are bums and clods at heart'' (Britt, 285).

Examples of documenting an idea borrowed from an author but not quoted are:

- Using the author's name to introduce:

   Suzanne Britt believes that neat people are weak in character (285).

- Not using the author's name to introduce:

   Although some maintain that neat people also are likely to have high values, at least one other well-known author and social critic says that neat people are weak in character (Britt, 284–285).

References in Block Quotations

Quotations longer than four typewritten lines are indented and typed without quotation marks, and their references are put outside end punctuation.

> Implicit in the concept of Strange Loops is the concept
> of infinity, since what else is a loop but a way of
> representing an endless process in a finite way? And
> infinity plays a large role in many of Escher's drawings.
> Copies of one single theme often fit into each other,
> forming visual analogues to the canons of Bach.
> (Hofstadter 15)

Sample Cover-Page Information:

The Effects of Child Abuse
by
Sarah Jo Johnson

English 1200
April 14, 1995

Sample Thesis Statement and Outline

See item 6 on page 403.

Sample page of text:

Sarah J. Johnson   Johnson 1
Professor Parsons
English 1200
14 April 1995

                The Effects of Child Abuse

    One of the most serious but least reported
crimes in the United States is child abuse, a
term which ''denotes a situation ranging from
the deprivation of food, clothing, shelter and
paternal love to incidences where children are
physically abused and mistreated by an adult,

---

resulting in obvious physical trauma to the
child and not infrequently leading to death"
(Fontana, *The Maltreated Child* 10). The number
of child abuse incidents in a given year cannot
be determined exactly because only about one
case in eight is reported ("Abused Child" 41).
But according to David Walters, "Child abuse
is pandemic in the United States" (3). Most of
these cases involve one or more of the following
types of maltreatment: physical abuse, sexual
abuse, emotional abuse, or neglect. All have
serious immediate consequences--especially
physical abuse, which frequently results in
death--but for the survivors, child abuse is
more than the momentary pain and humiliation of
a blow or an insult or even a sexual attack; it
is a lifelong trauma.

    To understand the effects of child abuse, we
must first understand what motivates or
provokes it. Some abusers are sadists or
psychopaths who inflict pain on others "for
the joy of it" (Fontana, Somewhere a Child Is
Crying 70). Most, however, are otherwise normal
people who have difficulty coping with stress
(Friedman and D'Agostino 31) or overcoming the
effects of "emotional deprivation in . . .
childhood, low levels of empathy, low self-
esteem, social aloofness, and a variety of
other personal characteristics" (Garbarino
and Stocking 7). The one characteristic that

Sample Works Cited Section (partial):

Works Cited

"Abused Child." Today's Education Jan. 1974: 40-42.
"Authorities Face up to the Child-Abuse Problem." U.S.
   News 3 May 1976: 83-84.
Bates, Robert. "Child Abuse and Neglect: A Medical
   Priority." Volpe, Breton, and Mitton 45-57.
Burgess, Ann W., and Nicholas Groth. "Sexual
   Victimization of Children." Volpe, Breton, and Mitton
   79-89.
Chase, Naomi. A Child Is Being Beaten. New York: Holt,
   1975.

Elmer, Elizabeth. <u>Children in Jeopardy</u>: A Study of Abused Minors and Their Families. Pittsburgh: U of Pittsburgh P, 1967.

Fontana, Vincent. <u>The Maltreated Child</u>: The Maltreatment Syndrome in Children. 2nd ed. Springfield: Thomas, 1971.

———. <u>Somewhere a Child Is Crying</u>: Maltreatment Causes and Prevention. New York: Macmillan, 1973.

TEXT CREDITS

Maya Angelou. From *I Know Why the Caged Bird Sings* by Maya Angelou. Copyright © 1969 by Maya Angelou. Reprinted by permission of Random House, Inc.

Anthony Brandt. "Children of Divorce" by Anthony Brandt from *Parenting*, October, 1991. Reprinted with permission from Parenting magazine.

Arthur L. Campa. "Anglo vs. Chicano: Why?" by Arthur L. Campa from *Western Reviews*, 1972.

Janice Castro. "Spanglish Spoken Here" by Janice Castro, with Dan Cook and Christina Garcia from *Time*, July 11, 1988. Copyright 1988 Time Inc. Reprinted by permission.

Sucheng Chan. "You're Short, Besides" by Sucheng Chan from *Making Waves* by Asian Women United, copyright © 1989 by Asian Women United. Reprinted by permission of Beacon Press.

Judith Ortiz Cofer. "The Myth of the Latin Woman: I Just Met a Girl Named Maria" by Judith Ortiz Cofer from *The Latin Deli* by Judith Ortiz Cofer, 1993. Reprinted by permission of The University of Georgia Press.

Willi Coleman. "Closets and Keepsakes" by Willi Coleman from *Double Stitch: Black Women Write about Mothers and Daughters* edited by Patricia Bell-Scott et al., Harper Perennial, 1993. Reprinted by permission of publisher and author.

Ferdinand M. de Leon. "Name Power" by Ferdinand M. de Leon and Sally Macdonald from *The Seattle Times*, June 29, 1992. Reprinted with permission of the Seattle Times.

Patty Fisher. "The Injustice System—Women Have Begun to Fight" by Patty Fisher from *San Jose Mercury News*, March 25, 1992. Reprinted by permission.

Margaret A. Gibson. "Cultural Barriers and the Press to Americanize" from Margaret A. Gibson, *Accommodation Without Assimilation: Sikh Immigrants in an American High School*. Copyright © 1988 by Cornell University Press. Used by permission of the publisher, Cornell University Press.

Joy Harjo. "Three Generations of Native American Women's Birth Experience" by Joy Harjo from *Ms. Magazine*, 1991. Reprinted by permission.

William Least Heat-Moon. "Tuesday Morning" from *Blue Highways* by William Least Heat-Moon. Copyright © 1982 by William Least Heat-Moon. By permission of Little, Brown and Company.

Linda Hogan. "Thanksgiving" by Linda Hogan from *ELLE*, November 1990.

Vance Horne. "Japanese Tea Ceremony" by Vance Horne from *The Olympian*, April 4, 1987, Olympia, WA. Reprinted by permission.

Jane Howard. "All Happy Clans Are Alike in Search of the Good" by Jane Howard from *Families*. Copyright © 1978 by Jane Howard. Reprinted by permission of Simon & Schuster, Inc.

John D. Hull. "A Boy and his Gun" by John D. Hull from *Time*, August 2, 1993. Copyright 1993 Time Inc. Reprinted by permission.

Zora Neale Hurston. "How it Feels to be Colored Me" by Zora Neale Hurston from *The World Tomorrow*.

NAME AND TITLE INDEX

SUBJECT INDEX